Llewellyn's 1999
Moon Sign Book
And Gardening
Almanac

With Lunar Forecasts by Gloria Star

Editor/Designer: Cynthia Ahlquist
Lunar Forecast Editing: Corrine Kenner
Cover Illustration: Brian Jensen
Cover Design: Anne Marie Garrison
Special thanks to Leslie Nielsen for astrological proofreading.

ISBN 1-56718-941-5
LLEWELLYN PUBLICATIONS
P.O. Box 64383 Dept. 941-5
St. Paul, MN 55164-0383 U.S.A.

Table of Contents

Planetary Business Rulerships; Advertising, General; Advertising, Newspaper; Advertising, Television, Radio, or Internet; Business, Education; Business, Opening; Business, Remodeling; Business, Starting; Buying; Buying Clothing; Buying Furniture; Buying Machinery, Appliances, or Tools; Buying Stocks; Collections; Consultants, Work With; Contracts; Contracts, Bid On; Copyrights/Patents, Apply For; Electronics, Buying; Electronics, Repair; Legal Matters; Loans; Mailing; Mining; New Job, Beginning; News; Photography, Radio, TV, Film, and Video; Promotions; Selling or Canvassing; Signing Papers; Staff, Fire; Staff, Hire; Travel; and Writing

Animals and Animal Breeding; Cultivating; Cutting Timber; Fertilizing and Composting; Grafting; Harvesting and Drying Crops; Irrigation; Lawn Mowing; Picking Mushrooms; Planting; Pruning; Spraying and Weeding; Transplanting; and Weather

How to Use This Book

Are you ready to harness the power of the Moon? With the *Moon Sign Book* you can do just that. The *Moon Sign Book* provides you with four essential tools to reap the benefits of the Moon. You can use these tools alone or in any combination to help you achieve success in 1999. The first tool is our unique, easy-to-use Astro Almanac: a list of the best dates in 1999 to begin important activities. The second tool is a complete how-to on using the Moon to fine-tune your timing. This takes the Astro Almanac one step further and teaches you *how* to choose the best dates for your activities. The third tool consists of insightful lunar astrological forecasts by astrologer Gloria Star. The fourth tool is informative articles on using the Moon in the home, business, garden, and everywhere you go. Read on to find out more about how to use each of these features.

The Astro Almanac

The simplest method for using the *Moon Sign Book* in lunar timing is to turn straight to the Astro Almanac, beginning on page 12. The Astro Almanac lists the best days to perform sixty different activities, based on the sign and phase of the Moon and on lunar aspects. All you need to do is find the particular activity that you are interested in, and the best dates for each month will be listed across the page. When working with the Moon's energies we consider two things—the inception, or beginning of an activity, and the desired outcome. We begin a project under a certain Moon sign and phase in order to achieve certain results. The results are influenced by the attributes of the sign and phase under which we started the project. Therefore, the Astro Almanac lists the best times to *begin* many activities.

The Moon Tables

The Astro Almanac is a general guide to the best days for the activities listed in it, but for a more in-depth exploration of lunar timing, the *Moon Sign Book* provides the Moon Tables. The Astro Almanac can't take everyone's special needs into account. This is partially because although we can provide generally favorable dates for everyone, not everyone will have the same goal for each activity that they start. Therefore, not everyone will want to start every activity at the same time. For example, let's say you decide to plant a flower garden. Which attributes would you like most in your flowers? Beauty? Then you may want to plant in Libra, because Libra is ruled by Venus, which in turn governs appearance. How about planting for quantity or abundance? Then you might try Cancer or Pisces, the two most fertile signs. What if you were going to be transporting the flowers somewhere, either in pots or as cut blooms? Then you might want to try Scorpio for sturdiness, or Taurus for hardiness. The Astro Almanac also does not take into account retrogrades, Moon void-of-course, or favorable and unfavorable days.

The procedure for using the Moon tables is more complex than simply consulting the Astro Almanac, but we encourage you to try it so that you can tailor the *Moon Sign Book* information to your needs and fully harness the potential of the Moon. The directions for using the tables to choose your own dates are in the section called "Using the Moon Tables," which begins on page 22. Be sure to read all of the directions, paying special attention to the information on the signs, Moon void-of-course, retrogrades, and favorable and unfavorable days. The sections titled "The Moon's Quarters & Signs" (page 52), the Moon Void-of-Course Table (page 56), and "Retrogrades" (page 54) are provided as supplementary material and should be read as well. These sections will give you a deeper understanding of how the process of lunar planning works, and give you background helpful in making use of the articles in this book.

Personal Lunar Forecasts

The third tool for working with the Moon is the Personal Lunar Forecasts section, written by Gloria Star. This section begins on page 361. Here Gloria tells you what's in store for you for 1999, based on your Moon sign. This approach is different than that of other astrology books, including Llewellyn's *Sun Sign Book*, which make forecasts based on Sun sign. While the Sun in an astrological chart represents the basic essence or personality, the Moon represents the internal or private you—your feelings, emotions, and subconscious. Knowing what's in store for your Moon in 1999 can give you great insight for personal growth. If you already know your Moon sign, go ahead and turn to the corresponding section in the back of the book (forecasts begin on page 365). If you don't know your Moon sign, you can figure it out using the procedure beginning on page 62.

Articles, Articles, Articles

Scattered throughout the *Moon Sign Book* are articles on using the Moon for activities from fishing to business. These articles are written by people who successfully use the Moon to enhance their daily lives, and are chosen to entertain you and enhance your knowledge of what the Moon can do for you. The articles can be found in the Home, Health, & Beauty section; the Leisure & Recreation section; the Business section; and the Gardening section. Check the table of contents for specific topics.

Some Final Notes

We get a number of letters and phone calls every year from readers asking the same types of questions. Most of these have to do with how to find certain information in the *Moon Sign Book* and how to use this information.

The best advice we can give is to read the *entire* introduction (pages 5–74), in particular the section on how to use the tables. We provide examples using the current Moon and aspect tables so that you can follow along and get familiar with the process. At first, using the Moon tables may seem confusing because there are several factors to take into account, but if you read the directions carefully and practice a little bit, you'll be a Moon sign pro in no time.

Remember, for quick reference for the best dates to begin an activity, turn to the Astro Almanac. To choose special dates for an activity that are tailor-made just for you, turn to "How to Use the Moon tables." For insight into your personal Moon sign, check out Gloria Star's lunar forecasts. Finally, to learn about the many ways you can harness the power of the Moon, turn to the articles in the Home, Health & Beauty; Leisure & Recreation; Business & Legal; and Farm, Garden, & Weather sections.

Get ready to improve your life with the power of the Moon!

Important!

All times given in the *Moon Sign Book* are set in Eastern Standard Time (EST). You must adjust for your time zone. There is a time zone conversion chart on page 8 to assist you. You must also adjust for Daylight Saving Time where applicable.

Time Zone Conversions

World Time Zones

(Compared to Eastern Standard Time)

(R) EST—Used
(S) CST—Subtract 1 hour
(T) MST—Subtract 2 hours
(U) PST—Subtract 3 hours
(V) Subtract 4 hours
(V*) Subtract 4½ hours
(W) Subtract 5 hours
(X) Subtract 6 hours
(Y) Subtract 7 hours
(Q) Add 1 hour
(P) Add 2 hours
(P*) Add 2½ hours
(O) Add 3 hours
(N) Add 4 hours
(Z) Add 5 hours
(A) Add 6 hours
(B) Add 7 hours
(C) Add 8 hours

(C*) Add 8½ hours
(D) Add 9 hours
(D*) Add 9½ hours
(E) Add 10 hours
(E*) Add 10½ hours
(F) Add 11 hours
(F*) Add 11½ hours
(G) Add 12 hours
(H) Add 13 hours
(I) Add 14 hours
(I*) Add 14½ hours
(K) Add 15 hours
(K*) Add 15½ hours
(L) Add 16 hours
(L) Add 16½ hours
(M) Add 17 hours
(M*) Add 17½ hours

Important!

All times given in the *Moon Sign Book* are set in Eastern Standard Time (EST). You must adjust for your time zone. You must also adjust for Daylight Saving Time where applicable.

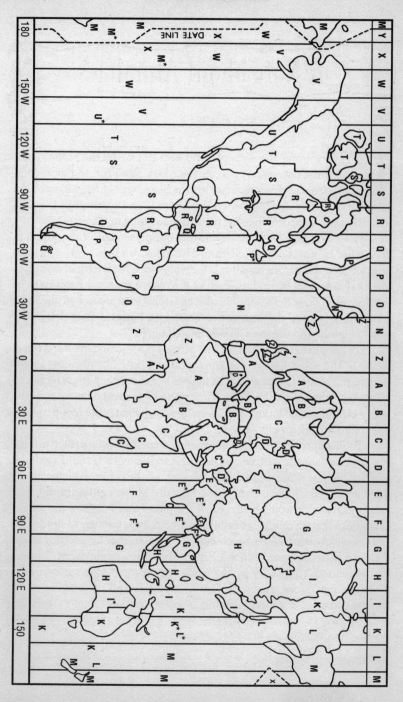

A Note about Almanacs

It is important for those people who wish to plan by the Moon to understand the difference between the *Moon Sign Book* and most common almanacs. Most almanacs list the placement of the Moon by the constellation. For example, when the Moon is passing through the constellation of Capricorn, they list the Moon as being in Capricorn.

The *Moon Sign Book*, however, lists the placement of the Moon in the zodiac by *sign*, not constellation. The zodiac is a belt of space extending out from the earth's equator. It is divided into twelve equal segments: the twelve signs of the zodiac. Each of the twelve segments happens to be named after a constellation, but the constellations are not in the same place in the sky as the segment of space (sign) named after them. The constellations and the signs do not "match up."

For *astronomical* calculations, the Moon's place in almanacs is given as being in the constellation. For *astrological* purposes, like planning by the Moon, the Moon's place should be figured in the zodiacal *sign*, which is its true place in the zodiac, and nearly one sign (30 degrees) different from the astronomical constellation. The *Moon Sign Book* figures the Moon's placement for *astrological* purposes.

To illustrate: If the common almanac gives the Moon's place in Taurus (constellation), its true place in the zodiac is in Gemini (zodiacal sign). Thus it is readily seen that those who use the common almanac may be planting seeds when they think that the Moon is in a fruitful sign, while in reality it would be in one of the most barren signs of the zodiac. To obtain desired results, planning must be done according to *sign*.

Some common almanacs confuse the issue further by inserting at the head of their columns "Moon's Sign" when they really mean "Moon's Constellation." In the *Moon Sign Book*, however, "Moon's sign" means "Moon's sign!" Use the *Moon Sign Book* to plan all of your important events and to grow a more beautiful, bountiful garden.

Using the Astro Almanac

Llewellyn's unique Astro Almanac (pages 12–21) is provided for quick reference. Use it to find the best dates for anything from asking for a raise to buying a car!

By reader request, we have included several new categories in the Astro Almanac relating to business, from hiring and firing staff to the best time to advertise on the internet. We hope you will find them useful. If you have suggestions for other activities to be added to the Astro Almanac, please write us at the address listed on the title page of this book.

The dates provided are determined from the sign and phase of the Moon and the aspects to the Moon. These are approximate dates only. We have removed dates that have long Moon void-of course periods from the list (we did not do this before 1998). Although some of these dates may meet the criteria listed for your particular activity, the Moon void would nullify the positive influences of that day. We have not removed dates with short Moon voids, however, and we have not taken planetary retrogrades into account. To learn more about Moon void-of-course and planetary retrogrades, see pages 54–61.

This year we have also removed days with lots of squares to the Moon, and eclipse dates. Like Moon voids, squares could nullify the "good" influences of a given day. Eclipses lend an unpredictable energy to a day, so we have removed eclipse dates so that you may begin your activities on the strongest footing possible.

Another thing to bear in mind when using the Astro Almanac is that sometimes the dates given may not be favorable for your Sun sign or for your particular interests. The Astro Almanac does not take personal factors into account, such as your Sun and Moon sign, your schedule, etc. That's why it is important for you to learn how to use the entire process to come up with the most beneficial dates for you. To do this, read the instructions under "Using the Moon Tables" (page 22). That way, you can get the most out of the power of the Moon!

Astro Almanac

Activity	Jan.	Feb.	Mar.	Apr.	May	Jun.	Jul.	Aug.	Sep.	Oct.	Nov.	Dec.
Advertise Sale				5	3, 31	27	25	12, 20	18	15	11	8
Advertise New Venture		11	22	5, 19	3, 17, 31	13, 14, 27	10, 11, 23, 25	20	18, 30	1, 15, 28	11, 24	8, 22
Advertise in the Paper	2, 5, 10, 12, 16, 17, 21, 26, 30	5, 9, 11, 14, 18, 21, 22, 26, 27	8, 13, 17, 18, 21, 22, 25, 26	4, 5, 9, 10, 13, 15, 18, 19, 22, 23	3, 8, 9, 12, 13, 14, 16, 17, 19, 21, 24, 31	5, 9, 10, 13, 18, 19, 25, 27	3, 5, 7, 10, 11, 14, 15, 18, 23, 25, 30	1, 3, 5, 8, 9, 12, 14, 20, 22, 26, 30, 31	4, 8, 9, 15, 18, 21, 23, 27, 30	1, 5, 15, 16, 20, 21, 24, 28, 30	1, 4, 9, 11, 13, 16, 18, 20, 24–26, 28, 30	5, 8, 11, 13, 16, 18, 22, 25, 31
Advertise on TV, Radio, Internet	18, 27	23	22	19	13	26	24, 29	20, 25	16, 21	13, 18	10, 15	12, 21
Apply for Job	6, 26	13, 22	12, 13, 21	25	5, 15		8, 17	22, 31	9, 21, 30		13	13
Apply for Copyrights, Patents	2, 5, 10, 12, 16, 17, 21, 26, 30	5, 9, 11, 14, 16, 18, 21, 22, 26, 27	8, 13, 17, 18, 21, 22, 25, 26	4, 5, 9, 10, 13, 15, 18, 19, 22, 23	8, 12, 13, 14, 16–21, 24, 31	5, 13, 18, 19, 25	3, 5, 7, 10, 11, 14, 15, 18, 23, 25, 30	1, 3, 5, 8, 9, 12, 14, 20, 22, 26, 30, 31	4, 8, 9, 15, 18, 21, 23, 27, 30	1, 5, 15, 16, 20, 21, 24, 28, 30	1, 4, 9, 11, 13, 16, 18, 20, 24–26, 28, 30	5, 8, 11, 13, 16, 18, 22, 26, 31

Astro Almanac

Activity	Jan.	Feb.	Mar.	Apr.	May	Jun.	Jul.	Aug.	Sep.	Oct.	Nov.	Dec.
Ask for Raise	5, 8, 12, 13, 18, 19, 21, 26	5, 9, 11, 16–18, 22	8, 10, 15, 17, 18, 21, 22, 25	4, 5, 9, 14, 15, 18, 19, 23	3, 8, 9, 12, 18, 21, 23, 24, 31	5, 8, 12, 13, 14, 18, 19, 21, 25	3, 5, 10, 11, 15, 18, 23, 30	1, 3, 5, 7, 12, 14, 16, 19–21, 22, 30	3, 4, 9, 12, 15, 17, 18, 26, 27	1, 5, 10, 16, 20, 28, 30	1, 3, 4, 9, 11, 14, 16, 18, 24, 25, 28, 30	3, 5, 8, 9, 11, 13, 14, 16, 18, 22, 23, 28
Bid on Contracts						19, 29	25	12, 13	18	16		9
Brewing			16, 17	13	10, 11	7	12	8, 9	4–6	2, 3	25, 26	23
Buy Stocks	17, 26	13, 22	13	7	5	1, 29	26	22, 23, 31	19	16	12	9
Buy Animals	18, 19	19, 21, 22	18, 20, 21–24	17–21	16–19, 21	14, 15, 18–20	13, 15–20	12–16	10–13, 16, 17	10, 13–17	10–13	8–11, 13
Buy Antiques	2, 16, 17, 29, 30	7–9, 12, 13, 25, 26	7, 8, 12, 13, 24, 25	3, 4, 7, 8, 9, 21, 22, 30	1, 2, 5–7, 18, 19, 27–29	1–3, 15, 24, 25, 29, 30	12, 13, 21, 22, 26, 27	8, 9, 17, 18, 22, 23	4–6, 14, 15, 19, 20	2, 3, 11, 12, 16, 17, 29, 30	7–9, 12, 13, 26, 27	4–6, 9–11, 23, 24, 31

Astro Almanac

Activity	Jan.	Feb.	Mar.	Apr.	May	Jun.	Jul.	Aug.	Sep.	Oct.	Nov.	Dec.
Buy Appliances	8, 13, 18, 23, 27	5, 10, 14, 15, 19, 21, 23	4, 9, 14, 18, 22	6, 10, 11, 15, 19, 23, 28	3, 8, 12, 14, 16, 25, 30	4, 9, 13, 21, 26	1, 6, 10, 19, 24	2, 4, 6, 15, 20, 25, 29	2, 11, 16, 21, 25, 26, 30	9, 11, 13, 18, 23, 27	5, 10, 15, 19, 23	2, 5, 7, 12, 17, 21, 29
Buy Cameras	7, 12, 22, 26	4, 9, 18, 22	3, 8, 18, 22, 31	5, 14, 18, 27	2, 11, 15, 24, 29	8, 12, 20, 25	5, 9, 18, 23	1, 5, 14, 19, 28	2, 10, 15, 25, 29	8, 13, 22, 26	4, 9, 18, 19, 23	1, 6, 16, 20, 29
Buy a Car	13, 27	10, 11, 23	9, 22	6, 19	3, 16, 30	13, 14, 26	10, 23, 24	6, 19, 20	16, 30	13, 27	9, 24	7, 21
Buy Electronics	8, 13, 18, 23, 27	5, 10, 14, 15, 19, 21, 23	4, 9, 14, 18, 22	6, 10, 11, 15, 19, 23, 28	3, 8, 12, 14, 16, 25, 30	13, 21, 26	1, 6, 10, 19, 24	2, 4, 6, 15, 20, 25, 29	2, 11, 16, 21, 25, 26, 30	9, 11, 13, 18, 23, 27	5, 10, 15, 19, 23	2, 5, 7, 12, 17, 21, 29
Buy a House		22	21	10, 11	18, 21	14–18	12	12				
Buy Real Estate	2, 8, 23		18, 19	15, 28	12, 13, 18	9, 21	7, 18	3, 8, 30	4	24, 29, 30	20	18

Astro Almanac

Activity	Jan.	Feb.	Mar.	Apr.	May	Jun.	Jul.	Aug.	Sep.	Oct.	Nov.	Dec.
Canning	2, 3, 6	2–4	2, 3				12	8, 9	4, 5, 6, 9	2, 3, 6, 7, 29, 30	2, 3, 26, 27, 30	1, 23, 24, 27, 28
Collect Money	8		18, 24	9, 15, 28	12, 18	21		3, 8, 16, 22, 30	4, 12, 26, 27	9, 24, 30		3, 9, 18, 23
Cut Hair to Increase Growth	20, 21, 22	17, 18	24	21, 22	18, 19	15	13					14, 15
Cut Hair to Decrease Growth	6, 7	2–4	2, 3	15	12, 13	9, 10, 13	6, 7, 10, 11	2, 3, 6, 7, 29, 30	9, 26, 27, 30	1, 6, 7, 27, 28	2, 3, 24, 30	1, 27, 28
Cut Hair to Thicken	29, 30	27, 28	1, 28			26					22	19, 20
Cut Timber	4–10, 13–17	1–6, 10–16	2–6, 9–15	1, 2, 5–12, 15	3–9, 12–15, 30, 31	1–5, 8–13, 29, 30	1, 2, 6–11, 29, 30	2–7, 10, 11, 29–31	1, 2, 7–9, 26–30	1, 4–9, 25–28, 31	1–6, 24, 28–30	1–3, 7, 25–30

Astro Almanac

Activity	Jan.	Feb.	Mar.	Apr.	May	Jun.	Jul.	Aug.	Sep.	Oct.	Nov.	Dec.
Dock or Dehorn Animals	10–20	9–16	10–15	10, 11, 19–22	8, 16–22	13–20	10–19	6–19	3–16	2–14, 31	1–11, 30	1–8
End a Relationship	2–17	1–16	2–17	1–15	1–15, 30, 31	1–13, 29, 30	1–12, 29–31	1–11, 27–31	1–9, 26–30	1–9, 25–31	1–7, 24–30	1–7, 23–31
Entertain	1, 4, 5, 8–10, 18, 19, 27, 28, 31	1, 5, 6, 14, 15, 23, 24, 27, 28	4–6, 14, 15, 22, 23, 26–28, 31	1, 10, 19, 20, 23, 24, 28, 29	8, 9, 16, 17, 20, 21, 25, 26	4, 5, 13, 14, 16–18, 21–23	1, 2, 10, 11, 14, 15, 18–20, 28–30	6, 7, 10–12, 15, 16, 24–26	3, 7, 8, 11–13, 21, 22, 30	1, 4, 5, 9, 10, 18–20, 27, 28	1, 5, 6, 15, 24, 25, 28, 29	2, 3, 12, 13, 21, 22, 25, 26, 29, 30
Extract Teeth	13, 14	9, 10	10, 22, 23	19	16, 17	13, 14, 19, 20	10, 11, 16, 17	6, 7, 13, 14	3, 9, 10, 16, 17	6–8, 13, 14	2–4, 10, 30	1, 7, 8
Get a Perm	4, 25, 26, 31	1, 21, 22, 27, 28	1, 20, 21, 26–28	17, 18, 23, 24	14, 15, 20, 21	11, 12, 16–18	8, 9, 14, 15	4, 5, 10–12, 31	1, 2, 7, 8, 28, 29	4, 5, 25, 26, 31	1, 22, 23, 28, 29	19, 20, 25, 26
Fire Staff	2–17	1–15	3–17	1–15	1–15, 31	1–13, 29, 30	1–12, 29–31	1–11, 27–31	1–9, 26–30	1–9, 25–31	1–7, 24–30	1–7, 23–31

Astro Almanac

Activity	Jan.	Feb.	Mar.	Apr.	May	Jun.	Jul.	Aug.	Sep.	Oct.	Nov.	Dec.
Hire Staff	21, 26, 30	18, 21, 22, 26, 27	18, 21, 22, 25, 26	18, 19, 22, 23	17, 18, 21, 24	14, 18, 19, 25, 28	15, 18, 23, 25	12, 14, 20, 22	18, 21, 23	9, 10, 15, 16, 20, 21, 24	9, 11, 13, 20	8, 11, 13, 16, 18
Legal Matters				5	3, 31	28	25		18	15	11	8
Marriage	2, 6, 8, 12, 13, 17–21, 22, 23, 26, 28, 30	5, 7, 9–11, 14, 16, 18, 20, 25, 27	7, 8, 12, 13, 15, 17–19, 21, 22, 26, 29	5, 6, 9–11, 14, 15, 18–20, 2–25, 28	3, 5, 9, 10, 12–19, 21, 23, 24, 28, 31	4, 5, 8, 9, 12, 13, 16, 18, 21, 23, 27	3, 7, 8, 11, 12, 15, 17, 22, 25	2, 3, 6, 8, 11, 12, 16, 21, 22, 30, 31	3, 4, 7–9, 12, 14, 18, 20, 23, 26, 27, 29, 30	4, 5, 9, 10, 14, 15, 20, 25, 28–30	1–3, 7, 9, 11, 13, 14, 18, 20, 24, 27, 28	2, 7–9, 13, 14, 18, 23, 26, 28
Marry to be Happy	8, 26	5, 25	21	19, 23, 28	14, 15, 18, 21	8, 12, 16, 18, 21, 23	8, 12, 15	8, 12, 16, 31	4, 7, 12, 29	4, 5, 9, 10, 28	1, 28	2
Marry for Long Term		22	21	18								
Mow Lawn for Less Growth	4–17	1–16	2–15	1–12, 15	3–9, 12–15, 30, 31	1–5, 8–13, 29, 30	1, 2, 6–11, 29	2–7, 10, 11, 29–31	1, 2, 7–9, 26, 27, 29	1, 4–9, 25–28, 31	1–6, 24, 25, 28–30	1–3, 7, 26, 28

Astro Almanac

Activity	Jan.	Feb.	Mar.	Apr.	May	Jun.	Jul.	Aug.	Sep.	Oct.	Nov.	Dec.
Neutering or Spaying Animals	16–19, 27–30	1, 12–16, 23, 27, 28	1, 12–15, 22	7–12, 19–23	14, 15, 17	12, 13	9, 10	13, 14	6–10, 19–21	3–5, 16–20	1–5, 15	1–3, 9–13, 21
Open a Business	26	22		25	21	18	15, 18, 25	13, 22, 23	21	16	12	9
Paint House	3, 4	1, 22, 27	15	10–12	14	8, 9, 12, 16	8, 9, 15	4, 12	6, 7	5, 25	28	
Pour Concrete	5, 19	1, 14, 15	14, 15	23, 24	14	5	8	5			29	
Remodel a Business	26	9, 14, 27	18, 22, 26	5, 10, 23	14	4, 26	1, 5, 14, 18, 23	10, 19	8, 25	4, 8, 13, 23, 31		
Remodel a House	5, 13–15, 26, 31	9–11, 27	1, 9–11, 26, 28	5, 10, 23	14	8, 16, 26	1, 5, 14, 23	10, 19	8, 16	4, 13, 31	9, 15, 19, 27	7, 25

Astro Almanac

Activity	Jan.	Feb.	Mar.	Apr.	May	Jun.	Jul.	Aug.	Sep.	Oct.	Nov.	Dec.
Repair Electronics	4, 18, 23	1, 5, 14, 15, 19, 23	1, 4, 7, 14, 20, 27	1, 6, 11, 15, 19, 28	8, 9, 25, 30	4, 5, 9, 13, 26	14, 15, 28–30	2, 6, 15, 20	2, 16, 21, 22, 25	4, 9, 13, 18, 23	5, 10, 15, 23	2, 12
Repair a Car	4, 18	15, 19, 23		11, 19, 23, 28	8	4, 13, 21, 26			2, 21		23	
Roofing	4, 5	1, 14, 16	14, 15	12	8, 9, 14, 15	5, 8, 11, 12	8, 30	4, 23	1, 2, 7, 8, 28, 29	4, 5, 25, 26, 31	1, 28, 29	25, 26
Seek Favors or Credit	13, 18, 19, 21, 22	9, 14–18, 27	9, 14, 18, 22, 27	5, 10, 15, 23	3, 8–10, 21, 31	5, 18, 27, 28	2, 3, 15, 25, 30	11, 12, 21, 22, 31	4, 8, 18	5, 15, 20, 24, 28	1, 11, 28	8, 13, 26
Set Fence Posts	5, 19	1, 16	1, 15, 28	12	9						21	
Sign Contracts	5, 26	14, 18, 22, 27	21, 26	10, 18, 23	5, 14, 21	5, 18	2, 9, 14, 15, 30	5, 12, 31	8, 21	5, 20	1, 13	13, 26

Astro Almanac

Activity	Jan.	Feb.	Mar.	Apr.	May	Jun.	Jul.	Aug.	Sep.	Oct.	Nov.	Dec.
Start Diet	4–7, 13–15	1–4, 10, 11, 14–16	2, 3, 9–11, 14, 15	5, 6, 10–12, 15	3, 4, 8, 9, 12, 13, 30, 31	4, 5, 9, 10	1, 2, 6, 7, 29, 30	2, 3, 10, 11, 29, 30	7–9, 26, 27	4–8, 31	1–4, 28–30	1, 7, 25–28
Start a Savings Account	26	22		18								
Sell Items		22		18	14	8, 12		31		25		
Sell Real Estate	2, 30	20, 25	18	15	12, 13, 19	9	12	2, 3, 8	4, 27	24	20, 27	18
Sports	4, 14	1, 27	18, 26	5, 15, 23	3, 4, 12, 13, 21, 31	9, 17, 18, 27, 28	15, 25	3, 12	8, 18, 26, 27	4, 5, 15, 24	1, 11, 20, 28	7, 8, 17, 18, 26
Start House Building	5, 19	1, 16	15, 28	12	9						28	

Astro Almanac

Activity	Jan.	Feb.	Mar.	Apr.	May	Jun.	Jul.	Aug.	Sep.	Oct.	Nov.	Dec.
Stop a Bad Habit	5, 7	1, 4	2, 3	25, 26	22–24	19, 20	16	13, 14	9, 10	6, 7	2–4, 29, 30	1, 25–28
Travel	13, 26, 27, 31	10, 11, 23, 24, 28	9, 22	6, 19	3, 16, 30	13, 14, 26, 27	10, 23, 24	6, 19, 20		13, 14, 27, 28	10, 11, 25, 28	7, 8, 21
Visit Dentist	5, 19	1, 16	1, 15, 28	12	10						30	
Visit Doctor			29, 30	25–27	22–24	19, 20	16, 17	13, 14	10			
Work with Consultants	2, 5, 10, 12, 16, 17, 21, 26, 30	5, 9, 11, 14, 16, 18, 21, 22, 26, 27	8, 13, 17, 18, 21, 22, 25, 26	4, 5, 9, 10, 13, 15, 18, 19, 22, 23	3, 8, 9, 13, 13, 17, 21, 24, 31	5, 9, 10, 13–15, 18, 19, 25, 28	3, 5, 11, 14, 15, 18, 23, 25, 30	1, 3, 5, 8, 9, 12, 14, 20, 22, 26, 30, 31	4, 8, 9, 15, 18, 21, 23, 27, 30	1, 5, 15, 16, 20, 21, 24, 28, 30	1, 4, 9, 11, 13, 16, 18, 20, 24, 26, 28, 30	5, 8, 11, 13, 16, 18, 22, 26, 31
Write Letters	6–8, 13–15, 21, 27, 28	2–4, 10, 11, 18, 23, 24	2, 3, 9–11, 17, 22, 23, 29, 30	5, 6, 13, 19–20, 25	3, 4, 10, 11, 17, 22–24, 31	13, 19, 26–28	5, 10, 11, 16–18, 23–25, 31	1, 6, 7, 13, 14, 19–21	3, 9, 10, 16–18, 23, 24, 25, 30	1, 13–15, 21, 27, 28	2–4, 10, 11, 17, 24, 25, 30	1, 7, 8, 14–16, 21, 22, 27, 28

Using the Moon Tables

Timing by the Moon

Timing your activities is one of the most important things you can do to ensure success. In many Eastern countries, timing by the planets is so important that practically no event takes place without first setting up a chart for it. Weddings have occurred in the middle of the night because that was when the influences were the best. You may not want to take it that far, and you don't really need to set up a chart for each activity, but you can still make use of the influences of the Moon whenever possible. It's easy and it works!

In the *Moon Sign Book* you will find the information you need to plan just about any activity: weddings, fishing, buying a car or house, cutting your hair, traveling, and more. Not all of the things you do will fall on favorable days, but we provide the guidelines you need to pick the best day out of the several from which you have to choose. The primary method in the *Moon Sign Book* for choosing your own dates is to use the Moon Tables, beginning on page 28. Following are instructions for choosing the best dates for your activities using the *Moon Sign Book*, several examples, directions on how to read the Moon Tables themselves, and more advanced information on using the Favorable and Unfavorable Days Tables, Void-of-Course, and Retrograde information to choose the dates that are best for you personally. To enhance your understanding of the directions given below, we highly recommend that you read the sections of this book called "A Note about Almanacs" (page 10), "The Moon's Quarters & Signs" (page 52), "Retrograde Table & Explanation" (page 54), and "Moon Void-of-Course Table & Explanation" (page 55). It is not essential that you read these before you try the examples below, but reading them will deepen your understanding of the date-choosing process.

The Four Basic Steps

Step One: Use the Directions for Choosing Dates

Look up the directions for choosing dates for the activity that you wish to begin. The directions are listed at the beginning of the following sections of this book: Home, Health, & Beauty; Leisure & Recreation; Business & Legal; and Farm, Garden, & Weather. Check the Table of Contents to see in what section the directions for your specific activity are listed. The activities contained in each section are listed in italics after the name of the section in the Table of Contents. For example, directions for choosing a good day for canning are listed in the Home, Health, & Beauty Section, and directions for choosing a good day to throw a party are in the Leisure Section. Read the directions for your activity, then go to step two.

Step Two: Check the Moon Tables

Next, turn to the Moon Tables, beginning on page 28. In the Moon Tables section, there are two tables for each month of the year. Use the Moon Tables to determine what dates the Moon is in the phase and sign listed in the directions for your particular activity. The Moon Tables are the tables on the left-hand pages, and include the day, date, the sign the Moon is in, the element of that sign, the nature of the sign, the Moon's phase, and the times that it changes sign or phase.

If there is a time listed after a date, such as 1 Fri. 3:16 am on January 1, that time is the time when the Moon moves into the zodiac sign listed for that day (which in this case would be Cancer). Until then, the Moon is considered to be in the sign for the previous day (Gemini in this example).

The abbreviation Full signifies Full Moon and New signifies New Moon. The times listed directly after the abbreviation are the times when the Moon changes sign. The times listed after the phase indicate when the Moon changes phase.

If you know the specific month you would like to begin your activity, turn directly to that month. When you begin choosing your own dates, you will be using the Moon's sign and phase information most often. All times are listed in Eastern Standard Time (EST). You need to adjust them according to your own time zone. (There is a time zone conversion map on page 8.)

When you have found some dates that meet the criteria for the correct Moon phase and sign for your activity, you may have completed the process. For certain simple activities, such as getting a haircut, the phase and sign information is all that is needed. For other activities, however, we need to meet further criteria in order to choose the best date. If the directions for your activity include information on certain lunar aspects, you should consult the Lunar Aspectarian. An example of this would be if the directions told you that you should not perform a certain activity when the Moon is square (Q) Mars.

Step Three: Turn to the Lunar Aspectarian

On the pages opposite the Moon Tables you will find the Lunar Aspectarian and the Favorable and Unfavorable Days Tables. The Lunar Aspectarian gives the aspects (or angles) of the Moon to the other planets. In a nutshell, it tells where the Moon is in relation to the other planets in the sky. Some placements of the Moon in relation to other planets are favorable, while others are not. To use the Lunar Aspectarian, which is the left half of this table, find the planet that the directions for your activity list, and run down the column to the date desired. For example, if you are planning surgery and in the Health & Beauty section it says that you should avoid aspects to Mars, you would look for Mars across the top and then run down that column looking for days where there are no aspects to Mars (these days are signified by empty boxes). If you want to find a favorable aspect (sextile [X] or trine [T]) to Mercury, run your finger down the column under Mercury until you find an X or T; positive or good aspects are signified by these letters. Negative or adverse aspects (square or opposition) are signified by a Q or O. A conjunction, C, is sometimes good, sometimes bad, depending on the activity or planets involved.

Step Four: Use the Favorable and Unfavorable Days Tables

The Favorable and Unfavorable Days Tables are helpful in choosing the best dates for you personally, because they take your Sun sign into account. The tables list all of the Sun signs. They are on the right-hand side of the Lunar Aspectarian table. Once you have determined which days meet the criteria for phase, sign, and aspects for your activity, you can check to see if those days are positive for you personally. To find out if a day is positive for you, find your Sun sign and then look down the column. If it is marked F, it is very favorable. If it is marked f, it is slightly favorable. U means very unfavorable and u means slightly unfavorable.

At this point, you have selected good dates for whatever activity you are about to begin. You can go straight to the examples section beginning on the next page. However, if you are up to the challenge and would like to learn how to fine-tune your selections even further, read on!

Step Five: Check for Moon Void-of-Course and Retrogrades

This last step is perhaps the most advanced portion of the procedure. It is generally considered a bad idea to make decisions, sign important papers, or start special activities during a Moon void-of-course period or during a planetary retrograde. Once you have chosen the best date for your activity based on steps one through four, you can check the Void-of-Course Table on page 55 to find out if any of the dates you have chosen have void periods. The Moon is said to be void-of-course after it has made its last aspect to a planet within a particular sign, but before it has moved into the next sign. Put simply, during the void-of-course period the Moon is "at rest," so activities initiated at this time generally don't come to fruition. You will notice that there are many void periods during the year, and it is nearly impossible to avoid all of them. Some people choose to ignore these altogether and do not take them into consideration when planning activities.

Next, you can check the Planetary Retrograde Table on page 54 to see what planets are retrograde during your chosen date(s). A planet is said to be retrograde when it appears to move backward in the sky as viewed from the Earth. Generally, the farther a planet is away from the Sun, the longer it can stay retrograde. Some planets will retrograde for several months at a time. Avoiding retrogrades is not as important in lunar planning as avoiding the Moon void-of-course, with the exception of the planet Mercury. Mercury rules thought and communication, so it is important not to sign papers, initiate important business or legal work, or make crucial decisions during these times. As with the Moon void-of-course, it is difficult to avoid all planetary retrogrades when beginning events, and you may choose to ignore this step of the process. Following are some examples using some or all of the steps outlined above.

Using What You've Learned

Example Number One

Let's say you need to make an appointment to have your hair cut. Your hair is thin and you would like it to look thicker. You look in the Table of Contents to see which section of the book lists the directions for hair care. You find that it is in the Home, Health, & Beauty section. Turning to that section you see that for thicker hair you should cut hair while the Moon is Full and in the sign of Taurus, Cancer, or Leo. You should avoid the Moon in Aries, Gemini, or Virgo. We'll say that it is the month of October. Look up October in the Moon Tables (page 46–7). The Full Moon falls on October 24 at 4:03 pm. It is in the sign of Taurus, beginning at 2:26 am, so this date meets both the phase and sign criteria.

Example Number Two

That was easy. Let's move on to a more difficult example using the sign and phase of the Moon. You want to buy a house for a permanent home. After checking the Table of Contents to see where the house purchasing instructions are, look in the Home, Health, & Beauty section under House. It says that you should buy a home when the Moon is in Taurus, Leo, Scorpio, or Aquarius (fixed signs). You need to get a loan, so you should also look in the Business & Legal section under Loans. Here it says that the third and fourth quarters favor the borrower (you). You are going to buy the house in January. Look up January in the Moon Tables. The Moon is in the third quarter from January 1–9, and in the fourth quarter from January 9–16. The best days for obtaining a loan would be January 3–4 while the Moon is in Leo or January 10–11 while it is in Scorpio. Just match up the best signs and phases (quarters) to come up with the best dates. With all activities, be sure to check the Favorable and Unfavorable Days for your Sun sign in the table adjoining the Lunar Aspectarian. If there is a choice between several dates, pick the one most favorable for you (marked F under your Sun sign). Because buying a home is an important business decision, you may also wish to see if there are Moon voids or a Mercury retrograde during these dates.

Example Number Three

Now let's look at an example that uses signs, phases, and aspects. Our example this time is fixing your car. We will use January as the example month. Look in the Home, Health, & Beauty section under automobile repair. It says that the Moon should be in a fixed sign (Taurus, Leo, Scorpio, or Aquarius) in the first or second quarter and well aspected to Uranus. (Good aspects are sextiles and trines, marked X and T. Conjunctions are also usually considered good if they are not conjunctions to Mars, Saturn, or Neptune.) It also tells you to avoid negative aspects to Mars, Saturn, Uranus, Neptune, and Pluto. (Negative aspects are squares and oppositions, marked Q and O.) Look in the Moon Tables under January. You will see that the Moon is in the first and second quarters from January 17–30. The Moon is in Aquarius on January 17 from 4:12 pm until 10:41 pm on January 19. It is in Taurus from 6:53 am on January 24 through 9:30 am on January 26, and it moves into Leo from 3:16 pm January 30. Although it is still in Leo on January 31, the Moon is Full that morning, beginning the third quarter, so you should avoid that day. Now, looking to the Lunar Aspectarian, we see that January 18 has a positive aspect to Uranus (conjunction), but that none of the other chosen dates do. In addition, there are no negative aspects to Mars, Saturn, Uranus, Neptune, and Pluto on January 18. There are no Moon voids or planetary retrogrades on January 18. Therefore, if you wanted to fix your car in January, this would be the best date.

Use Common Sense!

Some activities depend on many outside factors. Obviously, you can't go out and plant when there is still a foot of snow on the ground. You have to adjust to the conditions at hand. If the weather was bad during the first quarter when it was best to plant crops, do it during the second quarter while the Moon is in a fruitful sign instead. If the Moon is not in a fruitful sign during the first or second quarter, choose a day when it is in a semi-fruitful sign. The best advice is to choose either the sign or phase that is most favorable when the two don't coincide.

To summarize, in order to make the most of your activities, check with the *Moon Sign Book*. First, look up the activity in the corresponding section under the proper heading. Then, look for the information given in the tables (the Moon Tables, Lunar Aspectarian or Favorable and Unfavorable Days, or all three). Choose the best date according to the number of positive factors in effect. If most of the dates are favorable, then there is no problem choosing the one that will best fit your schedule. However, if there just don't seem to be any really good dates, pick the ones with the least number of negative influences. We know that you will be very pleased with the results if you use nature's influences to your advantage.

Key of Abbreviations for the Moon Tables

X: sextile/positive

T: trine/positive

Q: square/negative

O: opposition/negative

C: conjunction/positive, negative, or neutral depending on planets involved; conjunctions to Mars, Saturn, or Neptune are sometimes negative.

F: very favorable

f: slightly favorable

U: very unfavorable

u: slightly unfavorable

Full: Full Moon

New: New Moon

January Moon Table

Date	Sign	Element	Nature	Phase
1 Fri. 3:16 am	Cancer	Water	Fruitful	Full 9:50 pm
2 Sat.	Cancer	Water	Fruitful	3rd
3 Sun. 5:31 am	Leo	Fire	Barren	3rd
4 Mon.	Leo	Fire	Barren	3rd
5 Tue. 10:49 am	Virgo	Earth	Barren	3rd
6 Wed.	Virgo	Earth	Barren	3rd
7 Thu. 7:53 pm	Libra	Air	Semi-fruit	3rd
8 Fri.	Libra	Air	Semi-fruit	3rd
9 Sat.	Libra	Air	Semi-fruit	4th 9:21 am
10 Sun. 7:48 am	Scorpio	Water	Fruitful	4th
11 Mon.	Scorpio	Water	Fruitful	4th
12 Tue. 8:23 pm	Sagittarius	Fire	Barren	4th
13 Wed.	Sagittarius	Fire	Barren	4th
14 Thu.	Sagittarius	Fire	Barren	4th
15 Fri. 7:29 am	Capricorn	Earth	Semi-fruit	4th
16 Sat.	Capricorn	Earth	Semi-fruit	4th
17 Sun. 4:12 pm	Aquarius	Air	Barren	New 10:47 am
18 Mon.	Aquarius	Air	Barren	1st
19 Tue. 10:41 pm	Pisces	Water	Fruitful	1st
20 Wed.	Pisces	Water	Fruitful	1st
21 Thu.	Pisces	Water	Fruitful	1st
22 Fri. 3:26 am	Aries	Fire	Barren	1st
23 Sat.	Aries	Fire	Barren	1st
24 Sun. 6:53 am	Taurus	Earth	Semi-fruit	2nd 2:16 pm
25 Mon.	Taurus	Earth	Semi-fruit	2nd
26 Tue. 9:30 am	Gemini	Air	Barren	2nd
27 Wed.	Gemini	Air	Barren	2nd
28 Thu. 11:57 am	Cancer	Water	Fruitful	2nd
29 Fri.	Cancer	Water	Fruitful	2nd
30 Sat. 3:16 pm	Leo	Fire	Barren	2nd
31 Sun.	Leo	Fire	Barren	Full 11:07 am

January

Lunar Aspectarian   **Favorable and Unfavorable Days**

	Sun	Mercury	Venus	Mars	Jupiter	Saturn	Uranus	Neptune	Pluto	Aries	Taurus	Gemini	Cancer	Leo	Virgo	Libra	Scorpio	Sagittarius	Capricorn	Aquarius	Pisces
1	0									f		F		f	u	f		U		f	u
2				Q	T					u	f		F		f	u	f		U		f
3			0			Q		0	T	u	f		F		f	u	f		U		f
4				X			0			f	u	f		F		f	u	f		U	
5		T				T				f	u	f		F		f	u	f		U	
6	T								Q		f	u	f		F		f	u	f		U
7		Q			0			T			f	u	f		F		f	u	f		U
8			T			T			X	U		f	u	f		F		f	u	f	
9	Q			C						U		f	u	f		F		f	u	f	
10		X			0			Q		U		f	u	f		F		f	u	f	
11			Q					Q			U		f	u	f		F		f	u	f
12	X				T			X			U		f	u	f		F		f	u	f
13			X				X		C	f		U		f	u	f		F		f	u
14				X	Q					f		U		f	u	f		F		f	u
15						T				f		U		f	u	f		F		f	u
16		C								u	f		U		f	u	f		F		f
17	C			Q	X	Q		C		u	f		U		f	u	f		F		f
18						C			X	f	u	f		U		f	u	f		F	
19			C	T		X				f	u	f		U		f	u	f		F	
20									Q		f	u	f		U		f	u	f		F
21		X		C							f	u	f		U		f	u	f		F
22	X						X	T		f	u	f		U		f	u	f		F	
23			X			X				F		f	u	f		U		f	u	f	
24	Q	Q		0		C		Q		F		f	u	f		U		f	u	f	
25						Q					F		f	u	f		U		f	u	f
26	T	T	Q		X			T			F		f	u	f		U		f	u	f
27						T		0		f		F		f	u	f		U		f	u
28			T	T	Q	X				f		F		f	u	f		U		f	u
29										u	f		F		f	u	f		U		f
30			Q	T	Q			0		u	f		F		f	u	f		U		f
31	0	0						0	T	f	u	f		F		f	u	f		U	

February Moon Table

Date	Sign	Element	Nature	Phase
1 Mon. 8:37 pm	Virgo	Earth	Barren	3rd
2 Tue.	Virgo	Earth	Barren	3rd
3 Wed.	Virgo	Earth	Barren	3rd
4 Thu. 4:55 am	Libra	Air	Semi-fruit	3rd
5 Fri.	Libra	Air	Semi-fruit	3rd
6 Sat. 4:06 pm	Scorpio	Water	Fruitful	3rd
7 Sun.	Scorpio	Water	Fruitful	3rd
8 Mon.	Scorpio	Water	Fruitful	4th 6:58 am
9 Tue. 4:38 am	Sagittarius	Fire	Barren	4th
10 Wed.	Sagittarius	Fire	Barren	4th
11 Thu. 4:10 pm	Capricorn	Earth	Semi-fruit	4th
12 Fri.	Capricorn	Earth	Semi-fruit	4th
13 Sat.	Capricorn	Earth	Semi-fruit	4th
14 Sun. 12:57 am	Aquarius	Air	Barren	4th
15 Mon.	Aquarius	Air	Barren	4th
16 Tue. 6:40 am	Pisces	Water	Fruitful	New 1:40 am
17 Wed.	Pisces	Water	Fruitful	1st
18 Thu. 10:07 am	Aries	Fire	Barren	1st
19 Fri.	Aries	Fire	Barren	1st
20 Sat. 12:29 pm	Taurus	Earth	Semi-fruit	1st
21 Sun.	Taurus	Earth	Semi-fruit	1st
22 Mon. 2:54 pm	Gemini	Air	Barren	2nd 9:43 pm
23 Tue.	Gemini	Air	Barren	2nd
24 Wed. 6:09 pm	Cancer	Water	Fruitful	2nd
25 Thu.	Cancer	Water	Fruitful	2nd
26 Fri. 10:44 pm	Leo	Fire	Barren	2nd
27 Sat.	Leo	Fire	Barren	2nd
28 Sun.	Leo	Fire	Barren	2nd

February

Lunar Aspectarian   Favorable and Unfavorable Days

	Sun	Mercury	Venus	Mars	Jupiter	Saturn	Uranus	Neptune	Pluto	Aries	Taurus	Gemini	Cancer	Leo	Virgo	Libra	Scorpio	Sagittarius	Capricorn	Aquarius	Pisces
1						T				f	u	f		F		f	u	f		U	
2			0	X					Q		f	u	f		F		f	u	f		U
3											f	u	f		F		f	u	f		U
4					0			T			f	u	f		F		f	u	f		U
5	T	T				T		X		U		f	u	f		F		f	u	f	
6							0	Q		U		f	u	f		F		f	u	f	
7			T	C			Q				U		f	u	f		F		f	u	f
8	Q	Q									U		f	u	f		F		f	u	f
9					T			X			U		f	u	f		F		f	u	f
10			Q				X		C	f		U		f	u	f		F		f	u
11	X	X			Q	T				f		U		f	u	f		F		f	u
12				X						u	f		U		f	u	f		F		f
13			X				Q			u	f		U		f	u	f		F		f
14			Q	X				C	X	f	u	f		U		f	u	f		F	
15						C				f	u	f		U		f	u	f		F	
16	C	C		T				X		f	u	f		U		f	u	f		F	
17									Q		f	u	f		U		f	u	f		F
18		C		C				X			f	u	f		U		f	u	f		F
19							X		T	F		f	u	f		U		f	u	f	
20	X					C		Q		F		f	u	f		U		f	u	f	
21		X		0			Q				F		f	u	f		U		f	u	f
22	Q		X		X			T			F		f	u	f		U		f	u	f
23						T			0	f		F		f	u	f		U		f	u
24		Q		Q	X					f		F		f	u	f		U		f	u
25	T		Q	T						u	f		F		f	u	f		U		f
26		T					Q			u	f		F		f	u	f		U		f
27			T	Q	T			0	T	f	u	f		F		f	u	f		U	
28								0		f	u	f		F		f	u	f		U	

March Moon Table

Date	Sign	Element	Nature	Phase
1 Mon. 5:05 am	Virgo	Earth	Barren	2nd
2 Tue.	Virgo	Earth	Barren	Full 1:59 am
3 Wed. 1:34 pm	Libra	Air	Semi-fruit	3rd
4 Thu.	Libra	Air	Semi-fruit	3rd
5 Fri.	Libra	Air	Semi-fruit	3rd
6 Sat. 12:23 am	Scorpio	Water	Fruitful	3rd
7 Sun.	Scorpio	Water	Fruitful	3rd
8 Mon. 12:47 pm	Sagittarius	Fire	Barren	3rd
9 Tue.	Sagittarius	Fire	Barren	3rd
10 Wed.	Sagittarius	Fire	Barren	4th 3:41 am
11 Thu.12:54 am	Capricorn	Earth	Semi-fruit	4th
12 Fri.	Capricorn	Earth	Semi-fruit	4th
13 Sat. 10:32 am	Aquarius	Air	Barren	4th
14 Sun.	Aquarius	Air	Barren	4th
15 Mon. 4:31 pm	Pisces	Water	Fruitful	4th
16 Tue.	Pisces	Water	Fruitful	4th
17 Wed. 7:13 pm	Aries	Fire	Barren	New 1:48 pm
18 Thu.	Aries	Fire	Barren	1st
19 Fri. 8:09 pm	Taurus	Earth	Semi-fruit	1st
20 Sat.	Taurus	Earth	Semi-fruit	1st
21 Sun. 9:05 pm	Gemini	Air	Barren	1st
22 Mon.	Gemini	Air	Barren	1st
23 Tue. 11:33 pm	Cancer	Water	Fruitful	1st
24 Wed.	Cancer	Water	Fruitful	2nd 5:18 am
25 Thu. 4:22 am	Leo	Fire	Barren	2nd
26 Fri.	Leo	Fire	Barren	2nd
27 Sat.	Leo	Fire	Barren	2nd
28 Sun. 11:35 am	Virgo	Earth	Barren	2nd
29 Mon.	Virgo	Earth	Barren	2nd
30 Tue. 8:50 pm	Libra	Air	Semi-fruit	2nd
31 Wed.	Libra	Air	Semi-fruit	Full 5:50 pm

March

Lunar Aspectarian　　　　　　　　Favorable and Unfavorable Days

	Sun	Mercury	Venus	Mars	Jupiter	Saturn	Uranus	Neptune	Pluto	Aries	Taurus	Gemini	Cancer	Leo	Virgo	Libra	Scorpio	Sagittarius	Capricorn	Aquarius	Pisces
1						T				f	u	f		F		f	u	f		U	
2	0			X					Q		f	u	f		F		f	u	f		U
3		0			0			T			f	u	f		F		f	u	f		U
4			0				T		X	U		f	u	f		F		f	u	f	
5										U		f	u	f		F		f	u	f	
6				C		0		Q			U		f	u	f		F		f	u	f
7	T						Q				U		f	u	f		F		f	u	f
8		T			T			X			U		f	u	f		F		f	u	f
9							X		C	f		U		f	u	f		F		f	u
10	Q		T							f		U		f	u	f		F		f	u
11		Q			Q	T				u	f		U		f	u	f		F		f
12	X		Q	X						u	f		U		f	u	f		F		f
13		X			X	Q		C		u	f		U		f	u	f		F		f
14				Q			C		X	f	u	f		U		f	u	f		F	
15			X				X			f	u	f		U		f	u	f		F	
16			T						Q		f	u	f		U		f	u	f		F
17	C	C									f	u	f		U		f	u	f		F
18					C		X	X	T	F		f	u	f		U		f	u	f	
19			C			C				F		f	u	f		U		f	u	f	
20			0			Q	Q				F		f	u	f		U		f	u	f
21	X	X									F		f	u	f		U		f	u	f
22						X	T	T	0	f		F		f	u	f		U		f	u
23		Q								f		F		f	u	f		U		f	u
24	Q		X	T	Q	X				u	f		F		f	u	f		U		f
25		T								u	f		F		f	u	f		U		f
26	T		Q		T	Q		0	T	f	u	f		F		f	u	f		U	
27				Q		0				f	u	f		F		f	u	f		U	
28					T					f	u	f		F		f	u	f		U	
29			T	X					Q		f	u	f		F		f	u	f		U
30		0									f	u	f		F		f	u	f		U
31	0				0			T	X	U		f	u	f		F		f	u	f	

April Moon Table

Date	Sign	Element	Nature	Phase
1 Thu.	Libra	Air	Semi-fruit	3rd
2 Fri. 7:49 am	Scorpio	Water	Fruitful	3rd
3 Sat.	Scorpio	Water	Fruitful	3rd
4 Sun. 8:08 pm	Sagittarius	Fire	Barren	3rd
5 Mon.	Sagittarius	Fire	Barren	3rd
6 Tue.	Sagittarius	Fire	Barren	3rd
7 Wed. 8:39 am	Capricorn	Earth	Semi-fruit	3rd
8 Thu.	Capricorn	Earth	Semi-fruit	4th 9:51 pm
9 Fri. 7:24 pm	Aquarius	Air	Barren	4th
10 Sat.	Aquarius	Air	Barren	4th
11 Sun.	Pisces	Water	Fruitful	4th
12 Mon.	Pisces	Water	Fruitful	4th
13 Tue.	Pisces	Water	Fruitful	4th
14 Wed. 5:46 am	Aries	Fire	Barren	4th
15 Thu.	Aries	Fire	Barren	New 11:22 pm
16 Fri. 6:07 am	Taurus	Earth	Semi-fruit	1st
17 Sat.	Taurus	Earth	Semi-fruit	1st
18 Sun. 5:39 am	Gemini	Air	Barren	1st
19 Mon.	Gemini	Air	Barren	1st
20 Tue. 6:28 am	Cancer	Water	Fruitful	1st
21 Wed.	Cancer	Water	Fruitful	1st
22 Thu. 10:06 am	Leo	Fire	Barren	2nd 2:02 pm
23 Fri.	Leo	Fire	Barren	2nd
24 Sat. 5:05 pm	Virgo	Earth	Barren	2nd
25 Sun.	Virgo	Earth	Barren	2nd
26 Mon.	Virgo	Earth	Barren	2nd
27 Tue. 2:47 am	Libra	Air	Semi-fruit	2nd
28 Wed.	Libra	Air	Semi-fruit	2nd
29 Thu. 2:13 pm	Scorpio	Water	Fruitful	2nd
30 Fri.	Scorpio	Water	Fruitful	Full 9:55 am

April

Lunar Aspectarian   Favorable and Unfavorable Days

Day	Sun	Mercury	Venus	Mars	Jupiter	Saturn	Uranus	Neptune	Pluto	Aries	Taurus	Gemini	Cancer	Leo	Virgo	Libra	Scorpio	Sagittarius	Capricorn	Aquarius	Pisces
1							T			U		f	u	f		F		f	u	f	
2						0		Q		U		f	u	f		F		f	u	f	
3			C					Q			U		f	u	f		F		f	u	f
4		T	0								U		f	u	f		F		f	u	f
5						T		X	C	f		U		f	u	f		F		f	u
6	T	Q						X		f		U		f	u	f		F		f	u
7						T				f		U		f	u	f		F		f	u
8	Q			X	Q					u	f		U		f	u	f		F		f
9		X	T							u	f		U		f	u	f		F		f
10				Q	X	Q		C	X	f	u	f		U		f	u	f		F	
11	X							C		f	u	f		U		f	u	f		F	
12			Q	T		X			Q		f	u	f		U		f	u	f		F
13		C									f	u	f		U		f	u	f		F
14			X					X	T		f	u	f		U		f	u	f		F
15	C				C		X			F		f	u	f		U		f	u	f	
16			0		C		Q			F		f	u	f		U		f	u	f	
17							Q				F		f	u	f		U		f	u	f
18		X	C		.		T	0			F		f	u	f		U		f	u	f
19				X		T				f		F		f	u	f		U		f	u
20	X	Q		T		X				f		F		f	u	f		U		f	u
21				Q						u	f		F		f	u	f		U		f
22	Q	T		Q		Q		0		u	f		F		f	u	f		U		f
23			X	T		0			T	f	u	f		F		f	u	f		U	
24										f	u	f		F		f	u	f		U	
25	T		Q	X		T			Q		f	u	f		F		f	u	f		U
26											f	u	f		F		f	u	f		U
27							T	X		U		f	u	f		F		f	u	f	
28		0	T		0		T			U		f	u	f		F		f	u	f	
29			C					Q		U		f	u	f		F		f	u	f	
30	0					0		Q			U		f	u	f		F		f	u	f

May Moon Table

Date	Sign	Element	Nature	Phase
1 Sat.	Scorpio	Water	Fruitful	3rd
2 Sun. 2:36 am	Sagittarius	Fire	Barren	3rd
3 Mon.	Sagittarius	Fire	Barren	3rd
4 Tue. 3:12 pm	Capricorn	Earth	Semi-fruit	3rd
5 Wed.	Capricorn	Earth	Semi-fruit	3rd
6 Thu.	Capricorn	Earth	Semi-fruit	3rd
7 Fri. 2:40 am	Aquarius	Air	Barren	3rd
8 Sat.	Aquarius	Air	Barren	4th 12:28 pm
9 Sun. 11:16 am	Pisces	Water	Fruitful	4th
10 Mon.	Pisces	Water	Fruitful	4th
11 Tue. 3:54 pm	Aries	Fire	Barren	4th
12 Wed.	Aries	Fire	Barren	4th
13 Thu. 4:57 pm	Taurus	Earth	Semi-fruit	4th
14 Fri.	Taurus	Earth	Semi-fruit	4th
15 Sat. 4:08 pm	Gemini	Air	Barren	New 7:06 am
16 Sun.	Gemini	Air	Barren	1st
17 Mon. 3:40 pm	Cancer	Water	Fruitful	1st
18 Tue.	Cancer	Water	Fruitful	1st
19 Wed. 5:38 pm	Leo	Fire	Barren	1st
20 Thu.	Leo	Fire	Barren	1st
21 Fri. 11:16 pm	Virgo	Earth	Barren	1st
22 Sat.	Virgo	Earth	Barren	2nd 12:35 am
23 Sun.	Virgo	Earth	Barren	2nd
24 Mon. 8:29 am	Libra	Air	Semi-fruit	2nd
25 Tue.	Libra	Air	Semi-fruit	2nd
26 Wed. 8:05 pm	Scorpio	Water	Fruitful	2nd
27 Thu.	Scorpio	Water	Fruitful	2nd
28 Fri.	Scorpio	Water	Fruitful	2nd
29 Sat. 8:37 am	Sagittarius	Fire	Barren	2nd
30 Sun.	Sagittarius	Fire	Barren	Full 1:40 am
31 Mon. 9:06 pm	Capricorn	Earth	Semi-fruit	3rd

May

| Lunar Aspectarian | | | | | | | | | Favorable and Unfavorable Days | | | | | | | | | | | |
	Sun	Mercury	Venus	Mars	Jupiter	Saturn	Uranus	Neptune	Pluto	Aries	Taurus	Gemini	Cancer	Leo	Virgo	Libra	Scorpio	Sagittarius	Capricorn	Aquarius	Pisces
1											U		f	u	f		F		f	u	f
2								X	C	f		U		f	u	f		F		f	u
3		T				T		X		f		U		f	u	f		F		f	u
4			0	X						f		U		f	u	f		F		f	u
5	T					T				u	f		U		f	u	f		F		f
6		Q			Q					u	f		U		f	u	f		F		f
7				Q		Q		C	X	f	u	f		U		f	u	f		F	
8	Q				X		C			f	u	f		U		f	u	f		F	
9		X	T	T						f	u	f		U		f	u	f		F	
10	X						X		Q		f	u	f		U		f	u	f		F
11			Q					X			f	u	f		U		f	u	f		F
12						X		T		F		f	u	f		U		f	u	f	
13				0	C			Q		F		f	u	f		U		f	u	f	
14		C	X			C	Q				F		f	u	f		U		f	u	f
15	C						T				F		f	u	f		U		f	u	f
16						T		0		f		F		f	u	f		U		f	u
17				T	X					f		F		f	u	f		U		f	u
18		C			X					u	f		F		f	u	f		U		f
19	X	X		Q	Q					u	f		F		f	u	f		U		f
20					Q	0	0	T		f	u	f		F		f	u	f		U	
21		Q		X	T					f	u	f		F		f	u	f		U	
22	Q				T			Q			f	u	f		F		f	u	f		U
23			X								f	u	f		F		f	u	f		U
24	T	T					T				f	u	f		F		f	u	f		U
25			Q		T		X		U		f	u	f		F		f	u	f	
26			C	0					U		f	u	f		F		f	u	f	
27			0		Q				U		f	u	f		F		f	u	f
28		T		Q				U		f	u	f		F		f	u	f
29				X			U		f	u	f		F		f	u	f
30	0	0		X	C	f		U		f	u	f		F		f	u
31		X	T		f		U		f	u	f		F		f	u

June Moon Table

Date	Sign	Element	Nature	Phase
1 Tues.	Capricorn	Earth	Semi-fruit	3rd
2 Wed.	Capricorn	Earth	Semi-fruit	3rd
3 Thu. 8:37 am	Aquarius	Air	Barren	3rd
4 Fri.	Aquarius	Air	Barren	3rd
5 Sat. 6:01 pm	Pisces	Water	Fruitful	3rd
6 Sun.	Pisces	Water	Fruitful	4th 11:21 pm
7 Mon.	Pisces	Water	Fruitful	4th
8 Tue. 12:09 am	Aries	Fire	Barren	4th
9 Wed.	Aries	Fire	Barren	4th
10 Thu. 2:44 am	Taurus	Earth	Semi-fruit	4th
11 Fri.	Taurus	Earth	Semi-fruit	4th
12 Sat. 2:49 am	Gemini	Air	Barren	4th
13 Sun.	Gemini	Air	Barren	New 2:03 pm
14 Mon. 2:14 am	Cancer	Water	Fruitful	1st
15 Tue.	Cancer	Water	Fruitful	1st
16 Wed. 3:07 am	Leo	Fire	Barren	1st
17 Thu.	Leo	Fire	Barren	1st
18 Fri. 7:12 am	Virgo	Earth	Barren	1st
19 Sat.	Virgo	Earth	Barren	1st
20 Sun. 3:10 pm	Libra	Air	Semi-fruit	2nd 1:13 pm
21 Mon.	Libra	Air	Semi-fruit	2nd
22 Tue.	Libra	Air	Semi-fruit	2nd
23 Wed. 2:18 am	Scorpio	Water	Fruitful	2nd
24 Thu.	Scorpio	Water	Fruitful	2nd
25 Fri. 2:51 pm	Sagittarius	Fire	Barren	2nd
26 Sat.	Sagittarius	Fire	Barren	2nd
27 Sun.	Sagittarius	Fire	Barren	2nd
28 Mon. 3:12 am	Capricorn	Earth	Semi-fruit	Full 4:38 pm
29 Tue.	Capricorn	Earth	Semi-fruit	3rd
30 Wed. 2:20 pm	Aquarius	Air	Barren	3rd

June

Lunar Aspectarian | Favorable and Unfavorable Days

	Sun	Mercury	Venus	Mars	Jupiter	Saturn	Uranus	Neptune	Pluto	Aries	Taurus	Gemini	Cancer	Leo	Virgo	Libra	Scorpio	Sagittarius	Capricorn	Aquarius	Pisces
1						T				u	f		U		f	u	f		F		f
2				Q	Q					u	f		U		f	u	f		F		f
3			0					C		u	f		U		f	u	f		F		f
4	T					Q	C		X	f	u	f		U		f	u	f		F	
5		T		T	X					f	u	f		U		f	u	f		F	
6	Q					X			Q		f	u	f		U		f	u	f		F
7											f	u	f		U		f	u	f		F
8		Q	T					X	T	F		f	u	f		U		f	u	f	
9	X			0	C		X			F		f	u	f		U		f	u	f	
10		X	Q		C			Q			F		f	u	f		U		f	u	f
11						Q					F		f	u	f		U		f	u	f
12			X					T	0	f		F		f	u	f		U		f	u
13	C			T	X		T			f		F		f	u	f		U		f	u
14					X					u	f		F		f	u	f		U		f
15		C		Q	Q					u	f		F		f	u	f		U		f
16			C				0	T		u	f		F		f	u	f		U		f
17			X		Q	0				f	u	f		F		f	u	f		U	
18	X				T			Q		f	u	f		F		f	u	f		U	
19		X			T						f	u	f		F		f	u	f		U
20	Q					T					f	u	f		F		f	u	f		U
21			X		T		X		U		f	u	f		F		f	u	f	
22		Q		C					U		f	u	f		F		f	u	f	
23	T			0			Q			U		f	u	f		F		f	u	f
24		Q		0	Q					U		f	u	f		F		f	u	f
25		T				X				U		f	u	f		F		f	u	f
26					X		C		f		U		f	u	f		F		f	u
27		T	X						f		U		f	u	f		F		f	u
28	0			T					f		U		f	u	f		F		f	u
29					T				u	f		U		f	u	f		F		f
30		0	Q	Q			C		u	f		U		f	u	f		F		f

July Moon Table

Date	Sign	Element	Nature	Phase
1 Thu.	Aquarius	Air	Barren	3rd
2 Fri. 11:35 pm	Pisces	Water	Fruitful	3rd
3 Sat.	Pisces	Water	Fruitful	3rd
4 Sun.	Pisces	Water	Fruitful	3rd
5 Mon. 6:22 am	Aries	Fire	Barren	3rd
6 Tue.	Aries	Fire	Barren	4th 6:57 am
7 Wed. 10:22 am	Taurus	Earth	Semi-fruit	4th
8 Thu.	Taurus	Earth	Semi-fruit	4th
9 Fri. 11:59 am	Gemini	Air	Barren	4th
10 Sat.	Gemini	Air	Barren	4th
11 Sun. 12:27 pm	Cancer	Water	Fruitful	4th
12 Mon.	Cancer	Water	Fruitful	New 9:24 pm
13 Tue. 1:25 pm	Leo	Fire	Barren	1st
14 Wed.	Leo	Fire	Barren	1st
15 Thu. 4:39 pm	Virgo	Earth	Barren	1st
16 Fri.	Virgo	Earth	Barren	1st
17 Sat. 11:19 pm	Libra	Air	Semi-fruit	1st
18 Sun.	Libra	Air	Semi-fruit	1st
19 Mon.	Libra	Air	Semi-fruit	1st
20 Tue. 9:30 am	Scorpio	Water	Fruitful	2nd 4:01 am
21 Wed.	Scorpio	Water	Fruitful	2nd
22 Thu. 9:49 pm	Sagittarius	Fire	Barren	2nd
23 Fri.	Sagittarius	Fire	Barren	2nd
24 Sat.	Sagittarius	Fire	Barren	2nd
25 Sun. 10:09 am	Capricorn	Earth	Semi-fruit	2nd
26 Mon.	Capricorn	Earth	Semi-fruit	2nd
27 Tue. 8:55 pm	Aquarius	Air	Barren	2nd
28 Wed.	Aquarius	Air	Barren	Full 6:25 am
29 Thu.	Aquarius	Air	Barren	3rd
30 Fri. 5:27 am	Pisces	Water	Fruitful	3rd
31 Sat.	Pisces	Water	Fruitful	3rd

July

Lunar Aspectarian   Favorable and Unfavorable Days

	Sun	Mercury	Venus	Mars	Jupiter	Saturn	Uranus	Neptune	Pluto	Aries	Taurus	Gemini	Cancer	Leo	Virgo	Libra	Scorpio	Sagittarius	Capricorn	Aquarius	Pisces
1						Q	C		X	f	u	f		U		f	u	f		F	
2			0	T						f	u	f		U		f	u	f		F	
3	T				X				Q		f	u	f		U		f	u	f		F
4					X						f	u	f		U		f	u	f		F
5		T						X	T		f	u	f		U		f	u	f		F
6	Q					X				F		f	u	f		U		f	u	f	
7			T	0	C			Q		F		f	u	f		U		f	u	f	
8	X	Q				C	Q				F		f	u	f		U		f	u	f
9			Q					T			F		f	u	f		U		f	u	f
10		X					T		0	f		F		f	u	f		U		f	u
11			X	T	X					f		F		f	u	f		U		f	u
12	C					X				u	f		F		f	u	f		U		f
13				Q	Q			0		u	f		F		f	u	f		U		f
14		C				Q	0		T	f	u	f		F		f	u	f		U	
15		C	X	T						f	u	f		F		f	u	f		U	
16						T			Q		f	u	f		F		f	u	f		U
17	X										f	u	f		F		f	u	f		U
18		X						T	X	U		f	u	f		F		f	u	f	
19							T			U		f	u	f		F		f	u	f	
20	Q	Q	X	C	0			Q		U		f	u	f		F		f	u	f	
21					0	Q					U		f	u	f		F		f	u	f
22	T										U		f	u	f		F		f	u	f
23		T	Q					X	C	f		U		f	u	f		F		f	u
24						X				f		U		f	u	f		F		f	u
25		T		T						f		U		f	u	f		F		f	u
26			X		T					u	f		U		f	u	f		F		f
27										u	f		U		f	u	f		F		f
28	0	0				Q	Q	C	X	f	u	f		U		f	u	f		F	
29						Q	C			f	u	f		U		f	u	f		F	
30			0		X				Q	f	u	f		U		f	u	f		F	
31				T	X						f	u	f		U		f	u	f		F

August Moon Table

Date	Sign	Element	Nature	Phase
1 Sun. 11:47 am	Aries	Fire	Barren	3rd
2 Mon.	Aries	Fire	Barren	3rd
3 Tue. 4:08 pm	Taurus	Earth	Semi-fruit	3rd
4 Wed.	Taurus	Earth	Semi-fruit	4th 12:26 pm
5 Thu. 6:57 pm	Gemini	Air	Barren	4th
6 Fri.	Gemini	Air	Barren	4th
7 Sat. 8:52 pm	Cancer	Water	Fruitful	4th
8 Sun.	Cancer	Water	Fruitful	4th
9 Mon. 10:55 pm	Leo	Fire	Barren	4th
10 Tue.	Leo	Fire	Barren	4th
11 Wed.	Leo	Fire	Barren	New 6:09 am
12 Thu. 2:22 am	Virgo	Earth	Barren	1st
13 Fri.	Virgo	Earth	Barren	1st
14 Sat. 8:25 am	Libra	Air	Semi-fruit	1st
15 Sun.	Libra	Air	Semi-fruit	1st
16 Mon. 5:41 pm	Scorpio	Water	Fruitful	1st
17 Tue.	Scorpio	Water	Fruitful	1st
18 Wed.	Scorpio	Water	Fruitful	2nd 8:48 pm
19 Thu. 5:32 am	Sagittarius	Fire	Barren	2nd
20 Fri.	Sagittarius	Fire	Barren	2nd
21 Sat. 5:59 pm	Capricorn	Earth	Semi-fruit	2nd
22 Sun.	Capricorn	Earth	Semi-fruit	2nd
23 Mon.4:49 am	Aquarius	Air	Barren	2nd
24 Tue.	Aquarius	Air	Barren	2nd
25 Wed.	Aquarius	Air	Barren	2nd
26 Thu. 12:49 pm	Pisces	Water	Fruitful	Full 6:48 pm
27 Fri.	Pisces	Water	Fruitful	3rd
28 Sat.6:09 pm	Aries	Fire	Barren	3rd
29 Sun	Aries	Fire	Barren	3rd
30 Mon. 9:40 pm	Taurus	Earth	Semi-fruit	3rd
31 Tue.	Taurus	Earth	Semi-fruit	3rd

August

Lunar Aspectarian | Favorable and Unfavorable Days

	Sun	Mercury	Venus	Mars	Jupiter	Saturn	Uranus	Neptune	Pluto	Aries	Taurus	Gemini	Cancer	Leo	Virgo	Libra	Scorpio	Sagittarius	Capricorn	Aquarius	Pisces
1		T						X			f	u	f		U		f	u	f		F
2	T							X	T	F		f	u	f		U		f	u	f	
3		Q				C		Q		F		f	u	f		U		f	u	f	
4	Q			T	0		C	Q			F		f	u	f		U		f	u	f
5		X						T			F		f	u	f		U		f	u	f
6	X		Q				T		0	f		F		f	u	f		U		f	u
7										f		F		f	u	f		U		f	u
8			X	T	X					u	f		F		f	u	f		U		f
9		C					X			u	f		F		f	u	f		U		f
10				Q			0	0	T	f	u	f		F		f	u	f		U	
11	C			Q			Q			f	u	f		F		f	u	f		U	
12			C		T				Q		f	u	f		F		f	u	f		U
13				X		T					f	u	f		F		f	u	f		U
14		X						T	X		f	u	f		F		f	u	f		U
15						T				U		f	u	f		F		f	u	f	
16	X		X					Q		U		f	u	f		F		f	u	f	
17		Q			0		Q				U		f	u	f		F		f	u	f
18	Q			C		0					U		f	u	f		F		f	u	f
19			Q					X	C		U		f	u	f		F		f	u	f
20		T					X			f		U		f	u	f		F		f	u
21	T		T							f		U		f	u	f		F		f	u
22						T				u	f		U		f	u	f		F		f
23				X		T				u	f		U		f	u	f		F		f
24					Q			C	X	f	u	f		U		f	u	f		F	
25		0				Q	C			f	u	f		U		f	u	f		F	
26	0		0	Q	X					f	u	f		U		f	u	f		F	
27							X		Q		f	u	f		U		f	u	f		F
28			T					X			f	u	f		U		f	u	f		F
29							X		T	F		f	u	f		U		f	u	f	
30		T	T							F		f	u	f		U		f	u	f	
31	T				C	C	Q	Q			F		f	u	f		U		f	u	f

September Moon Table

Date	Sign	Element	Nature	Phase
1 Wed.	Taurus	Earth	Semi-fruit	3rd
2 Thu. 12:25 am	Gemini	Air	Barren	4th 5:18 pm
3 Fri. 3:10 am	Cancer	Water	Fruitful	4th
4 Sat.	Cancer	Water	Fruitful	4th
5 Sun.	Cancer	Water	Fruitful	4th
6 Mon. 6:29 am	Leo	Fire	Barren	4th
7 Tue.	Leo	Fire	Barren	4th
8 Wed. 10:57 am	Virgo	Earth	Barren	4th
9 Thu.	Virgo	Earth	Barren	New 5:03 pm
10 Fri. 5:16 pm	Libra	Air	Semi-fruit	1st
11 Sat.	Libra	Air	Semi-fruit	1st
12 Sun.	Libra	Air	Semi-fruit	1st
13 Mon. 2:09 am	Scorpio	Water	Fruitful	1st
14 Tue.	Scorpio	Water	Fruitful	1st
15 Wed. 1:35 pm	Sagittarius	Fire	Barren	1st
16 Thu.	Sagittarius	Fire	Barren	1st
17 Fri.	Sagittarius	Fire	Barren	2nd 3:06 pm
18 Sat. 2:13 am	Capricorn	Earth	Semi-fruit	2nd
19 Sun.	Capricorn	Earth	Semi-fruit	2nd
20 Mon.1:38 pm	Aquarius	Air	Barren	2nd
21 Tue.	Aquarius	Air	Barren	2nd
22 Wed. 9:51 pm	Pisces	Water	Fruitful	2nd
23 Thu.	Pisces	Water	Fruitful	2nd
24 Fri.	Pisces	Water	Fruitful	2nd
25 Sat. 2:34 am	Aries	Fire	Barren	Full 5:31 am
26 Sun.	Aires	Fire	Barren	3rd
27 Mon. 4:51 am	Taurus	Earth	Semi-fruit	3rd
28 Tue.	Taurus	Earth	Semi-fruit	3rd
29 Wed. 6:21 am	Gemini	Air	Barren	3rd
30 Thu.	Gemini	Air	Barren	3rd

September

Lunar Aspectarian									Favorable and Unfavorable Days												
	Sun	Mercury	Venus	Mars	Jupiter	Saturn	Uranus	Neptune	Pluto	Aries	Taurus	Gemini	Cancer	Leo	Virgo	Libra	Scorpio	Sagittarius	Capricorn	Aquarius	Pisces
1			Q	0		C					F		f	u	f		U		f	u	f
2	Q	Q					T	T	0	f		F		f	u	f		U		f	u
3			X							f		F		f	u	f		U		f	u
4	X	X			X					u	f		F		f	u	f		U		f
5						X				u	f		F		f	u	f		U		f
6				T	Q			0	T	u	f		F		f	u	f		U		f
7			C		Q	0				f	u	f		F		f	u	f		U	
8			Q	T						f	u	f		F		f	u	f		U	
9	C	C				T			Q		f	u	f		F		f	u	f		U
10								T			f	u	f		F		f	u	f		U
11			X			T		X	X	U		f	u	f		F		f	u	f	
12			X							U		f	u	f		F		f	u	f	
13					0			Q			U		f	u	f		F		f	u	f
14	X		Q		0	Q					U		f	u	f		F		f	u	f
15		X						X			U		f	u	f		F		f	u	f
16				C		X			C	f		U		f	u	f		F		f	u
17	Q		T							f		U		f	u	f		F		f	u
18		Q			T					u	f		U		f	u	f		F		f
19					T					u	f		U		f	u	f		F		f
20	T				Q			C		u	f		U		f	u	f		F		f
21		T		X	Q	C			X	f	u	f		U		f	u	f		F	
22			0							f	u	f		U		f	u	f		F	
23				Q	X				Q		f	u	f		U		f	u	f		F
24					X						f	u	f		U		f	u	f		F
25	0							X	T	F		f	u	f		U		f	u	f	
26		0	T	T			X			F		f	u	f		U		f	u	f	
27				C				Q		F		f	u	f		U		f	u	f	
28			Q		C	Q					F		f	u	f		U		f	u	f
29	T							T	0		F		f	u	f		U		f	u	f
30		T	X	0		T				f		F		f	u	f		U		f	u

October Moon Table

Date	Sign	Element	Nature	Phase
1 Fri. 8:32 am	Cancer	Water	Fruitful	4th 11:03 pm
2 Sat.	Cancer	Water	Fruitful	4th
3 Sun. 12:14 pm	Leo	Fire	Barren	4th
4 Mon.	Leo	Fire	Barren	4th
5 Tue. 5:40 pm	Virgo	Earth	Barren	4th
6 Wed.	Virgo	Earth	Barren	4th
7 Thu.	Virgo	Earth	Barren	4th
8 Fri. 12:52 am	Libra	Air	Semi-fruit	4th
9 Sat.	Libra	Air	Semi-fruit	New 6:34 am
10 Sun. 10:01 am	Scorpio	Water	Fruitful	1st
11 Mon.	Scorpio	Water	Fruitful	1st
12 Tue. 9:18 pm	Sagittarius	Fire	Barren	1st
13 Wed.	Sagittarius	Fire	Barren	1st
14 Thu.	Sagittarius	Fire	Barren	1st
15 Fri. 10:03 am	Capricorn	Earth	Semi-fruit	1st
16 Sat.	Capricorn	Earth	Semi-fruit	1st
17 Sun. 10:17 pm	Aquarius	Air	Barren	2nd 9:59 am
18 Mon.	Aquarius	Air	Barren	2nd
19 Tue.	Aquarius	Air	Barren	2nd
20 Wed. 7:33 am	Pisces	Water	Fruitful	2nd
21 Thu.	Pisces	Water	Fruitful	2nd
22 Fri. 12:42 pm	Aries	Fire	Barren	2nd
23 Sat.	Aries	Fire	Barren	2nd
24 Sun. 2:26 pm	Taurus	Earth	Semi-fruit	Full 4:03 pm
25 Mon.	Taurus	Earth	Semi-fruit	3rd
26 Tue. 2:34 pm	Gemini	Air	Barren	3rd
27 Wed.	Gemini	Air	Barren	3rd
28 Thu. 3:09 pm	Cancer	Water	Fruitful	3rd
29 Fri.	Cancer	Water	Fruitful	3rd
30 Sat. 5:47 pm	Leo	Fire	Barren	3rd
31 Sun.	Leo	Fire	Barren	4th 7:04 am

October

Lunar Aspectarian   Favorable and Unfavorable Days

	Sun	Mercury	Venus	Mars	Jupiter	Saturn	Uranus	Neptune	Pluto	Aries	Taurus	Gemini	Cancer	Leo	Virgo	Libra	Scorpio	Sagittarius	Capricorn	Aquarius	Pisces
1	Q		X		X					f		F		f	u	f		U		f	u
2						X				u	f		F		f	u	f		U		f
3		Q			Q			0		u	f		F		f	u	f		U		f
4	X					Q	0		T	f	u	f		F		f	u	f		U	
5		X	C	T	T					f	u	f		F		f	u	f		U	
6						T			Q		f	u	f		F		f	u	f		U
7			Q								f	u	f		F		f	u	f		U
8								T	X	U		f	u	f		F		f	u	f	
9	C					T				U		f	u	f		F		f	u	f	
10			X	X	0			Q		U		f	u	f		F		f	u	f	
11		C			0	Q					U		f	u	f		F		f	u	f
12											U		f	u	f		F		f	u	f
13			Q			X	X		C	f		U		f	u	f		F		f	u
14	X									f		U		f	u	f		F		f	u
15			T	C	T					f		U		f	u	f		F		f	u
16		X				T				u	f		U		f	u	f		F		f
17	Q				Q					u	f		U		f	u	f		F		f
18						C	C	X		f	u	f		U		f	u	f		F	
19		Q			Q					f	u	f		U		f	u	f		F	
20	T			X	X				Q	f	u	f		U		f	u	f		F	
21		T	0			X					f	u	f		U		f	u	f		F
22			Q					X			f	u	f		U		f	u	f		F
23						X		T		F		f	u	f		U		f	u	f	
24	0			T	C			Q		F		f	u	f		U		f	u	f	
25			T			C	Q				F		f	u	f		U		f	u	f
26		0						T			F		f	u	f		U		f	u	f
27			Q			T			0	f		F		f	u	f		U		f	u
28	T				X					f		F		f	u	f		U		f	u
29				0	X					u	f		F		f	u	f		U		f
30		T	X			Q		0		u	f		F		f	u	f		U		f
31	Q					Q	0		T	f	u	f		F		f	u	f		U	

November Moon Table

Date	Sign	Element	Nature	Phase
1 Mon. 11:07 pm	Virgo	Earth	Barren	4th
2 Tues.	Virgo	Earth	Barren	4th
3 Wed.	Virgo	Earth	Barren	4th
4 Thu. 6:56 am	Libra	Air	Semi-fruit	4th
5 Fri.	Libra	Air	Semi-fruit	4th
6 Sat. 4:45 pm	Scorpio	Water	Fruitful	4th
7 Sun.	Scorpio	Water	Fruitful	New 10:53 pm
8 Mon.	Scorpio	Water	Fruitful	1st
9 Tue. 4:15 am	Sagittarius	Fire	Barren	1st
10 Wed.	Sagittarius	Fire	Barren	1st
11 Thu. 5:00 pm	Capricorn	Earth	Semi-fruit	1st
12 Fri.	Capricorn	Earth	Semi-fruit	1st
13 Sat.	Capricorn	Earth	Semi-fruit	1st
14 Sun. 5:46 am	Aquarius	Air	Barren	1st
15 Mon.	Aquarius	Air	Barren	1st
16 Tue. 4:21 pm	Pisces	Water	Fruitful	2nd 4:04 am
17 Wed.	Pisces	Water	Fruitful	2nd
18 Thu. 10:58 pm	Aries	Fire	Barren	2nd
19 Fri.	Aries	Fire	Barren	2nd
20 Sat.	Aries	Fire	Barren	2nd
21 Sun. 1:26 am	Taurus	Earth	Semi-fruit	2nd
22 Mon.	Taurus	Earth	Semi-fruit	2nd
23 Tue. 1:14 am	Gemini	Air	Barren	Full 2:04 am
24 Wed.	Gemini	Air	Barren	3rd
25 Thu. 12:29 am	Cancer	Water	Fruitful	3rd
26 Fri.	Leo	Fire	Barren	3rd
27 Sat.	Leo	Fire	Barren	3rd
28 Sun.	Leo	Fire	Barren	3rd
29 Mon. 5:11 am	Virgo	Earth	Barren	4th 6:19 pm
30 Tue.	Virgo	Earth	Barren	4th

November

Lunar Aspectarian   Favorable and Unfavorable Days

	Sun	Mercury	Venus	Mars	Jupiter	Saturn	Uranus	Neptune	Pluto	Aries	Taurus	Gemini	Cancer	Leo	Virgo	Libra	Scorpio	Sagittarius	Capricorn	Aquarius	Pisces
1					T					f	u	f		F		f	u	f		U	
2	X	Q		T					Q		f	u	f		F		f	u	f		U
3			C			T					f	u	f		F		f	u	f		U
4		X						T			f	u	f		F		f	u	f		U
5				Q			T		X	U		f	u	f		F		f	u	f	
6			0					Q		U		f	u	f		F		f	u	f	
7	C						0	Q			U		f	u	f		F		f	u	f
8				X							U		f	u	f		F		f	u	f
9		C	X					X	C		U		f	u	f		F		f	u	f
10							X			f		U		f	u	f		F		f	u
11			Q	T						f		U		f	u	f		F		f	u
12					T					u	f		U		f	u	f		F		f
13	X	X		C						u	f		U		f	u	f		F		f
14			T	Q				C		u	f		U		f	u	f		F		f
15						Q	C		X	f	u	f		U		f	u	f		F	
16	Q	Q		X						f	u	f		U		f	u	f		F	
17							X		Q		f	u	f		U		f	u	f		F
18	T	T		X							f	u	f		U		f	u	f		F
19			0				X	X	T	F		f	u	f		U		f	u	f	
20				Q	C					F		f	u	f		U		f	u	f	
21						C	Q	Q			F		f	u	f		U		f	u	f
22		0		T							F		f	u	f		U		f	u	f
23	0						T	T	0	f		F		f	u	f		U		f	u
24			T	X						f		F		f	u	f		U		f	u
25						X				u	f		F		f	u	f		U		f
26		T	Q	Q						u	f		F		f	u	f		U		f
27	T			0		Q		0	T	f	u	f		F		f	u	f		U	
28		Q	X	T		0				f	u	f		F		f	u	f		U	
29	Q								Q	f	u	f		F		f	u	f		U	
30		X				T					f	u	f		F		f	u	f		U

December Moon Table

Date	Sign	Element	Nature	Phase
1 Wed. 12:29 pm	Libra	Air	Semi-fruit	4th
2 Thu.	Libra	Air	Semi-fruit	4th
3 Fri. 10:36 pm	Scorpio	Water	Fruitful	4th
4 Sat.	Scorpio	Water	Fruitful	4th
5 Sun.	Scorpio	Water	Fruitful	4th
6 Mon. 10:28 am	Sagittarius	Fire	Barren	4th
7 Tue.	Sagittarius	Fire	Barren	New 5:32 pm
8 Wed. 11:14 pm	Capricorn	Earth	Semi-fruit	1st
9 Thu.	Capricorn	Earth	Semi-fruit	1st
10 Fri.	Capricorn	Earth	Semi-fruit	1st
11 Sat. 11:59 am	Aquarius	Air	Barren	1st
12 Sun.	Aquarius	Air	Barren	1st
13 Mon. 11:18 pm	Pisces	Water	Fruitful	1st
14 Tue.	Pisces	Water	Fruitful	1st
15 Wed.	Pisces	Water	Fruitful	2nd 7:50 pm
16 Thu. 7:30 am	Aries	Fire	Barren	2nd
17 Fri.	Aries	Fire	Barren	2nd
18 Sat.11:45 am	Taurus	Earth	Semi-fruit	2nd
19 Sun.	Taurus	Earth	Semi-fruit	2nd
20 Mon. 12:39 pm	Gemini	Air	Barren	2nd
21 Tue.	Gemini	Air	Barren	2nd
22 Wed. 11:52 am	Cancer	Water	Fruitful	Full 12:31 pm
23 Thu.	Cancer	Water	Fruitful	3rd
24 Fri. 11:32 am	Leo	Fire	Barren	3rd
25 Sat.	Leo	Fire	Barren	3rd
26 Sun. 1:34 pm	Virgo	Earth	Barren	3rd
27 Mon.	Virgo	Earth	Barren	3rd
28 Tue. 7:15 pm	Libra	Air	Semi-fruit	3rd
29 Wed.	Libra	Air	Semi-fruit	4th 9:05 am
30 Thu. 4:37 am	Scorpio	Water	Fruitful	4th
31 Fri.	Scorpio	Water	Fruitful	4th

December

Lunar Aspectarian — Favorable and Unfavorable Days

	Sun	Mercury	Venus	Mars	Jupiter	Saturn	Uranus	Neptune	Pluto	Aries	Taurus	Gemini	Cancer	Leo	Virgo	Libra	Scorpio	Sagittarius	Capricorn	Aquarius	Pisces
1				T				T			f	u	f		F		f	u	f		U
2	X						T		X	U		f	u	f		F		f	u	f	
3			C		O					U		f	u	f		F		f	u	f	
4				Q	O			Q			U		f	u	f		F		f	u	f
5		C				Q					U		f	u	f		F		f	u	f
6								X			U		f	u	f		F		f	u	f
7	C			X			X		C	f		U		f	u	f		F		f	u
8						T				f		U		f	u	f		F		f	u
9			X			T				u	f		U		f	u	f		F		f
10										u	f		U		f	u	f		F		f
11		X			Q			C		u	f		U		f	u	f		F		f
12			Q	C		Q	C		X	f	u	f		U		f	u	f		F	
13	X			X						f	u	f		U		f	u	f		F	
14		Q	T				X		Q		f	u	f		U		f	u	f		F
15	Q										f	u	f		U		f	u	f		F
16		T						X	T	F		f	u	f		U		f	u	f	
17			X				X		T	F		f	u	f		U		f	u	f	
18	T					C		Q		F		f	u	f		U		f	u	f	
19			O	Q			C	Q			F		f	u	f		U		f	u	f
20								T			F		f	u	f		U		f	u	f
21		O		T		T			O	f		F		f	u	f		U		f	u
22	O			X						f		F		f	u	f		U		f	u
23			T				X			u	f		F		f	u	f		U		f
24					Q			O		u	f		F		f	u	f		U		f
25						Q	O		T	f	u	f		F		f	u	f		U	
26	T	T	Q	O	T					f	u	f		F		f	u	f		U	
27						T			Q		f	u	f		F		f	u	f		U
28		Q	X								f	u	f		F		f	u	f		U
29	Q						T	T	X	U		f	u	f		F		f	u	f	
30				T	O					U		f	u	f		F		f	u	f	
31	X	X				O		Q		U		f	u	f		F		f	u	f	

The Moon's Quarters & Signs

Everyone has seen the Moon wax and wane through a period of approximately twenty-nine and a half days. This circuit from New Moon to Full Moon and back again is called the lunation cycle. The cycle is divided into parts, called quarters or phases. There are several methods by which this can be done, and the system used in the *Moon Sign Book* may not correspond to those used in other almanacs.

The Quarters

First Quarter

The first quarter begins at the New Moon, when the Sun and Moon are in the same place, or conjunct. (This means that the Sun and Moon are in the same degree of the same sign.) The Moon is not visible at first, since it rises at the same time as the Sun. The **New Moon** is the time of new beginnings, beginnings of projects that favor growth, externalization of activities, and the growth of ideas. The first quarter is the time of germination, emergence, beginnings, and outwardly directed activity.

Second Quarter

The second quarter begins halfway between the New Moon and the Full Moon, when the Sun and Moon are at right angles, or a 90 degree square to each other. This half Moon rises around noon and sets around midnight, so it can be seen in the western sky during the first half of the night. The second quarter is the time of growth, development, and articulation of things that already exist.

Third Quarter

The third quarter begins at the Full Moon, when the Sun and Moon are opposite one another and the full light of the Sun can shine on the full sphere of the Moon. The round Moon can be seen rising in the east at sunset, and then rising a little later each evening. The **Full Moon** stands for illumination, fulfillment, culmination, completion, drawing inward, unrest, emotional expressions, and hasty actions leading to failure. The third quarter is a time of maturity, fruition, and the assumption of the full form of expression.

Fourth Quarter

The fourth quarter begins about halfway between the Full Moon and New Moon, when the Sun and Moon are again at 90 degrees, or square. This decreasing Moon rises at midnight, and can be seen in the east during the last half of the night, reaching the overhead position just about as the Sun rises. The fourth quarter is a time of disintegration, drawing back for reorganization and reflection.

The Signs

Moon in Aries is good for starting things, but lacking in staying power. Things occur rapidly, but also quickly pass.

With Moon in Taurus, things begun last the longest and tend to increase in value. Things begun now become habitual and hard to alter.

Moon in Gemini is an inconsistent position for the Moon, characterized by a lot of talk. Things begun now are easily changed by outside influence.

Moon in Cancer stimulates emotional rapport between people. It pinpoints need, and supports growth and nurturance.

Moon in Leo accents showmanship, being seen, drama, recreation, and happy pursuits. It may be concerned with praise and subject to flattery.

Moon in Virgo favors accomplishment of details and commands from higher up while discouraging independent thinking.

Moon in Libra increases self-awareness. It favors self-examination and interaction with others, but discourages spontaneous initiative.

Moon in Scorpio increases awareness of psychic power. It precipitates psychic crises and ends connections thoroughly.

Moon in Sagittarius encourages expansionary flights of imagination and confidence in the flow of life.

Moon in Capricorn increases awareness of the need for structure, discipline, and organization. Institutional activities are favored.

Moon in Aquarius favors activities that are unique and individualistic, concern for the humanitarian needs, society as a whole, and improvements that can be made.

During Moon in Pisces, energy withdraws from the surface of life, hibernates within, secretly reorganizing and realigning for a new day.

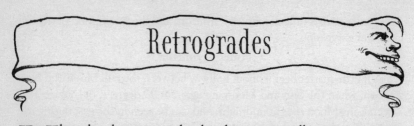

Retrogrades

W hen the planets cross the sky, they occasionally appear to move backward as seen from Earth. When a planet turns "backward" it is said to be *retrograde*. When it turns forward again, it is said to go *direct*. The point at which the movement changes from one direction to another is called a *station*.

When a planet is retrograde, its expression is delayed or out of kilter with the normal progression of events. Generally, it can be said that whatever is planned during this period will be delayed, but usually it will come to fruition when the retrograde is over. Of course, this only applies to activities ruled by the planet that is retrograde. Mercury retrogrades are easy to follow.

Mercury Retrograde

Mercury rules informal communications—reading, writing, speaking, and short errands. Whenever Mercury goes retrograde, personal communications get fouled up or misunderstood. The general rule is *when Mercury is retrograde, avoid informal means of communication*.

Planetary Retrogrades for 1999 (EST)

Planet	Begin		End	
Mercury	3/10/99	4:07 am	4/2/99	4:15 am
Pluto	3/13/99	10:56 am	8/18/99	5:59 pm
Mars	3/18/99	8:40 am	6/4/99	1:12 am
Neptune	5/6/99	1:33 pm	10/13/99	5:01 pm
Uranus	5/21/98	1:43 pm	10/22/99	10:34 pm
Mercury	7/12/99	6:26 pm	8/5/99	10:20 pm
Venus	7/29/99	8:41 pm	9/10/09	7:25 pm
Jupiter	8/24/99	8:46 pm	12/20/99	10:23 am
Saturn	8/29/99	7:09 pm	1/11/00	11:59 pm
Mercury	11/4/99	9:51 pm	11/24/99	10:53 pm

Moon Void-of-Course

By Kim Rogers-Gallagher

The Moon makes a loop around the Earth in about twenty-eight days, moving through each of the signs in two and a half days (or so). As she passes through the 30 degrees of each sign, she "visits" with the planets in numerical order by forming angles or aspects with them. Because she moves one degree in just two to two and a half hours, her influence on each planet lasts only a few hours, then she moves along. As she approaches the late degrees of the sign she's passing through, she eventually reaches the planet that's in the highest degree of any sign, and forms what will be her final aspect before leaving the sign. From this point until she actually enters the new sign, she is referred to as void-of-course, or void.

Think of it this way: The Moon is the emotional "tone" of the day, carrying feelings with her particular to the sign she's "wearing" at the moment. After she has contacted each of the planets, she symbolically "rests" before changing her costume, so her instinct is temporarily on hold. It's during this time that many people feel "fuzzy" or "vague"—scattered, even. Plans or decisions we make now will usually not pan out. Without the instinctual "knowing" the Moon provides as she touches each planet, we tend to be unrealistic or exercise poor judgment. The traditional definition of the void Moon is that "nothing will come of this," and it seems to be true. Actions initiated under a void Moon are often wasted, irrelevant, or incorrect—usually because information is hidden or missing, or has been overlooked.

Now, although it's not a good time to initiate plans, routine tasks seem to go along just fine. However, this period is really ideal for what the Moon does best: reflection. It's at this time that we can assimilate what the world has tossed at us over the past few days.

On the lighter side, remember that there are other good uses for the void Moon. This is the time period when the universe seems to be most open to loopholes. It's a great time to make plans you don't want to fulfill or schedule things you don't want to do. See the table on pages 56–61 for a schedule of the 1999 void-of-course Moons.

Moon Void-of-Course

Last Aspect		Moon Enters New Sign		
Date	Time	Date	Sign	Time
		January		
3	2:35 am	3	Leo	5:31 am
5	6:31 am	5	Virgo	10:49 am
7	6:07 am	7	Libra	7:53 pm
10	1:32 am	10	Scorpio	7:48 am
12	7:53 am	12	Sagittarius	8:23 pm
15	1:43 am	15	Capricorn	7:29 am
17	10:49 am	17	Aquarius	4:12 pm
19	5:44 pm	19	Pisces	10:41 pm
21	7:35 pm	22	Aries	3:26 am
24	5:26 am	24	Taurus	6:53 am
26	4:44 am	26	Gemini	9:30 am
28	7:52 am	28	Cancer	11:57 am
30	11:17 am	30	Leo	3:16 pm
		February		
1	4:40 pm	1	Virgo	8:37 pm
4	1:18 am	4	Libra	4:55 am
6	12:22 pm	6	Scorpio	4:06 pm
9	3:01 am	9	Sagittarius	4:38 am
11	3:40 pm	11	Capricorn	4:10 pm
13	10:32 pm	14	Aquarius	12:57 am
16	4:42 am	16	Pisces	6:40 am
18	2:42 am	18	Aries	10:07 am
20	11:12 am	20	Taurus	12:29 pm
21	4:36 pm	22	Gemini	2:54 pm
24	5:28 pm	24	Cancer	6:09 pm
26	10:24 pm	26	Leo	10:44 pm
28	12:18 am	1 (March)	Virgo	5:05 am
		March		
2	1:59 am	3	Libra	1:34 pm

Moon Void-of-Course

Last Aspect		Moon Enters New Sign		
Date	Time	Date	Sign	Time
4	5:44 pm	6	Scorpio	12:23 am
7	9:38 am	8	Sagittarius	12:47 pm
10	5:41 am	11	Capricorn	12:54 am
12	10:33 pm	13	Aquarius	10:32 am
15	10:40 am	15	Pisces	4:31 pm
17	1:48 pm	17	Aries	7:13 pm
18	8:07 pm	19	Taurus	8:09 pm
21	3:52 pm	21	Gemini	9:05 pm
23	3:11 pm	23	Cancer	11:33 pm
25	4:46 pm	25	Leo	4:22 am
27	8:46 am	28	Virgo	11:35 am
30	4:03 am	30	Libra	8:50 pm
		April		
1	3:39 am	2	Scorpio	7:49 am
4	2:01 am	4	Sagittarius	8:08 pm
6	4:07 pm	7	Capricorn	8:39 am
9	1:06 pm	9	Aquarius	7:24 pm
12	2:02 am	12	Pisces	2:35 am
13	11:53 pm	14	Aries	5:46 am
15	11:22 pm	16	Taurus	6:07 am
17	7:56 am	18	Gemini	5:39 am
20	6:22 am	20	Cancer	6:28 am
21	9:32 am	22	Leo	10:06 am
23	3:58 pm	24	Virgo	5:05 pm
25	11:15 pm	27	Libra	2:47 am
28	4:08 pm	29	Scorpio	2:13 pm
30	11:35 pm	2 (May)	Sagittarius	2:36 am
		May		
4	5:37 am	4	Capricorn	3:12 pm
7	1:45 am	7	Aquarius	2:40 am

Moon Void-of-Course

Last Aspect		Moon Enters New Sign		
Date	Time	Date	Sign	Time
9	9:01 am	9	Pisces	11:16 am
10	10:51 pm	11	Aries	3:54 pm
13	12:59 pm	13	Taurus	4:57 pm
15	7:06 am	15	Gemini	4:08 pm
17	10:05 am	17	Cancer	3:40 pm
19	2:52 pm	19	Leo	5:38 pm
21	3:15 pm	21	Virgo	11:16 pm
23	5:37 am	24	Libra	8:29 am
26	9:56 am	26	Scorpio	8:05 pm
28	4:08 pm	29	Sagittarius	8:37 am
31	10:54 am	31	Capricorn	9:06 pm
		June		
3	3:39 am	3	Aquarius	8:37 am
5	1:27 pm	5	Pisces	6:01 pm
6	11:21 pm	8	Aries	12:09 am
9	9:28 pm	10	Taurus	2:44 am
11	5:35 am	12	Gemini	2:49 am
13	10:20 pm	14	Cancer	2:14 am
15	11:39 pm	16	Leo	3:07 am
18	4:10 am	18	Virgo	7:12 am
20	1:13 pm	20	Libra	3:10 pm
23	12:36 am	23	Scorpio	2:18 am
25	12:50 pm	25	Sagittarius	2:51 pm
28	3:11 am	28	Capricorn	3:12 am
30	11:37 am	30	Aquarius	2:20 pm
		July		
2	10:22 pm	2	Pisces	11:35 pm
4	2:26 am	5	Aries	6:22 am
7	5:07 am	7	Taurus	10:22 am
9	9:09 am	9	Gemini	11:59 am

Moon Void-of-Course

Last Aspect		Moon Enters New Sign		
Date	Time	Date	Sign	T
11	11:37 am	11	Cancer	12:27
12	9:24 pm	13	Leo	1:25 p
14	3:54 pm	15	Virgo	4:39 pn
17	1:28 pm	17	Libra	11:19 p
20	4:01 am	20	Scorpio	9:30 am
22	9:28 pm	22	Sagittarius	9:49 pm
24	4:52 am	25	Capricorn	10:09 am
26	6:06 pm	27	Aquarius	8:55 pm
29	3:56 am	30	Pisces	5:27 am
		August		
1	11:03 am	1	Aries	11:47 am
3	2:12 pm	3	Taurus	4:08 pm
5	4:35 pm	5	Gemini	6:57 pm
6	7:43 pm	7	Cancer	8:52 pm
9	10:01 pm	9	Leo	10:55 pm
11	6:09 am	12	Virgo	2:22 am
13	10:31 am	14	Libra	8:25 am
16	4:12 pm	16	Scorpio	5:41 pm
19	1:07 am	19	Sagittarius	5:32 am
21	2:36 pm	21	Capricorn	5:59 pm
23	5:13 pm	24	Aquarius	4:49 am
26	4:31 am	26	Pisces	12:49 pm
28	12:41 pm	28	Aries	6:09 pm
30	7:39 pm	30	Taurus	9:40 am
		September		
1	11:46 pm	2	Gemini	12:25 am
3	9:59 am	3	Cancer	3:10 am
5	8:23 am	6	Leo	6:29 am
7	3:31 pm	8	Virgo	10:57 am
9	7:34 pm	10	Libra	5:16 pm

Moon Void-of-Course

| Last Aspect | | Moon Enters New Sign | | |
Date	Time	Date	Sign	Time
12	4:38 am	13	Scorpio	2:09 am
15	10:24 am	15	Sagittarius	1:35 pm
17	3:06 pm	18	Capricorn	2:13 am
20	8:04 am	20	Aquarius	1:38 pm
22	5:38 am	22	Pisces	9:51 pm
24	3:27 am	25	Aries	2:34 am
26	5:34 pm	27	Taurus	4:51 am
28	9:01 pm	29	Gemini	6:21 am
		October		
1	1:09 am	1	Cancer	8:32 am
3	7:53 am	3	Leo	12:14 pm
5	3:15 pm	5	Virgo	5:40 pm
7	12:27 pm	8	Libra	12:52 am
10	12:33 am	10	Scorpio	10:01 am
11	4:42 pm	12	Sagittarius	9:18 pm
15	7:49 am	15	Capricorn	10:03 am
17	9:59 am	17	Aquarius	10:17 pm
20	12:53 am	20	Pisces	7:33 am
21	11:25 pm	22	Aries	12:42 pm
24	2:05 pm	24	Taurus	2:26 pm
26	9:22 am	26	Gemini	2:34 pm
28	1:55 pm	28	Cancer	3:09 pm
30	4:00 pm	30	Leo	5:47 pm
		November		
1	8:43 pm	1	Virgo	11:07 pm
3	9:03 pm	4	Libra	6:56 am
6	1:01 pm	6	Scorpio	4:45 pm
8	12:57 am	9	Sagittarius	4:15 am
11	11:53 am	11	Capricorn	5:00 pm
14	12:08 am	14	Aquarius	5:46 am

Moon Void-of-Course

Last Aspect		Moon Enters New Sign		
Date	Time	Date	Sign	Time
16	10:31 am	16	Pisces	4:21 pm
18	4:04 pm	18	Aries	10:58 pm
20	7:42 pm	21	Taurus	1:26 am
22	9:24 pm	23	Gemini	1:14 am
24	6:21 pm	25	Cancer	12:29 am
26	6:35 pm	27	Leo	1:18 am
28	9:43 pm	29	Virgo	5:11 am
30	2:11 pm	1 (December)	Libra	12:29 pm
		December		
3	6:04 pm	3	Scorpio	10:36 pm
5	9:30 pm	6	Sagittarius	10:28 am
8	1:36 pm	8	Capricorn	11:14 pm
11	2:14 am	11	Aquarius	11:59 am
13	1:46 pm	13	Pisces	11:18 pm
15	7:50 pm	16	Aries	7:30 am
18	5:03 am	18	Taurus	11:45 am
19	5:46 pm	20	Gemini	12:39 pm
22	4:03 am	22	Cancer	11:52 am
24	3:31 am	24	Leo	11:32 am
26	5:07 am	26	Virgo	1:34 pm
28	1:52 pm	28	Libra	7:15 pm
30	10:35 pm	30	Scorpio	4:37 am

Find Your Moon Sign

E very year we give tables for the position of the Moon during that year, but it is more complicated to provide tables for the Moon's position in any given year because of its continuous movement. However, the problem was solved by Grant Lewi in *Astrology for the Millions* (available from Llewellyn).

Grant Lewi's System

1. Find your birth year in the Natal Moon Tables (pages 64–74).

2. Run down the left-hand column and see if your date is there.

3. If your date is in the left-hand column, run over this line until you come to the column under your birth year. Here you will find a number. This is your base number. Write it down, and go directly to the direction under the heading "What to Do with Your Base Number" on the next page.

4. If your birth date is not in the left-hand column, get a pencil and paper. Your birth date falls between two numbers in the left-hand column. Look at the date closest after your birth date; run across this line to your birth year. Write down the number you find there, and label it "top number." Having done this, write directly beneath it on your piece of paper the number printed just above it in the table. Label this "bottom number." Subtract the bottom number from the top number. If the top number is smaller, add 360 to it and then subtract. The result is your difference.

5. Go back to the left-hand column and find the date before your birth date. Determine the number of days between this date and your birth date. Write this down and label it "intervening days."

6. Note which group your difference (found at 4, above) falls in. If your difference was 80–87, your daily motion was 12 degrees. If your difference was 88–94, your daily motion was 13 degrees. If your difference was 95–101, your daily motion was 14 degrees. If your difference is 102–106, your daily motion is 15 degrees. *Note: If you were born in*

a leap year and use the difference between February 26 and March 5, then the daily motion is slightly different. If you fall into this category and your difference is 94–99, your daily motion is 12 degrees. If your difference is 100–108, your daily motion is 13 degrees. If your difference is 109–115, your daily motion is 14 degrees. If your difference is 115–122, your daily motion is 15 degrees.

7. Write down the "daily motion" corresponding to your place in the proper table of difference above. Multiply daily motion by the number labeled "intervening days" (found at step 5).

8. Add the result of step 7 to your bottom number (under step 4). This is your base number. If it is more than 360, subtract 360 from it and call the result your base number.

What to Do with Your Base Number

Turn to the Table of Base Numbers and locate your base number in it. At the top of the column you will find the sign your Moon was in. In the far left-hand column you will find the degree the Moon occupied at: 7 AM of your birth date if you were born under Eastern Standard Time (EST); 6 AM of your birth date if you were born under Central Standard Time (CST); 5 AM of your birth date if you were born under Mountain Standard Time (MST); or 4 AM of your birth date if you were born under Pacific Standard Time (PST).

If you don't know the hour of your birth, accept this as your Moon's sign and degree. If you do know the hour of your birth, get the exact degree as follows:

If you were born after 7 AM Eastern Standard Time (6 AM Central Standard Time, etc.), determine the number of hours after the time that you were born. Divide this by two. Add this to your base number, and the result in the table will be the exact degree and sign of the Moon on the year, month, date, and hour of your birth.

If you were born before 7 AM Eastern Standard Time (6 AM Central Standard Time, etc.), determine the number of hours before the time that you were born. Divide this by two. Subtract this from your base number, and the result in the table will be the exact degree and sign of the Moon on the year, month, date, and hour of your birth.

Table of Base Numbers

	♈ (13)	♉ (14)	♊ (15)	♋ (16)	♌ (17)	♍ (18)	♎ (19)	♏ (20)	♐ (21)	♑ (22)	♒ (23)	♓ (24)
0°	0	30	60	90	120	150	180	210	240	270	300	330
1°	1	31	61	91	121	151	181	211	241	271	301	331
2°	2	32	62	92	122	152	182	212	242	272	302	332
3°	3	33	63	93	123	153	183	213	243	273	303	333
4°	4	34	64	94	124	154	184	214	244	274	304	334
5°	5	35	65	95	125	155	185	215	245	275	305	335
6°	6	36	66	96	126	156	186	216	246	276	306	336
7°	7	37	67	97	127	157	187	217	247	277	307	337
8°	8	38	68	98	128	158	188	218	248	278	308	338
9°	9	39	69	99	129	159	189	219	249	279	309	339
10°	10	40	70	100	130	160	190	220	250	280	310	340
11°	11	41	71	101	131	161	191	221	251	281	311	341
12°	12	42	72	102	132	162	192	222	252	282	312	342
13°	13	43	73	103	133	163	193	223	253	283	313	343
14°	14	44	74	104	134	164	194	224	254	284	314	344
15°	15	45	75	105	135	165	195	225	255	285	315	345
16°	16	46	76	106	136	166	196	226	256	286	316	346
17°	17	47	77	107	137	167	197	227	257	287	317	347
18°	18	48	78	108	138	168	198	228	258	288	318	248
19°	19	49	79	109	139	169	199	229	259	289	319	349
20°	20	50	80	110	140	170	200	230	260	290	320	350
21°	21	51	81	111	141	171	201	231	261	291	321	351
22°	22	52	82	112	142	172	202	232	262	292	322	352
23°	23	53	83	113	143	173	203	233	263	293	323	353
24°	24	54	84	114	144	174	204	234	264	294	324	354
25°	25	55	85	115	145	175	205	235	265	295	325	355
26°	26	56	86	116	146	176	206	236	266	296	326	356
27°	27	57	87	117	147	177	207	237	267	297	327	357
28°	28	58	88	118	148	178	208	238	268	298	328	358
29°	29	59	89	119	149	179	209	239	269	299	329	359

Month	Date	1901	1902	1903	1904	1905	1906	1907	1908	1909	1910
Jan.	1	55	188	308	76	227	358	119	246	39	168
Jan.	8	149	272	37	179	319	82	208	350	129	252
Jan.	15	234	2	141	270	43	174	311	81	213	346
Jan.	22	327	101	234	353	138	273	44	164	309	84
Jan.	29	66	196	317	84	238	6	128	255	50	175
Feb.	5	158	280	46	188	328	90	219	359	138	259
Feb.	12	241	12	149	279	51	184	319	90	221	356
Feb.	19	335	111	242	2	146	283	52	173	317	94
Feb.	26	76	204	326	92	248	13	136	264	60	184
Mar.	5	166	288	57	211	336	98	229	21	147	267
Mar.	12	249	22	157	300	60	194	328	110	230	5
Mar.	19	344	121	250	24	154	293	60	195	325	105
Mar.	26	86	212	334	116	258	22	144	288	69	192
Apr.	2	175	296	68	219	345	106	240	29	155	276
Apr.	9	258	31	167	309	69	202	338	118	240	13
Apr.	16	352	132	258	33	163	304	68	204	334	115
Apr.	23	96	220	342	127	267	31	152	299	77	201
Apr.	30	184	304	78	227	354	114	250	38	164	285
May	7	267	40	177	317	78	210	348	126	249	21
May	14	1	142	266	42	172	313	76	212	344	124
May	21	104	229	350	138	275	40	160	310	85	210
May	28	193	313	87	236	2	123	259	47	172	294
Jun.	4	277	48	187	324	88	219	358	134	258	30
Jun.	11	11	151	275	50	182	322	85	220	355	132
Jun.	18	112	238	359	149	283	48	169	320	93	218
Jun.	25	201	322	96	245	11	133	267	57	180	304
Jul.	2	286	57	197	333	97	228	8	142	267	40
Jul.	9	21	160	283	58	193	330	94	228	6	140
Jul.	16	121	247	7	159	291	57	178	330	102	226
Jul.	23	209	332	105	255	18	143	276	66	188	314
Jul.	30	295	66	206	341	105	239	17	151	275	51
Aug.	6	32	168	292	66	204	338	103	237	17	148
Aug.	13	130	255	17	168	301	65	188	339	111	234
Aug.	20	217	341	113	265	27	152	285	76	197	323
Aug.	27	303	77	215	350	113	250	25	160	283	62
Sep.	3	43	176	301	75	215	346	111	246	27	157
Sep.	10	139	263	27	176	310	73	198	347	121	242
Sep.	17	225	350	123	274	35	161	294	85	205	331
Sep.	24	311	88	223	358	122	261	33	169	292	73
Oct.	1	53	185	309	85	224	355	119	256	35	166
Oct.	8	149	271	36	185	320	81	207	356	130	250
Oct.	15	233	359	133	283	44	169	305	93	214	339
Oct.	22	319	99	231	7	130	271	42	177	301	83
Oct.	29	62	194	317	95	233	5	127	266	44	176
Nov.	5	158	279	45	193	329	89	216	5	139	259
Nov.	12	242	6	144	291	53	177	316	101	223	347
Nov.	19	328	109	239	15	140	280	50	185	311	91
Nov.	26	70	203	325	105	241	14	135	276	52	185
Dec.	3	168	288	54	203	338	98	224	15	148	268
Dec.	10	251	14	155	299	61	185	327	109	231	356
Dec.	17	338	118	248	23	150	289	59	193	322	99
Dec.	24	78	213	333	115	249	23	143	286	61	194
Dec.	31	176	296	61	213	346	107	232	26	155	277

Month	Date	1911	1912	1913	1914	1915	1916	1917	1918	1919	1920
Jan.	1	289	57	211	337	100	228	23	147	270	39
Jan.	8	20	162	299	61	192	332	110	231	5	143
Jan.	15	122	251	23	158	293	61	193	329	103	231
Jan.	22	214	335	120	256	23	145	290	68	193	316
Jan.	29	298	66	221	345	108	237	32	155	278	49
Feb.	5	31	170	308	69	203	340	118	239	16	150
Feb.	12	130	260	32	167	302	70	203	338	113	239
Feb.	19	222	344	128	266	31	154	298	78	201	325
Feb.	26	306	75	231	353	116	248	41	164	286	60
Mar.	5	42	192	317	77	214	2	127	248	26	172
Mar.	12	140	280	41	176	311	89	212	346	123	259
Mar.	19	230	5	136	276	39	176	308	87	209	346
Mar.	26	314	100	239	2	124	273	49	173	294	85
Apr.	2	52	200	326	86	223	10	135	257	35	181
Apr.	9	150	288	51	184	321	97	222	355	133	267
Apr.	16	238	14	146	286	48	184	318	96	218	355
Apr.	23	322	111	247	11	132	284	57	181	303	96
Apr.	30	61	208	334	96	232	19	143	267	43	190
May	7	160	296	60	192	331	105	231	4	142	275
May	14	246	22	156	294	56	192	329	104	227	3
May	21	331	122	255	20	141	294	66	190	312	105
May	28	69	218	342	106	240	29	151	277	51	200
Jun.	4	170	304	69	202	341	114	240	14	151	284
Jun.	11	255	30	167	302	65	200	340	112	235	11
Jun.	18	340	132	264	28	151	304	74	198	322	114
Jun.	25	78	228	350	115	249	39	159	286	60	209
Jul.	2	179	312	78	212	349	122	248	25	159	293
Jul.	9	264	39	178	310	74	209	350	120	244	20
Jul.	16	349	141	273	36	161	312	84	206	332	123
Jul.	23	87	237	358	125	258	48	168	295	70	218
Jul.	30	187	321	86	223	357	131	256	36	167	302
Aug.	6	272	48	188	319	82	219	360	129	252	31
Aug.	13	359	150	282	44	171	320	93	214	342	131
Aug.	20	96	246	6	133	268	57	177	303	81	226
Aug.	27	195	330	94	234	5	140	265	46	175	310
Sep.	3	281	57	198	328	90	229	9	138	260	41
Sep.	10	9	158	292	52	180	329	102	222	351	140
Sep.	17	107	255	15	141	279	65	186	312	91	234
Sep.	24	203	339	103	244	13	149	274	56	184	319
Oct.	1	288	68	206	337	98	240	17	148	268	52
Oct.	8	18	167	301	61	189	338	111	231	360	150
Oct.	15	118	263	24	149	290	73.	195	320	102	242
Oct.	22	212	347	113	254	22	157	284	65	193	326
Oct.	29	296	78	214	346	106	250	25	157	276	61
Nov.	5	26	177	309	70	197	348	119	240	7	161
Nov.	12	129	271	33	158	300	81	203	329	112	250
Nov.	19	221	355	123	262	31	164	295	73	202	334
Nov.	26	305	88	223	355	115	259	34	165	285	70
Dec.	3	34	187	317	79	205	359	127	249	16	171
Dec.	10	138	279	41	168	310	89	211	340	120	259
Dec.	17	230	3	134	270	40	172	305	81	211	343
Dec.	24	313	97	232	3	124	267	44	173	294	78
Dec.	31	42	198	325	87	214	9	135	257	25	181

Month	Date	1921	1922	1923	1924	1925	1926	1927	1928	1929	1930
Jan.	1	194	317	80	211	5	127	250	23	176	297
Jan.	8	280	41	177	313	90	211	349	123	260	22
Jan.	15	4	141	275	41	175	312	86	211	346	123
Jan.	22	101	239	3	127	272	51	172	297	83	222
Jan.	29	203	325	88	222	13	135	258	34	184	306
Feb.	5	289	49	188	321	99	220	359	131	269	31
Feb.	12	14	149	284	49	185	320	95	219	356	131
Feb.	19	110	249	11	135	281	60	181	305	93	230
Feb.	26	211	334	96	233	21	144	266	45	191	314
Mar.	5	297	58	197	343	107	230	8	153	276	41
Mar.	12	23	157	294	69	194	328	105	238	6	140
Mar.	19	119	258	19	157	292	68	190	327	104	238
Mar.	26	219	343	104	258	29	153	275	70	200	323
Apr.	2	305	68	205	352	115	240	16	163	284	51
Apr.	9	33	166	304	77	204	337	114	247	14	149
Apr.	16	130	266	28	164	303	76	198	335	115	246
Apr.	23	227	351	114	268	38	161	285	79	208	331
Apr.	30	313	78	214	1	123	250	25	172	292	61
May	7	42	176	313	85	212	348	123	256	23	160
May	14	141	274	37	173	314	84	207	344	125	254
May	21	236	359	123	277	47	169	295	88	217	339
May	28	321	88	222	11	131	259	34	181	301	70
Jun.	4	50	186	321	94	220	358	131	264	31	171
Jun.	11	152	282	45	182	324	93	215	354	135	263
Jun.	18	245	7	134	285	56	177	305	96	226	347
Jun.	25	330	97	232	20	139	268	44	190	310	78
Jul.	2	58	197	329	103	229	9	139	273	40	181
Jul.	9	162	291	54	192	333	101	223	4	144	272
Jul.	16	254	15	144	294	65	185	315	104	236	355
Jul.	23	338	106	242	28	148	276	54	198	319	87
Jul.	30	67	208	337	112	238	20	147	282	49	191
Aug.	6	171	300	62	202	341	110	231	15	152	281
Aug.	13	264	24	153	302	74	194	324	114	244	4
Aug.	20	347	114	253	36	157	285	65	206	328	95
Aug.	27	76	218	346	120	248	29	156	290	59	200
Sep.	3	179	309	70	213	350	119	239	25	161	290
Sep.	10	273	32	162	312	83	203	332	124	252	13
Sep.	17	356	122	264	44	166	293	75	214	337	105
Sep.	24	86	227	354	128	258	38	165	298	70	208
Oct.	1	187	318	78	223	358	128	248	35	169	298
Oct.	8	281	41	170	322	91	212	340	134	260	23
Oct.	15	5	132	274	52	175	303	85	222	345	115
Oct.	22	97	235	3	136	269	46	174	306	81	216
Oct.	29	196	327	87	232	7	137	257	44	179	307
Nov.	5	289	50	178	332	99	221	349	144	268	31
Nov.	12	13	142	283	61	183	313	93	231	353	126
Nov.	19	107	243	12	144	279	54	183	315	91	225
Nov.	26	206	335	96	241	17	145	266	52	189	314
Dec.	3	297	59	187	343	107	230	359	154	276	39
Dec.	10	21	152	291	70	191	324	101	240	1	137
Dec.	17	117	252	21	153	289	63	191	324	99	234
Dec.	24	216	343	105	249	28	152	275	60	199	322
Dec.	31	305	67	197	352	115	237	9	162	285	47

Month	Date	1931	1932	1933	1934	1935	1936	1937	1938	1939	1940
Jan.	1	60	196	346	107	231	8	156	277	41	181
Jan.	8	162	294	70	193	333	104	240	4	144	275
Jan.	15	257	20	158	294	68	190	329	104	239	360
Jan.	22	342	108	255	32	152	278	67	202	323	88
Jan.	29	68	207	353	116	239	19	163	286	49	191
Feb.	5	171	302	78	203	342	113	248	14	153	284
Feb.	12	267	28	168	302	78	198	339	113	248	8
Feb.	19	351	116	266	40	161	286	78	210	332	96
Feb.	26	77	217	1	124	248	29	171	294	59	200
Mar.	5	179	324	86	213	350	135	256	25	161	306
Mar.	12	276	48	176	311	86	218	347	123	256	29
Mar.	19	360	137	277	48	170	308	89	218	340	119
Mar.	26	86	241	10	132	258	52	180	302	69	223
Apr.	2	187	334	94	223	358	144	264	34	169	315
Apr.	9	285	57	185	321	95	227	355	133	264	38
Apr.	16	9	146	287	56	178	317	99	226	349	128
Apr.	23	96	250	18	140	268	61	189	310	80	231
Apr.	30	196	343	102	232	7	153	273	43	179	323
May	7	293	66	193	332	103	237	4	144	272	47
May	14	17	155	297	64	187	327	108	235	357	139
May	21	107	258	28	148	278	69	198	318	90	239
May	28	205	351	111	241	17	161	282	51	189	331
Jun.	4	301	75	201	343	111	245	13	154	280	55
Jun.	11	25	165	306	73	195	337	117	244	5	150
Jun.	18	117	267	37	157	288	78	207	327	99	248
Jun.	25	215	360	120	249	28	169	291	60	200	339
Jul.	2	309	84	211	353	119	254	23	164	289	64
Jul.	9	33	176	315	82	203	348	125	253	13	160
Jul.	16	126	276	46	165	297	87	216	336	108	258
Jul.	23	226	8	130	258	38	177	300	69	210	347
Jul.	30	317	92	221	2	128	262	33	173	298	72
Aug.	6	41	187	323	91	211	359	133	261	21	170
Aug.	13	135	285	54	175	305	97	224	346	116	268
Aug.	20	237	16	138	267	49	185	308	78	220	355
Aug.	27	326	100	232	10	136	270	44	181	307	80
Sep.	3	49	197	331	100	220	8	142	270	31	179
Sep.	10	143	295	62	184	314	107	232	355	125	278
Sep.	17	247	24	147	277	58	194	317	89	228	4
Sep.	24	335	108	243	18	145	278	55	189	316	88
Oct.	1	58	206	341	108	229	17	152	278	40	188
Oct.	8	151	306	70	193	322	117	240	4	134	288
Oct.	15	256	32	155	287	66	203	324	100	236	13
Oct.	22	344	116	253	27	154	287	64	198	324	98
Oct.	29	68	214	350	116	239	25	162	286	49	196
Nov.	5	161	316	78	201	332	126	248	12	145	297
Nov.	12	264	41	162	298	74	212	333	111	244	22
Nov.	19	353	125	262	36	162	296	73	207	332	108
Nov.	26	77	222	0	124	248	33	172	294	58	205
Dec.	3	171	325	87	209	343	135	257	19	156	305
Dec.	10	272	50	171	309	82	220	341	120	253	30
Dec.	17	1	135	271	45	170	306	81	217	340	118
Dec.	24	86	231	10	132	256	43	181	302	66	214
Dec.	31	182	333	95	217	354	142	265	27	167	313

Month	Date	1941	1942	1943	1944	1945	1946	1947	1948	1949	1950
Jan.	1	325	88	211	353	135	258	22	165	305	68
Jan.	8	50	176	315	85	219	348	126	256	29	160
Jan.	15	141	276	50	169	312	87	220	340	123	258
Jan.	22	239	12	133	258	52	182	303	69	224	352
Jan.	29	333	96	221	2	143	266	32	174	314	75
Feb.	5	57	186	323	95	227	358	134	265	37	170
Feb.	12	150	285	58	178	320	96	228	349	131	268
Feb.	19	250	20	142	267	62	190	312	78	234	359
Feb.	26	342	104	231	11	152	274	43	182	323	83
Mar.	5	65	196	331	116	236	8	142	286	46	179
Mar.	12	158	295	66	199	328	107	236	10	139	279
Mar.	19	261	28	150	290	72	198	320	102	243	8
Mar.	26	351	112	242	34	161	281	53	204	332	91
Apr.	2	74	205	340	125	244	16	152	294	55	187
Apr.	9	166	306	74	208	337	117	244	19	148	289
Apr.	16	270	36	158	300	81	206	328	112	252	17
Apr.	23	360	120	252	42	170	290	63	212	340	100
Apr.	30	83	214	350	133	254	25	162	302	64	195
May	7	174	316	82	217	346	127	252	27	158	299
May	14	279	45	166	311	90	215	336	123	260	26
May	21	9	128	261	50	179	299	72	221	349	110
May	28	92	222	1	141	263	33	173	310	73	204
Jun.	4	184	326	91	226	356	137	261	36	168	307
Jun.	11	287	54	174	322	98	224	344	134	268	34
Jun.	18	17	137	270	60	187	308	81	231	357	119
Jun.	25	102	231	11	149	272	42	183	318	82	213
Jul.	2	194	335	99	234	7	145	269	44	179	316
Jul.	9	296	63	183	332	106	233	353	144	277	43
Jul.	16	25	147	279	70	195	318	89	241	5	129
Jul.	23	110	240	21	157	280	52	192	327	91	224
Jul.	30	205	343	108	242	18	153	278	52	190	324
Aug.	6	304	71	192	341	115	241	3	153	286	51
Aug.	13	33	156	287	80	203	327	98	251	13	138
Aug.	20	119	250	30	165	289	63	201	336	99	235
Aug.	27	216	351	117	250	28	162	287	61	200	332
Sep.	3	314	80	201	350	125	249	13	161	296	59
Sep.	10	41	165	296	90	211	336	108	260	21	146
Sep.	17	127	261	39	174	297	74	209	345	107	246
Sep.	24	226	359	126	259	38	170	295	70	209	341
Oct.	1	323	88	211	358	135	257	22	170	306	67
Oct.	8	49	174	306	99	220	344	118	269	30	154
Oct.	15	135	272	47	183	305	84	217	353	116	256
Oct.	22	236	8	134	269	47	180	303	80	217	351
Oct.	29	333	95	220	7	144	265	31	179	315	75
Nov.	5	58	181	317	107	229	352	129	277	39	162
Nov.	12	143	283	55	192	314	94	225	1	125	265
Nov.	19	244	18	141	279	55	189	311	90	225	0
Nov.	26	343	104	229	16	153	274	39	189	323	84
Dec.	3	67	189	328	115	237	360	140	284	47	171
Dec.	10	153	292	64	200	324	103	234	9	136	274
Dec.	17	252	28	149	289	63	199	319	100	234	9
Dec.	24	351	112	237	27	161	282	47	199	331	93
Dec.	31	76	198	338	123	246	9	150	293	55	180

Month	Date	1951	1952	1953	1954	1955	1956	1957	1958	1959	1960
Jan.	1	194	336	115	238	6	147	285	47	178	317
Jan.	8	297	67	199	331	107	237	9	143	278	47
Jan.	15	30	150	294	70	200	320	104	242	9	131
Jan.	22	114	240	35	161	284	51	207	331	94	223
Jan.	29	204	344	124	245	17	155	294	55	189	325
Feb.	5	305	76	207	341	116	246	18	152	287	56
Feb.	12	38	159	302	80	208	330	112	252	17	140
Feb.	19	122	249	45	169	292	61	216	340	102	233
Feb.	26	215	352	133	253	27	163	303	63	199	333
Mar.	5	314	96	216	350	125	266	27	161	297	75
Mar.	12	46	180	310	91	216	351	121	262	25	161
Mar.	19	130	274	54	178	300	86	224	349	110	259
Mar.	26	225	14	142	262	37	185	312	72	208	356
Apr.	2	324	104	226	358	135	274	37	169	307	83
Apr.	9	54	189	319	100	224	360	131	271	34	170
Apr.	16	138	285	62	187	308	97	232	357	118	269
Apr.	23	235	23	150	271	46	194	320	82	217	5
Apr.	30	334	112	235	6	146	282	48	177	317	91
May	7	62	197	330	109	232	8	142	279	42	177
May	14	146	296	70	196	316	107	240	6	127	279
May	21	243	32	158	280	54	204	328	91	225	15
May	28	344	120	244	15	155	290	55	187	326	100
Jun.	4	71	205	341	117	241	16	153	288	51	186
Jun.	11	155	306	79	204	325	117	249	14	137	288
Jun.	18	252	42	166	290	63	214	336	101	234	25
Jun.	25	354	128	253	26	164	298	63	198	335	109
Jul.	2	80	214	351	125	250	24	164	296	60	195
Jul.	9	164	315	88	212	335	126	259	22	147	297
Jul.	16	260	52	174	299	72	223	344	110	243	34
Jul.	23	3	137	261	37	173	307	71	209	343	118
Jul.	30	89	222	2	134	258	33	174	304	68	205
Aug.	6	174	324	97	220	345	134	268	30	156	305
Aug.	13	270	62	182	308	82	232	353	118	254	42
Aug.	20	11	146	269	48	181	316	79	220	351	126
Aug.	27	97	232	11	143	267	43	183	314	76	215
Sep.	3	184	332	107	228	355	143	278	38	166	314
Sep.	10	280	71	191	316	92	241	2	127	265	50
Sep.	17	19	155	278	58	189	325	88	230	359	135
Sep.	24	105	242	20	152	274	54	191	323	84	225
Oct.	1	193	341	116	237	4	152	287	47	174	324
Oct.	8	291	79	200	324	103	249	11	135	276	58
Oct.	15	27	163	287	68	198	333	98	239	8	143
Oct.	22	113	252	28	162	282	64	199	332	92	235
Oct.	29	201	350	125	245	12	162	295	56	182	334
Nov.	5	302	87	209	333	114	256	19	144	286	66
Nov.	12	36	171	297	76	207	341	109	247	17	150
Nov.	19	121	262	37	171	291	73	208	341	101	244
Nov.	26	209	0	133	254	20	173	303	65	190	345
Dec.	3	312	95	217	342	124	265	27	154	295	75
Dec.	10	45	179	307	84	216	348	119	255	27	158
Dec.	17	129	271	46	180	299	82	218	350	110	252
Dec.	24	217	11	141	263	28	184	311	73	199	355
Dec.	31	321	103	225	352	132	273	35	164	303	84

Month	Date	1961	1962	1963	1964	1965	1966	1967	1968	1969	1970
Jan.	1	96	217	350	128	266	27	163	298	76	197
Jan.	8	179	315	89	217	350	126	260	27	161	297
Jan.	15	275	54	179	302	86	225	349	112	257	36
Jan.	22	18	141	264	35	189	311	74	207	359	122
Jan.	29	105	225	1	136	275	35	173	306	85	206
Feb.	5	188	323	99	225	360	134	270	35	171	305
Feb.	12	284	64	187	310	95	235	357	121	267	45
Feb.	19	26	150	272	46	197	320	81	218	7	130
Feb.	26	113	234	11	144	283	45	182	315	93	216
Mar.	5	198	331	109	245	9	142	280	54	180	313
Mar.	12	293	73	195	332	105	244	5	142	277	54
Mar.	19	34	159	280	71	205	329	90	243	15	139
Mar.	26	122	243	19	167	291	54	190	338	101	226
Apr.	2	208	340	119	253	18	151	290	63	189	323
Apr.	9	303	82	204	340	116	252	14	150	288	62
Apr.	16	42	167	288	81	213	337	99	253	23	147
Apr.	23	130	253	28	176	299	64	198	347	109	235
Apr.	30	216	349	128	261	27	161	298	71	197	333
May	7	314	90	213	348	127	260	23	158	299	70
May	14	51	176	298	91	222	345	109	262	32	155
May	21	137	263	36	186	307	74	207	357	117	245
May	28	225	359	137	270	35	172	307	80	205	344
Jun.	4	325	98	222	357	137	268	31	168	309	78
Jun.	11	60	184	308	99	231	353	119	270	42	163
Jun.	18	146	272	45	195	315	82	217	6	126	253
Jun.	25	233	10	145	279	43	183	315	89	214	355
Jul.	2	336	106	230	6	147	276	40	178	318	87
Jul.	9	70	191	318	108	241	1	129	279	51	171
Jul.	16	154	281	56	204	324	91	227	14	135	261
Jul.	23	241	21	153	288	52	193	323	98	223	5
Jul.	30	345	115	238	16	156	286	47	188	327	97
Aug.	6	79	200	327	116	250	10	138	288	60	180
Aug.	13	163	289	66	212	333	99	238	22	144	270
Aug.	20	250	32	161	296	61	203	331	106	233	14
Aug.	27	353	124	246	27	164	295	55	199	335	106
Sep.	3	88	208	336	126	259	19	147	297	68	189
Sep.	10	172	297	77	220	342	108	249	30	152	279
Sep.	17	260	41	170	304	72	212	340	114	244	23
Sep.	24	1	134	254	37	172	304	64	208	344	115
Oct.	1	97	217	344	136	267	28	155	308	76	198
Oct.	8	180	306	88	228	351	117	259	38	161	289
Oct.	15	270	50	179	312	82	220	350	122	254	31
Oct.	22	10	143	262	47	182	313	73	217	353	123
Oct.	29	105	226	352	146	275	37	163	318	84	207
Nov.	5	189	315	97	237	359	127	268	47	168	299
Nov.	12	281	58	188	320	93	228	359	130	264	39
Nov.	19	19	151	271	55	191	321	82	225	3	131
Nov.	26	113	235	1	157	282	45	172	328	92	215
Dec.	3	197	326	105	245	7	138	276	55	176	310
Dec.	10	291	66	197	328	102	237	7	139	273	48
Dec.	17	30	159	280	63	202	329	91	234	13	139
Dec.	24	121	243	11	167	291	53	183	337	101	223
Dec.	31	204	336	113	254	14	149	284	64	184	320

Month	Date	1971	1972	1973	1974	1975	1976	1977	1978	1979	1980
Jan.	1	335	109	246	8	147	279	56	179	318	90
Jan.	8	71	197	332	108	243	6	144	278	54	176
Jan.	15	158	283	69	207	328	93	240	18	139	263
Jan.	22	244	20	169	292	54	192	339	102	224	4
Jan.	29	344	117	255	17	156	288	64	188	327	99
Feb.	5	81	204	342	116	253	14	153	287	63	184
Feb.	12	167	291	79	216	337	101	251	26	147	271
Feb.	19	252	31	177	300	62	203	347	110	233	14
Feb.	26	353	126	263	27	164	297	72	199	334	109
Mar.	5	91	224	351	124	262	34	162	296	72	204
Mar.	12	176	312	90	224	346	122	262	34	156	203
Mar.	19	261	55	185	309	72	226	356	118	243	37
Mar.	26	1	149	270	37	172	320	80	208	343	130
Apr.	2	100	233	360	134	270	43	170	307	80	213
Apr.	9	184	320	101	232	355	131	273	42	164	302
Apr.	16	271	64	194	317	82	235	5	126	254	46
Apr.	23	9	158	278	47	181	329	88	217	352	139
Apr.	30	109	242	8	145	278	52	178	318	88	222
May	7	193	329	111	240	3	141	282	50	173	312
May	14	281	73	203	324	92	243	14	134	264	54
May	21	19	167	287	55	191	337	97	226	3	147
May	28	117	251	16	156	286	61	187	328	96	231
Jun.	4	201	339	120	249	11	151	291	59	180	323
Jun.	11	291	81	213	333	102	252	23	143	273	63
Jun.	18	29	176	296	64	201	346	106	234	13	155
Jun.	25	125	260	25	167	295	69	196	338	105	239
Jul.	2	209	349	129	258	19	162	299	68	188	334
Jul.	9	300	90	222	341	111	261	32	152	282	72
Jul.	16	40	184	305	72	212	354	115	243	24	163
Jul.	23	133	268	35	176	303	78	206	347	114	248
Jul.	30	217	0	137	267	27	172	308	77	197	344
Aug.	6	309	99	230	350	120	271	40	161	290	83
Aug.	13	51	192	314	81	223	2	124	252	34	171
Aug.	20	142	276	45	185	312	86	217	356	123	256
Aug.	27	225	10	146	276	36	182	317	86	206	353
Sep.	3	317	109	238	360	128	281	48	170	299	93
Sep.	10	61	200	322	90	232	10	132	262	43	180
Sep.	17	151	284	56	193	321	94	228	4	132	264
Sep.	24	234	20	155	284	45	191	326	94	215	2
Oct.	1	325	120	246	9	136	291	56	179	308	103
Oct.	8	70	208	330	101	241	19	140	273	51	189
Oct.	15	160	292	66	202	330	102	238	12	140	273
Oct.	22	243	28	165	292	54	199	336	102	225	10
Oct.	29	334	130	254	17	146	301	64	187	318	112
Nov.	5	79	217	338	112	249	27	148	284	59	197
Nov.	12	169	300	76	210	339	111	247	21	148	282
Nov.	19	253	36	175	300	63	207	347	110	234	18
Nov.	26	344	139	262	25	156	310	73	195	329	120
Dec.	3	87	226	346	122	257	36	157	294	67	206
Dec.	10	177	310	84	220	347	121	255	31	156	292
Dec.	17	261	45	185	308	72	216	356	118	242	28
Dec.	24	355	148	271	33	167	318	81	203	340	128
Dec.	31	95	235	355	132	265	44	166	303	76	214

Month	Date	1981	1982	1983	1984	1985	1986	1987	1988	1989	1990
Jan.	1	226	350	129	260	36	162	300	71	205	333
Jan.	8	315	89	225	346	126	260	36	156	297	72
Jan.	15	53	188	309	73	225	358	119	243	37	168
Jan.	22	149	272	35	176	319	82	206	348	129	252
Jan.	29	234	0	137	270	43	172	308	81	213	343
Feb.	5	324	98	234	354	135	270	44	164	306	82
Feb.	12	64	196	317	81	236	6	128	252	48	175
Feb.	19	157	280	45	185	328	90	217	356	138	260
Feb.	26	242	10	145	279	51	182	316	90	222	353
Mar.	5	332	108	242	15	143	280	52	185	313	93
Mar.	12	74	204	326	104	246	14	136	275	57	184
Mar.	19	166	288	55	208	337	97	227	19	147	268
Mar.	26	250	20	154	300	60	191	326	111	230	1
Apr.	2	340	119	250	24	151	291	60	194	322	103
Apr.	9	84	212	334	114	255	22	144	286	66	192
Apr.	16	175	296	66	216	346	106	237	27	156	276
Apr.	23	259	28	164	309	69	199	336	119	240	9
Apr.	30	349	130	258	33	160	302	68	203	331	113
May	7	93	221	342	124	264	31	152	297	75	201
May	14	184	304	75	225	355	114	246	36	165	285
May	21	268	36	175	317	78	207	347	127	249	18
May	28	358	140	266	41	170	311	76	211	341	122
Jun.	4	102	230	350	135	272	40	160	307	83	210
Jun.	11	193	313	84	234	3	123	255	45	173	294
Jun.	18	277	45	185	325	87	216	357	135	258	27
Jun.	25	8	149	275	49	180	320	85	219	352	130
Jul.	2	110	239	359	146	281	49	169	317	92	219
Jul.	9	201	322	93	244	11	133	263	55	181	304
Jul.	16	286	54	196	333	96	225	7	143	266	37
Jul.	23	19	158	284	57	191	328	94	227	3	138
Jul.	30	119	248	7	155	290	57	178	327	101	227
Aug.	6	210	331	101	254	19	142	272	66	189	313
Aug.	13	294	64	205	341	104	236	16	152	274	48
Aug.	20	30	166	293	66	202	337	103	236	13	147
Aug.	27	128	256	17	164	299	65	187	335	111	235
Sep.	3	218	340	110	264	27	151	281	75	197	321
Sep.	10	302	75	214	350	112	247	24	160	282	59
Sep.	17	40	174	302	74	212	345	112	245	23	156
Sep.	24	138	264	26	172	309	73	197	343	121	243
Oct.	1	226	349	119	274	36	159	292	84	206	329
Oct.	8	310	86	222	359	120	258	32	169	291	70
Oct.	15	50	183	310	84	220	354	120	255	31	165
Oct.	22	148	272	35	181	319	81	206	352	130	251
Oct.	29	234	357	130	282	44	167	303	92	214	337
Nov.	5	318	96	230	8	129	268	40	178	300	79
Nov.	12	58	193	318	93	229	4	128	265	39	175
Nov.	19	158	280	44	190	329	90	214	2	139	260
Nov.	26	243	5	141	290	53	175	314	100	223	345
Dec.	3	327	106	238	16	139	277	49	185	310	88
Dec.	10	66	203	326	103	237	14	136	274	48	185
Dec.	17	167	288	52	200	337	98	222	12	147	269
Dec.	24	252	13	152	298	62	184	324	108	232	355
Dec.	31	337	114	248	24	149	285	59	193	320	96

Month	Date	1991	1992	1993	1994	1995	1996	1997	1998	1999	2000
Jan.	1	111	242	15	145	281	53	185	317	92	223
Jan.	8	206	326	108	244	16	136	279	56	186	307
Jan.	15	289	54	210	337	99	225	21	147	270	37
Jan.	22	18	158	299	61	190	329	110	231	2	140
Jan.	29	119	252	23	155	290	62	193	326	101	232
Feb.	5	214	335	116	254	24	145	287	66	193	315
Feb.	12	298	63	220	345	108	235	31	155	278	47
Feb.	19	29	166	308	69	201	337	119	239	12	148
Feb.	26	128	260	32	164	299	70	202	335	111	240
Mar.	5	222	356	124	265	32	166	295	76	201	337
Mar.	12	306	87	229	354	116	259	39	164	285	72
Mar.	19	39	189	317	77	211	360	128	248	22	170
Mar.	26	138	280	41	172	310	90	212	343	121	260
Apr.	2	230	5	133	275	40	175	305	86	210	345
Apr.	9	314	98	237	3	123	270	47	173	294	83
Apr.	16	49	198	326	86	220	9	136	257	31	180
Apr.	23	148	288	50	180	320	98	221	351	132	268
Apr.	30	238	13	143	284	48	183	315	95	218	353
May	7	322	109	245	12	132	281	55	182	302	93
May	14	57	207	335	95	228	18	144	267	39	190
May	21	158	296	59	189	330	106	230	1	141	276
May	28	247	21	154	292	57	191	326	103	227	1
Jun.	4	330	119	253	21	141	291	64	190	311	102
Jun.	11	66	217	343	105	236	28	152	276	48	199
Jun.	18	168	304	68	199	340	114	238	11	150	285
Jun.	25	256	29	165	300	66	199	337	111	236	10
Jul.	2	339	129	262	29	150	300	73	198	321	111
Jul.	9	74	227	351	114	245	38	160	285	57	209
Jul.	16	177	313	76	210	348	123	246	22	158	293
Jul.	23	265	38	175	309	75	208	347	120	245	19
Jul.	30	349	137	272	37	160	308	83	206	331	119
Aug.	6	83	237	359	123	255	48	169	293	67	218
Aug.	13	186	322	84	221	356	132	254	33	166	302
Aug.	20	273	47	185	318	83	218	356	129	253	29
Aug.	27	358	146	282	45	169	317	93	214	340	128
Sep.	3	93	246	7	131	265	56	177	301	78	226
Sep.	10	194	331	92	231	4	141	263	43	174	311
Sep.	17	281	56	194	327	91	228	5	138	261	39
Sep.	24	8	154	292	53	178	326	102	223	349	137
Oct.	1	104	254	16	139	276	64	186	310	89	234
Oct.	8	202	339	101	241	13	149	273	53	183	319
Oct.	15	289	66	202	337	99	238	13	148	269	49
Oct.	22	16	164	301	61	187	336	111	231	357	148
Oct.	29	115	262	25	148	287	72	195	318	100	242
Nov.	5	211	347	111	250	22	157	283	61	193	326
Nov.	12	297	76	211	346	107	247	22	157	277	58
Nov.	19	24	174	309	70	194	346	119	240	5	159
Nov.	26	126	270	33	156	297	80	203	328	109	251
Dec.	3	220	355	121	258	31	165	293	69	202	334
Dec.	10	305	85	220	355	115	256	31	165	286	67
Dec.	17	32	185	317	79	203	357	127	249	13	169
Dec.	24	135	278	41	166	306	89	211	338	117	260
Dec.	31	230	3	131	266	41	173	303	78	211	343

Home, Health, & Beauty

How to Choose the Best Dates

Automobile Purchase

The Moon is helpful when in favorable aspect to Mercury and Uranus and in the signs of Gemini or Sagittarius, which correspond to travel. Also try the fixed signs (Aquarius, Taurus, Leo, and Scorpio), which correspond to reliable purchases.

Automobile Repair

The Moon should be in favorable aspect to Uranus and in the signs of Taurus, Leo, Aquarius, or Virgo. The first and second quarters are best. Avoid any unfavorable aspects between the Moon and Mars, Saturn, Uranus, Neptune, or Pluto.

Baking

Baking should be done when the Moon is in Cancer. Bakers who have experimented say that dough rises higher and bread is lighter during the increase of the Moon (first or second quarter). If it is not possible to bake under the sign of Cancer, try Aries, Libra, or Capricorn.

Beauty Care

For beauty treatments, skin care, and massage, the Moon should be in Taurus, Cancer, Leo, Libra, or Aquarius, and sextile, trine, or conjunct [X, T, C] Venus and/or Jupiter.

Plastic surgery should be done in the increase of the Moon, when the Moon is not square or opposite (Q or O) Mars. Nor should the Moon be in the sign ruling the area to be operated on. Avoid days when the Moon is square or opposite Saturn or the Sun.

Fingernails should be cut when the Moon is not in any aspect with Mercury or Jupiter. Saturn and Mars must not be marked Q or O because this makes the nails grow slowly or thin and weak. The Moon should be in Aries, Taurus, Cancer, or Leo. For toenails, the Moon should not be in Gemini or Pisces. Corns are best cut in the third or fourth quarter.

Brewing

It is best to brew during the Full Moon and the fourth quarter. Plan to have the Moon in Cancer, Scorpio, or Pisces.

Building

Turning the first sod for the foundation of a home or laying the cornerstone for a building marks the beginning of the building. Excavate, lay foundations, and pour cement when the Moon is Full and in Taurus, Leo, or Aquarius. Saturn should be aspected, but not Mars.

Canning

Can fruits and vegetables when the Moon is in either the third or fourth quarter, and when it is in Cancer or Pisces. For preserves and jellies, use the same quarters but see that the Moon is in Cancer, Pisces, or Taurus.

Cement and Concrete

Pour cement and concrete during the Full Moon in the fixed signs of Taurus, Leo, or Aquarius.

Dental Work

Pick a day that is marked favorable for your Sun sign. Mars should be marked X, T, or C and Saturn, Uranus, and Jupiter should not be marked Q or O. Teeth are best removed during the increase of the Moon in the first or second quarter in Gemini, Virgo, Sagittarius, Capricorn, or Pisces. Avoid the Full Moon! The day should be favorable for your lunar cycle, and Mars and Saturn should be marked C, T, or X. Fillings should be done in the third or fourth quarters in the signs of Taurus, Leo, Scorpio, or Aquarius. The same applies for plates.

Dieting

Weight gain occurs more readily when the Moon is in a water sign (Cancer, Scorpio, Pisces). Experience has shown that weight may be lost if a diet is started when the Moon is decreasing in light (third or fourth quarter) and when it is in Aries, Leo, Virgo, Sagittarius, or Aquarius. The lunar cycle should be favorable on the day you wish to begin your diet.

Dressmaking

Design, cut, repair, or make clothes in Taurus, Leo, or Libra on a day marked favorable for your Sun sign. First and second quarters are best.

Venus, Jupiter, and Mercury should be aspected, but avoid Mars or Saturn aspects. William Lilly wrote in 1676, "Make no new clothes, or first put them on when the Moon is in Scorpio or afflicted by Mars, for they will be apt to be torn and quickly worn out."

Eyeglasses

Eyes should be tested and glasses fitted on a day marked favorable for your Sun sign and on a day that falls during your favorable lunar cycle. Mars should not be in aspect with the Moon. The same applies for any treatment of the eyes, which should also be started during the increase of the Moon (first or second quarter).

Fence Posts and Poles

Set the posts or poles when the Moon is in the third or fourth quarters. The fixed signs Taurus, Leo, and Aquarius are best for this.

Habits

To end any habit, start on a day when the Moon is in the third or fourth quarter and in a barren sign. Gemini, Leo, or Virgo are the best times, although Aries and Capricorn may be suitable as well. Make sure your lunar cycle is favorable. Avoid lunar aspects to Mars or Jupiter. Aspects to Neptune or Saturn are helpful. These rules apply to smoking.

Hair Care

Haircuts are best when the Moon is in a mutable (Gemini, Sagittarius, Pisces) or earthy sign (Taurus, Capricorn), well placed and aspected, but not in Virgo, which is barren. For faster growth, hair should be cut when the Moon is in Cancer or Pisces in the first or second quarter. To make hair grow thicker, cut it when the Moon is Full or in opposition to the Sun (marked O in the Lunar Aspectarian) in the signs of Taurus, Cancer, or Leo up to and at, but not after, the Full Moon. However, if you want your hair to grow more slowly, the Moon should be in Aries, Gemini, or Virgo in the third or fourth quarter, with Saturn square or opposite the Moon.

Permanents, straightening, and hair coloring will take well if the Moon is in Taurus or Leo and Venus is marked T or X. You should avoid doing your hair if Mars is marked Q or O, especially if heat is to be used. For permanents, a trine to Jupiter is helpful. The Moon also should be in the first quarter, and check the lunar cycle for a favorable day in relation to your Sun sign.

Health

Diagnosis is more likely to be successful when the Moon is in a cardinal sign (Aries, Cancer, Libra, Capricorn), and less so when in a mutable sign (Gemini, Sagittarius, Pisces, Virgo). Begin a program for recuperation when the Moon is in a cardinal or fixed sign and the day is favorable to your sign. Enter hospitals at these times. For surgery, see Surgical Procedures. Buy medicines when the Moon is in Virgo or Scorpio.

House Furnishings

Days when Saturn is aspected make things wear longer and tend to a more conservative purchase. Saturn days are good for buying, and Jupiter days are good for selling.

House Purchasing

If you desire a permanent home, buy when the Moon is in Taurus, Leo, Scorpio, Aquarius, or Cancer, preferably when the Moon is New. If you're buying for speculation and a quick turnover, be certain that the Moon is not in a fixed sign, but in Aries, Cancer, or Libra.

Lost Articles

Search for lost articles during the first quarter and when your Sun sign is marked favorable. Also check to see that the planet ruling the lost item is trine, sextile, or conjunct the Moon. The Moon governs household utensils, Mercury letters and books, and Venus clothing, jewelry, and money.

Marriage

The best time for marriage to take place is during the increase of the Moon, just past the first quarter, but not under the Full Moon. Good signs for the Moon to be in are Taurus, Cancer, Leo, and Libra. The Moon in Taurus produces the most steadfast marriages, but if the partners later want to separate they may have a difficult time. Avoid Aries, Gemini, Virgo, Scorpio, and Aquarius. Make sure that the Moon is well aspected (X or T), especially to Venus or Jupiter. Avoid aspects to Mars, Uranus, or Pluto.

Moving

Make sure that Mars is not aspected to the Moon. Try to move on a day that is favorable to your Sun sign, or when the Moon is conjunct, sextile, or trine the Sun.

Mowing the Lawn

Mow the lawn in the first or second quarter to increase growth. If you wish to retard growth, mow in the third or fourth quarter.

Painting

The best time to paint buildings is during the decrease of the Moon (third and fourth quarter). If the weather is hot, do the painting while the Moon is in Taurus; if the weather is cold, paint while the Moon is in Leo. Another good sign for painting is Aquarius. By painting in the fourth quarter, the wood is drier and the paint will penetrate; when painting around the New Moon the wood is damp and the paint is subject to scalding when hot weather hits it. It is not advisable to paint while the Moon is in a water sign if the temperature is below 70 degrees, as it is apt to creep, check, or run.

Pets

Take home new pets when the date is favorable to your Sun sign, or the Moon is well aspected by the Sun, Venus, Jupiter, Uranus, or Neptune. Avoid days when the Moon is badly aspected (Q or O) by the Sun, Mars, Saturn, Uranus, Neptune, or Pluto. Train pets starting when the Moon is in Taurus. Neuter them in any sign but Virgo, Libra, Scorpio, or Sagittarius. Avoid the week before and after the Full Moon. Declaw cats in the dark of the Moon. Avoid the week before and after the Full Moon and the sign of Pisces. When selecting a new pet it is good to have the Moon well aspected by the planet that rules the animal. Cats are ruled by the Sun, dogs by Mercury, birds by Venus, horses by Jupiter, and fish by Neptune.

Predetermining Sex

Count from the last day of menstruation to the day next beginning, and divide the interval between the two dates into halves. Pregnancy occurring in the first half produces females, but copulation should take place when the Moon is in a feminine sign.

Pregnancy occurring in the latter half, up to within three days of the beginning of menstruation, produces males, but copulation should take place when the Moon is in a masculine sign. This three-day period to the end of the first half of the next period again produces females.

Romance

The same principles hold true for starting a relationship as for marriage. However, since there is less control of when a romance starts, it is sometimes necessary to study it after the fact. Romances begun under an increasing Moon are more likely to be permanent, or at least satisfying. Those started on the waning Moon will more readily transform the participants. The general tone of the relationship can be guessed from the sign the Moon is in. For instance, romances begun when the Moon is in Aries may be impulsive and quick to burn out. Those begun in Capricorn will take greater effort to bring them to a desirable conclusion, but they may be very rewarding. Good aspects between the Moon and Venus are excellent influences. Avoid Mars, Uranus, and Pluto aspects. Ending relationships is facilitated by a decreasing Moon, particularly in the fourth quarter. This causes the least pain and attachment.

Sauerkraut

The best tasting sauerkraut is made just after the Full Moon in a fruitful sign (Cancer, Scorpio, or Pisces).

Shingling

Shingling should be done in the decrease of the Moon (third or fourth quarter) when it is in a fixed sign (Taurus, Leo, Scorpio, or Aquarius). If shingles are laid during the New Moon, they have a tendency to curl at the edges.

Surgical Procedures

The flow of blood, like the ocean tides, appears to be related to the Moon's phases. *Time* magazine (June, 6, 1960, page 74) reported that on 1,000 tonsillectomy case histories analyzed by Dr. Edson J. Andrews, only 18 percent of associated hemorrhaging occurred in the fourth and first quarters. Thus, an astrological rule: To reduce hemorrhage after a surgical procedure, plan to have the surgery within one week before or after the New Moon. Avoid surgery within one week before or after the Full Moon. Operate in the increase of the Moon if possible.

Also select a date when the Moon is not in the sign governing the part of the body involved in the operation. The further removed the Moon sign from the sign ruling the afflicted part of the body, the better for healing. The signs and the body parts they rule are as follows: Aries, head;

Zodiac Signs & Their Corresponding Body Parts

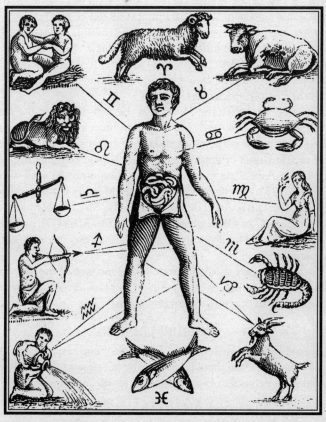

♈ = Aries	♎ = Libra
♉ = Taurus	♏ = Scorpio
♊ = Gemini	♐ = Sagittarius
♋ = Cancer	♑ = Capricorn
♌ = Leo	♒ = Aquarius
♍ = Virgo	♓ = Pisces

Taurus, neck and throat; Gemini, lungs, nerves, arms, shoulders, hands, and fingers; Cancer, breast, chest, and stomach; Leo, heart, spine, and back; Virgo, nervous system and intestines; Libra, kidneys; Scorpio, reproductive organs; Sagittarius, thighs, hips, and liver; Capricorn, knees, bones, and teeth; Aquarius, circulatory system, shins, and ankles; and Pisces, feet.

For successful operations, there should be no lunar aspects to Mars, and favorable aspects to Venus and Jupiter should be present. Do not operate when the Moon is applying to (moving toward) any aspect of Mars, which tends to promote inflammation and complications after the operation. See the Lunar Aspectarian (pages 28–51) to determine which days have Mars aspects. There should be good aspects to Venus and Jupiter (X or T in the Lunar Aspectarian).

Never operate when the Moon is in the same sign as at the patient's birth (the person's Sun sign). Let the Moon be in a fixed sign, but not in the same sign as the patient's ascendant (rising sign). The Moon should be free of all manner of impediment. There should be no Q or O aspects in the Lunar Aspectarian, and the Moon should not be void-of-course. (See pages 28–51.) Do not cut a nerve when Mercury is afflicted (marked Q or O in the Lunar Aspectarian). When the Moon is conjunct or opposed the Sun (C or O) or when it is opposed by Mars (O), avoid amputations. Good signs for abdominal operations are Sagittarius, Capricorn, or Aquarius.

Cosmetic surgery should be done in the increase of the Moon, when the Moon is not in square or opposition to Mars. Avoid days when the Moon is square or opposite Saturn or the Sun.

Weaning Children

This should be done when the Moon is in Sagittarius, Capricorn, Aquarius, or Pisces. The child should nurse for the last time when the Moon is in a fruitful sign. Venus should then be trine, sextile, or conjunct the Moon.

Wine and Drinks Other Than Beer

It is best to start brewing when the Moon is in Pisces or Taurus. Good aspects (X or T) to Venus are favorable. Avoid aspects with Mars or Saturn.

Candle Dipping

By K. D. Spitzer

No one can be sure of the actual year that someone took a little bit of braided fiber, dipped it in wax or pitch, and lit it. Undoubtedly, this was done by some anonymous ancient woman who was tired of getting up in dark predawn hours to start her daily chores; she was probably just sick of scrubbing the soot off the walls from the torches. If the idea had been her husband's, you know they would have erected an inscribed monument so enduring that 2,000 years later we would have proof that an early ancestor of Edison's had, on a particular day, started civilization down the path toward staying up all night!

The Egyptians have left evidence that they had candles as early as the fourth century BCE, because we have carbon dated their candlesticks. This approximate date is corroborated by the Minoans on Crete, who left candle holders dated to the same time. We know that the Romans had candles because Pliny wrote about them. They were made of flax rope and soaked in pitch and wax. The word *candle* comes from the Latin word *candere*, which means to shine.

It was the wick, of course, that separated the candle from the earlier lighting equipment of torches, rushes, and crude oil lamps. The wick provided the means of controlling the shape and size of the candle, and thus the burning time and amount of brightness. Beeswax was the most obtainable wax and its hardness meant a candle would burn long and clear.

Beeswax was also part of the trilogy of honey, honey wine, and wax— all products of the bee that were sacred to ancient goddesses. Indeed, the humming of the bees was believed to be the actual voice of a goddess. It was also believed that the hardworking bees could reproduce without sex, which indicated their industry and purity. The Vestal Virgins of Rome were charged with guarding the sacred fire and the bee and its products were sacred to them and the goddess Vesta. The chastity of the bees was symbolic of the vows of the Vestal Virgins to their goddess.

These priestesses were the only ones considered pure enough to blow on the sacred fire. A vestige of this custom could be found through the

Middle Ages, as girls who could respark a dying flame where considered virgins, but were not if they couldn't! In use up until the advent of matches was a bit of fiber covered with wax and then dipped in a flammable mixture. It was called a *vesta*, and was used for lighting.

Wax was always big business because as a commercial venture it was clean, solid, and easily shipped. Alert merchant princes were always on the lookout for a product to substitute for the costly and increasingly rare beeswax, a commodity that was purchased in great quantity by the Catholic Church. More than 50 percent of each vigil candle had to be virgin beeswax. Beeswax was so precious that the wax that didn't burn was collected and reused, and thus was not virgin.

Quality in beeswax became so important that master beekeepers fed their bees special diets. One recommended diet included six pounds of honey to a quarter liter of pureed lentils, white wine, and one fish. This would ensure that the candle would burn virtually smokeless and without bad odors.

Poor people melted the fat from pigs to make tallow candles and soap. Pig fat makes a particularly soft soap and a particularly sooty, foul-smelling, and fast-burning candle. Beef suet was firmer, but was also more difficult to come by.

Candles were always dipped until the fifteenth century, when someone took up the idea of making wooden molds to shape the tapers. Certainly this speeded up the process, but major strides came with the discovery of spermaceti, a crystalline substance from the head of a sperm whale. The standard measurement of light—one candlepower—was based on the light of one spermaceti candle weighing about two and a half ounces, burning at a rate of 120 grams per hour.

This candle was still quite pricey, but certainly more available than beeswax. Things changed, however, in 1811, when Michel Chevreul figured out how to separate the fatty acids in fat from the glycerin. Eventually, he discovered that glycerin can be spun off into stearic acid, which is a very cheap additive used to harden candles. Braided wicks of cotton or linen rather than a single spun thread were introduced in 1825, further ensuring a cleaner, long-burning product.

In 1830, they were able to separate paraffin from the petroleum found at oil seeps in the ground. By 1854, paraffin and stearic acid were being combined and the whole lighting industry took off.

Fortunes were foretold in the shapes formed by the drips from a candle. A triangle meant success, while a tear-shaped drip meant sorrow. Like reading tea leaves, all the milestones of life could be predicted: birth, death, journeys, and marriage.

The sacred power of the flame can be found in the candles on Christmas trees and the lights in each house window. There is also an association between choirs and candles that relates to the old custom of singing until the candle burns out. This was a Celtic ritual to lure the Sun back at the Winter Solstice and longest night, which leads to the festival of Candlemas.

Candles were made with medicinal herbs or even opium, and burned to ease the suffering of the ill. Some were lit to drive demons away from the dying. Lighted tapers at the four corners of the funeral bier meant that the soul of the deceased could not be grabbed by Satan's minions.

How To Dip Candles

Candle dipping is a fun craft that, while messy, does not require too much skill. Supplies can be gathered from craft stores or natural food stores. Paraffin can be obtained where canning supplies are sold.

Choose a day when the Moon is in a fixed sign and after it is Full. Put down newspapers to cover all surfaces and find an old double boiler at a yard sale to use for the process. (A discarded percolator makes an ideal container for pouring wax if you're thinking of doing some molded candles.) An electric skillet filled with water also makes a useful melter. Save tin cans in several sizes in which to melt wax, but be sure they are as deep as the length of your candle. Paraffin is a petroleum product and thus flammable. Heating it directly over flame is dangerous.

Melt 1 pound of paraffin with 1 teaspoon of stearic acid or perhaps ¼ to ½ pound of beeswax. Add color chips if desired. Fragrance can also be added, essential oils being the purest and longest lasting of scents to use.

Choosing the correct wick is important. The smaller the wick, the smaller the circumference of the candle should be. A thickly braided wick would not burn as fast as the wax in a taper, so you need to choose a medium size.

Candles are dipped in pairs, so you need to measure a length of wicking equal to two candles plus another four to five inches that you can use to grip while dipping. Dip the wicking into the prepared wax, which should be warmed to about 160 degrees, and let soak for a minute or two. Remove and dunk into a container of cool water. Straighten the wick by running your fingers down the length of it from the dry part of the wicking to its waxed end. Remember not to get the middle four to five inches in the wax.

The other technique is to weight the bottom tails of the wicking with metal washers to keep the candles straight. At the end of the dipping process, you can cut off the weights to leave a flat bottom to the candle.

Once you have completed the initial soaking and straightening of the wick, you can dip more quickly. The idea is to give a quick coating of wax without a messy build-up on the bottom or the end of the wicking. After each dip in the wax, dip the candle in the cool water. You can't allow the wax to get too hot as it will melt what is already on the wicking. If it is too cool then it will not coat as well.

Some people first dip in clear paraffin and save the colored paraffin for the last few dips. There is no particular reason to do this because you really don't save anything, including money. If you have several containers of colored wax, on the last dip, you can make a rainbow effect by dipping in each successive color up to evenly spaced segments.

The trickiest part of the process is dipping both candles in the wax at the same time without sealing them both together. You can salvage this attempt by cutting the candles apart and paring down the lump of wax at the joint. Then smooth the taper by rolling it with your palm on a flat surface within twenty minutes of its last dip. Candles should air-dry to a high gloss, but after they have aged for four to five days, you can polish them by rubbing gently with felt.

If you want to make your own vesta, cut a length of wicking and dip and straighten no more than three times. These are handy to use for ritual if you don't like using matches for lighting candles. Some craft stores sell vestas to use as the wick in a mold if you don't wish to make your own.

Bayberry Candles

Bayberry candles enjoy a certain romance here in the U.S., a tradition that goes back to the Pilgrims and the first settlers on Nantucket. To produce an eight-ounce bayberry candle, you need 1½ quarts of berries. To release the wax, boil the berries in water for five minutes and skim the wax from the surface. Do this in small batches until you have used all the berries. Then re-melt all the wax and strain out the impurities. The candles can be molded, or dipped in the traditional fashion.

As long as candles offer a flattering light in the service of romance, carry petitions in their smoke to the heavens, or hide salamanders in their flames, and they will remain an ever present symbol of the element of fire and a powerful tool for the working of all magic. They can never be rendered obsolete by the power of electricity.

The Scented Home

By Caroline Moss

For anyone who loves herbs, essential oils, and natural fragrances, a wonderful way to improve daily happiness is to use them in scenting the home. I have listed some suggestions, room by room, that I have found enjoyable. Many also make easy and unusual gift ideas.

Kitchen

Kitchen wreaths using spices as well as herbs can be as simple or complex as you wish. You can purchase a ready-made wreath and add a few sprigs from your garden, or make one up from scratch. Many books are available on this art. Small bunches of dried herbs and spices are fast, effective, and fragrant additions to wreaths. Try rosemary and purple sage cut to three-inch lengths and tied with mauve and green ribbons, or bunches of cinnamon sticks tied with red. Tiny muslin bags of mixed herbs, called *bouquet garni*, can be tied on to a wreath and cut off to add to soups and casseroles. Just pinch the herbs as you walk past to release a scent.

Plants on a window sill add fragrance and oxygenate the air. The list of scented herbs and flowers suited to pot growth is immense. Try jasmine, balm of Gilead, lemon thyme, marjoram, lemon verbena, and scented geraniums (pelargoniums). The cultivation of scented geraniums can become a hobby in itself. These fascinating plants come in many fragrances such as lemon, rose, mint, spice, and even chocolate! They are easily propagated, so you will soon have lots for a big display or to give away, and the leaves retain their scent when dried for use in potpourri. Note that the flowers are not spectacular and the showy red and pink geraniums do not carry the scents.

Don't just keep the pleasure of scent for yourself and your family— make a catnip mouse for your cat. No time to sew? Simply take a small fabric toy or cushion, snip a seam open, poke in some dried cat mint and sew it up. The cat won't mind if it's not too tidy.

Glue cinnamon sticks onto a stiff board base for a scented pot stand that will release its fragrance each time warm pots are placed on it. This won't last forever, but should give good service if you try to keep it fairly dry. Muslin sachets of herbs stitched into fabric mats have the same effect.

Dried herbs need to be in dark, airtight containers to retain their scent. However, be sure to string up some bunches of fresh and dried herbs for pinching as you pass. Rosemary, sage, and lavender are particularly long-lasting and fragrant. For a change, hang bunches of southernwood which, in addition to a haunting scent, has insect repellent qualities.

To fill the home with a lovely fragrance there is no need to spend a lot on specially marketed simmering potpourris. Just throw orange peel, cinnamon sticks, cloves, and bay leaves into a pan of water and boil it up to fill the home with a warm smell. Alternatively, sprinkle a few drops of your favorite essential or fragrance oil, with some potpourri if you have it, into a pan of water and warm on the stove. This is fast and effective and gives a good strong scent, where scented candles and the like can be too subtle.

Sitting Room

Potpourri is an age-old way of scenting the home and can be cozy, elegant, spicy, or flowery according to your mood and the season. Try making your own from one of the many recipes available, or simply add your own touches to a purchased base. Throw some small fir cones, cinnamon sticks, or gold-painted bay leaves to a Christmas mix. Dry petals from a special bouquet to add to a flower base. Don't worry if they are not too scented, as color and form are important too, and essential oils can be added to a bowl that has lost its aroma.

If you become interested in potpourri you might like to try making the old-fashioned version where rose petals were sandwiched in alternate layers with salt in a lidded china pot. The mixture should be pressed down and kept lidded other than when you are in the room. Add to the pot as more petals become available. This mixture turns black and is not attractive to look at, but the aroma is very long-lasting.

Rub cool light bulbs with cotton wool soaked with scented oil and enjoy the fragrance pervading the room as the bulb heats.

Scented cushions can be made using the principles of aromatherapy, with sachets of herbs sewn into larger cushions. Try chamomile or lavender for relaxing qualities, or rosemary and pine for stimulation. For general use, however, you can't go wrong with perennial favorites such as rose. As with potpourri, boost the petals with a drop of oil when the fragrance fades.

If you, or a friend, have an open fire, a lovely touch is to throw scented cones into the flames. Melt some beeswax (or old candle stubs) in a washed can placed in a pan of water. Using a can inside the pan means you can simply throw it away and are not left with a waxy pan to try to clean.

Add a few drops of scented oil. Leave to cool and thicken very slightly and drop cones in. Remove the cones with tongs and leave them to drain and dry on aluminum foil. Don't waste expensive essential oils on this—cheaper fragrance oils are just fine. Keep a big basket full of these by the fire.

When cooking or crafting, save all your stalks and twigs. Dry them well and bag them up into small brown paper bags. Tie them up with string or raffia and throw them into a log fire for a burst of scent. A basket full of cones or twig bags makes a charming holiday gift for friends—be sure to attach a label explaining their use!

Don't confine herb and spice wreaths to the kitchen. A large circle can make an unusual and spectacular year-round display—try making a wreath with alternate bunches of green and purple sage.

As an alternative to the wall, place your wreath on a (protected) table top, perhaps with a bowl of fruit or flowers in the center. If the wreath base is bound with damp moss, herb cuttings have even been known to take root in wreath bases bound with damp moss.

One of the most popular ways of incorporating perfume into the home is the scented candle. These can be expensive. If you have a bottle of fragrance oil around, light a wide candle and add a drop or two of oil into the little pool of melted wax around the flame. Relax and enjoy.

Add fragrance to the bookshelf by pressing costmary (alecost) leaves, with their minty balsam scent, between the pages of favorite books to deter silverfish. Large, rose-scented geranium leaves also add an ethereal Victorian aura to precious journals, and are a joy to discover nestling between the pages of a book unread for a few years.

In a food processor, mix dried herbs with equal parts of bicarbonate of soda and salt. Sprinkle liberally on the carpet and vacuum up an hour or so later. This is a natural carpet freshener.

Bathroom

Oils can be added to the bath for scent alone or for their beneficial properties. Full details are outside the scope of this article, so consult any good aromatherapy book or practitioner. Just remember that if you are using essential oil (rather than a synthetic fragrance), only a few drops are needed.

To use herbs and flower petals for your bath, put them into small muslin bags that can be fished out before you get in. The idea of fragrant herbs floating on the water may be temptingly romantic, but the reality is a mass of soggy brown herbage clinging to and scratching the body—believe me, stick to bags! A soggy rose petal is a depressing thing.

There are, of course, endless possibilities for incorporating fragrance into one's daily bathroom routine and an easy and effective one is the herbal hair rinse. Make a strong infusion of an herb of your choice. Strain it, then add two drops of essential oil if you wish and use as your final hair rinse. Try roses and lavender combined for a feminine scent or rosemary or bay for something less flowery for men or women.

Bedroom

The sleep pillow is a comforting use of natural fragrance and many people swear by its effectiveness. Calming and soporific herbs include hops, chamomile, and lavender. Just take care to make moderate use of lavender, as it can be overpowering.

Potpourri can, of course, be delightful in a bedroom, and a bowlful on a dressing table is especially welcome in the guest room. Beware of putting it on the bedside table as it may be knocked over in the night as people reach for clocks or water.

We have all seen lavender bags, but do break the mold by making little sachets filled with something different—a handful of a fine potpourri is a good substitute. Slip these sachets into drawers or sew on ribbons so that they can be tied onto coat hangers. Use pine, bayberry, and rosemary for a more masculine scent.

If stitching little bags is not your thing, then simply hang bunches of *eau de cologne* mint in your wardrobe.

Pressed herb bookmarks may retain some scent themselves or can be made using scented cards. Choose a fairly porous card and place it in a box with a pad of cotton wool soaked with essential oil. After a few weeks the card will retain the scent for quite a long period.

I do hope you try at least one of the above ideas and have fun scenting your home with fresh herbs and natural oils.

America's Favorite Brew

By Louise Riotte

E very day now we are warned of the rising price of coffee. The delicious brew so vital to getting us going in the morning is becoming ever more valuable due to crop failure in the coffee-producing countries. This has happened before, and the price has gone down again when the coffee bushes yielded abundantly the following year. But, as with all plant crops, nothing is certain. Another freeze could wipe out the crop again. Even so, coffee is a little luxury we will not willingly do without, so most of us will pay the price and go right on drinking our favorite brew.

Coffee was also highly prized in colonial times and was often hard to come by, so various substitutions were tried rather than doing without it entirely. Some substitutions, of course, were more palatable than others. The plants used also varied from one area to another, depending on what was available or abundant, or what substitute was found to be more pleasing.

According to Grace Firth in her book A *Natural Year*, colonial gardeners often cultivated coffee substitutes that in later years escaped and now grow wild. Some people like the taste of these substitutes, others do not. "Like any food or beverage," she warns, "the product should be weighed on its own merits. To taste parched and perked seeds, roots, or nuts with the thought 'coffee' in mind is unfair to the substitute."

Coffee As We Know It

Coffee, ruled by Neptune, Mars, and Pluto, is the favorite hot drink in almost every country in temperate or cold climates. The scientific name is *Coffea arabica*. It originally grew wild in Ethiopia. It now grows under cultivation in Java, Sumatra, India, Arabia, equatorial Africa, Hawaii, Mexico, Central and South America, and the West Indies. *Coffee arabica* is a shrub with evergreen leaves, reaching a height of fifteen to twenty feet when fully grown. The flowers are white and the berry begins to grow while the tree is blossoming, and ripens from green to yellow to red. The average tree produces a pound and a half of berries a year, enough for one pound of roasted coffee. It is usually five years old before it bears a full crop.

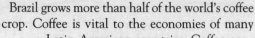

Brazil grows more than half of the world's coffee crop. Coffee is vital to the economies of many Latin American countries. Coffee contains caffeine, a drug that acts as a stimulant to mental and physical energy. The drink tends to expand blood vessels mildly so that more blood flows to the heart and brain.

Chicory

Roasted chicory roots (*Cichorlum intybus*), ruled astrologically by Jupiter and Virgo, do not taste like coffee, but when used as an additive, some people believe they improve the color and flavor of South American coffee. Personally I do not care for the additive. Some years ago I had a dentist who loved the taste, and when I had an appointment with him he always presented me with a cup of chicory flavored coffee. After the first sip or two I tried to find a way to surreptitiously get rid of it without offending my host, who apparently believed he was bestowing upon me a great delicacy.

Chicory, which grows on roadsides and in waste clay soils from Canada southward, is identifiable when young by its leaves, which resemble those of dandelions. As the plants mature, a rigid, loosely branched, two-foot stem develops, and blue flowers bloom in midsummer. The tubular roots, which grow horizontally, should be dug in September after flowering is over.

As a matter of fact, September is the best month for gathering most coffee substitutes, and best results are usually obtained if seeds, roots, and leaves are harvested during the waning Virgo Moon.

To use chicory as a substitute or as a coffee additive, the roots should be washed, coarsely ground, dried in a very slow oven for two or three hours, then roasted in a clean skillet. The roasting or browning process should be done very slowly and the granulated chicory should be repeatedly stirred until the proper color and flavor are reached.

The chicory may then be ground a second time and dry-roasted again if the flavor and color do not quite meet your taste. Roasting should be done a little at a time until the desired taste is achieved.

In *Eat the Weeds*, Ben Charles Harris waxes eloquent as he attests to the value of chicory as a coffee substitute, declaring it to be one of the best, cheapest, and most easily available, often growing in your own back yard or immediate environs. He found that ½ to 3 ounces of prepared chicory added to one pound of coffee increases the yield by 30 percent, approximately ten extra cups.

He says that the method of preparing chicory for use is quite simple. "In mid-summer on a rainy day, after you have properly identified the herb...dig up the roots and wash them clean, preferably with a brush. After slicing the roots in long thin strips, you are ready for either of two methods of preparing the roots for roasting. The first consists of tying together five or six of the strips with a thin wire, or leaving them untied, and allowing them to dry on, under or in an oven, in direct sunlight, or of course up in the dear old attic."

The other method is to cut the sliced roots into thin transverse sections and then into quarters and allow them to dry. The roasting process for the quarter-sections is about the same as for the coffee bean. You may even place these smaller sections when dry inside a hot oven or directly on the clean surface of your kitchen stove. The time limit is about one hour. However, the better method of roasting chicory roots is to place several packages of the tied-up root right in the midst of an outdoor fireplace. After a few minutes, the whites of the root centers will have turned a uniform brown; then these roots are ready to be ground.

My friendly dentist was a Native American and it was not surprising that he liked chicory coffee for, according to Virginia Scully in *A Treasury of American Indian Herbs*, the Indians roasted the roots and used them as they did the dandelion. Dandelion roots make an especially bitter brew, but some like it. In France and in our own South, subject to French influence, the roots are dug, dried, ground, and added to coffee, not as an adulterant but for its distinctive flavor.

Cleavers

Cleavers, or goose grass (*Galium aparine*), a member of the madder family, seems to be the most popular coffee substitute after chicory. Cleavers grow in Alaska, southward across Canada, and down into Texas, and are found on seashores and in rocky woods. Although cleaver sprouts may be eaten in the spring, the tiny twin burr-seeds ripen later.

Says Grace Firth, "The seeds are less than an eighth of an inch in diameter and are usually not ground. After roasting, they are simply brewed into coffee. The taste and smell of cleaver is similar to full-bodied coffee. I have found cleaver brew to be pleasant and mildly stimulating."

Euell Gibbons, in *Stalking the Healthful Herbs*, also has a good word to say about cleavers: "I do not hesitate to use the word substitute, for cleavers really try to imitate coffee. This may be a family resemblance, for cleavers belong to the *Rubiaceae*, the natural order of plants to which the coffee tree also belongs, so they are at least distant cousins."

Chufa

The Chufa (*Cuperus esculentus*), ruled by the Sun, is a fine food and medicinal herb with an almost universal distribution. It is found in Europe, Africa, Asia, and America. In North America it is found from New Brunswick to Minnesota and southward to Florida and Texas. The botanical name means "edible sedge," and the chufa is related to the tules and bulrushes. It has grasslike leaves at the base, and its stout, triangular seedstalk rises one to two feet. Near its top is another circle of leaves in the flower cluster, consisting of five to eight rays, each bearing numerous little flat spikelets. The edible part grows underground, and while it is called a nut, it is really a small tuber, about half an inch long, dark colored, and wrinkled. The chufa likes rich, wet, alluvial soil. In poor soil it sets a poor crop.

If chufa tubers are roasted until they are a very dark brown all through, then pulverized in a blender or coffee mill, they make a very palatable hot drink when brewed exactly as you do coffee. This brew tastes more like some of the roasted-cereal health food drinks than it does coffee, but it is a good hot beverage of that class. I have several times tried chufa coffee for dinner when I was afraid that real coffee would keep me awake too long, and have always found it a pleasant drink. It contains no harmful stimulants and can be freely given to children who insist on having coffee when the grown-ups do.

Chufa tubers are tender and sweet and have a nutty almond or filbert flavor. They may be eaten untreated or roasted like chestnuts. They were highly prized by the Indians as a food source and are also known in Europe, especially in the Mediterranean countries, where they are used to make an "orgeat." This is a syrupy drink usually made from almonds and a water prepared from orange flowers.

Sunflower

The common sunflower (*Helianthus annus*) is an American plant that has been widely cultivated, much improved, and may be found anywhere in the United States. According to Scully, of approximately fifteen species of sunflower, four are spread throughout the Rockies. The little sunflower is small and grows from the valleys to the timberline, where it is joined by the alpine sunflower that is found from 10,000 to 12,000 feet. The Native Americans dried the highly nutritious seeds and gathered them into meal for gruel and cakes. Frequently they added water to the meal as a drink, and crushed roasted seeds to make a drink like coffee.

Ground Nut

The ground nut (*Apius tuberosa*) is an herb of Venus and it is also known as the wild potato. The Native Americans called it *hopness*. It likes to grow along sandy roadsides, and the tubers, roots, and seed pods are all used. Like many other coffee substitutes, the tubers are best gathered after September when they are mature. We may utilize the ground nut as a coffee dilutent (thinner), says Harris, by scraping out the meaty interior of the tuber and then roasting the balance, which must be first cut into smaller segments.

The ever-traveling ground nut is a poor and honest relation of the soya bean, which is also used as a coffee substitute. The early pilgrims were taught by the Native Americans to respect this wild plant as a source of nutrients. In the sandy soil attached to the root system are found the edible tubers, or small potatoes, growing in a rather long chain, somewhat like a string of enlarged beads. For this reason they were called "rosary roots" by the French Jesuit missionaries in Canada, who observed how the small tubers grew as the Indians gathered them. These are the "potatoes" that Sir Walter Raleigh's expeditions took back to England. The tubers contain protein, natural sugar and starch, and minerals.

Some people will try to make a coffee substitute out of just about anything. Recently a woman told me that she saved the seeds from dried okra pods, browned them, and made what was to her an acceptable brew.

References

Bills, Rex. *The Rulership Book*. Richmond, VA: MacCoy Publishing and Masonic Supply Co., Inc., 1967.

Coon, Nelson. *Using Plants for Healing*. New York: Hearthside Press, Inc.

Firth, Grace. *A Natural Year*. New York: Simon and Schuster.

Gibbons, Euell. *Stalking the Healthful Herbs*. New York: David McKay Company, Inc., 1967.

Harris, Ben Charles. *Eat the Weeds*. Barre, MA: Barre Publishing.

Scully, Virginia. *A Treasury of American Indian Herbs*. New York: Bonanza Books.

Apple Cider Vinegar

By Chandra Moira Beal

People have been making and using vinegar for at least the past five millennia. In 400 BCE, Hippocrates, who is regarded as the father of medicine, treated his patients with vinegar. During the Middle Ages, bands of outlaws roamed the countryside robbing victims of the black plague after dousing themselves with a vinegar, now known as Four Thieves Vinegar, to protect themselves from getting sick. When they successfully resisted the disease, they were granted their freedom in exchange for the vinegar recipe (see below). Thousands of lives were saved during the Civil War by using vinegar as a disinfectant and anti-bacterial agent.

Making your own vinegar is easy, and it has many uses. Herbs, flowers, fruits, and spices can be added as flavoring agents. Vinegar can be used internally and externally.

Vinegar is a useful beauty agent, too. Make a facial wash from a few crushed strawberries in a cup of vinegar. Let the mixture sit for two hours. Strain the vinegar and pat it over your face and neck before bed, then rinse it off in the morning. This facial nourishes the skin and clears your complexion of blemishes. Vinegar diluted with water makes a beneficial hair rinse that strips the hair of residue build-up and makes it shine.

Vinegar is a great degreasing cleanser around the house, especially on glass. Soak the rinds of several kinds of citrus fruits in vinegar for several weeks and then strain out the peels.

Making Vinegar

To make your own apple cider vinegar, wash, peel, and chop several fresh apples. Mash or press the apples to release their juices. Some recipes suggest combining sweet apples with tart ones. Sweet apples have a higher sugar content, which produces more alcohol and therefore more acid. Tart apples will produce a sharper-tasting vinegar. Place the apples in a large enamel crock or wide-mouthed glass jar and cover them with cold water. Cover the container tightly and store it in a warm place. Check the mixture occasionally until the liquid has turned to cider, a process that takes anywhere from one to six weeks, depending on the sugar content and temperature of the mixture. Skim off the foam that occasionally rises to the surface. If you want to speed up the fermentation process, add yeast, brown sugar or molasses to the initial mixture and keep it warm. Allow this cider mixture to ferment a second time by removing the lid and covering it with cheesecloth or a towel to expose it to air and keep dirt and bugs out. Aeration is the key to giving the vinegar a tart flavor. The vinegar will be ready when it smells and tastes to your liking. Strain out the apple pieces, pour the vinegar into sterilized bottles, and cork.

Vinegar of the Four Thieves

 2 quarts apple cider vinegar

 2 tablespoons lavender petals

 2 tablespoons rosemary

 2 tablespoons sage

 2 tablespoons wormwood

 2 tablespoons rue

 2 tablespoons peppermint

 Several cloves of peeled garlic

Combine the herbs and steep in vinegar in the sun for two weeks. Add several cloves of garlic and steep again for several days. Strain the vinegar and bottle. Melt wax around the rim or add glycerin to preserve it.

Midlife by the Moon

By Gretchen Lawlor

I n the next ten years more women will be entering menopause than in all of recorded history. There are forty million women scheduled to go though menopause in the next twenty years. The Baby Boomers, born in the 1940s and early 1950s, are five times more numerous than any preceding generation. Menopause will not be the same thing once this flood of women have gone through it.

In our culture menopause is cast as a disease. Menopausal women are the largest commercial market in history, with the estrogen Premarin the most prescribed drug in the United States. Descriptions of the horrors of depressed, irritable, shriveled old women fill medical journals and pop magazines.

This prevailing attitude, promoted largely by the medical establishment, is that no woman will be able to cope with menopausal changes without the intervention of doctors, through surgery or drugs. Ninety percent of women in their forties visiting their doctors are recommended hormone replacement therapy.

Modern medicine and better nutrition are allowing women to live longer, often another thirty-five to forty years after the midlife transition. They are living longer, but not better.

Lack of Rituals for Midlife Transformation

In many cultures the post-menopausal woman is considered powerful and wise. There are social roles or positions that are not available until a woman has made this crossing. The most powerful shamaness or healer is the woman in her late fifties or older. In many tribal situations the older woman, with her intimate wisdom gained from the years of nurturing children and managing the family, moves on to nurture and manage the tribe through her position on the tribal council.

Studies indicate symptoms are rarer in cultures where post-menopausal women gain power and status that they didn't have in reproductive years. In China, influenced by the knowledge gained through 7,000 years of Chinese medicine, distressing physical symptoms are uncommon, or seen in a very different light. For example, hot flashes are considered valuable for their cleansing qualities. Heat or fevers are the best means of clearing toxic material, viruses, and cancerous cells from the body.

In Western society, midlife is just not recognized for the profound transformational journey it can be. Women who are going through this period of flux and internal change are held up to ridicule. The surgical removal of the uterus, a hysterectomy, is our only cultural ritual to help women mark the shedding of an old life and the taking up of new powers. Consider the roots of the word *hysterectomy:* "The surgical removal of the uterus, believed to be responsible for the generation of abnormal emotional fears or hysteria."

Cycles of the Moon in Women's Lives

At midlife, a woman begins to make her transition to the powerful third cycle of life. These three cycles are symbolized in the roles of maiden, mother, and crone. Each cycle lasts for approximately twenty-eight years, and ebbs and flows in a manner similar to the cycle of the Moon, from New, to waxing, to Full, and then waning. The light increases to peak at the Full Moon, then decreases and disappears, just before the next New Moon begins.

The timing and duration of each of these cycles corresponds precisely to the cycles of the progressed Moon. The progressed Moon's movement can be used by a woman as a timing tool for anticipating opportunities and challenges within each cycle. Peak moments where the significant shifts happen are always associated with Moon changes.

The First Cycle: Maiden

The first cycle, that of the maiden, is from birth to age twenty-eight, approximately (the timing for each woman will be slightly different, and can be seen in the astrological chart). This is the cycle of youth, of the woman coming into her first flowering, experimenting with life.

The Second Cycle: Mother

The second cycle is that of the mother, from age twenty-eight to fifty-six. In this cycle a woman is focused on giving birth to and nurturing something she creates, whether it be a family, or a relationship, a talent, or a profession.

These roles are symbolic ones as not all women will become mothers, and certainly not all right around age twenty-eight. A woman who becomes a mother in the maiden cycle of her life experiences this role in a different, more childlike, naive way than does a woman who commences parenting in the mother cycle. A woman needs to nourish and feed an emerging aspect of life during her cycle as mother.

The Third Cycle: Wise Woman or Crone

The third cycle, which begins around age fifty-six, is the cycle of the wise woman or crone. This is the one we have neglected in our youth-oriented culture. This is the time a woman comes into her wisdom. All the experience she has gathered in her lifetime becomes her wealth, to pass on to her tribe or community. She steps beyond the purely personal realms of experience to share her accumulation of knowledge with others. Her presence becomes a stabilizing force for those around her.

This is a profoundly neglected and ignored cycle in a woman's life. Powerful wise women cool their heels alone and lonely in empty nests. They are undervalued by our culture, unable to re-enter the work force in any position that reflects the richness and value of their abounding wisdom and understanding.

There are many women who are entering this phase now, and these are women who are unwilling to "go quiet into that good night." This is a generation of women who reclaimed birth as a natural process, and know the power in doing so. In increasing numbers these women are saying no to sedating themselves through their midlife transformations. They want to be awake and alert to the power they are coming into, and are looking for signs and tools along the way with which to navigate the journey.

The Progressed Moon Illuminates the Path

The progressed Moon is a remarkable tool in the navigation of this profound midlife transformation. The phases of the progressed Moon are the major marking stones along the journey.

Progressions are a system astrologers use to predict developmental stages along the path of life. It takes approximately twenty-eight years for the Moon to complete a progressed lunar cycle. The Moon goes through each cycle, moving from New to Full and back to New just as it does in the sky every month. The progressed Moon is a symbolic journey, encompassing years rather than days, though possessing similar attributes. As it reaches New and Full, as it waxes and wanes, it provides clues regarding the nature of opportunities and challenges in a woman's journey.

Progressed Full Moon—Age Forty-Two

Around the age of forty-two there is a peak in the second cycle of life. This is the high point of the cycle of the mother, which began around age twenty-eight. At this time the progressed Moon opposes itself, creating a symbolic Full Moon in every woman's life.

The progressed Full Moon comes at a slightly different time and lasts for a varying period for each of us, but consists of a period from between three months to two and a half years, when the progressed Moon opposes the position of the Moon at birth. During this time, a woman reaches a life peak, a culmination of effort of the last fourteen years. Children are reaching a point of maturity, and in our work we are achieving some of the goals we set for ourselves in our thirties. This is the time to celebrate the fullness of whatever it is a woman has brought to life and nourished. It can be a professional peak of acknowledgment or the gratifying maturation of gifts and skills in a child.

The Full Moon is a time of culmination, emotional peak, and fullness, as well as potential emotional overload. This is a time many women sense the beginning of a total reorganization of life, a turn of the tide that is going to move them in very different directions in their lives.

The Full Moon is always a time of emotional intensity and volatility, and this is similar for the progressed Full Moon at age forty-two. This phase is full of powerful emotions that flood the system. One is filled with emotions, overloaded with the emotional care of mate and family. The bowl of motherhood begins to overflow, discharged through rages and tears.

Forty-two is often a watershed year in a woman's life. Most women experience profound changes in this year—signs of the shift in orientation that is beginning to happen. There is usually some crisis—some break in the weave and rhythm of life as it has been—that acts as an omen of imminent change.

The Full Moon has been reached, and the light begins to decrease, preparing for another cycle. After the peak begins the process of dissolution and shedding of this old way of relating to others and to the world.

The Waning Square of the Moon: Age Forty-Nine

Between forty-two and forty-nine (remember, we each have our personal timing; look to the progressed Moon in your own chart for the exact years), the old life loses its hold. Boredom, apathy, and disinterest in family and work illustrate the shift. Physical symptoms of aging appear: the hot flashes and irritability, and fluctuations or cessation in menstrual flow.

Within a woman's life and her body appear the signs of the greatest wisdom: that dissolution must precede new life. We forget and are reminded that all of life is cyclic. There is a great round of birth, of flowering and of death, and then of birth again. All of our lives we have this mystery revealed within the cycle of the Moon, and in the cycle of our monthly fertility and blood.

The dominant patterns of a woman's personality are dissolving. She becomes itchy and irritable, uncomfortable like a snake that must shed its skin. She needs solitude and time to reflect.

This is the time a woman is challenged to shed the role of caretaker of all the souls around her. She becomes difficult to live with, she pushes people away with her irritability. She needs to be alone, to discover what it is she needs to nourish herself. Some of her work is to rediscover what it was that she gave away as she entered the cycle of the Mother. The talents and passions that were put aside in order to get along with mate or family or community and the pleasures or interests that she had no time for when she was nurturing her family all come back clamoring for attention.

Regret and depression are common as a woman senses a fading of the light. She has peaked with the Full Moon, and is this all there is? Is there enough time to pursue some of those neglected gifts and passions? Personal failures and weakness loom large in her vision, as do the frailties of those around her. Life is hard, yet those hard places can facilitate this metamorphosis into a new power.

The expectations of family and society have formed a woman's personal traits and characteristics up to this point, and they no longer work. She is bored and disillusioned with life. Depression, nostalgia, and regret drag her down as she witnesses the ending of this way of relating to her world, yet she does not know what, if anything, will come in its place.

The progressed waning square of a woman's Moon to the position it held at her birth, often at age forty-nine, signals an intensification of the dissolution process. Some crisis provides the impetus to surrender more, to shed more skins. In Chinese, the symbol for the word "crisis" is the same as the word "opportunity." At forty-nine, there comes an opportunity.

Solitude becomes a desperate hunger, a necessity in order to listen, to give in to whatever begs to be let loose into her new life ahead. She may appear lost and floundering. She is shedding, clearing away the past, in her dreams, her rages, and her tears.

New Moon, New Life, at Age Fifty-Six

So what is this new life, this new promise, rumbling just beneath the surface in the late forties and early fifties? How does a woman find this new life, and what does she do to let it out? What is it?

In each of us the journey and the outcome will be somewhat different, and much of the work is actually done in the dark of the Moon, in the months preceding the New Moon around age fifty-six. There must be a separation from the comfort of life as it has been. This is not always our choice. Sometimes it is brought to us at this time in our lives, through an illness, a death, the loss of a job, a love affair, or a terrible depression.

The pattern of the Moon, myths of women's journeys, stories of those who have gone before, and the wisdom of the body all are signs along the way. The promise of a New Moon and the experience of cycles must lend some trust that there will be another chance. At the New Moon there is a new cycle starting, yet, in those first few nights of the New Moon, the crescent is not yet visible. This wisdom is paralleled in the progressed New Moon. A woman must act on impulse. She has nothing but her own deep wisdom that leads her in the direction she must go. Yet there is nothing tangible for her to hold on to, just an act of faith, a knowledge that she cannot go back, she must step forward.

Each challenge that she responds to, each demon that she faces in her fears, the blocks and obstacles along the way from people who doubt her or want to hold her back—these are all the gathering of power.

Tools and Rituals of Renewal

There are tools that can help a woman navigate the midlife journey. The body needs tending, nourishing in a different way to do the work well. Use the allies that nature provides as much as possible. There are herbs and foods to help the body and attitudes and experiences that help the spirit.

Exercise is important in keeping the body supple and strong. Even walking for twenty minutes three times a week will make a big difference in the life force available to you. Take time for yourself. Some kind of withdrawal from your ordinary life is absolutely necessary in order to make a successful midlife crossing. It is only in solitude that a woman can really face the changes in her body and her life. In silence and alone she can come to terms with what needs to die in order for something else to be born.

In other times, when signs of menopause and the darkening of the Moon showed that a woman was ready, she was allowed to leave the tribe and go away for a while. These days, we have no positive ritual withdrawal, unless we manage it through a serious health crisis. Perhaps this is something midlife women will begin to demand and create.

Have fun. One of the greatest lessons of midlife is that you no longer have to live by other people's rules and needs. You are the mistress of your own life. Pick your own company, find your own daily rhythms, and sleep less or at different times.

Eat more fresh plant-based foods, vegetables, grains, and tofu. Reduce dairy and animal fats. Eat less red meat, although fish and organic chicken (no hormones) are okay. Avoid additives and preservatives, and keep salt, sugar and hydrogenated fats, like margarine, to a minimum.

Vitamin E is about the best thing to keep hot flashes to a manageable level, and it strengthens the heart. Calcium with magnesium keeps the bones strong, and essential fatty acids, found in flax seed or borage oil, are fabulous sources of anti-inflammatories. They are good for the joints and nerves and help keep skin and hair hydrated.

Herbs for the body to help the physical symptoms of the metamorphosis include estrogenic herbs (best for women who have short, irregular, or absent periods), such as black cohosh, sage, alfalfa, red clover, or licorice. For women who experience heavy bleeding and frequent periods, try progesterone-rich herbs, such as vitex (also know as chaste-tree berry), sarsaparilla, or wild yam. The mineral-rich herbs such as nettle, oat straw, horsetail, or even raspberry leaf make great daily tea beverages that strengthen the nerves and the bones.

If you have unavoidable stress, consider an herb that is known as a stress adapter, raising your energy levels and increasing your tolerance for stress, such as Siberian ginseng. It isn't a real ginseng, which is generally too stimulating for a woman's body at midlife.

For support to the nervous system and better sleep, use skullcap or oats, which not only calm the system but also help rebuild it. If you are thin and hyperactive, licorice or borage may be your best allies, nourishing your hard-working adrenal glands.

With the New Moon in the fifties a woman moves to become mistress of her own life. She begins another cycle of creativity. In this cycle, the cycle of the wise woman, a truly wise woman pursues what gives her the greatest joy and the gratest sense of meaning. The more a woman does what brings her joy, the more physical energy is available to her. Follow your bliss, and wherever that takes you has nothing to do with striving for success or keeping anyone happy but yourself. In following this bliss and in radiating the happiness that comes with this journey, you do such great service to others, which is another part of this cycle. You inspire the women coming after you, you remind everyone that all things are cyclic, that the New Moon will always follow the dark, that new life always comes out of the old.

Herbal Tonics

By Carly Wall, C.A.

As the Moon waxes and wanes and then renews itself once again, we too wish we could renew ourselves and become vigorous as we were in our youth. This is on all of our minds especially as the generation of baby boomers edges toward its fifties. We all want to maintain the vibrancy and exude the health of our younger days, but can we really rejuvenate our bodies and actually become young again? Look to the shelves of health food and retail stores and you would think so. DHEA, Melatonin, Retin-A, shark cartilage, and other myriad creams, pills, and elixirs come on the scene and fade as another miracle fad takes their place. That's not to say these products don't do what their makers claim, in whatever degree. But as a fountain of youth, they just don't fit the bill. A magic youth fountain would not merely mask or stave off the inevitable, but really rejuvenate from the ground up—namely work on a cellular level to renew and rebuild—in essence, make young again! You may laugh and sneer, but as I delve deeper into the study of herbs and plant medicines, it seems that this fountain can be found easily for each one of us. Tonic herbs seem to be the key, along with the sensible attention to diet and exercise.

Plant Magic

At the Australian Aromatherapy Conference held in April 1996, researchers revealed a startling discovery. Recent experiments have found that some essential oils, those with antioxidant properties, have been shown to slow down, if not reverse, the aging process. Older mice fed these essential oils were found to have a 50 percent increase in polyunsaturated fatty acids in the liver, seemingly reversing the process of aging. Other experiments were done on pregnant animals. The animals ingested thyme essential oil and there were indications that even the unborn young were gaining benefits from these plant extracts. Although ingestion of essential oils is not recommended to the general public without the advice of a professional aromatherapist or other natural health care practitioner, there are other ways we can squeeze out the benefits of these plant juices—ways that are easy and safe.

The easiest method I know of gaining benefits of the herbs in this way is through creating your own medicinal extracts—specifically, rejuvenating medicinal herbal extracts made from herbs that contain antioxidants.

What Are Antioxidants?

Our bodies must fight every day to protect themselves. One of the biggest fights is in protecting from invading atoms or groups of atoms that can damage our cells and cause our immune system to shut down, leading to degeneration and disease. These damaging atoms are called "free radicals." They are formed from various different exposures, mainly from toxic chemicals, radiation, and pollution.

Our bodies have enzymes called "free radical scavengers" with the job of fighting off these bad atoms. They neutralize the free radicals. But what happens if through stress, bad diet, and an environment inundated with pollution and other toxic stressors these scavengers are overwhelmed? Well, you can supplement these scavenger enzymes by eating a diet rich in antioxidants, which are also scavengers in a sense, gobbling up and ridding the body of these unwanted invaders. The result is that the body stays strong and vital and in the peak of health. Scientists claim oxidation damage caused by free radicals is one of the main mechanisms causing aging. Perhaps, some would say, aging is really just a disease. If we lived in a perfect environment, and ate the right foods, we would not only live longer, but look good while doing it.

Although many foods can contain antioxidants, there is a group of herbs that contains large amounts of antioxidants as well as having other medicinal properties to help the body renew and rejuvenate itself. There is a method of extracting the good qualities of the herb quite easily, called tincturing. This method extracts all the medicinal qualities of the herbs into an easy, compact, and long-lasting liquid that you can add to juices, teas, or other drinks. It is quite easy.

Ideally you should use fresh herbs just picked from your own back yard. These plants contain the highest amounts of "life-force" as well as all the nutrients and vitamins. Use dried herbs if you must, but to do the best job, learn to grow your own fresh specimens to make tinctures in spring, summer, and fall that will carry you through the year.

Making Tinctures

Basically, tincturing requires four steps. First is to pack fresh, clean herbs (or dried) tightly into a Mason jar. Then cover the herbs in the jar with vodka or rum. Seal and store this in a sunny window for two weeks, shaking occasionally. Next, strain the mixture, pressing out the plant material to get every bit of glorious liquid. You may repeat the process by adding fresh herbs to the liquid, then straining out, to obtain a stronger tincture. Then all you have to do is pour the strained liquid into clean, dark bottles. Seal and store away for use. It will keep indefinitely, but it is best to use it up within the year and make a fresh batch so you know you are obtaining the best benefits. To make a tincture of more than one herb, add equal amounts of herbs to the jar and proceed as before, but you may want to repeat this process three times to get a strong enough quantity of all herbs.

To use, add an eyedropper of your tincture to a cup of water, fruit juice, or tea (cooled to room temperature). Honey can be added for flavor. Drink this once a day and over the course of some weeks you should feel a difference in energy and vitality, according to the herbs you use. You are adding a boost of antioxidants to your diet in this way. Author's note of caution: You may want to talk to your doctor before trying any herbal remedies. Also, avoid herbal treatments when you are pregnant or nursing, unless advised by a natural health care practitioner. Many of these herbs listed are stimulating and can cause uterine contractions. Here are some herbs you may want to try.

Thyme

The pungency of the smell of thyme is clean and fresh. It is anti-bacterial and anti-fungal, as well as being good for respiratory problems and digestive complaints. It stimulates the immune system and calms the nerves. There are many different types of thyme to choose from. The best to use are wild thyme or mother of thyme, English thyme, lemon thyme or nutmeg thyme. All thymes are perennial and most are pretty hardy. They require light, sandy, well-drained soil, and full Sun.

Tea Tree

The worldwide demand for the antiseptic properties of the oil contained within this tree has exploded. It is a powerful antiseptic oil obtained from the leaves of this small tree or shrub. The Australian aborigines have long used the crushed leaves for skin infections. It is a powerful immunostimulant and is unusual in that it fights bacteria, fungi, and viruses. It is good for colds, fevers, flus, and infectious illnesses. Seeds of this easy-to-grow shrub are available for purchase. It is a tender perennial so it will grow outdoors only in the more temperate climes. It has narrow, bright green leaves.

Evening Primrose

All parts of this plant are edible and nutritious—including the seeds. It soothes and protects mucous membranes, acts as an antispasmodic, and serves as a weak astringent. Studies show it reduces high blood pressure, guarding against coronary artery disease. It is good for premenstrual syndrome, improves rheumatoid arthritis, and contains gamma-linoleic acid to help suppress inflammation and strengthen the immune system. It has been shown to regenerate liver cells damaged in alcoholism. It helps headaches and depression too. These night-blooming plants are easily grown in full Sun and light, well-drained soil. They bloom in summer.

Celery Seed

Widely used as a domestic spice, celery seed is useful medicinally to help gout, arthritis, and in regenerating the liver. It gets rid of toxic buildups in the blood. It is also useful in stomach and digestive complaints. It is a great diuretic. It is useful in helping the kidneys and is an energy stimulant. In the past, it was used as a cleansing tonic after winter. Harvest the seeds after the plant flowers its second year, or use the root. It isn't very difficult to grow. It is a heavy feeder plant, so it requires lots of manure (poultry, stable, or sheep). Moisture is essential, so mulch heavily.

Garlic

A prized medicinal favorite, garlic strengthens the body in every way. It has strong anti-bacterial effects, and is antiseptic. It has been known to prevent many diseases and lowers blood cholesterol. It is also effective against flu, asthma, and stomach ulcers. An expectorant, it also reduces blood clots and prevents heart attacks, lowering blood pressure. It is good for inflammations and arthritis. It contains vitamins A, B_1, B_2, C, and various minerals. Garlic is easily grown in the garden and prefers full Sun. Use fresh bulbs and grind in the blender before making the tincture.

Rose Hips

Rose hips are a powerhouse of nutrition! Packed with vitamins A, B_1, B_2, pectin, zinc, and especially vitamin C. It is a tonic with laxative and astringent properties. Powerful, yet safe, it is stimulating and energy-giving. Many herbalists suggest these should be a part of our daily diet. Gather the round "berries," or hips, when they appear on your rosebush just as they turn bright scarlet—this should be right after the first frost. Grind them in the blender before making your tincture.

Violet

A mild stimulant, the leaves and flowers contain rutin, a substance that strengthens capillaries. It also has large amounts of vitamins A and C. Experiments have shown it has anti-tumor properties. It also contains an aspirin-like substance, helps sinus congestion, and is good for arthritis as well as respiratory infections. It purifies blood, acts as a laxative, and lowers blood pressure. Only the odorless wild American violet is used medicinally. You can purchase the seed from many wildflower catalogs. They spread rapidly.

Clover

This grows like a weed, but clover actually has a high protein content and was used as a food source by tribes of North American Indians. It aids in reducing fevers, helps kidney ailments, and strengthens the blood. Anticancer chemicals have been discovered in the plant, and experiments have been conducted using it on breast cancer patients. A mild sedative, it detoxifies, rebuilds, stimulates, and cleanses. It is good for asthma, skin disorders, and constipation. It contains large amounts of anti-oxidants. It is a short-lived perennial, preferring full Sun. Use the flowers. Clover seeds can be found through farm seed supply stores. It also grows wild and is easy to identify.

Sage

The Latin word from which sage is taken, *salvia*, means "to save," referring to its many healing properties. It was believed by old-time herbalists that sage prolonged life. No wonder, as it is a strong anti-oxidant with antibacterial qualities. It fights cold and flu germs, and studies confirm it is effective against staph infections. It is a hardy perennial with gray-green leaves. It likes full Sun, but can stand partial shade. The leaves are highly aromatic, with a camphor-like, slightly bitter taste.

Rosemary

Studies show rosemary increases circulation, reduces headaches, fights bacterial and fungal infections, and strengthens fragile blood vessels. It has also been shown to fight cancer cell formation. Do not use this if you have high blood pressure. It is a diuretic, helpful for colds and flu, gout, muscular pain, and palpitations. It was one of the herbs used to protect one against the plague during the Middle Ages. A beautiful tender perennial shrub that originated in the Mediterranean area, it has a piney taste and is quite refreshing.

Licorice

This is one herb that is easy to take. It is fifty times sweeter than sugar. A recent study has shown licorice root actually stimulates the production of interferon, a chemical critical to enhancing the immune system and keeping many immune-response deficiency diseases at bay. It has a diuretic action, clears respiratory passages, is good for urinary and bowel disorders, and is called the great detoxifier. A hardy perennial with a stringy taproot, it is the root that is used. Cut the root in pieces. You may need to soak this tincture longer than two weeks, perhaps up to a month, as the root is tough and thick and it will take longer to extract the properties. Heating the vodka or rum (careful, it's flammable) also speeds the process.

Purple Coneflower

Also called echinacea, Native Americans used purple coneflower for many of their toughest illnesses, from infections and skin diseases to cancer. It is a powerful immune stimulant, increasing the chances of fighting off almost any disease. Clinical studies show extracts of this herb improve white blood cell count. It is a mild antibiotic that fights strep and staph infections, and a great natural antibiotic. You don't want to take this long term, as the body can become immune to its effects. You may wish to take it for two weeks, rest for one week, and then resume taking it. Also, it cannot repair a damaged immune system such as one with advanced AIDS or cancer, but is good for general use. It is easy to grow the plants. After plants die back in fall, dig out three to four-year-old roots, slice them, and make the tincture. You may also want to soak this root up to a month, or warm the alcohol to speed the process of extraction.

Parsley

Parsley is rich in chlorophyll, and it is thought to be the basis for many tonics and cure-alls of the Middle Ages. It is helpful in arthritis and rheumatism, asthma, urinary disorders, and contains a rich abundance of vitamins, as well as iron, iodine, phosphorus, potassium, and calcium. Studies show it also contains a substance that inhibits cancer cells. The root is considered a stimulant, and good for alleviating fluid retention and gas. A member of the carrot family, parsley can grow in partial shade. Use leaves and stems, or roots. If roots are used, slice them and soak in the tincture up to a month, or heat the alcohol carefully to speed the release of the plant's healing qualities.

Health by the Seasons

By Gretchen Lawlor

It used to be that we cared for our bodies the way we now care for our cars—with regular maintenance and periodic tune-ups. When I was growing up, we children knew it was really spring when we got our annual dose of worm medicine. Molasses in hot water gave us the iron we needed just before spring. In the spring we ate greens fresh from the woods. Summer was the time to lighten the diet and eat from the garden.

Now we have year-round access to tropical fruits and vegetables flown in from all around the world. No one has the time to relax into a holiday or pause long enough to really notice any change that comes with the turn of a season. Modern medicine pulls us back from serious health crises without a break in our work schedule or a loss of a school day. *Convalescence* is a funny word from the past.

Yet we aren't healthier. Serious medical problems are on the increase. People are living longer, but often in a compromised state. Immune disorders, Epstein-Barr, and chronic fatigue reflect the confusion and disorder of immune systems that have experienced so much interference from drugs. We are the most medicated group of people to ever live on the planet. Most adults can't even manage to raise a good fever, and if a fever were to manifest, it's likely to be immediately suppressed with aspirin or Tylenol.

There is an enthusiastic trend in our culture today toward returning to a simpler life, closer to nature. People are relocating to small towns and looking toward creating a better relationship with the Earth. Seasonal celebrations are found in church and school, cutting across religious and philosophical lines.

Seasonal living—living with the natural order, taking our guidelines from the laws of nature—is one way to restore health and reduce stress. It's not new information. The Chinese, in their Five Element medicine theory, have developed sophisticated guidelines of appropriate behavior, diet, and treatment for each season that have been around for thousands of years. Even the early practitioners of Western medicine—the alchemists and the early Western herbalists, healers, and astrologers—worked with the elements and their interrelationship with body types. They used seasonal, timely application of diet, herbs and other healing modalities. Seasonal living resurrects some of those old folk rhythms in hopes of taking back the responsibility for our own health through the preventive maintenance of a healthy, natural rhythmic lifestyle. Each seasonal change provides an opportunity to stop and reorganize our lives. For example, in spring we all feel a burst of fresh enthusiasm for new projects and new connections and are more active than we were in slumbering winter. Winter is our time of short days and long nights, when we were less active, with more time to ponder and reflect. Winter is a time to wait for the new directions in our lives to come to us, through our dreams and our reveries.

Use the indicators for seasonal changes in diet and exercise, as well as herbs and supplements, to better align yourself to healthy action and attitude. Depending on your climate, your activity and optimum foods will vary, but consider these guidelines.

Spring Awakening—New Beginnings

Let's start with spring, the time of emergence. In spring we waken from winter's slumbers and hibernation. The inward focus of winter has finally revealed new directions to pursue. Now is the time to move, to begin something new, to break new ground in the eternally cyclic journey of life—especially during the time of the year when the Sun is is the sign of Aries, roughly March 21 to April 19.

The months of spring encompass the signs of Aries, Taurus, and Gemini. There are activities and attitudes that are most effective in each of these signs. While the Sun is in Aries it is a good time to step out into something new, to be adventurous. Increased physical activity stimulates enthusiasm and courage. Taurus (April 21–May 20) is the time to establish or ground the new direction you have embarked upon. Look at your fresh spark of inspiration with a practical eye.

In Gemini time (May 21–June 22), connect this new reality with the existing aspects of your life. Share what you are doing with your family and link it with your community.

Spring is the season of the greatest obvious shifts in diet and health. Coming out of the heavy, warming diet of winter, the body is in need of cleansing. It is a time for light, fresh foods from local sources. Foods should be simply prepared and lightly cooked. Raw foods may be too much of an adjustment—wait until late spring or summer. For now, steaming or grilling will make food easily digestable.

Spring is the best time for fasting and purification. A liquid fast one day a week will leave you feeling more alert and vital. If you aren't able to do that, designate one day in the week to take leave from your ordinary routine and eat very lightly.

One well-known body cleanser is a lemon drink regime, called the Master Cleanser. Take two tablespoons of fresh-squeezed lemon juice, one to two tablespoons of maple syrup, and a pinch of cayenne pepper. Stir it into an eight-ounce glass of good spring water. The lemon juice is an excellent liver cleanser, causing it to contract and function more efficiently in its work of clearing deep tissue and organ toxins. The cayenne pepper eliminates mucus (it also clears parasites from the system) and stimulates the blood circulation. The maple syrup not only improves the taste but provides a light, transitional source of energy. Drink six to eight glasses of this daily for one to two weeks.

Vermifuges are herbal worming agents—agents of internal spring cleaning. Eating a half teaspoon of garlic, whole or in capsules, or cayenne (*Capsicum annum*) in yogurt daily for a week, can clear the system of parasites acquired during the winter months. A tea of wormwood (*Artemesia vulgaris*) or tansy (*Tanacetum vulgare*) is safe for the same purpose.

Spring fevers burn off viruses and fight disease. The high temperatures and sudden acute inflammations that occur frequently in this season help to remove toxins. Physical exercise helps strengthen the digestion and awaken the fires of enthusiasm.

Herbs of spring are digestive stimulants such as cayenne, ginger, mustard, and cloves, and circulatory stimulants such as cinnamon, garlic, ginger, and hawthorn berries.

Summer Light—Be in Nature

Summer is the time of manifestation and profusion in the outer world. We enter summer at the Solstice, around June 21, the longest day of the year. This is also the entry of the Sun into Cancer (June 21–July 19). Cancer, Leo, and Virgo are the signs of summer (in the Northern Hemisphere).

Plants, animals, and children undergo growth spurts in summer. We all are at maximum manifestation at this energetic peak in the external world. The spark of change we have witnessed at spring matures. This is the time of peak engagement with the passion and intensity of nature— through exercise, sports, walks, picnics in the sunlight, and fresh air.

Cancer time (June 21–July 19) is time to nourish the new growth of spring by finding a home for it, making it ours by personalizing it with our own emotions. In Leo time (July 20–August 19), we celebrate and playfully enjoy and share our new creations. Be bold and proud of who you are and what you are doing.

In Virgo time (August 20–September 22), digestion and assimilation are enhanced. There is an exquisite sensitivity at this time to the details of what we have created and its part in the natural order of life.

In summer we need a diet that brings us close to nature. Bond with your environment by eating locally grown organic fruits and vegetables. Eat more salads, grains, and nuts, and less meat and dairy. The summer diet is light and cooling, which not only allows for winter weight to drop off, but keeps your energy levels high in the warmer temperatures.

Eat upward-growing vegetables and soft leafed greens. Steam them, quick-boil them, or eat them raw. Enhance flavors simply—with balsamic vinegar, lemon juice, fresh ginger, parsley, or other fresh herbs.

Autumn Harvest

Autumn begins with a powerful shift in focus from the outer world of manifestation to the inner world of stillness and potential at the Equinox. This sudden change, with a coolness in the air and the shorter evenings as we move toward winter's deep, can hit hard. The delights of the senses and the pleasures of the outer world begin to fade. Autumn is a reminder of change, and of the familiar cycle of death, rebirth, life, and decay.

Autumn begins with celebration of the harvest. Starting with the Autumn Equinox around September 23, the days and nights return to equal length. Now we gather and give thanks for the fruits of our efforts in spring and summer.

Autumn is a time of letting go and releasing our creations. We begin to gather in what we will need for another inward journey.

In Libra time (September 23–October 21), one's creation is given away and received by others. It is time to refine your projects so as to make them socially valid, acceptable and usable by others.

Scorpio time (October 22–November 21) is a time to shed skins, to allow the passing of whatever is no longer relevant in order to reveal the essence. It is time to deepen your focus, to increase your determination.

During Sagittarius time (November 22–December 20), your vision expands, through contact with the larger social order, and gains a religious, political, or philosophical component.

Apples, grapes, tomatoes, beans, and grains are all the gifts of autumn, and perfect nourishment for this time of year. Berries strengthen the blood and increase circulation to deep organs as the life force moves inward from the skin in preparation for winter.

Depending on the weather, a light diet of harvest fruits and vegetables may be fine for early Autumn. However, as the cycle of the year becomes more darkness than light, root crops and grains are harvested and are at their energetic peak as a food.

The diet should begin to have more protein content. The heating fuel of whole grains begins to stoke the inner fires, as we will need to generate our own heat as the heat of the Sun diminishes. Meat eaters can add more fish and chicken, with occasional red meat—best as a garnish rather than as the focus of the meal. Organic meat tends to be raised with more consciousness and compassion, which passes on energetically into our systems as we digest the meal. Vegetarians should have more beans, seeds, and a variety of grains.

Autumn is another critical time for fasting. Because spring and autumn are the most radical alterations of direction and physical needs, fasting at these times is more powerful in terms of providing opportunity for the body to shift gears. From a purely practical perspective, this is a great time to fast because of the abundance of harvest fruits and vegetables available for eating or juicing. Fasting allows the surface eliminative organs to discharge excess toxicity and recharges the system for the deep organ activity of the colder months.

This is another season where colds and flu, fevers and inflammations are predictable—especially around the Equinox. Don't suppress them. Use the opportunity to allow the body to discharge through fevers, sweat, mucus, or even through coughing. It is better that this happen before winter's low vitality sets in and the body is less able to throw things off.

Winter Stillness—Turn Inward

Winter is a time when minimal plant growth occurs, when seeds and subterranean stores are held in reserve. Nature is in her resting season, the life force is deep in the roots, preparing for spring.

Winter is time to still oneself, where activity is lessened and inner processes hold sway. Seek inner warmth. It is time to conserve energy and not be wasteful with it. Soon enough in spring you will be ready to let it out. We are meant to be waiting, dreaming, contemplating, and preparing for another cycle of outward manifestation.

Winter begins with the Winter Solstice on or around December 21. This is the beginning of the month of Capricorn. At the Solstice there is a profound turn in the annual cycle, where the Sun begins its return and the days begin to grow longer.

Capricorn (December 21–January 19) is a time to plan, to acknowledge the necessary passage of time required for anything to develop into something truly useful and well formed. Aquarius (January 20–February 19) is time to find your tribe, your community of peers to link with for the next outer cycle of manifestation. Set long-term goals. Pisces (February 20–March 20) is the closure just before the new activity of Aries and spring so soon to come. Release personal will to the guidance of spirit.

In winter, eat hearty, more compact vegetables, sturdy leafed greens such as kale or bok choy, winter squashes and downward-growing roots, such as carrots, turnips, onions, and potatoes (versus the light leafy greens, such as lettuce, which better suit summer). Use more contractive cooking methods, ones that help hold the energy in the food, such as slow simmering, pressure cooking, or baking. Some fried or sautéed foods are tolerated at this time of year. Serve foods warm. For seasoning use sea salt, miso, tamari, and sauerkraut.

Winter sweats and saunas help elimination and cleansing of the body when eating winter's concentrated diet. If your ability to handle and eliminate waste is weak, or if you take in more than you need during winter, garbage may pile up in the large intestine, which will have to be dealt with by other organs and functions of the body.

Winter colds and sinus infections are the body's efforts to discharge waste through mucus or pus. Colds are treated best with rest, fluids and sweating, a perfect cleansing and replenishing regime for winter.

The old practice of taking cod liver oil for its vitamin A and D content improves the condition of the immune system, especially through greater resilience of the mucus membranes. Molasses, particularly in the month of Pisces, replenishes iron sources depleted through the winter diet. Keep in mind that unexpressed feelings and blocked creative energy lower your resistance, leaving you open to passing viruses.

Winter is a season to store up energy in preparation for a new cycle of activity. Exercise is important for physical and emotional well-being, but it is also critical to recharge your batteries in winter. Plenty of sleep and relaxation are appropriate for this season and are the best preparation for new life ahead.

Every year is a journey through the elements and the seasons. Be healthy in accordance with the wisdom of spring, summer, autumn, and winter, and you will stay well.

Raw Milk: Forsaken Food

By Penny Kelly

When I was a girl the milkman used to deliver milk to our house two or three times a week. He put the milk, which came in one-quart glass bottles, in a covered metal box on the front porch. The glass bottles had a thick lip around the top edge, and a thick layer of cream floating on the milk. I thought having a milkman was extremely modern and sophisticated compared to my grandma, who had to go out and milk her cow, then separate milk from cream before putting it in a pitcher in the refrigerator.

Much later, a large modern grocery store opened in town and we began to buy milk in wax-coated cardboard cartons that declared the milk inside to be both "pasteurized" and "homogenized." The milk didn't have any cream floating on the top, and at that time, I thought how wonderful it was that we didn't have to deal with that darn cream any more!

Today, I have a cow and calf, and every day I go out to milk, just like Grandma, then bring the milk in and run it through the separator before putting it in a pitcher in the refrigerator.

"Why bother when you can just go to the store and buy it?" people often ask.

Why? Lots of reasons! One is because I want raw milk. Pasteurized milk has been heated to high temperatures, supposedly to kill bacteria. This process got started back in the early half of the century when people were looking for answers to the unsolved mystery of tuberculosis, and believed it could be transmitted through milk.

When Louis Pasteur published his discovery of bacteria and the fact that heating could destroy bacteria, the authorities ordered the heating of milk, which came to be known as "pasteurization," just in case TB was caused by mysterious bacteria in raw milk.

As it turned out, it wasn't, but a whole industry had sprung up to pasteurize milk and no authority wanted to put people out of work, so the processing of milk became a law. The huge loss in this was that during heating, the natural enzymes in the milk were destroyed, enzymes that

Mother Nature put there to help human bodies digest the milk and absorb the nutrients in it.

Without the help of the enzymes in the milk, not only did the human pancreas have to work harder to digest it, it was much more difficult to find anything nutritionally useful in this new form of milk.

Next came the process of homogenizing. Either someone didn't like dealing with the bit of leftover cream that settled on top of the milk after it went through the separator, or they figured they could skim it off and sell a pint of it for the same price as an entire quart of milk. Whatever it was, "homogenization" was developed. This was a simple process of shaking or agitating the milk so violently that the large fat globules present in the milk were shattered into tiny, irregular pieces. This shattering was so complete and so effective that the fat globules were unable to regroup and remained suspended in the milk.

The result of this was that as people drank the milk, they took in these shattered fat globules, which then proceeded to slip through the body's natural barriers and get into forbidden places in the body where a big, round, jolly fat globule would never have gotten through. Thus it passed into the bloodstream to collect and harden in veins and arteries, it collected in globs on organs, or was stored as a waste material in layers of padded cells just under the skin.

The fact that fat was getting into places it shouldn't be was aided by the subtle degeneration of activity in liver and gall bladder function in millions of people as a result of poor nutrition. Without plenty of bile to emulsify fats, even more of it got into the system.

As time went on, other factors began to complicate the problem. Cows were fed corn and crops containing the residues of seriously toxic chemicals, which had a great affinity for lodging in the fat cells of the cows' milk. Later dangerous hormones were added to animal diets.

Now not only was the milk seriously lacking from both an enzyme and a nutritional angle, its structure was destroyed and the shattered pieces of the fat globule, carrying the load of toxic chemicals, were getting past the bile duct without enough emulsifying and into the cells of the body. It wasn't long before doctors and researchers were reporting all kinds of difficulties from drinking pasteurized, homogenized milk.

As we here at Lily Hill Farm continued to investigate the history of milk, the store-bought version began to look more and more like a source of serious trouble that we just didn't want to risk. This brought us to the point where we decided that having a good supply of milk, cream, butter, yogurt, sour cream, and cheeses was essential. It has forced us to answer a lot of questions from family and friends who, at first, couldn't quite fathom why on earth we would take on the work, time, expense, and trouble of being tied to a cow and her milking schedule.

"The reasons," we told them, "are simple. We have made a deep commitment to learn the truth about food and then work to bring that into our daily lives in a real way. Since both of us like milk and have inherited the ability to digest it, we decided to investigate, and the history, as well as the nonsense, of pasteurization and homogenization was what we uncovered."

We also learned that fat is absolutely necessary in everyone's life and without it you will not be able to absorb and utilize the fat-soluble vitamins A, D, E, and K. Without these four vitamins in good supply and readily available in your body, you simply won't be healthy and you won't be able to heal from anything, not even the common cold. Since we were already eating a majority of fruits, steamed vegetables, salads, fresh-ground whole wheat bread, and an occasional piece of meat, we didn't have much high-nutrition fat in our diet. So we decided to buy a cow.

A glass of raw milk on my granola in the morning, a tablespoon of butter on my muffin at noon, a dish of homemade yogurt, and a nibble of cheese now and then have done what three and a half years of intense detoxification plus a ton of vitamins and minerals did not do. They have brought a smoothness to my skin, shine to my hair, firm strength to my fingernails, and a tremendous sense of well-being.

The law says that we cannot sell milk that is unpasteurized, and we hope fervently that this will change as people begin to understand that many foods that are really very good for them are being rendered either useless or destructive, or both, by the government's laws and processing requirements. Gladys, my brown-eyed Holstein beauty, produces three gallons of milk a day, plus cream. This is far more than we need, and when we first started offering to give away raw, unpasteurized, unhomogenized milk, butter, and yogurt to family and friends, they were dubious. After trying a gallon or two, and a dab of butter, the reaction changed dramatically to increasing requests and exclamations of astounded pleasure in the taste, flavor, and texture of these foods in their whole, natural form.

My friend Luanne summed it up very well the other day when I overheard her tell someone about her early morning visit here. "I had a cup of my favorite tea with real cream in it, a giant, homemade oatmeal muffn with real butter and fresh strawberry jam on it, and my god, I felt like I had just been to the gourmet coffeehouse!"

Children's Moon Signs

By Gretchen Lawlor

The Moon in your child's astrological birth chart is an immediately available indicator of what he or she needs to feel safe, emotionally nourished, and happy. The Moon sign shows what a person's most basic needs are, and how and where to get them met.

The Moon is the primary planetary influence in a child's first seven years. These are the years when the emotional foundations are laid for the rest of a person's life. If you are a parent and you know your children's Moon signs, you know what your children will need in their early environment. You have a major insight into what they will respond to in order to feel safe and well cared for. In doing what you can to provide these needs in the first years of their lives, you lay healthy emotional foundations for their future happiness and well-being.

Even after the age of seven, the Moon will still describe the emotional nature and what will always be needed for emotional equilibrium and well-being. The Moon will always need tending, though the foundational work of the first seven years of life is critical in the establishment of healthy emotional patterns throughout adulthood.

The Moon by sign is representative of a child's deeply imprinted ways of seeking nourishment and support. This is often an instinctive part of the personality—more unconscious than the Sun sign.

We all share the same survival needs for food, water, companionship, and shelter. The degree that each of us experiences or craves even these basic needs differs, and the Moon can guide you to those differences.

For example, Moon in Aries needs frequent new challenges and a sense of independence, whereas Moon in Cancer needs a sense of roots, of dependable traditions and family containment around them. The Moon in Aquarius is happiest being a rebel, most comfortable swimming upstream against the flow, and finds great comfort in the companionship of a tribe of friends. Moon in Capricorn is emotionally reserved, serious, and responsible as a child, and gains comfort from consistent traditional home and family settings.

To find the Moon in your child's chart requires your child's birth date, time and place. Many popular books contain tables to approximate this, including the *Moon Sign Book,* or you can contact an astrologer or astrological computing service to calculate this for you. Because the Moon moves so swiftly and changes sign every two and a half days, it's easy to make a mistake if you look it up yourself in an astrological ephemeris.

Following are tips on the emotional needs of each Moon sign, how each Moon responds to stress and what will help them cope, Moon environments, Moon foods, and Moon moods. The Moon in children's charts also shows how they experience their mothers, which can help you know what behavior in you, the parent, will be most supportive of them.

Moon in Aries

Moon in Aries children need to move, and tend to be fussy and irritable as infants. This changes suddenly when they earn to crawl or walk, through which they have achieved some autonomy and independence. They are easily bored with routine and want to be busy and active all the time. They can be compulsive about staying busy, using this to stave off any emotions.

Aries Moons naturally expect to be the center of attention in the family, and can profoundly resent the arrival of a sibling, who gets in the way of what they want to do. Teasing and goading siblings into reacting comes instinctively for the Aries Moon child, who thrives on the energy this creates.

Moon in Aries experiences the mother as adventurous, courageous, lively, and assertive. On the flip side, mother may give the impression of being irritable or even resentful of a child's needs.

They tend to be quite spontaneous and uncomplicated in their emotional responses—quick to fire, quick to recover and forget. They get annoyed by the inability of others to just get on with things.

They need to be physical with their emotions and may find it hard to explain why they are feeling as they are. They can get more in touch with feelings if they are being active at the same time.

Moon in Aries is happiest when leading or inspiring others. In a park or preschool or playground, it is the Moon in Aries child whose enthusiasm and vitality sparks all the other children to play at Aries' game.

Aries Moon children should be encouraged in sports, in physical activities, and in situations where their natural enthusiasm for life stimulates and inspires others.

Moon in Taurus

Moon in Taurus children have exquisitely attuned senses. Textures, smells, and tastes are all very important means through which these children experience or absorb life. They respond best to a steady, consistent, conservative home environment, where changes are introduced slowly and smoothly. Objects have a soothing, stabilizing quality to them, particularly those with engaging textures.

Moon in Taurus children are collectors, having a natural ability to acquire beautiful things. They may have some trouble sharing their bounty with friends or siblings, though this is one of their greatest life lessons. As a parent you can help them, perhaps through involving them in collecting for underprivileged children.

Where a Moon in Taurus person lives, the garden is often prolific, even if they are not the gardeners. They are soothed in crisis through contact with nature, with being outdoors in a tranquil setting.

Mother for the Moon in Taurus child comes across as a real earth goddess, a sensible, practical, solid, down-to-earth dependable force in the child's life. Mother can also feel extremely rigid and not to be crossed for her fierce temper when aroused.

Moon in Taurus receives emotional nourishment from food, from being fed. Mealtimes are important grounding rituals for these children. They will enjoy being involved in the preparation of food for others, as this is a primary way of showing affection for this sign. They are uncomfortable around strong emotions and are prone to eating disorders when surrounded by stressful circumstances from which they cannot escape.

Moon in Gemini

Children with the Moon in Gemini can drive everyone around them crazy with their incessant questioning of life. They need explanations and are incessantly curious. Emotions can be confusing to these children, who change mood like quicksilver, their ruling metal. They would enjoy those refrigerator word magnets that they can use to identify a feeling with a word. It is in giving something a name that they feel safe and secure.

Tending to be fussy as infants, they thrive on constant change and interaction, and get bored easily without plenty of stimulation. They are definitely adaptable and cope well with change.

Mother is usually perceived as very communicative and the early home environment exciting, though seldom in a conventional sense. Mother herself is frequently seen as a rebel, and may be more of a companion to the child than a pillar of stability. However, she is likely to do well at encouraging the child's curiosity and independent style.

There's plenty of mental energy in these children. They are naturally and instinctively witty. Humor is often their way of dealing with emotional upsets—though compulsive clowning may block them from facing issues that need attention. Confronted with emotional overload, they are likely to look for escape through wild activity or distraction through books, television, or computer.

The right educational environment is critical to the emotional nourishment of this Moon sign. They need a situation that fosters creativity and experimentation, which can accommodate their restless spirit. An academic foundation is important, especially in language, communication, and literature.

Moon in Cancer

Children with the Moon in Cancer will always be sentimental about their early family circumstances. The relationship with the mother will continue to influence their relationships long after they leave home. Cancer Moons will either make supreme efforts to duplicate their early family conditions in their own adult lives, or react in total opposition to those early circumstances, dedicating all their efforts to pursuing a life in total contradiction to those early years. In either case, their attention continues to focus on the circumstances of the early years. They don't forget anything.

In schooling they respond best to a teacher who takes on the maternal nourishing model as these children need that safety envelope longer than other signs.

Memories are important to Moon in Cancer. Give them scrapbooks of early years. Respect their need for repetitive or recurring cycles that they can anticipate and depend on, whether this be the annual holiday to the beach or the dependable Christmas traditions.

They don't relocate easily. If this is necessary, make sure you respect their sentimental attachments to objects, pets, and even the old home. Here's where photo albums can be helpful. Give the little Cancer Moons the opportunity to make memorials and embrace their strong feelings by gathering photos of the life passing. All the water Moon signs (Cancer, Scorpio, and Pisces) benefit through learning to manage their strong emotional reactions through expressing them in art or music.

Moon in Cancer has profound mood swings, and needs opportunities to retreat and recover from the emotions of those around them. When they do this they can appear cold and distant. Let them do this, and they will return to the family happier.

The waxing and waning of the Moon affects them more than the other signs. They may be more outgoing during the waxing Moon, more clingy or retiring during the waning Moon, and easily overloaded at the New or Full Moon.

Moon in Leo

The Moon in Leo child is hard to overlook. Warm, loving, generous, loud, and dramatic, they gravitate instinctively toward being center stage. Give Moon in Leo plenty of opportunity to shine through tools and props of play acting, or even drama classes. These outlets may make it easier for the siblings of this child who may feel overshadowed or squeezed out if all the Leonine drama needs to happen on the home front.

Moon in Leo children will express how they feel readily and boldly as they dramatize their feelings. However, they are excruciatingly sensitive to any loss of face, and negative emotions will not be put on public display. You will know by their dignified withdrawal that they are going through something. If this Moon sign child needs discipline, it is better to do it in a way that allows them to save face. Take them aside, and appeal to their strong sense of idealism. Respect their pride.

Moon in Leo is comfortable in a home where emotions are tossed about in a loud and theatrical manner, with plenty of roaring and posturing and carrying on. Mother can be a real drama queen, sometimes taking up the stage with her own concerns about the neglect of the child's well-being. Moon in Leo tends to see Mother as possessing style and pride, and appreciates her ability to keep up a good image in front of others. Despite all difficulties she might encounter, Mother is a rich character in the drama of a Leo Moon's home and family life.

Moon in Virgo

The Moon in Virgo child needs to be needed and appreciated, and gets emotional satisfaction from caring for and about others. Frequently animals are the first loves in their lives. The opportunity to learn to tend to an animal provides this child with a sense of skillful accomplishment.

Moon in Virgo, being an earth sign, receives a sense of emotional well-being from physical affection, from objects, and tangible care. A stuffed animal (important that it be an animal that exists in nature rather than in fantasy) will be consoling to this sensitive little one. This child's system needs regularity and natural rhythms in daily life. Virgo Moons thrive on a home situation that reflects the natural world through its simplicity and access to nature.

Their health is directly connected to their emotions, and in particular their digestion. They appreciate emotional support from attention to their diet. Moon in Virgo children can be fussy about what they eat, and they usually know just what they need. Food combinations affect children of this Moon sign more than most, so keep their diet very simple.

The Moon in Virgo child can be quite critical of self, and exceptionally aware of the shortcomings of others, too. Mother may have been quite a perfectionist, with very high personal standards as well as being particularly efficient around the home. Moon in Virgo children want to learn from the mother, and will imitate until they get it perfect.

As a parent, your awareness of these children's tendency to be extremely hard on themselves can alert you to the danger of casual critical comments, which so many other children would ignore, but not Moon in Virgo. Moon in Virgo children can lose sight of the larger picture and fixate on small details. They love crafts that help them develop skills.

Moon in Libra

Moon in Libra children are acutely attuned to the harmony and emotional balance in the family—especially between the parents. Instinctive peacemakers, they may throw themselves into the center of the parental dynamic from a very early age. Because they can so easily put themselves in another person's shoes, they naturally become the counselor or mediator to whom disgruntled family members come for soothing.

They respond best to a refined home environment, where music and the arts are a part of daily life. They appreciate the good things in life. Being an air sign, they want to exchange feelings with another through words and ideas. A diary can provide the reflective surface for the Libran soul to try out and clarify their feelings. Often it is in speaking or giving names to the feelings that clarity, peace, and equilibrium can emerge.

They hate upheaval and are willing to do just about anything for a peaceful home. They may choose to gloss over serious difficulties, pretending to the world that all is fine. Here is the great Libran dilemma—to balance needs of other with needs of self, and to develop boundaries that encourage interaction without ignoring their own best interests.

They tend to compare themselves to others, and are acutely aware of fairness, that all receive an equal share of whatever is going around. They are not solitary players, and have best friends very early in their social lives. They are instinctively graceful, love beautiful objects, and easily acquire them.

Mother is seen by the Moon in Libra child as graceful, dedicated to her relationships, artistic, and fair. If there is a dark side to the picture, Moon in Libra will notice where Mother compromised herself for the well-being of others.

Moon in Scorpio

Infants with Moon in Scorpio are acutely aware of the emotional undercurrents in the home environment from birth. They love to ferret out mysteries and secrets and are instinctively aware of the subtle plays occurring around them. These children learn early on how to surf the emotional waters of the family, often in order not to be hurt.

Scorpio Moons thrive on crisis. They seem to need emotional highs and lows in order to develop to their full potential. This can be exhausting to a parent with a more low-key or steady Moon.

These children need encouragement to release their emotions in nondestructive ways, and will need help to find alternative outlets. In this way their feelings become an asset rather than an exhausting liability.

They are often the emotional barometers of the family, sometimes acting out the shadow or unspoken element of the family dynamic. What we call psychosomatic health problems reflect this child's intense mind-body link. If they are disturbed, their whole system will respond, sometimes with serious health problems. Sometimes this is the only way these children feel they can get the intense attention they need from their parents.

The Moon in Scorpio child is very territorial and needs some space in the home to retreat, a place where they feel all powerful. They tend to be particularly aware of ghosts and are prone to childhood terrors. Treat their fantasies seriously. They need to know that it is okay to have strong feelings, and that they have the skills to share them with the world.

Moon in Sagittarius

The Moon in Sagittarius child, being a fire sign, needs to be able to move around and explore. Instinctively adventurous, they are always on the go, looking for new territory. They are lively and enthusiastic, and tend to tell wonderful stories that don't need to bear any resemblance to the truth.

Their early home environment may have included a lot of travel, or at least an influence of other cultures. Moon in Sagittarius souls are often at home in a culture other than the one of their birth, and can relocate easily. Their restlessness may keep them moving as they are more at home on the road than with the steadiness of home life.

They respond well to early religious or philosophical exposure. Mother may have been religious, although it's best if she encouraged a wide, expansive viewpoint. She probably pondered larger issues than the other mothers on the block. Moon in Sagittarius feels at home with politics, religion, and asking many large questions about life.

Moon in Sagittarius can feel very hemmed in by emotional intensity. They resolve problems and care for themselves by getting away and focusing on distant horizons or the larger picture. A faith or philosophy that they can refer to for general guidelines for morals and principles is essential.

Moon in Capricorn

The child with Moon in Capricorn can appear quite reserved and tends to be slow to warm emotionally to others. However, once a connection has been made, children born of this Moon are intensely loyal. They respond best to a home situation that is steady, predictable, and based on traditional values.

The mother of a Moon in Capricorn, no matter what her own Sun or Moon sign is, is perceived by the child as a capable manager, serious and responsible. This mother tends to discourage dependency, and many young Moon in Capricorn children are quite serious and capable for their age.

"Old when young, and young when old" is the astrologer's phrase, reflecting the early maturity, or even tough early years that frequently accompany this sign. A strong influence of Capricorn in the chart indicates a life that tends to get better with age.

Moon in Capricorn loves projects and is soothed by organizing their toys or their rooms, or planning an outing or holiday. They have excellent rapport with older people. An older relative, such as a grandparent, can provide extra parenting and care that will make a profound difference.

Being an earth sign, this child needs tangible demonstrations of affection. They may not find it easy to initiate cuddles, but they respond well to receiving them. Gifts tell them they are appreciated and that all is well with their world.

Moon in Aquarius

The Moon in Aquarius is emotionally unpredictable, with frequent and sudden changes in mood. They thrive in lively, constantly changing home environments, and prefer plenty of comings and goings of family members and friends.

This is the infant who smiles and engages with strangers at the grocery store, and the young child who takes well to preschool social life. However, they may be less happy about the discipline and conformity required of these school situations. They are rule breakers and innovators and blossom in situations that accommodate their spontaneous, unconventional way of thinking about everything.

Moon in Aquarius children are very aware of the eccentric soul of their mothers. The mother is seen more as peer than as parent. The Moon in Aquarius child's irreverence can be the source of a tremendous amount of chaos in a conservative or traditional family format, but can lead to wonderful friendships as parent and child get older.

Sometimes these children are the ones who act out the suppressed wildness of other family members. Being the emotionally independent souls they are, as they grow they may prefer to spend much of their time at friends' homes. They are essentially more happy in a crowd than alone, though their unconventional approach to life may keep them searching for the group that suits them—their special "tribe."

Moon in Pisces

Moon in Pisces children, being water signs, are highly sensitive, imaginative, and impressionable. They do well in a home and family that appreciates the arts and enjoys playing with the imagination. Some form of spiritual direction in their early years will endure as a source of comfort for their whole lives.

Moon in Pisces tends to be an emotional sponge—easily becoming waterlogged by the feelings of others around them. They need their own private place in the family home, preferably their own bedroom, where they can retreat and recover from the impressions of life they so easily collect. Without periodic withdrawal these children may resort to escape through excess television or computer games, or excesses in food (or even drugs or alcohol as they grow older).

If you have a Pisces Moon child who seems disconnected from reality, he or she is likely to be in a state of overload. These are children who may have trouble discerning reality from fantasy. Their imagination is an important part of them and needs to be nourished, with respect for their extreme impressionability. You may need to teach them to care for themselves by modeling boundary-making for them, or stepping in when you see your child awash and in overload.

Moon in Pisces children find comfort in tending to the wounds of others, and they are instinctive healers, especially to emotional wounding. This is a wonderful trait, a precursor to their later dedication to causes and issues concerned with relieving the suffering of others.

As a mother and as an astrologer who has looked at many charts of parents and children, I find it fascinating to look at the diversity within each family setting. Each child in a family is likely to have a different Moon sign, yet they share the same mother. Each child's perceptions of the mother are colored by the filter of their own Moon sign. Moon in Leo sees mother as bold and dramatic, where Moon in Virgo may see mother as careful, meticulous, and reserved. Moon in Libra sees mother as the diplomat and artist and Moon in Scorpio sees mother as intense and emotionally explosive. This can happen in the same family. This is the mother of all four of these diverse Moon sign children. She also has her own filters—her own Moon sign needs coloring any effort at nuturing she attempts is colored by her own history, how she was mothered herself.

It is not easy to articulate or to even be consciously aware of what you need to feel happy and safe, especially when you are a child. Yet the chart lays it out so clearly. Use the knowledge the Moon provides. It is a fabulous window into your own child's deep and instinctive needs, which they cannot easily tell you. Give them the best you can, a good start for a rich and satisfying life.

Mead

By K. D. Spitzer

I f you start now, you can lay down the ideal beverage to celebrate the turn of the century and millennium. Mead is as old as fermentation and can still hold its own against the more popular grape wines. Properly aged, its flavor is unparalleled. It can be made at any time of the year, as long as the Moon, its ruler, is in a waxing fertile sign. After fermentation is complete, you will want to bottle it when the Moon is in a third quarter dry sign, especially one other than Leo.

People associate mead with the Vikings, but mead-making is about 12,000 years old and has an ancient place in most world cuisines. It maintained its popularity until less expensive cane sugar became readily accessible. Mead is honey-based and all the mystery and lore about honey has glamorized mead as well.

Surely everyone has heard the history of the word *honeymoon*. A "Moon" is the length of time from one phase of the Moon until it returns to that same phase, in about twenty-eight days, or as we describe it, a month. This was the amount of time that Saxon wedding guests expected to be entertained and to serve as witnesses that the marriage "took." Every day for that Moon, in the hall of the manor, they would toast the bridal pair with a round of mead to encourage them to their "duties," while in the bridal chamber, the bride and groom would drink from the dynastic cup to increase their fertility and the ability to produce sons. Thanks to the magic and power of mead, when they finally emerged from their chambers, the bride was likely to have the heir firmly on board.

Mead is as easy to make as any country wine, and while it is drinkable after six months, it gets even smoother the longer it ages. Some say that it doesn't peak until it is five to seven years old. The important thing is to use a good quality honey. A clover honey will produce a delicate, simple mead that will stand on its own, while a strong honey-like buckwheat can sustain the additives that will produce a stronger-flavored drink.

Add hops and you will have a mead ale that is close to the original northern version of beer. This was a standard ration for British troops during the Napoleonic wars and supposedly caused a mutiny when the drink was watered down. The British Navy did the opposite and often watered the mead ale with rum for its seamen.

If you use more honey to the gallon and no hops, you will have a potent drink called sack mead, that is, a mead with a higher alcohol content. Using a strong honey to begin with will produce a strongly flavored sack mead.

As you are beginning to suspect, there are many versions of a potent drink as old as mead. Melomels are meads that are made with fruit: raspberries, cherries, blueberries, and cranberries. Cherry melomels must have been the medieval flavor of choice, as so many recipes have survived to this day. On the other hand, it may have had something to do with thrifty housewives, with wimples askew, sampling the alcoholic fruit after straining off the melomel for bottling. (Of course, then they didn't have ice cream to serve it up on. Waste not, want not!) Using a little bit more honey to water (one and a half parts honey to two parts water) will make a sweeter melomel that can be served with pastries or fruit as a dessert wine.

There are two noteworthy melomels that are so good that they have their own name. Cyser is honey and apple juice combined in a subtle blend that has spanned centuries because it is a very fine wine. It has been glorified in ancient verse and recent country western lyrics. Pyment is a blend of grapes and honey so historically popular that we know it was drunk in ancient Egypt. Warmed and with spices added before drinking, it becomes the Hyppocras of medieval fame. Red wine was preferred, but white was used as well.

It's fooling around with the metheglins that will really hook you. These honey wines are flavored with herbs and spices and the variety is endless. Its name *metheglin* comes from the old Welsh word *meddyglyn*, which means medicine. Not surprisingly, because of the healing properties of the herbs and honey, an assortment of metheglins was kept around the Tudor household for dosing the sick. The list of additives for metheglin is limited only by your imagination and palate.

Wine making does not come with interchangeable parts, so it is not always possible to obtain the same ingredients each time you make it. The bees cannot always produce the same flavor honey because one year their favorite apple orchard may become a parking lot or their meadow a housing development. Experimentation is the hallmark of wine making. Always use the best ingredients and keep careful notes.

Honey is not acidic enough to sustain the entire fermentation process, and thus acid in some form must be added to mead. It can be citrus fruit juice, such as orange and lemon, or you can use the nineties version—a couple teaspoons of citric acid. If you want to make a traditional mead without the use of citrus, then you will need to use a yeast nutrient.

It is very difficult to clear mead and it requires racking several times. Racking is siphoning off the liquid from the sediment. However, you can also use some pectin enzyme to absorb the pectin in fruit and the waxy substances in honey in order to get rid of the cloudiness. Understand that the cloudiness will not hurt you, but it will detract from the beauty of your wine.

Campden tablets are routinely added to homemade wine now. Each tablet contains about seven grains of potassium metabisulfite, which release four grains of sulfur dioxide in a slightly acid solution. Campden tablets are added to the must (initial mixture of honey and water), or fermenting liquid. A Campden tablet is an effective sterilizing agent that stops the growth of wild yeasts and any spoilage organisms. It also adds a tiny bit more acid. However, Campden tablets, along with pectin enzymes and yeast nutrients ("food" for the yeast organisms in the mead), are optional ingredients.

A couple of further notes: never boil the honey. Only simmer, as the high heat will kill off its qualities. Also be sure to skim any scum from the heated surface, as this is where the minute particles of wax will rise and collect. Most old recipes for mead make several gallons. I have cut the recipes down so that you can make smaller batches and more of them.

Traditional Mead

3   pounds honey
1   tablespoon citric acid
1   teaspoon pectin enzyme
1   Campden tablet, optional
1   package champagne yeast
1   teaspoon yeast nutrient
    Peel from 2 oranges—pare but do not get bitter white pith
    Juice from 2 freshly squeezed and strained oranges

Empty the honey into a pot, and, using the honey jar, add 2 jars of water. Simmer for a half hour, skimming off the foam that forms. Transfer into a 2-gallon container and add the citric acid, pectin enzyme, Campden tablet, and enough water to make 2 gallon. Let stand overnight. Mix the yeast and yeast nutrient with the orange juice and let it proof until it bubbles, about 1 hour. Add to the honey mixture (or must) along with the orange zest.

Keeping the container loosely covered but secure against fruit flies, let the mixture ferment until the bubbling slows. Then rack it off into another container with an airlock and continue to rack it off every 3 months until the wine clears (some mead makers recommend racking the mixture once a month). Naturally you will need to taste it each time you rack it off.

When the wine is clear, rack it off into bottles and cork them about a quarter of the way. The tricky thing about mead is that it is very slow to ferment and may shoot its corks. Keep an eye on your bottles or store them in a place you can clean easily. Once you are certain the mead has completed fermentation, you can push in the corks. Give the mead a year to mellow before tippling.

Melomel

Use the recipe for traditional mead and add 2 to 3 pounds of crushed fruit to the heated and skimmed honey and water. Add more water to make 1 gallon if needed and continue with recipe. You don't need pectin enzyme for this recipe.

Cyser

- 3 pounds honey
- 1 gallon best quality unpasteurized apple cider
- 1 Campden tablet, optional
- Juice of 2 oranges and 1 lemon
- Peel of 1 orange and 1 lemon (do not include pith)
- 1 package champagne yeast
- 1 teaspoon yeast nutrient

Bring the honey and apple cider almost to a boil and let simmer until foam rises and can be skimmed. Skim the foam. Pour off into a 2-gallon container and add Campden tablet if desired. Let sit 24 hours. Dissolve yeast and yeast nutrient in orange and lemon juice; let proof about 1 hour. Add to honey and apple juice along with citrus peels. Let ferment about 5 days, and then rack off and let ferment 10 days. Rack again. Store in a 1-gallon airlocked container until fermentation is complete. Bottle and cork, and let age about 6 months before sampling.

Metheglin

3   pounds honey

3   ounces dried sage or 1 quart fresh sage leaves

   Juice of 1 lemon

1   teaspoon citric acid

½   pound raisins

1   Campden tablet, optional

1   packet champagne yeast

1   teaspoon yeast nutrient

   Juice of 2 oranges and 1 lemon

Mix the honey with 2 parts water, using the honey jar to measure. Bring almost to a boil and let simmer until foam rises and can be skimmed off. Pour off into a 2-gallon container. Add raisins, sage, citric acid, lemon juice, and Campden tablet, if desired, with enough added water to make 1 gallon and let stand overnight. Pare oranges with sharp vegetable peeler to get zest without bitter pith. Dissolve yeast into the orange and lemon juice. When it has proofed, add yeast, yeast nutrient, and orange zest to must and stir. Let stand until fermentation has slowed, then rack off into a 1-gallon airlocked container. When fermentation is complete and wine has cleared, then bottle, cork and let age at least 6 months before sampling.

To experiment with metheglins, plan on 2 to 3 ounces of dried herbs per gallon or 1 to 2 quarts of fresh herbs. These can be single spices or herbs or a combined use of your favorite flavors. Why not use the ingredients of your favorite herb tea? The herbs can be bagged and added to the must, or a tea can be made and used in place of clear water. There will be a subtle difference in flavors depending on technique.

Use 1 to 3 cinnamon sticks or a tablespoon of cloves per gallon, or bruise 3 ounces of peeled ginger root.

Zest from any of the citrus fruits can be used; a sharp vegetable peeler will take the zest and leave the pith. Use the zest from 2 or 3 pieces of fruit per gallon.

Keep a record of your recipes and don't throw out any of your experiments until they have aged a couple of years.

You can use your metheglins to flavor marinades, glazes, or soups and stews. Pour them over vegetables in a casserole, or use them to steam bratwurst and kielbasa.

Leisure & Recreation

How to Choose the Best Dates

Everyone is affected by the lunar cycle. Your lunar high occurs when the Moon is in your Sun sign, and your lunar low occurs when the Moon is in the sign opposite your Sun sign. The handy Favorable and Unfavorable Dates Tables on pages 28–52 give the lunar highs and lows for each Sun sign for every day of the year. This lunar cycle influences all your activities: your physical strength, mental alertness, and manual dexterity are all affected.

By combining the Favorable and Unfavorable Dates Tables and the Lunar Aspectarian Tables with the information given in the list of astrological rulerships, you can choose the best time to begin many activities.

The best time to perform an activity is when its ruling planet is in favorable aspect to the Moon—that is, when its ruling planet is trine, sextile, or conjunct the Moon (marked T, X, or C in the Lunar Aspectarian), or when its ruling sign is marked F in the Favorable and Unfavorable Days tables. Another option is when the Moon is in the activity's ruling sign.

For example, if you wanted to find a good day to train your dog, you would look under animals, and find that the sign corresponding to animal training is Taurus, and that the planet that rules this activity is Venus. Then, you would consult the Favorable and Unfavorable Days Tables to find a day when Venus (the ruling planet) is trine, sextile, or conjunct (T, X, or C) the Moon; or when Taurus (the ruling sign) is marked F in the Favorable and Unfavorable Days table; or when the Moon is in Taurus.

Animals and Hunting

Animals in general: Pisces, Neptune; Sagittarius, Jupiter; Virgo, Mercury

Animal training: Taurus, Venus

Cats: Leo, Sun; Virgo, Mercury

Dogs: Virgo, Mercury

Fish: Pisces, Neptune; Cancer, Moon

Birds: Gemini, Mercury; Libra, Venus

Horses, trainers, riders: Sagittarius, Jupiter

Arts

Acting, actors: Pisces, Neptune; Leo, Sun
Art in general: Libra, Venus
Ballet: Pisces, Neptune; Libra, Venus
Ceramics: Capricorn, Saturn
Crafts: Virgo, Mercury; Libra, Venus
Dancing: Taurus, Venus; Pisces, Neptune
Drama: Taurus, Venus; Pisces, Neptune
Embroidery: Libra, Venus
Etching: Aries, Mars
Films, filmmaking: Pisces, Neptune; Leo, Sun; Aquarius, Uranus
Literature: Gemini, Mercury
Music: Libra, Taurus, Venus
Painting: Libra, Venus
Photography: Pisces, Neptune; Aquarius, Uranus
Printing: Gemini, Mercury
Theaters: Leo, Sun; Libra, Venus

Fishing

During the summer months the best time of the day for fishing is from sunrise to three hours after, and from about two hours before sunset until one hour after. In cooler months, the fish are not biting until the air is warm. At this time the best hours are from noon to 3:00 pm. Warm and cloudy days are good. The most favorable winds are from the south and southwest. Easterly winds are unfavorable. The best days of the month for fishing are those on which the Moon changes quarters, especially if the change occurs on a day when the Moon is in a watery sign (Cancer, Scorpio, Pisces). The best period in any month is the day after the Full Moon.

Parties & Friends

Barbecues: Moon, Cancer; Aries, Mars
Casinos: Taurus, Venus; Leo, Sun; Sagittarius, Jupiter
Festivals: Taurus, Libra, Venus
Parades: Jupiter, Sagittarius; Libra, Venus

The best time for parties is when the Moon is in Gemini, Leo, Libra, or Aquarius, with good aspects to Venus and Jupiter. There should be no aspects (positive or negative) to Mars or Saturn. The need for friendship is greater when Uranus aspects the Moon, or the Moon is in Aquarius. Friendship prospers when Venus or Uranus is trine, sextile, or conjunct the Moon. The chance meeting of acquaintances and friends is facilitated by the Moon in Gemini.

Sports

The Sun rules physical vitality, Mars rules coordination and competition, and Saturn rules strategy but hinders coordination. Plan activities to coincide with good aspects (X or T in the Lunar Aspectarian) from the planets. Accidents are associated with squares or oppositions (Q or O in the Lunar Aspectarian) to Mars, Saturn, or Uranus. Below is a list of sports and the planets and signs that rule them.

Acrobatics: Aries, Mars

Archery: Sagittarius, Jupiter

Ball games in general: Venus

Baseball: Aries, Mars

Bicycling: Gemini, Mercury; Aquarius, Uranus

Boxing: Aries, Mars

Calisthenics: Aries, Mars; Pisces, Neptune

Chess: Gemini, Mercury; Aries, Mars

Competitive sports: Aries, Mars

Coordination: Aries, Mars

Deep-sea diving: Pisces, Neptune

Exercising: Leo, Sun

Football: Aries, Mars

Horse racing: Sagittarius, Jupiter

Jogging: Gemini, Mercury

Physical vitality: Leo, Sun

Polo: Aquarius, Uranus; Sagittarius, Jupiter; Capricorn, Saturn

Racing (other than horse): Leo, Sun; Aquarius, Uranus

Ice skating: Pisces, Neptune

Roller skating: Gemini, Mercury

Sporting equipment: Sagittarius, Jupiter
Sports in general: Leo, Sun
Strategy: Capricorn, Saturn
Swimming: Neptune, Pisces; Moon, Cancer
Tennis: Gemini, Mercury; Taurus, Venus; Aquarius, Uranus; Aries, Mars
Wrestling: Aries, Mars

Travel

Air travel: Gemini, Mercury; Sagittarius, Jupiter; Aquarius, Uranus
Automobile travel: Gemini, Mercury
Boating: Cancer, Moon; Pisces, Neptune
Camping: Leo, Sun
Helicopters: Aquarius, Uranus
Hotels: Moon, Cancer; Taurus, Venus
Journeys in general: Leo, Sun
Parks: Leo, Sun
Picnics: Taurus, Venus; Sun, Leo
Rail travel: Aquarius, Uranus; Gemini, Mercury
Restaurants: Cancer, Moon; Virgo, Mercury; Sagittarius, Jupiter
Vacations, holidays: Pisces, Neptune; Taurus, Venus

Short journeys are ruled by Mercury, long ones by Jupiter. The Sun rules the actual journey itself. Long trips that threaten to exhaust the traveler are best begun when the Sun is well aspected to the Moon, and the date is favorable for the traveler. If traveling with other people, good aspects from Venus are desirable. For enjoyment, aspects to Jupiter are profitable. For visiting, aspects to Mercury are good. To avoid accidents, avoid squares or oppositions to Mars, Saturn, Uranus, or Pluto.

For air travel, choose a day when the Moon is in Gemini or Libra, and well aspected by Mercury and/or Jupiter. Avoid adverse aspects of Mars, Saturn, or Uranus.

Writing

Write for pleasure or publication when the Moon is in Gemini. Mercury should be direct. Favorable aspects to Mercury, Uranus, and Neptune promote ingenuity.

Hunting & Fishing Dates

From/To	Quarter	Sign
January 1, 3:16 am–January 3, 9:50 pm	2nd	Cancer
January 10, 7:48 am–January 12, 8:23 pm	4th	Scorpio
January 19, 10:41 pm–January 22, 3:26 am	1st	Pisces
January 28, 11:57 am–January 30, 3:16 pm	2nd	Cancer
February 6, 4:06 pm–February 9, 4:38 am	3rd	Scorpio
February 16, 6:40 am–February 18, 10:07 am	1st	Pisces
February 24, 6:09 pm–February 26, 10:44 pm	2nd	Cancer
March 6, 12:23 am–March 8, 12:47 pm	3rd	Scorpio
March 15, 4:31 pm–March 17, 7:13 pm	4th	Pisces
March 23, 11:33 pm–March 25, 4:22 am	1st	Cancer
April 2, 7:49 am–April 4, 8:08 pm	3rd	Scorpio
April 12, 2:35 am–April 14, 5:46 am	4th	Pisces
April 20, 6:28 am–April 22, 10:06 am	1st	Cancer
April 29, 2:13 pm–May 2, 2:36 am	2nd	Scorpio
May 9, 11:16 am–May 11, 3:54 pm	4th	Pisces
May 17, 3:40 pm–May 19, 5:38 pm	1st	Cancer
May 26, 8:05 pm–May 29, 8:37 am	2nd	Scorpio
June 5, 6:01 pm–June 8, 12:09 am	3rd	Pisces
June 14, 2:14 am–June 16, 3:07 am	1st	Cancer
June 23, 2:18 am–June 25, 2:51 pm	2nd	Scorpio
July 2, 11:35 pm–July 5, 6:22 am	3rd	Pisces
July 11, 12:27 pm–July 13, 1:25 pm	4th	Cancer
July 20, 9:30 am–July 22, 9:49 pm	2nd	Scorpio
July 30, 5:27 am–August 1, 11:47 am	3rd	Pisces
August 7, 8:52 pm–August 9, 10:55 pm	4th	Cancer
August 16, 5:41 pm–August 19, 5:32 am	1st	Scorpio
August 26, 12:49 pm–August 28, 6:09 pm	2nd	Pisces
September 3, 3:10 am–September 6, 6:29 am	4th	Cancer
September 13, 2:09 am–September 15, 1:35 pm	1st	Scorpio
September 22, 9:51 pm–September 25, 2:34 am	2nd	Pisces

Hunting & Fishing Dates

From/To	Quarter	Sign
October 1, 8:32 am–October 3, 12:14 pm	3rd	Cancer
October 10, 10:01 am–October 12, 9:18 pm	1st	Scorpio
October 20, 7:33 am–October 22, 12:42 pm	2nd	Pisces
October 28, 3:09 pm–October 30, 5:47 pm	3rd	Cancer
November 6, 4:45 pm–November 9, 4:15 am	4th	Scorpio
November 16, 4:21 pm–November 18, 10:58 pm	2nd	Pisces
November 25, 12:29 am–November 27, 1:18 am	3rd	Cancer
December 3, 10:36 pm–December 6, 10:28 am	4th	Scorpio
December 13, 11:18 pm–December 16, 7:30 am	1st	Pisces
December 22, 11:52 am–December 24, 11:32 am	2nd	Cancer

Editor's Note: This chart lists the best hunting and fishing dates for this year, but not the only possible dates. To accommodate your own schedule, you may wish to try dates other than those listed above. To learn more about choosing good fishing dates, see the fishing information on page 136. To learn more about hunting dates, see the animal and hunting information on page 135.

Moon Lore

By Verna Gates

Before the Sun burns away the mysteries of the night, the Moon presides over the hidden forces of shadow. While the Moon shines as the lesser light, its beams shone over the campfires of our ancestors, where young and old gathered together.

The old ones offered wisdom: Never let a child sleep in the moonlight for fear of lunacy. Don't let the New Moon catch you without money or you'll have little all month. Never point at the Moon; pointing nine times will anger the man on the Moon, and he will deny your entrance to heaven. Start new habits and new projects on the New Moon and work vigorously while it waxes. Francis Bacon, whom many believe is the true Shakespeare, claimed his mighty intellect grew with the waxing Moon. Sensitive to the Moon's influence, Bacon once fainted during an eclipse.

Beware the Full Moon, also. Humanity grows restless at its pull. The mob demanded the life of Jesus and crucified him by the light of a Full Moon. Caesar cried out to Brutus as a mob of Roman senators placed their knives into his flesh during a Full Moon. Lincoln was attending Ford Theater just three days before the Full Moon. Alexander II of Russia had his royal family dragged out into a wooded area and murdered during a Full Moon. It was reported in 1978 that a Full Moon beamed over a heat wave in the Islamic religious capital of Mecca, and more than a hundred people tried to commit suicide. Suicide is most common during the Full Moon.

On the other hand, maternity wards staff extra helpers during the Full Moon. Human gestation is nine lunar months. In the Niger area of West Africa, it was believed that all babies were delivered not by a stork, but by the Moon bird. The Great Moon Mother blesses her children with babies and other gifts. In some cultures, such as the Mongolian Buriats and the natives of Greenland, it is believed that the Moon is a man and actually aids the husband (if he doesn't actually act alone) in the impregnation of women. In Southern Italy, women wore crescent-shaped charms to appeal to the Moon goddess. They desired her assistance in bringing about an easy labor. If you want many healthy children, marry during a Full Moon.

Birth and death, the cycle of life, is embodied in the ever-changing Moon. Some believe that the Moon represents our own eternal life, ebbing and flowing, but always renewing and growing into fullness. According to the Hottentots, the Moon once sent a rabbit to deliver its message of eternal life. The Moon said, "People will be born, grow fat and healthy, then shrivel into old age, then come back new again, just as I do." However, the rabbit scrambled the message and told people they would only have one life. The Moon was obligated to keep his garbled word and introduce death. The angry Moon threw a Moon stick at the rabbit, splitting his lip forever. In retaliation, the rabbit scraped the face of the Moon with his paw.

Moon Stories

The beacon of the night did more than speak of life, it inspired tales of the supernatural. The Moon shone over the ancients as they told their fantastic stories. She inspired their romantic tales of brave men and great ladies, of hearts won and lost. The Moon curved her crescent as laughter wafted up to her, as she heard the stories of tricksters and fools. Her fullness lit the night as wide-eyed children heard tale of restless spirits. Many eyes turned toward the Moon herself to tell stories of her mysteries.

Chang-O

No one could really blame Chang-O for being upset. She was a shining, immortal goddess, now condemned to live among dreary humans. Even worse, her punishment revoked her immortality. She not only was limited to living out one lifetime, but she would grow old and ugly, weak and sick, and then, she would die. It was all Yi's fault. Yi, her husband, the heavenly archer, had brought this punishment on them because he couldn't resist loading his bow and letting arrows fly at the nine Suns. He shot eight of the suns out of the sky, leaving only one to light the world. As punishment, the god and goddess were banished from the realm of the gods and sent to Earth.

Chang-O missed her heavenly life and begged Yi to find the goddess Hsi Wang Mu, keeper of immortality. Hsi Wang Mu brewed an elixir of eternal life from magic peaches. These powerful fruits took three thousand years to ripen in her own garden of paradise. The compassionate Hsi

Wang Mu agreed to make enough of the elixir to restore their immortality, but she stopped short of reversing their fortunes totally. She refused to make enough elixir to renew their status as god and goddess.

When Yi brought back the elixir, Chang-O brought out the cups to drink to immortality. However, Yi wanted one more good hunting trip with all of the thrill and risk of human mortality. Chang-O had to wait. And wait. She grew increasingly impatient. The longer she waited, the more of the elixir Chang-O wanted to drink. She remembered her anger at Yi for shooting down the Suns and bring this punishment on them. After all, she had done nothing to deserve this lonely life on Earth.

So Chang-O drank the elixir. All of it. As she swallowed, she felt herself getting lighter and lighter. She began to float upward. Up and up she went, high into the sky. She is a beautiful goddess once again, but she is now lonelier than ever. Her weightlessness prevents her from leaving the cold sky. Her husband Yi eventually forgave her greediness and built her a house of cinnamon on the Moon. She shares her home with a white rabbit. Yi can only visit once a month during the dark of the Moon.

Europa

The young women of the Phoenician court were dancing in the surf, splashing and indulging in the sunlit day. While all were lovely in their bloom of youth, one maiden stood out above the others in beauty and grace. The regal loveliness of the Princess Europa did not escape the watchful eye of Zeus, king of the Greek gods.

As the girls laughed and played, suddenly, out of the waves strutted a beautiful white bull. At first frightened, the maidens soon realized that the bull was quite tame. They made a game of hanging garlands from his neck and horns. Lovely Europa even dared to climb onto his back. That's when the bull took off. Zeus carried the bewildered Europa to Crete, where he ravished her. The result was a son, King Minos.

Interrupted in her earthly life, Minos' mother Europa nightly relives the transforming event that plucked her from her courtiers. As the sky darkens, shy Europa emerges to race across the sky, chased by her solar bull lover. Once a month, the Sun catches the lovely Europa, and the two celestial bodies enjoy a heavenly conjunction with earthly pleasures (the New Moon). Every ninth year, they converge at their original meeting place in the sky. During this time, Minos ordered a great festival complete with the sacrifices of seven boys and seven girls sent from Athens to dance to death before the Minotaur.

The Werewolf

In 1580, in the Auvergne district of France, Monsieur Sanroche lived with his wife in an elegant chateau. The Sanroche woods were a popular sporting area and Sanroche often received visiting huntsmen asking his company for the chase. One day, Monsieur Fayrolle invited him to go deer hunting. Declining, Sanroche explained that he was awaiting a call from his lawyer. Completing his business in surprising good time, Sanroche decided to try to catch up with Fayrolle.

The Sun was setting and a glorious Full Moon rising when Sanroche found his friend. Fayrolle was lying, pale and bloody, upon the ground. As they walked back to Sanroche's chateau, Fayrolle told of a vicious wolf attack. In the fray, Fayrolle had drawn his knife and cut off the wolf's paw. Now at the chateau, Fayrolle offered to show Sanroche the severed limb. As he pulled it from his bag, both men gasped in shock at the sight of a human hand.

Sanroche grabbed the hand and studied its long, shapely fingers, its fine white skin, and especially its jewelry. One finger bore a blue topaz set in swirling spirals of gold. Sanroche took the hand and called for the doctor.

The doctor was already at Sanroche's house. He was trying desperately to save Sanroche's wife from a profusely bleeding stump at the end of her arm. Sanroche kept quiet about the severed paw/hand for weeks, letting his wife recover from her wound. Then, when she was strong again, he demanded answers. Through tears, the wife confessed to turning into a werewolf upon the rising of the Full Moon. In this true and amazing story, she was tried, tortured and burned at the stake in one of history's best-known werewolf trials.

Enanna

Enanna, queen of the Sumerian heavens, should never have gone to visit her sister, Ereshkigal, queen of the dead. Ereshkigal lived in the place of shadows and spirits, called Kur-nu-gi-a. Into this dark place, Enanna emanated brightness as she walked in with the rainbow curled around her neck, the zodiac circling around her waist, and stars dotting her tunic from top to bottom. She wore a crown topped with the crescent Moon.

The shining goddess, ruler of the heavens, inspired hatred and envy in the sister who was surrounded with faint ghosts and dark murmuring. Ereshkigal killed her sister and staked her corpse among the dead.

The Moon, which brought water to the parched land of Sumeria (Iraq), stopped shining in the sky. The rain clouds vanished into the merciless Sun. The crops withered. After three days of starless skies, the water god missed the tugging of the Moon, who pulled his tides and stole precious moisture from him to return to Earth. He searched for Enanna. His fears were confirmed when he found the lifeless body of the Queen of Heaven in Kur-nu-gi-a. As the water god, he controlled the waters of life, which he now called forth and anointed on the starry forehead of Enanna. She revived and ascended back

into the heavens. The waxing and waning Moon reminds Earth people of the treachery that you can find even among your own kind.

The Mandrake

The evil one had a spell of hatred to cast. For years, she had searched for the exact instrument she needed. It took the death of her own son to bring the prize within her grasp. According to the evil ones, her son was born completely bad. He came out the birth canal biting and scratching her womb. He devoted every breath to evil thoughts and dirty deeds. As a young man, he was an accomplished criminal. To celebrate his twenty-first birthday, he ravished and murdered the town mayor's daughter. For this vicious act, he was hanged by the light of the Full Moon. The conditions were perfect.

Under his gallows tree grew the mandrake, reaching its maturity, ready for harvest. This harbinger of evil grows a root resembling a man, with arms, legs, torso, and head. This root figure can be used to cast spells on enemies, much like the voodoo doll. Shavings of it can be mixed with vipers' tongues, bat's blood, and the fat of dead children for potent charms.

Now, under the light of the Full Moon, the evil one released a black chicken, because the devil will chase a black chicken. He had to be occupied in order for the evil one to steal his special plant. With her silver sword, she took the mandrake cleanly from the earth, for not to do so means certain death. A mandrake root, not totally dislodged with the first stroke, will pull you deep into its earthly lodge for a slow dance with death.

Mandrake in hand, the evil one returned to her den. She cleaned the mandrake, dressed it in little silk pajamas, and hung a gallows noose around its fleshy neck. Until the next Full Moon, she fed it stolen communion wafers. Set out into the full light of the round orb, her charm was now ready for her evil deeds.

From this evil one comes many of the ills of the world. Beware of the Full Moon, for then she stands in her greatest power.

Tsuki-Yomi

The Moon god Tsuki-yomi lived in a shimmering sky palace with his radiant sister, Amaterasu, the Sun. The Sun and Moon shared the palace and shared the sky, happily gazing down on the faces that smiled at them from Earth. Everyone who lived on Earth was content because the food goddess, Ukemochi, fed them bountifully from her body.

One day, an old man died. The people didn't smile up at Tsuki-yomi and Amaterasu. They looked to Earth in sadness. Not understanding what happened, Amaterasu sent her brother to Earth to see if Ukemochi had failed at her duties. The Sun did not want to shine over hungry people.

Ukemochi was delighted to receive such a magnificent guest as the Moon. To honor Tsuki-yomi, the food goddess summoned a splendid feast. She stretched out her hand to the ground, and rice and vegetable dishes poured out of her mouth. She stretched her hand to the sea and fish leapt onto plates, perfectly seasoned and cooked. Her hand reached toward the mountains, and all manner of cooked game sprang from her mouth.

Tsuki-yomi watched Ukemochi pour out food from her mouth. He stared at the heavily burdened tables and the overabundance of food. Rather than seeing the honor Ukemochi intended, he saw waste and gluttony. Rather than appreciating the bounty of her body, he disapproved of her oral delivery. Tsuki-yomi cried out in disgust and drew his Moon-forged crescent sword. In his anger, he slew his hostess, Ukemochi, the food goddess.

As she died, her body transformed. Her head divided into cows and sheep, who gathered on the green fields of the mountain. Grain sprouted from her arms and legs and took root in the land. From her melting organs, rice grew in puddles and formed the first rice paddies. Her hair stretched into worms, silk worms for clothes, earthworms to nourish the soil.

When the Moon returned to the palace he shared with the Sun, Amaterasu was furious at his reckless folly. To avoid more of her blows, Tsuki-yomi raced to the other side of the sky. To this day, he avoids her anger and comes out only at night.

Bizarre Moon Theories

By Kirin Lee

History abounds with the bizarre and strange when it comes to the Moon. Many ancient people had odd beliefs and rituals associated with our satellite, but none compare to the downright crazy theories proposed by more modern humans. Here are a dozen wild theories straight from the files of bizarre astronomy.

Theory Number One

A common belief in the sixth century BCE was that the Earth was a flat disk floating on a vast expanse of water. The Greeks took this one step further, believing that the heavens formed a dome above, and the underworld formed a second dome below. A sphere, after all, is much more pleasing to visualize than a half-sphere.

Anaximander of Miletus (611 BCE) also held this belief, but tried to explain the heavens even further. His theory was that the sphere around the Earth was encased in fire contained in tubes. These tubes needed vents, which were the stars seen at night.

He tried to fit the Moon into this wild theory as well. Claiming it was a very large tube vent, he said that it constantly changed shape, creating the lunar phases. It seems that he had no explanation as to why the Moon appeared solid with fixed features such as craters.

Theory Number Two

Johannes Hevelius made several contributions to astronomy, but is best known for becoming one of the first men to produce an atlas of the Moon. Produced in 1647, his atlas named the various features of the Moon's surface. Even though his system was superseded by Riccoioli's in 1651, his atlas was very accurate for its time. Unfortunately, rumor has it that his original engraving on copper was melted down to make a tea set.

Theory Number Three

In 1824 Franz von Paula Gruithuisen theorized that the Moon's craters were formed by the impact of other space-going bodies. Before that, in

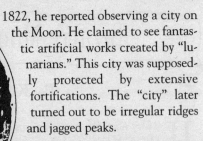

1822, he reported observing a city on the Moon. He claimed to see fantastic artificial works created by "lunarians." This city was supposedly protected by extensive fortifications. The "city" later turned out to be irregular ridges and jagged peaks.

Theory Number Four

Sir William Herschel firmly believed in lunar inhabitants. In 1789, in his journals, he reported seeing many odd things regarding the Moon. Herschel also saw towns, forests, and roads on the lunar surface. He even went so far as to say he saw a circus! Weirdly enough, his son, Sir John, was later used in a huge Moon alien hoax in 1835.

Theory Number Five

In 1835 a debt-ridden newspaper, the *New York Sun*, got a boost from a major hoax. Reporter Robert Locke made up a story of unbelievable proportions, yet people ate it up hook, line, and sinker.

He claimed to have information from a good source that a Sir John Herschel had discovered a civilization on the Moon made up of bat people with yellow skin. Animals and plants, up to 130 species, had also been found. Moon alien fever raged through the general population. A group of ministers even made plans to Christianize their new neighbors. Finally, some Yale scientists traced Locke down and forced him to admit to fraud.

Theory Number Six

On a night in October 1939, a weather balloon caught fire and hit the ground near Strafford, Missouri. The next day, the local paper announced that the Moon had crashed and burned on a nearby highway. Not everyone believed it this time, especially when the Moon mysteriously reappeared in the sky that night.

Theory Number Seven

In 1942 a Mr. Weisberger declared that the geological formations visible on the Moon weren't really there at all. He said that what we were seeing was nothing more than disturbances in the super-thick atmosphere around the Moon.

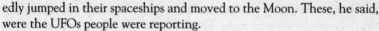

Theory Number Eight

A man named M. K. Jessup theorized that pygmies traced their lineage back to Atlantis. Claiming that they were clever, he said that they had invented space ships. When Atlantis was in its last days, these pygmies supposedly jumped in their spaceships and moved to the Moon. These, he said, were the UFOs people were reporting.

Theory Number Nine

In 1951 a Mr. Ocampo spread wild statements saying that the craters on the Moon were the result of two powerful races who destroyed themselves with nuclear weapons of incredible force.

Theory Number Ten

Also in 1951, George Adamski, using a small telescope in his back yard, reported that the Moon was being used as a base of operations by aliens. He claimed to observe their comings and goings regularly.

In 1952, Adamski said that he met a real Venusian in California. He published his story, and naturally people believed it.

Theory Number Eleven

Howard Menger published a book in 1959 claiming that he made regular trips to the Moon on an alien space craft. He even had photos to prove it. His photos, however, were quite out of focus.

Theory Number Twelve

In a book, Don Wilson claims that NASA is covering up alien activity on the Moon. He takes his claims a step further by saying that the Moon is a hollow alien spacecraft. What he doesn't say is why they parked it there.

Grandfather Bristlecone

By Bernyce Barlow

Once there was a tree called Bristlecone. Bristlecone grew on the top of a very rugged mountain whose slopes were steep and quick to slip during winter storms, but Bristlecone was as strong as the mountain and had survived the harshest of conditions while growing into maturity. Bristlecone grew very slowly, one inch every hundred years. Some of Bristlecone's family were eight thousand years old. These were indeed the elders of the forest! Other trees, animals, and flora lived in the forest with Bristlecone, but most went on their way in what seemed to Bristlecone a very short time.

There was one exception to this rule. Her name was Grandmother Moon. Grandmother Moon had been around when Bristlecone was just a young seedling growing in his mother's shadow. For as long as he could remember, Grandmother Moon had kept him company when everything else on the mountain was sleeping, cloaked in an icy blanket.

Grandmother Moon and Bristlecone became the best of friends, watching all the changes that occurred on and at the foot of the mountain as centuries passed. From the top of the mountain they could see a great distance, giving them much to talk about during the evenings and mornings they spent together. Sometimes they would talk about the snow geese traveling north or south, or about the latest comet or eclipse. Once in a while a couple of bears or a cougar would wander through the forest, or an elk looking for a mate. With so much going on every day and night on the mountain there was always something to talk about, even over thousands of years!

As time passed Bristlecone became an elder. His stay on the mountain had taught him many lessons. His wisdom was sought out by the other trees and creatures of the forest. He strived to speak honestly about his experiences so others would know how to survive on the mountain as he had. When a question was beyond his time and knowledge he would ask Grandmother Moon to shed her insight on the subject. Her time above the mountain was longer than Bristlecone's on the mountain, so her wisdom stretched in light of time. Once, a two-legged came to Bristlecone and asked to make a flute from a branch from his limb. Bristlecone was somewhat hesitant, and rightfully so, since that branch had taken two thousand years to grow. Bristlecone decided to ask Grandmother Moon her opinion. She thought it was a splendid idea and offered her counsel. The next day Bristlecone gave the two-legged permission to cut the branch that would fill his need.

Bristlecone was thousands of years old and very close to the end of his growing cycle. Grandmother Moon knew that Bristlecone would soon be leaving the forest, just as so many other Bristlecones had; their time on Earth was long but not endless. There were only a few pine bundles left on the ancient tree and when they dropped no others would grow. It seemed appropriate that a branch from the Bristlecone be made into a flute. That way, after the last pine bundle dropped next winter, the Bristlecone would live on in a windtune whenever a two-legged played the Bristlecone flute.

Two winters later the two-legged returned to visit the Bristlecone but all that was left of him was an old stump. Saddened by this discovery, the two-legged made camp near the place the Bristlecone once grew and later that night played the flute made from the elder's branch. As he played a beautiful windtune, Grandmother Moon rose in the midnight sky and shed moonbeams on the flute player. His music became haunting and magical as if he had been touched by some kind of spirit of place. Grandmother Moon recognized the tune. She had heard it many times when the wind blew through the branches of her friend—a distinct melody of ancient scale. Grandmother Moon took delight in the memory of her friend as she listened to the flute carry the song across the mountain.

Every year after that, the two-legged returned to the site where the Bristlecone had once grown. Sometimes he brought his son with him and they played their flutes together. Grandmother Moon always looked forward to their visits. When the elder two-legged left this world his son continued to come to the mountain and play the Bristlecone song, as did his son and his and for many generations following. Whenever Grandmother heard the flute song she beamed with light and love for the cherished memory of her friend, Grandfather Bristlecone. It is said whenever the Bristlecone song is played by the light of the Moon, Grandmother Moon will send magic through the night on moonbeams of light and love.

Author's note: The Bristlecone Forest is located in Central California off of Highway 395 one hour south of Bishop, California. The Bristlecone tree does indeed grow one inch every hundred years and matures for thousands of years, making it the oldest living tree on the planet.

Pearls: Jewels of the Moon

By Louise Riotte

Long before gold, diamonds, and other precious stones came to be considered symbols of divine grace and worldly power among the people who lived by the sea, the pearl was the central object in a great cult of worship, the cult of the shells. The cult still echoes down to us, whispering through the winds of time and tradition; for the pearl is still valued as a symbol of modesty, chastity, and tranquillity, and beloved for its natural beauty.

It is no surprise that in the beginning the pearl was an object of great wonder, as all natural things were. The first great religion was a simple worship of the great forces of nature—the earth, water, fire, and air—controlled by the powers of the Moon and the Sun. The marriage between the sky and the earth was the central point—the place where the action took place, the action we call "creation"—not only of man, but of trees, fish, animals, fruits and grains, and their spirits.

It is believed that the first deity worshipped was the Moon, the special ruler of the sea and the rain and the menses of women, the earth mother. The "face" within the Moon, its waxing and waning, was a recognizable touchstone to the passage of time. An old man was many Moons old—a child just a few. It was recognized early that there was some connection between the Moon and the tides, and the tides buffeted the beaches and tossed up shells, fish, and stones under the Moon's power. By watching the Moon's phases the tides could be calculated. It was observed that as the air cooled the night, the rains came; clearly they too were under control of the Moon. So was sleep. Inevitably the Moon god, later to be worshipped as the Moon goddess, was the god who brought the rains and thus fertility.

In the early world of seafarers and fishermen, three shells and three shell products were symbols of the great religion of the elements: the cowry, the snail, and the conch were the shells, and the shellfish, the pearl shell, and the pearl were the shell products.

The cowry was the smallest and the most widely used symbol. It was thought to have the power of creating life, and was thus a special shell of women, worn on girdles, and given as dowries to aid in fertility. Other uses for these shells were money, good luck charms, amulets, and tokens of games of chance. In isolated places today they are still used as money.

The snail shell, though equally esteemed as a parent of life, had a separate role. Its spiral, more easily portrayed than the curves of the cowry, seems to have been used as a symbol of a cowry. Even today it may be seen on pillars of government that are architecturally derived from the Ionians of Greece.

The conch, known in India as the "chank," is the third shell of importance. It, too, is considered the "bringer of life," but of spiritual life—the Word—the Sacred Law. Perhaps this was because, when held to the ear, the voice of the sea god murmured through it. Even today in Crete it is still used by shepherds as we might use a siren to call for help. It was still employed as a call for rain in Mexico when the Spanish conquered the Aztecs.

The pearl, which they believed was guarded in the sea by dragons, has always been renowned for a characteristic unique among gems. It came from the creator god to the sea worshippers in shining tranquil perfection and unity out of the shell of God's humblest of creatures—the mollusk we call the oyster. They believed it to be at once new life and the promise of life everlasting. The serpent-dragon was a symbol of masculine fertility, the cowry and snail symbols of female fertility. The pearl, guarded between them, was akin to man's life, a gift of the creator god.

Pearls from the Persian Gulf

Long before oil became important, the pearls found in the Persian Gulf were greatly valued. It is believed the sacred use of pearls derived from India. Coins have been found showing the ancient kings of Persia wearing a single pearl hanging from the right ear and there are paintings of women wearing a ring through the left nostril with three pearls strung from it—symbolic that the wearer was noble and properly married in the eyes of God.

When the Roman Empire declined and lost Constantinople, the rulers of India and Persia regained control of the Persian Gulf pearls and of the shipping channels. As in the past they then brought pearls from Tamil land (Northern India, then called Malabar and Ceylon). The Romans were not notable as traders, either by temperament or desire. The supply of Eastern pearls to the West slowed and the Europeans fell back on river pearls. The Orient began to accumulate vast numbers of pearls and there were many stories of the splendor in which the far Eastern kings garbed themselves.

The most famous reporter of his century, Marco Polo (1254–1324), who was probably the prototype for the merchant of Venice, was not published in his own country but in France. His maps, eagerly sought by navigators (one of which was Christopher Columbus, who had one annotated in the Venetian's own hand) were "corrected" so often in reproduction that they became thoroughly confusing. Polo himself was not confused, and it is surprising just how accurate and keen an observer he was. His friends called him "Marco Million" in reference to the jewels sewn into his ragged garments, which were all that was left of his fine raiment when he returned home.

Polo dictated his book and only the first part is in the first person. Even today his story is one of marvelous adventure, and gives a picture of not only central Asia and the great Genghis Khan, but of certain parts of Siberia as well as Africa and a few references to Japan.

What is of interest to us here is his descriptions of pearls, the most elaborate being that of King Malabar, who was adorned with a great "rosary" consisting of 104 pearls and rubies. On his ankles and toes, Polo relates, blossomed pearl bracelets and rings worth more than a city's ransom. The pearls were found in his kingdom. No one was permitted to remove a pearl weighing more than half a saggio—all others belonged to the king—which resulted in an incredible quantity.

The Malabar pearls came from the shell called the *Margaritifera vulgaris*, or the lingah shell. These are known to be the most fertile pearl-bearing shells in the world, native to the area and to the Persian Gulf. To control their breeding was to have a corner on the pearl market of the world.

The Pearls of America

Native Americans were keenly aware of the beauty and value of pearls. When the mysterious mounds (tombsites of an ancient people) were opened, jars of pearls and pearls on ceremonial robes were found in abundance. The people who built the mounds at Spiro, Oklahoma, must have found quantities of pearl-bearing mollusks in the region, abundant in the unpolluted waters of the time. There is also evidence that the Indians of both North and South America honored pearls, using them both ritualistically and ornamentally. Virginia chronicles speak of Indians of both sexes wearing pearls. They have been described by Captain John Smith, who related that they wore them in the same fashion as the women of ancient India, Greece, and Egypt—three at a time hanging from pierced ears. They were further adorned with bone carvings and pieces of shell. The men also, like the Egyptians, wore necklaces of pearls over the heart.

In the Powhatan tribe tribute was often paid in pearls. It is said that a necklace of pearls was used by Powhatan himself in the same manner as the Tudor kings used signet rings. Powhatan gave it to the colonial leader, Sir Thomas Dale, telling him that any messenger sent to him by the English should wear the necklace as proof of good faith.

While the Native Americans used pearls for ornaments and sewn on ceremonial robes, it seems that freshwater pearls were largely ignored by the early colonists. The Puritans disdained jewels not so much as jewels but as symbols of the Pagan religion of the monarchy. They even passed laws forbidding the wearing of silk by the lower classes. However, the influence of the Puritans was offset by another pioneer group, the Dutch. Dutch girls liked earrings of beads of pearl and chip diamonds, and their men liked buckles, watches, and gold-headed canes. There was generally more luxury in the colonies than has been supposed.

While the affluent were buying pearls at auctions and in jewelry stores, the poor were enjoying another sort of pearl rush entirely. Suddenly, pearls were found growing in local river mussels. David Howell, a shoemaker, made the first find. He liked mussels prepared with garlic and butter, and while feasting bit down on something large and hard—a pearl of great size but, because of being cooked, unfortunately of no value. The news of his find spread far and wide, and a few days later a carpenter named Jacob Quackenbush found a fine pink pearl, which was harvested in flawless condition.

The news brought people from far and wide with dreams of getting rich by harvesting the pearl-bearing mussels. Whole families came and set up tents. Pearling was enjoyable, and simple equipment was all that was needed. The work was casual—a simple water telescope made at home with a tin can and a piece of glass was just about all a pearl fisher had to carry, though some hopefuls brought baskets. Pearl fishing, while not highly profitable because the competition was fierce, was fun. After wading most of the day the pearl hunters gathered at night around the campfire, frying fish and playing the banjo or the harmonica. On

Saturdays they went to the nearest town to sell their pearls, to shop, to dance, and perhaps to drink. The first great mussel beds found were soon fished out, but by that time pearls were being found in many other places. These new pearls were green, pink, purplish brown, cream, rose-pink and white. In one area they were even a metallic green, in another a dark blue.

Remember, this pearl frenzy took place in the nineteenth century, before the waters of many lakes and rivers became polluted with industrial waste. The find at Notch Brook came about in 1857. Other pearl-bearing streams were soon found in many other places, mostly by small boys wading in the streams. The freshwater pearls were for the most part baroque, that is, irregularly shaped. Even so, there was a ready sale for them and some lucky pearlers made thousands of dollars. Sometime around World War I, United States river pearling ceased being profitable, although shell collecting continued. About this time increasing industrial use of the rivers changed the tranquil currents so necessary to the Unio (mollusks). Dams and bridges destroyed coves (small sheltered inlets or bays) and altered streams, and in many areas the mussels were actually killed off.

While the wives of Eastern millionaires preferred their jewels of the Moon goddess to be round, and therefore usually derived from the oyster, a great many Midwestern women prized the pearls of their own rivers and paid handsomely for them. More than one jewelry store got its start by selling American river pearls. The story is told of Evarts and Company of Dallas, Texas, which began in 1897 when the first Evart brought a basket of pearls from the Coronado River to the city, advertised, and sold them. American women loved the brooches, necklaces, and earrings of the baroque pearls found in American waters. By 1909, Kunz (George Frederick), the great gemologist of the early part of the nineteenth century, was able to say that pearls were America's most popular jewel, and that never in the world's history had so many owned such fine pearls.

Are all the pearl-bearing mollusks gone? No, but now they must be searched for more diligently. Pink pearls are still found in the Mississippi River. My husband was at one time a member of a skin divers club and they occasionally met at a clear lake, Lake Tenkiller, in Oklahoma. He returned from one such trip bringing me several lovely pink pearls that I have always treasured.

Care of Pearls

It must be remembered that pearls are organic in origin and therefore subject to deterioration if not properly cared for. Such care is not difficult.

They should be wiped off after a few wearings and given a little polishing with vegetable oil. They need an occasional washing with gentle soap and warm water when the thread gets grubby, and they should be checked by a jeweler at regular intervals.

The pearls may need restringing. A jeweler should perform this service, and may charge different prices for different necklaces. If you tend to "play with" your pearls or finger them you might loosen the threads sooner than those who leave them alone. If your perspiration is acidic it may injure your pearls. Knots are important to keep the pearls from slipping to and fro and wearing away. Silk string is inclined to stretch, and the knots may loosen. Knots are also important to keep the pearls from scattering should the string break. It is wise for those who wear their pearls frequently to have them restrung every year by a good jeweler who will count them beforehand. Pearls left in vaults may dry up and should be checked from time to time. Some of the great natural pearls are centuries old but have been cared for properly. Pearls, when not in use, are best stored in a soft velvety bag or box so they will not rot or be scratched by other jewelry.

The cult of the shells, the worship of the Moon goddess, is probably our most ancient religious tradition. There is an interesting example. In 1901 in a bronze sarcophagus in a tomb of the winter palace of the kings of Persia at Shushan, or as it is now called, Susa, a lovely pearl necklace was found belonging to an Achaemenid princess buried there. This pearl neckpiece is the oldest and finest of all pearl pieces found anywhere, and dates from at least the fourth century BCE and possibly earlier. The arrangement of the beads, consisting of three strings of seventy-two pearls, each string being divided by round gold discs into nine equal sections, is strongly suggestive of the cult of the shells, the pearls that were thought to be the Moon-substance. "The precious gifts of the gods, the shining, tranquil symbol of the Moon, of life-giving unity, of radiant harmony, and immortal perfection."

Bibliography

Devore, Nicholas. *Encyclopedia of Astrology*.

Dickinson, Joan Younger. *The Book of Pearls*. New York: Crown Publishing, 1968.

Goodavage, Joseph E. *Astrology, the Space Age Science*. The New American Library, 1966.

World Book Encyclopedia. New York: Merchandise Mart Plaza.

Interview with the Moon

By Kim Rogers-Gallagher

As I started up the wide, winding path that led to the Moon's home, I listened to the assortment of animal sounds that filled the woods. The chipmunks, squirrels, and birds were easy enough to identify, but there were many others—a chorus of voices. I walked deeper into the forest, unable to shake the feeling that I was being watched, but for some reason, I wasn't afraid. Suddenly, I saw a pair of deer tiptoe toward me out of the woods. It was a doe and her fawn. I froze and stood very still, afraid I'd frighten them. To my amazement they came right to me, nuzzling in my pockets like horses looking for carrots. Tentatively extending my hand, still expecting them to run, I was even more astounded when the fawn licked my fingers. As I rubbed her behind the ear, her mother nudged my other hand, and let me stroke her face. I lingered there with them for a while, quite taken with the gentle creatures.

When I finally resumed my walk, the deer walked beside me, right up to the door of the charming little house. It was made of stone, with a thatched roof, and was set snugly in the middle of a grove of trees. There was smoke coming from the chimney, and as I stepped up on the porch, I noticed bird feeders everywhere, full to the brim. Several tiny gold finches landed bravely on my shoulders, peeping loudly as I caught my first glimpse of the Moon.

I didn't have to knock. The door opened, and a small round woman with teeny glasses perched on the end of her nose stood in front of me. She wore a blue apron and the warmest smile I'd ever seen. She wiped her hands on her apron, hugged me, and said, "Welcome home, dear," in a voice that somehow sounded familiar. I can't remember ever feeling more welcome anywhere—or safer.

"Come in, come in," she said, stepping aside so that I could enter. "I see you've made friends with some of my little ones, haven't you?" She reached into her apron pocket, took out a handful of sliced apples, and dropped them into a wooden bowl on the porch. The deer began to munch them as she petted their heads tenderly. Two golden retrievers and a tiny Yorkshire terrier ran up to me and covered my face with wet dog kisses. I snuggled them and thought about how good they smelled as she hung up my coat. I noticed a neat line of boots just inside the door, and bent to untie my shoes as the Moon handed me a pair of slippers. "Here, dear, put these on," she said. I did as she asked, and followed her down a hallway toward a bright, wonderful room where a medley of wonderful aromas filled the air. Two cups of steaming hot tea sat on the round wooden table on well-worn calico placemats. "Now, you just sit down there and have your tea, and we'll have a nice visit, dear," she said. She took two huge oven mitts from a hook near the oven and reached inside. "I've baked you an apple pie, and there's vanilla ice cream, too."

Before I could thank her—and ask her how she knew—she set the pie on top of the stove, smiled, and said, "Apple is your favorite, isn't it?"

"Well, yes, it is—how did you know that?"

She chuckled, set a crock of honey on the table, and sat down, smiling fondly at me. "Oh, I know all about you, dear. I remember the first apple pie you ever tasted, in fact—even though you probably don't. You were three, it was a Sunday afternoon, and your grandparents had just taken you to church. The three of you stopped at a little diner on your way home. Your grandfather gave you a quarter, and held you up so that you could reach the buttons on the jukebox. Oh, it was a fine time, and you were always such a well-mannered child. I was sorry to see them go, and I knew you were, too. They loved you very much."

My eyes filled up with tears. My grandparents had raised me, and somehow she knew that, too. I wiped my eyes and sniffled. "Sorry," I said.

She stroked my hair and squeezed my hand. "Oh, there's no need to apologize for crying, dear. You have a perfect right to express all your feelings. I know that's always been difficult for you, but it's quite safe for you to let them out here." I sniffled again and hugged her. I could feel my own Twelfth House Moon's amazement at how readily I'd let her out, for once. "Thank you so much," I said.

I took a bite of my pie, and watched as she pulled a huge scrapbook from one of the bookshelves in the living room. She set it between us and opened to the first page.

Amazingly, the photos were of me. I didn't know quite what to say. She smiled at my surprise, and said, "Oh, now, don't be so surprised, dear. I have scrapbooks of all my children."

We sat there for some time, going through the album. It seemed she had a story for each photo—and although they were my stories, she remembered things I never would have. The day my great-aunt gave me my first teddy bear, which still sits on my bed, to this very day. How hard I cried when my dog ran away when I was nine. I had managed to hold back the tears pretty well until then—but when she reminded me of how happy I'd been when he came home, unharmed, I dabbed my eyes with the fresh white handkerchief she pulled from her pocket. For once, it felt good to cry. The Moon was here with me, soothing me and letting me know it was all right. We finally closed the book after she showed me a photo of my present home. It looked quite cozy in the picture, with several bird feeders of its own hanging from the trees, and a stone bird bath in front. I ran my finger over the picture and sighed. There were lots of blank pages left over—and I smiled at the thought of her filling those pages with everything else that would ever happen to me.

During the course of the afternoon, a huge orange and white tiger cat with long fur and the biggest feet I'd ever seen settled comfortably on my lap. "That's Tigger," she said, as he began to knead and purr. "He'll stay there all day if you let him."

I let him. In fact, I let all of her cats come and sit with me—and there were quite a few, each as fat and happy as the last. The Moon and I chatted until well after dark, mostly about animals, and my childhood. I found myself pouring my heart out to her, about everything that had every frightened, delighted, or hurt me. She understood everything—and made me understand many things I hadn't. More than anything, I remember thinking about how wonderful it was to be so unconditionally loved and accepted. When I told her I had to go, she frowned. "Oh, you can't leave just yet," she said. "I've prepared your room for you. Stay the night, have a good sleep, and we'll fix you a nice breakfast in the morning and send you on your way. Besides, you haven't had your dinner yet, and I'm sure you're tired."

I was delighted she asked. I didn't want to leave—not yet. I asked her if I'd be imposing, and she laughed again. "Of course not, dear—this is your home. I'm just glad you're here."

She had prepared a wonderful dinner, of course. Homemade sauce over stuffed pasta shells. She set out fresh-baked bread and creamy herb butter, and a fresh pitcher of milk. She made me finish my salad, too—because, she said, "Greens are good for you, and you need your vitamins." I offered to help with the dishes, and she agreed to let me dry them. As we stood side by side, in front of the sink, I looked out the window onto a small stone patio. At one point, she tapped me on the arm and pointed. "Look," she said, "she's brought her baby to meet you." I peered out through the back door, and saw a vixen and her kit. "Go on out and see them, dear," she said. "I'll finish up here." I stepped out onto the patio and the two foxes came to me, letting me stroke their beautiful red coats. The kit rolled onto her back like a puppy, and I scratched her belly. The vixen made her way up onto my lap, forcing me to sit down, and licked my chin. I laughed out loud, delighted, and looked up through the window to see The Moon standing there smiling at me. Everything was magical here—and every creature knew it had a safe home with this wonderful woman.

When I reluctantly went back inside, torn between visiting with the foxes and wanting to spend more time close to the Moon, she was waiting for me. "Why don't you change into your nightgown and robe, and we'll sit in front of the fire and chat?"

I said I'd love to, and followed her into a small, cozy bedroom, right next to hers—my room. Laid out on the bed were a flannel nightgown, a long white robe, and a pair of warm wool socks. "Now, you just get comfy, and I'll see you in front of the fire." She kissed my forehead, and I just couldn't resist hugging her again. I wrapped my arms around her, and she began to hum, rocking me as if I were four, not forty. We stood there like that for a moment, and finally, she patted me on the back and squeezed me. I sniffled again, and she wiped my eyes—and read my mind.

"There, there, darling. You can come back any time you want to. I'm always going to be here—always. Now you just change up."

When I joined her in the living room, she was sitting in one of two overstuffed chairs in front of a huge stone fireplace. While she knitted, the cats took turns on my lap, and the dogs dozed in front of the fire.

We were silent for a long, long, comfortable time, and finally, she began to speak. "I know you have questions for me, don't you, dear?" I nodded, realizing for the first time since I'd arrived that my original reason for coming was to interview her. Then I laughed. I couldn't think of a single thing to ask her—nothing she hadn't already told me just by being with me.

She looked right into my eyes, and patted my hand, reading my mind again. "That's right, dear. You already know everything you came here to ask. Just remember to always trust your instinct—the same instinct that's made you know you're safe here—and never try to deny your feelings." She smiled, as if it were all so simple, and returned to her work. "That's all, dear." I wondered if it wasn't that simple.

We sat in silence again for some time. The only sounds in the room, in fact, were the crackling of the fire, the clicking of her knitting needles, and the purring of her cats. I found myself yawning, but reluctant to go to bed and leave her. Finally, she stood up. "Come, dear, let's get you tucked in."

She brought me to my room, then, and when I got into bed—the softest, warmest bed I'd every known—she did indeed tuck me in. She sat down on the bed next to me, and smoothed the hair from my forehead. "Are you warm enough, dear?" I told her I was—on the outside and the inside. "Good," she said. She kissed my cheek, and turned to go. At the door, she stopped and said, "You know, you're a good girl. Be nice to yourself and you'll be fine, dear. Sleep well."

After the most peaceful night's sleep I'd had in a long time, I woke to the Moon tapping on the bedroom door. "I'll be right there," I called to her, and sat up, recalling my dreams, all of them wonderful.

The Moon had prepared French toast for us with powdered sugar. There was a fresh pitcher of orange juice and a bowl of berries on the table. We chatted easily for a long time, mostly about me. Every time I tried to change the subject, she brought it back. "It's all right to talk about you, dear. That's what I'm here for."

I admitted that my Moon was in the Twelfth House, and she waved me off. "Oh, well, that may be true, but you've still got feelings, don't you?" I smiled, and admitted that I certainly did.

Finally, it was time to go. After I'd changed and taken one last look at the room where I'd spent the most peaceful night in my life, I returned to the kitchen, where she handed me a brown paper lunch bag, stuffed to the brim. "This is for the ride home." At the front door, she hugged me again, and said, "I want you to know that this is your home, and you're always welcome."

"I love you," I said, and she smiled.

"And I love you," she said. "And tell that Twelfth House Moon of yours to let those feelings out more often." I said I'd try, and I stepped off the porch, ready to head back into the real world armed with the knowledge that the Moon would always be there.

The Lunar Love Boat

By Jeraldine Saunders

E veryone knows that the most glamorous, mysterious, romantic glow imaginable is that of moonlight shining through sweet ocean mists. Having lived at sea for ten years (my book about it, *The Love Boats*, became the television series), I have observed firsthand that moonrise—any size Moon, at any time of evening—over a dark, gently rocking sea is the ultimate romantic stimulus. Lunar charisma is naturally magnified and intensified in the environment of Neptune—and it is the business of astrologers and poets from the beginning of time to apply the lessons of this natural phenomenon to the task of enriching the love lives of earth folk.

Astrology draws a very direct analogy between water, the liquid element in nature, and emotion, the liquid element of human nature. Your personal love boat is constantly stimulated and influenced by the ever-shifting moods of the Moon because we are all sailing on an open sea of emotions. With a little knowledge of the Moon's cycles and its powerful resonance in our love relationships, you can chart a smoother, straighter course for your love relationship.

The mood created by the Moon is determined by several factors, whose influences farmers and astrologers have been tracking and observing since time began.

First, there's the regular monthly cycle of the Moon's waxing and waning. Every month, the New Moon begins the cycle, and it waxes a little each day, until it is Full halfway through the month, whereupon it begins to wane daily until it disappears (the "dark of the Moon") just prior to being once again reborn as a New Moon.

The next factor we consider is which of the twelve signs the Sun is in. The Sun spends a month in each sign during a year. The Moon travels through each sign of the zodiac every month (spending two or three days in each), but it renews itself and waxes Full in a different sign each month through the year, reflecting the path of the Sun as we observe it from Earth.

Spring begins with a New Moon in Aries and a Full Moon, one of the most beautiful of the whole year, in the Venus-ruled sign of Libra, opposite Aries. The following New Moon, usually in May, is in the sign of Taurus, and two weeks later, the Full Moon is opposite, in Scorpio. In between, of course, the Moon scoots through all the other signs.

As it passes through each sign each month, the Moon spotlights the twelve houses of your individual horoscope and highlights the areas of your life into which they fall. For example, if you are a Sun sign Aries, a Taurus Moon highlights your sector of basic necessities and job income. Under this Moon, you may go job- or house-hunting with the natural attunement of the cosmos acting as a tail wind to help speed you to the right place or right time. The sign-by-sign descriptions below include love House positions for each sign.

Moon in Aries

When the Moon is in Aries, a youthful spirit is at the helm of your love boat, especially if your Sun sign is Libra or Sagittarius. It's a wonderful time for renewing or refreshing a long-lasting relationship with a new kind of togetherness. Youth can be awfully foolish, though, and when the Moon is in Aries, we tend to be quicker to take offense, to argue, and perhaps to say or do something regrettable. Normally diplomatic but very marriage-minded Libra may be tempted to serve an ultimatum on a lover when the Moon is in Aries. Freedom-loving Sagittarians might get carried away and make a verbal commitment that they aren't really prepared to keep.

Men may be more affected by the "macho" element of the Aries Moon than women, and although some men may be more inclined to stop and rescue a damsel in distress when the Moon is here, others may be more inclined to aggression. Set an example of consideration during the Aries Moon each month, and your love boat can avoid stormy scenes.

The new Aries Moon is one of the best new-start days of the whole year for all of us. Use this day to make a few personal adjustments. Take an honest look at your own contribution to your relationship: You have the power to make immediate changes in your relationship by changing your own attitudes and behavior. Plan a romantic surprise for your lover under this Moon. When you're together, concentrate on giving.

Your reward for being a "giver" at the Aries new Moon time is true togetherness when the Full Moon in Libra, the sign of harmonious partnership, comes a couple of weeks later.

Sun-sign Aries, you will find yourself making important relationship decisions near the time of the Full Moon in your birthday month. Each spring, you can use these New and Full Moons to create new relationship patterns and to release whatever (or whomever!) you've outgrown.

A Full Moon in Aries is impetuous and impulsive. It comes during the autumn time of marriage-oriented Libra, so elopements and other dramatic romantic gestures are encouraged by the Aries energy. It is frequently a time for sudden break-ups among young lovers, many of which will be repaired once the ego pressures of Aries are lifted. Those who have been hanging on for lack of strength to say the painful word "good-bye" will finally hear themselves come out with it.

Moon in Taurus

The Taurus Moon is sensual and sexy (especially for Capricorns!). The Aries Moon is sexy, too, but the Taurus Moon is for "making love" in the sense of putting a creative, personal, loving touch on the everyday aspects of your relationship. You can strengthen or stabilize love during the Taurus Moon by fixing a favorite dinner, massaging tired shoulders, or otherwise providing basic needs in a tender, loving way. Our senses seem more sensitive during the time of Taurus Moon, so all the little everyday physical comforts and joys take on a more meaningful role on your love boat.

Taurus Moon isn't a propitious time to try to change your lover's mind about anything important, but you can probably come to an agreement on practical matters. For Capricorns, you may spot the person of your dreams on a Taurus Moon day. Perhaps you will interview this person for a job in your company and quietly fall in love behind your poker face as you discuss their resume and job description.

A shrewd Scorpio may find that "making it permanent" is the subject under a Taurus Moon, and if you've been trying to have your cake and eat it too, romance-wise, the Moon may be in Taurus when you finally decide to settle down and focus on that solid, permanent relationship.

The New Moon in Taurus each spring is the perfect time for couples to set basic, long-term material goals. This is a time of comfortable togetherness. Marrieds find that their love boat is kept bobbing happily by the simple security of having someone to come home to and depend on, and we don't mind if our mate isn't perfect. Singles are not looking for excitement, but for someone they can relax and enjoy themselves with. It's interesting that the placid, patient, Venus-ruled Taurus Sun has as its partnership sign deep, seething, power-seeking Scorpio. When the Taurus Sun is opposed by the Full Scorpio Moon, two weeks after the stabilizing Taurus New Moon, relationships for all signs are often tested in the areas of trust, fidelity, and deep values. No amount of Moon-mood savvy can save a relationship that is not innately compatible to begin with.

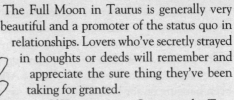

The Full Moon in Taurus is generally very beautiful and a promoter of the status quo in relationships. Lovers who've secretly strayed in thoughts or deeds will remember and appreciate the sure thing they've been taking for granted.

If Taurus is your Sun sign, the Taurus Moon strengthens and sensitizes you. Use this Moon every month to introduce yourself to someone you want to impress, to make resolutions designed to improve your self-image and self-esteem, and to enlarge your horizon of personal goals.

Moon in Gemini

The Gemini Moon is usually plenty of fun, and it's a terrific time to have a getaway together, even if it's just an evening jaunt to a restaurant. Sometimes we become more communicative under a Gemini Moon, but we might also feel edgy and oversensitive about criticism.

Under Gemini Moons, you may be full of curiosity about your lover's life during the hours you're away from each other, but refrain from getting too nosy. We all require lots of freedom at this time, although we thoroughly enjoy chats and companionship with those with whom we feel we can be ourselves. A Gemini Moon sharpens our sense of humor, and you can get through to your lover more easily with a lighthearted, wittily pointed remark than with a lecture.

The New and Full Moons while the Sun is in Gemini (late May and June) often find lovers too busy to take time to be alone. Schedule a getaway together at the New Moon time, if you can. It's a great influence under which to have a talk about any little thing that the two of you need to catch up on and to make plans for the future.

The Full Moon in Gemini calls for letting things happen spontaneously. Whatever you have planned for "just the two of you" is very likely to be interrupted. Friendship may turn to romance under this Moon, and vice versa. By setting your lover free during a Gemini Moon period, or by going along with his or her program, the bonds of confidence are strengthened, and you remind your loved one of how much fun it is to be with you.

Aquarians, Gemini Moon of any month is the time to strike up a first conversation, ask for a first date, or take a day off for sheer, carefree, loving fun with your loved one. You're never bored under this Moon, and visiting new places together should be particularly delightful, whether you find a new book store or take a little trip.

Sagittarians can make lots of points with a partner by practicing listening skills during any Gemini Moon time. What are some of your love's most endearing qualities? Make a point of mentioning how proud you are of them!

Gemini Sun sign natives will enjoy running errands for their lovers during this Moon, or picking up an amusing card or little gift while they're buzzing about on their daily rounds. Later, plan to talk a new lover into playing what you want to play, because while the Moon is in your sign each month, we all enjoy your imaginative charm and wit and find it easy to succumb to your many whims.

Moon in Cancer

The Moon rules watery Cancer, and as Moon children know all too well, emotions run very close to the surface when the Moon comes home for a visit. We all need lots of reassurance and coddling during a Cancer Moon, but that's not necessarily a bad thing, is it? It gives us an excuse to cuddle and express sentiments that we all need to share but may sometimes feel silly expressing or asking for. If your love is a reserved Virgo or a stoic Scorpio who may normally seem uncomfortable with that mushy stuff, Cancer Moon is your (and their) big chance!

There's no better time than Cancer Moon for showing off your homemaking skills to someone about whom you're serious. Family matters may come forward in your relationship, and it's a wonderful time, usually, to meet the family of your intended, or to introduce your family to him/her.

Capricorns can take time off from keeping up a dignified front and retreat behind closed doors to enrich and refresh long-term relationships. This Moon falls in Capricorn's partnership sector, so if your partner is Capricorn you can draw closer and have warm, intimate times during these days.

Sun sign Pisces, the Cancer Moon is in your romantic sector. Your fancy is very likely to be struck at this time. It is frequently the time when Pisceans, noted for their indecision in emotional matters, may be talked into commitment.

The whole world celebrates the nurturing spirit at the New Moon in Cancer in late June or early July, and it favors (and promotes!) proposals of marriage, conceptions, weddings, honeymoons, and family vacations, as well as family reunions and gatherings at home.

A Full Moon in Cancer, each year while the Sun is in Capricorn, is a powerful catalyst for commitment, especially among Capricorns. For all of us, the week of this Moon is highly emotional, and many couples can gain greatly from marriage counseling at this time. The Pisceans must try to enjoy the rich creative potential of this Moon without losing their perspective in love affairs.

When the Moon is in Cancer, Sun sign Cancerians do well to remember that the world around them is more emotionally sensitive than usual. You may be giving advice in love matters to dear ones during Cancer Moons, and this is good, because the less you allow yourself to worry and doubt the security of your own relationship, the better. Realize that this is a time of personal power for you and be ready to receive the needs of others, rather than reaching out for help with your own.

Moon in Leo

Leo Moons are for celebrating romance for its own sweet sake. Lovers are inspired by artistic experiences and entertaining events of all kinds. You may use such a Moon-supported activity to put ideas into the head of someone you'd like to have a deep relationship with.

Light-hearted romances, flirtations first dates, and rekindling the flames in your long-time relationship are all favored. All you need to keep your love boat bobbing contentedly in Leo Moon time is an activity that you both enjoy, and the feeling of romantic excitement will follow. Go ahead and wear something colorful—we all respond to a little dramatic touch at this time. If you're a reserved Virgo or Capricorn, ask a Leo pal to lend you something from their attention-getting wardrobe.

Leo Suns are full of themselves when their Moon time comes. Use one of your well-timed entrances to make a spectacular impression on a love prospect at this time. An air of mystery augments your personal power enormously at this time. If your love is a Leo Sun, make plenty of room for them at center stage when the Moon enters Leo; wait a few days to ask for a starring role for yourself.

Aries Sun signs wax particularly ardent with a Leo Moon firing up their ever-ready romance sector. Be oh-so careful that you don't lead some sincere heart astray at this time, magnetic Aries. You know how quickly you may fall passionately and utterly in and out of love; have mercy on those more constant hearts who take you at your word.

Aquarians need their mates and lovers at Leo Moon time, and that's good, because Aquarians sometimes neglect their intimate lives until this need arises. Express your need in sweet, romantic ways; just make it up as you go along and go with it—innovation is your strong point!

A New Leo Moon comes in late summer and is deliciously sexy. Use your imagination to please yourselves at this time, lovers. First love is often born at this time; it's a time to caution teens that the fervor of first love can carry consequences.

The Full Leo Moon falls during the Sun's transit of Aquarius, and it sends a vibration reminiscent of the full-strength summer Sun through the cold winter week in which it occurs. All Full Moons have a volatile quality, but this one usually brings vitality, and is more likely to provide a boost of confidence that helps us to handle problems. If the Full Moon rocks your love boat, as any Full Moon may, the most effective use of this energy is to remind yourself and your loved one of the original delight that you found in each other's true selves. Build your lover's ego with extravagant compliments that emphasize true strengths and talents.

Moon in Virgo

When the Moon is in the Virgo position, practical matters come forward, so you may assume that your lover, no matter what the Sun sign, is thinking about work, health, and the maintenance of the household. This love boat in ship shape is the happiest one on the water. It promotes a feeling of security and emotional harmony simply by demonstrating level headedness and thoughtful caring.

A Virgo Moon sharpens our vision and our awareness of "little things." We all notice more detail in our surroundings. This works nicely when putting finishing touches on a job of skill, such as balancing the checkbook or tidying the files, but when we begin to "nitpick" about the little things we see out of place, we can upset the love boat. Stress the usefulness of the sharpened critical faculty that Virgo Moon brings, and try to wait a few days, until the Moon is in diplomatic Libra, before entering a discussion with your lover about the haircut they still haven't bothered to get. This advice goes double for Sun sign Virgos.

Romances that begin under Virgo Moon are often between customers and service people. You may meet a charming nurse at the doctor's office, or fall for the mechanic who fixes your car. For heaven's sake, schedule checkups and repairs when the new Moon in Virgo occurs, just in case some skilled professional is the right one for you!

Sun sign Virgos can use the Virgo Moon to make a confident overture in the direction of a new love. This is sometimes rather a shy group, whose perfectionism often gives them a sense of never quite making the grade, although to the rest us Virgo may seem dauntingly perfect. When the Moon is with them, Virgo can stop fretting over whether they look good enough or sound interesting enough and simply extend a lunch invitation to someone they're interested in.

The new Moon in Virgo, early in the fall, is when shy lovers and school valedictorians find romance. Use this Moon for making a list of ways you can improve your own half of your relationship. How can you be more giving? More considerate? More supportive?

For Taurus, the Virgo Moon is an important romantic moment. You have been admiring a self-effacing but highly conscientious co-worker for months—Virgo Moon is the moment to show interest and ask for a first date. For Pisceans, a Virgo Moon may help you end vacillation about getting married, or it may prompt you to return to the stable relationship that you've been neglecting!

A Full Virgo Moon during the Sun's sojourn in Pisces, just as winter begins to give way to spring, is usually a quieter event than other Full Moons. It is a marvelous time to take stock of affairs on your love boat, make a list together of the changes you both agree are needed, and make up a budget and schedule for getting them underway.

Moon in Libra

Moon in Libra is made for lovers! Libra is the sign of partnership, of one-to-one harmony, and, as a bonus, of beauty. Many couples can safely air differences under the Libra Moon, as this is the sign of fair play and diplomacy. However, the negative manifestation of this Moon may sometimes be that smooth talking lovers put a "snow job" over on their mate.

You can use this Moon to present your case to a lover who has opposed you on an issue that's important to you. If you are already harmonious in your relationship, this Moon is delicious for taking some time to purely enjoy each other. You can socialize with the crowd successfully now, but for most of us the real fulfillment of Libra Moon is special time with just the two of you. The New Moon in Libra comes when the leaves are turning in autumn. Marriage proposals and ceremonies, honeymoon voyages and anniversary celebrations, are all greatly favored. Do a little something special to revive the romantic side of things with your long-time love. Your partner won't think it's corny if you light candles at dinner!

Gemini is even more silver-tongued and charming than usual under Libra Moons, but sometimes a normally un-catchable Gems will allow themselves to be talked to the altar, forgetting for the duration of the Moon their own innate love of fickleness and freedom.

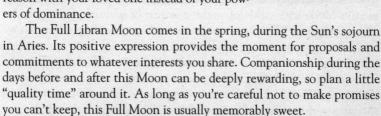

Aries Sun signs are particularly amenable under Libra Moon influence. As an Aries, you very wisely may use this Moon to practice listening skills and to exercise your excellent powers of reason with your loved one instead of your powers of dominance.

The Full Libran Moon comes in the spring, during the Sun's sojourn in Aries. Its positive expression provides the moment for proposals and commitments to whatever interests you share. Companionship during the days before and after this Moon can be deeply rewarding, so plan a little "quality time" around it. As long as you're careful not to make promises you can't keep, this Full Moon is usually memorably sweet.

Many June weddings are the aftermath of an April Full Moon in Libra, when lovers are reminded of the potential for complete oneness that is inherent in the concept of marriage. Use this Moon to pop the question or to renew understanding in an existing relationship.

Sun sign Librans glow with even more fascinatingly elusive grace than usual when the Moon doubles his or her Sun power. Your reserves of wile are considerable, Libra. Exercise your romantic strategy with all the subtlety and finesse at your command or begin a partnership that will lead you where you want to go. This is the time to link up with the partner who can put you on the fast track to goals.

Moon in Scorpio

Scorpio Moons are unmistakable. The twinkle of Libra gives way to a more intense, often yellowish, glow, sometimes accompanied by scary weather or serious news events that capture the public attention. In our personal lives, too, a Scorpio Moon brings up emotional issues that run deep within us. Your relationship may be relatively recent, but the emotional issues that surface may come from the deep and distant past of childhood and formative love experiences.

Often, behavior on your lover's part that has puzzled you becomes clearly understandable in Scorpio moonlight. Insight is one of the great benefits available during this period. Bear in mind that some of the emotions triggered by Scorpio Moon may be fears and insecurities that can pollute your insight with unfounded suspicions. Let an insight stand the test of time before feeling sure that you've seen the truth.

If you're a well-adjusted Sun sign Scorpio, you are a winner when the Moon is on your side. This planet augments your magnetism and your personal power casts a potent spell. There is nearly always someone in their sphere that a Scorpio would like to exercise influence over—make your move when the Moon is with you.

When it is New in the autumn, the Scorpio Moon is a birthday in the truest sense for all of us. Scorpio is the sign that governs conception, so use this Moon for meditation and the setting of spiritual goals, individually and together. This Moon urges surrender to the deep urges that we may have been suppressing.

Cancerians are romantically possessed when the Moon is in Scorpio. If you're currently flirting with a Cancerian, there's no better time to get really close. The object of Cancer's affections becomes the center of their thoughts at this time, and romance is creative motivation for them.

Taureans, usually so level-headed, can be emotionally vulnerable at the time of Scorpio Moon. If your Taurean has been neglecting you for late hours of work, Scorpio Moon is the time that they can hear your protests. Make your needs known gently in a soft voice with lots of touching, if possible, and Taurus will drop into your lap like a ripe fruit!

The Full Scorpio Moon, buried deceptively like a land mine in the middle of fragrant, balmy spring days, is a famous trigger of world events, as well as local and personal upheaval. It merely brings to fulfillment what we have designed with our intentions and attitudes. This Moon demonstrates to us that our thoughts, feelings, and, daily choices are the building blocks—or stumbling blocks—of our lives and relationships. As a vehicle for understanding karmic patterns, it is unique.

Moon in Sagittarius

When a Sagittarius Moon takes over, the whole world begins to buzz. It's another moment for freedom lovers, with lots of enthusiastic energy promoting a feeling of self-reliance and perhaps a little selfishness. Lovers who enjoy travel, learning, good conversation, and gatherings of all sorts feel the closeness of understanding under this Moon. Possessive members of all signs, however, may feel uncomfortable with the independent air that this Moon gives their mate or lover. Don't fight it, dear Cancerian, Leo, Taurean, or Piscean; remember, your loved one will be hanging around home when the Moon enters Capricorn in a few days.

A New Moon in Sag is the time for lovers to sign up for a class together, join a church or study group of any kind, or to start a workout program together. You're more likely to stick with it if you start on this day, as long as you're both really interested. Make a resolution at Sag New Moon time to develop the friendship in your intimate relationship. Sagittarian Moons remind us that over-dependence on another person for a feeling of self-worth is cheating the spiritual system!

For a Sun-sign Sag, the always-abundant energy surges in Sag Moonlight. If emotional difficulties have been nagging you, you may be tempted to overindulge in comfort food or drink. Instead, indulge in a good physical workout or one of those spur-of-the-moment trips that you enjoy so much.

Leos are in their romantic element under a Sag Moon. In this Moon time, Leo stalks the quarry. Single Leos take the lead in taking an acquaintance one step further or dress to kill and go hunting at a social spot. Married Leos feel sociable and will expect to be allowed to flirt at a party unopposed, purely for fun and vanity.

The Full Sagittarian Moon during the Gemini Sun's sojourn enhances the vibrations of Jupiter, and we are usually inclined to feel optimistic at this time, though we may become restless with routine and begin to plan a nice, long trip. Is it a coincidence that this Full Moon kicks off vacation season in many parts of the world? Conversely, professional colleagues or neighbors or classmates may expand their involvement to include romance.

If the love boat hits a stormy patch during the Full Moon in Sagittarius, it is usually best not to try to talk it out right then and there. Suggest a "time out" from talk, affirm your faith in the relationship to the heavens, and busy yourself with whatever little independent tasks will take your mind off of emotional matters.

Moon in Capricorn

Capricorn is a clear, cool Moon. It's a matter-of-fact sort of Moon, not renowned for its romance, but it certainly is a period when your love boat can float contentedly on its emotional sea if you and your lover's goals and direction in life are the same. If there are basic differences in your values or ambitions, Capricorn Moon may be the time that these fundamental

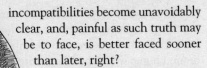

incompatibilities become unavoidably clear, and, painful as such truth may be to face, is better faced sooner than later, right?

Capricorn Moon usually provides a good emotional climate for business, but the rock-solid elements of the home-and-family structure are also emphasized. If the foundation of your relationship is strong, this will be a time of progress and the satisfaction that comes from shared goals. If all isn't what it should be, you'll feel closed in, curtailed, and restricted. The resulting anger and frustration may cause this Moon period to bring depression for some. If you find you're inclined to look on the gloomy side of life during this Moon, try not to make any permanent relationship decisions at this time, but do take your moodiness as a warning that your needs are not being met.

The Capricorn New Moon comes in the middle of the holiday season each year, and therefore accompanies family doings and emphasizes our traditions and family ways. Sometimes the "holiday blues" may visit at this time, because Saturn, Capricorn's ruler, may remind us of areas of our lives in which we feel we don't measure up. Although we tend to be too hard on ourselves at this Moon, it is very useful for clarifying what's truly important to us.

Enjoyable times for Virgo accompany this Moon. Virgo's sense of order is creatively activated, and they become the most handy and useful of mates, proving that you can't overestimate the power of becoming indispensable in your lover's life! Often, single Virgo will meet someone during this Moon period who finally measures up to their perfectionist standards.

Cancer is inspired to secure the relationship (a relationship can never be secure enough for Cancer) by making the home more comfy and inviting, usually filling it with delicious cooking smells. Single Cancerians sometimes become fearful at Capricorn Moon that they will never have the relationship they need. Please, Moonchild, try to remember not to take your emotions too seriously if the chilly Capricorn Moon feeds your longings and dampens your hopes. It's only a Moon mood you're passing through, and you are used to those!

Capricorn Sun sign natives are in their element when the Moon doubles their confidence, which is not always as strong as they pretend. In the spirit of their Saturn ruler, Caps are serious about life. That doesn't mean they aren't having a good time. They like to work that hard. When you do get home, Cap, remember to point out to your loved one just how important, how very vital, their contribution to your life is. If your love is a Cap, keep in mind that you are at the center of their existence, no matter how it appears. Remember that they're shy; they often don't know how to express how much a strong relationship and home life mean to them. Make tender moves when the Moon is here.

The Full Moon in Capricon comes in the middle of summer, and though it may bring some over-romantic dreams to an end, the reality we are left with is where the real love and fulfillment lie. What matters most becomes clear at this time. Couples who are in it for the long-term will make solid plans at this time. Those who aren't really meant for happiness with each other will be able to release and move on to better prospects.

Moon in Aquarius

An Aquarian Moon may have little effect on your love life, or it may affect it strongly. That's the way Aquarian influence works—unpredictably. Plans you've made may be changed suddenly, or spur-of-the-moment plans, including a date with someone you didn't even know was interested, may pop up. An old friend may turn into a love prospect quite unexpectedly. A series of unusual events may result in your meeting the right one completely by "accident."

Someone who calls late deserves to be heard when the Moon is in Aquarius. It's good to keep a flexible frame of mind regarding emotional matters when the Moon is here. Your love may come up with a new idea, and so may you. You may see a routine relationship in a whole new light under Aquarian Moon influence. It is another period when independence is emphasized. For lovers who've developed an imbalance of dominant/subordinate roles, it may be the moment when the apple cart is upset.

For Librans, colleagues and friends confess their romantic interest in you when the Moon is in Aquarius. Your wish to join forces romantically with someone who can also help you realize a dream or ambition crystallizes, and may become real, under this Moon.

The Aquarian Moon reminds Leos of their great need for the regard of the one they love. A Leo needs lots of reassurance when the Moon is in Aquarius, and if they've taken a lover for granted, this Moon time will

bring a comeuppance, as the cherished one shows a spirit of independence—perhaps not being available when Leo snaps fingers.

Aquarians have a powerful moment at this time—your charms are always bewitching, but the Moon in Aquarius turns you into a wizard! Your mate may or may not enjoy the extra charisma, however, because you may feel like enjoying the rapt attention of new friends under this Moon.

A new Aquarian Moon spawns innovative thinking, creative problem-solving, and new group associations. If your loved one comes home with a crazy new notion, enjoy it. If someone new comes into your romantic life around this time, count on a very interesting relationship for as long as it lasts.

Important changes for all of us take place under the Full Aquarian Moon. Your love boat requires a skilled hand at the helm, because the weather may change quite without warning, and then that change may change into another condition altogether. It is a catalyst for insights and discoveries; surprising truths will help you in surprising ways. Through the early twenty-first century, this Full Moon will be a catalyst for world events as well as unexpected developments in our personal lives.

Moon in Pisces

A Pisces Moon is a powerful emotional time, although it is subtle. Just when you think you're being objective about a relationship, when you think you've got it all under control, a little doubt, a little uncertain moment, may find its way in and leave a nagging emotional hangover the next morning.

This capturing of your deep psyche's attention has a beautifully positive side as well. It's all because of Neptune, the ruler of Pisces, whose domain is that shifting sea where your love boat sails. You can explore areas of physical and emotional love during this Moon that neither of you ever thought of before. This Moon stimulates the emotional imagination, and it's important to keep this in mind. The next time you find yourself wondering whether you've got something to worry about in a relationship, whether something's going on behind your back, check the Moon position before you jump to conclusions. Remember, we can make things up out of our own fearful thinking when Pisces holds the Moon.

Scorpio Sun signs are drawn by their deepest motivations in this Moon. Scorpio is very controlled, but they are entirely at home in the dark depths of the Piscean sea; Scorpio can be every bit as subtle in a much more forceful way. The attraction of opposites is what it's all about here, and there's no sexier combination than the overpowering Scorpio with the apparently passive Pisces. Mysteries of the deep, indeed!

Virgo can become a little obsessive when the Moon is in Pisces. Virgo loves logic and precision, and Pisces Moon is vague by definition. The never-ending search for perfection that creates such superb craftspersons and artists among those with Virgo birthdays meets the ultimate challenge in nebulous Pisces Moon time. These opposite signs meet wherever there is giving and sacrifice required, however, so Virgo can spend this time serving, helping, and healing the object of your affection.

Pisces Sun signs are sometimes a little undone during this Moon, as the siren song of the inner spirit makes focus foggy and concentration impossible. Musical interludes, poetic jottings and treasure-hunting at the thrift store are all good uses of this Moon energy. One more thing: your lover's motivations are as clear as glass at this time; you cannot be fooled, unless you are desperately trying to avoid seeing an unpleasant truth. Have faith and face your own insights unafraid; you may find out you're doing better than you thought.

A New Moon in Pisces marks the beginning of the end of winter. The ambiguity of this Moon is expressed in the March weather, which is famous for being changeable. Lovers will feel sentimental. Put on your favorite songs, write each other poetry, plan to sleep late and have breakfast in bed, if possible, near this time. Have a pencil and paper nearby while you sleep, because dreams may bring valuable clues to your personal love secrets.

The Full Pisces Moon in early fall is called the Harvest Moon, and there are often important fulfillments associated with this Moon. What you have sown is reaped. Lovers frequently take a long look at the give-and-take patterns in their relationships. Occasionally, this Full Moon may mark an occasion when one partner is called upon to make a great "sacrifice" for the other—perhaps being the caregiver during a health crisis, or taking on an extra load of responsibility during job or career transition.

May your love boat always sail smoothly!

Your Lunar Soul Mate

By Alice DeVille

Your astrological chart is a wondrous blueprint of your plans for this lifetime. The array of planets and their location in various houses of the chart (there are twelve signs and twelve houses, or departments of life) show evidence of the quests you plan to undertake this time around. Each degree of a planet, point, or house cusp contains a soul code that speaks to the experiences you are planning, how you expect to do them, why you might be interested, who may be part of your journey, and the end result.

Since every human being is unique, your astrological chart is not going to be duplicated in the universe for thousands of years—not until the planets line up in the same array as they were on your day of birth. If you have not had an astrology chart constructed, you may want to consult an astrologer or order a natal chart from Llewellyn's Computerized Astrological Services (see coupon in the back of this book).

The personal planets (Sun, Moon, Mercury, Venus, and Mars) spell out your fundamental emotional response pattern to the people you encounter. Mercury describes how you communicate your feelings to others; Venus, your love qualities and romantic style; and Mars, your passion and energy; but the Sun, Moon, and Ascendant carry greater weight in determining the true nature of your emotions. The Sun sign represents your essence, dominant traits, zest for life, and emotional triggers. If you have other planets in the same sign as your Sun, these qualities increase in importance.

Your Ascendant or Rising sign (sign and degree on the cusp of your first house that are determined by your time of birth) carries the signature of your personal style and approach to life, and how others see you. Consider it an expression of attraction because people who are drawn to you probably have planets in good aspect to your Ascendant and will be enamored of your looks, personality, and mannerisms. The Ascendant's opposite house, the seventh house, strongly relates to the type of people you attract as partners. The planet that rules the Seventh House is significant because it often characterizes the behavior or a mini profile of your potential partners.

If you long to plumb the very depth of your emotions and the memory of all that you hold dear, look to the Moon. Your Moon's sign conveys your feelings and your innate need to be understood. Intuitions about people and the workings of your subconscious mind surface when you invoke your Moon's power. You have locked away your hurts, anxieties, and sensitivities and need to examine them to grow emotionally. If you are true to your Moon sign and have high self-esteem, you will have done some serious soul searching to first understand yourself and your needs. When you feel comfortable and love who you are, you'll be ready to include a life partner.

If relationships have been a struggle and you find yourself making excuses for your core beliefs, you may be drawing partners whose planets are in provocative aspect to your own. When your primary complaint is that your partner doesn't seem to understand you, your Moon signs may not be compatible. This condition is true for all types of partnerships. You may have to do a relationship inventory and assess the merits of staying in them. Don't let fears about being out in the cold haunt you. If you know it is time to close a door, let go quietly. Losing yourself in stressful, abusive, or unfulfilling relationships suggests you are not taking accountability for your life. You owe it to yourself to resonate to your Moon's inner drive. When you are drawn toward more harmonious directions, new doors open.

The Moon is a powerful love link that may hold clues about your karmic past and the people you would like to draw into your life this time around. In a woman's chart, the Moon's aspects from her partner's planets need to be harmonious to draw out her feminine side and support the expression of her emotions. If the partner's Sun is compatible, the chances of understanding one another increase. A man needs a partner whose planets are complements to his Sun and give him latitude to express himself. Both men and women need positive connections with their Moons, otherwise they may be unable to show their true feelings in the other's presence.

Suppression of innermost feelings is at the core of relationship problems. Your romantic souls want to know you are understood and that you provide a nurturing environment for your partners. When the bonds you have with another are straining to find equilibrium, you start questioning the durability and depth of the partnership. A feeling of uncertainty often leads to closer examination of your life purpose and a trip to your astrologer.

As an astrologer who specializes in relationship dynamics, I see a significant number of clients who are looking for the perfect mate or analyzing current relationships. I find that individuals want to know whether they have known partners in previous incarnations, why they came together this time, whether this partnership is going to last, and what they are supposed to do to keep love alive. Most want to know whether they have found their soul mate or are likely to in the near future. If they have met someone who seems compatible, they want to examine individual beliefs and philosophies, see where ideas merge unobtrusively, and explore the depths of the emotional and physical responses. On the other hand, individuals in combative relationships convey angst that they have not met their soul mates, for surely they would not have chosen this program of clashing wills.

I start by comparing clients' charts to look at the dynamics and patterns between the two parties or by examining the questioner's chart for the type of partner that is likely to be sought. Questions pour from the seekers' hearts. Should I date this person? What's in it for the two of us? Do we have compatible chart connections? Why don't we get along? Is karma a factor in why we came together? Am I destined to a life without a meaningful relationship? Why are we on such a rocky road now when things were so good in the beginning? Almost without exception, clients express an interest in the law of magnetic attraction—the soul mate encounter.

Perhaps you don't fully understand all the mysteries of life—few of us do—yet love is one area that begins with you and grows unconditionally when you learn to give of yourself. When you cherish and embrace all that you stand for, it is easy to attract a mate who is at ease with him or herself. If you're down on yourself, you are more likely to pair up with another who carries the baggage of the disenchanted. You may not be listening to the message of your Moon. At any rate, your Moon is a strong indicator of the path your soul is taking in this lifetime and of the people you are drawing toward you to fulfill your spiritual mission.

I'm surprised that individuals feel it is beyond their control to manifest a soul mate relationship along with other goals. You use positive thoughts and actions to plant seeds that nurture the ideal career to express your talents and reward you with prosperity that is far beyond the material. When you likewise heed the inner knower, you are able to direct your energy toward a relationship that resonates on all levels: physical, mental, emotional, and spiritual. You are sensing the higher planes of love that you have known in past lives reflected by your natal Moon. You answer the wake-up call. People you meet seem more attuned to your purpose. You find them friendlier, easier to talk to, and somewhat familiar. Impressions from the past are about to surface. Symbol-laden dreams punctuate your sleep patterns and coincidences accelerate. Are you ready to make the connection?

Partners Across Time

Soul mates are spiritual partners whose
love is tied to a universal response or
pure form of love. The very core of your
soul carries with it the memory of all
soul mate encounters since the time
that you first descended upon the
Earth plane. Most of you understand
the soul mate relationship to be the
highest potential of an intimate loving relationship. Such a relationship is
possible only to the extent the lovers are

expressing their highest potential as individuals. The souls have reached
a level of balance that allows them to experience the splendor that has
been promised since creation. A soul mate relationship is the expression
of your innermost dream of intimate love and union with another. In the
depth of your consciousness, you and your soul mate have already joined
forces. If this is an incarnation where you will be together in body and
spirit, you and your soul mate are most likely meeting on the causal plane
(the upper area of the mental plane where the soul designs the blueprints
for current and future incarnations). Even if your primary soul mate is not
on the planet, this soul serves as a guide in your life, so you are never
alone. The major purpose of the soul mate connection is to help each other ascend, whether or not both of you are in body in any given lifetime.
God does not look at soul mates as separate entities.

Soul Mate Types

The concept of soul mate usually gives us a picture of happy, embracing
partners in a love relationship. As you will see later in this article, other
facets of the soul mate relationship unfold based on the criteria you choose
for coming back on the Earth plane in a given lifetime—in other words,
what did you come here to do? Although not all astrologers study soul mate
phenomena or support it, clients of the majority of relationship astrologers
express an interest in finding their mate and linking up with the perfect
partner. In my practice, probably eight out of ten clients explore this topic
in depth at some time. When I present soul mate workshops, the lecture
room fills quickly with interested men and women seeking insight into the
search and discovery of their higher selves through the sacred partnership of

the soul mate. Anyone who wants love must first internalize a life wish—it is the magnet for drawing their age-old reunion in this incarnation.

If you are researching information about soul mates, you will find a variety of definitions from experts and authors. You'll discover there are different types of soul mates.

Secondary soul mates are individuals who may be either the opposite sex or of the same sex. These individuals may be part of your soul cluster (group of souls who incarnate together over various lifetimes and come from the same soul). You often marry secondary soul mates and they make very suitable partners when aspects are right; they may also be souls with whom you have karma to complete; they may be blood relatives, friends, or spiritual teachers, or combinations of these descriptions.

Twin flames, also known as twin souls or primary soul mates, can be the spiritual and often physical partner who knows the very essence of your soul. When you first incarnated on the Earth plane, you came from the same atom and are able to recognize one another, on some level, across time. Although your goal is to grow spiritually, you and your twin flame do make karma with each other in various embodiments, and that karma has to be balanced when you find each other again. Sometimes couples who seem to bicker, battle, and squabble more than most planetary pairs are twin flames in search of balance. If you recognize yourself as one of these, your search for spirit must become the end result.

What About Age Differences?

Although their souls are the same age, sometimes soul mates have a significant age difference in body that may affect their relationship in a given lifetime. You don't necessarily link up physically with your soul mate, especially primary, in each incarnation, yet you are always in touch. You and your primary soul mate may decide not to marry or pair as lovers. Here are some of the reasons soul mates may not reincarnate in the primary soul mate role:

- ·☾ One of the partners has chosen other issues to work on in this particular incarnation.
- ·☾ One partner is working on necessary karma with others before reuniting with the twin flame, who may be significantly more advanced spiritually.
- ·☾ One of the twin flames chooses the parent, child, friend, or relative relationship to help the other twin progress spiritually.

- ☽ Circumstances prohibit a marriage between the two because one of the flames is significantly younger or older than the other.

- ☽ The twin flame may be the soul's teacher and the purpose of meeting in this particular lifetime is to fill the other partner with spiritual learning. One of the partners may have chosen a less evolved path for several lifetimes. The errant twin flame chooses what the teacher flame has to offer and both of them advance in their spiritual ascension through the infusion of transformational love.

When Soul Mates Connect

Several scenarios describe the circumstances under which soul mates connect in love relationships in a given lifetime. Remember, they have chosen the road taken. Here are a few examples.

Twin flames make detours in other relationships before eventually finding each other. The souls may have made other commitments with destiny before their Moons' powerful love links matured to the level of recognition. Individuals may know their soul mates for years without recognizing them in that role. All of a sudden the relationship turns romantic and the partners discover the bliss of transformational love, delighted to find that someone they already know is the love of their life. This situation may also occur with married couples who have mixed feelings about the strength of the union until spiritual awakenings take the partners to new levels of understanding.

The twin flame marries the teacher who may not have much time remaining on the planet, even though age differences may not be that significant. Their time together is nurturing, yet higher callings beckon. The lingering flame, inspired by the connection, carries out the spiritual essence of the work. Here the Moons are likely to be compatible, with understanding and philosophical attunement as the bonding agent.

Despite considerable age differences, a marriage takes place, yet the partners have a limited number of years together. The Moon and other planets are creating the condition to reunite, however briefly. The partners connect, the tension is high, the Moons are awry, yet the flames recognize they are partners for all time. Mars and Venus take the center stage in the attraction game. The Moon may create tension.

The twin souls are clones. They intuit without words what is going on and mutually feel the slightest energy shift. These souls are working on the same issues and may not be objective in making recommendations for change. The Moons reflect powerful understanding and empathy and key planetary conjunctions are likely. Astrological indicators are strong in both charts that twin souls will connect. Those Moons are cooking!

If one of the flames is functioning as an enlightened soul and the other as a dormant personality (spiritual growth is at a different frequency level), a common juncture occurs between them only through the awakened flame. In other words, the soul-infused entity can supply material to the "sleeper" to accelerate spiritual growth, but that twin flame's soul will not have the capacity in one lifetime to absorb all that the enlightened one has to offer. In future incarnations, the soul seeking infusion may choose to continue the growth cycle. On the other hand, the enlightened being has the capacity to absorb and understand all that the emerging soul has to offer. The Moons are harmoniously aspected—one has the patience and skill to release the knowledge when the partner is ready, while the other has the determination to absorb and the insight to trust that this teacher/soul mate is part of the divine plan.

The bells ring, the whistles blow, rockets go off, and you feel like you are going to the Moon in sheer delight when you meet this fascinating creature who could be your soul mate. All conditions seem compatible starting with the natal chart: harmony between the Suns and Moons, compatible Ascendants (sometimes one's Ascendant is the other's Seventh House of partners, indicating that you recognize something of your shadow self and your potential partner's qualities). Mars aspects show biorhythmic connections, and Venus inspires romance and courtship. Transits (current movement of the planets in the heavens) activate natal planets in each chart that signify the possibility of romance. Progressed planets (the forward movement of your natal planets based on your age, with one ephemeris day equaling one year of life) form aspects that show love or marriage or both are imminent. Each party's chart needs analysis to determine the staying power of the new directions.

If this person is truly your primary soul mate, the level of intimacy you already share will rekindle in record time. This soul knows your very essence—you resonate on all chakra levels (seven main vortexes of concentrated etheric energy located at the root, spleen, solar plexus, heart, throat, mid point of forehead between the brows, and the crown of the head). This soul is the one who remembers how you like to be held, hugged, kissed, and touched. Your two souls blend magnificently in an unrestricted flow of passion, understanding, feeling, mental attunement, compassion, and love, and become inseparable companions in record time because you know so much about each other's needs.

Soul mates may marry each other, but the marriage does not last and isn't meant to. Your astrological charts contain enough compatible aspects to draw you into the relationship, but the dynamics can't be too perfect this time around or you won't want to let go when the experience cycle ends. Some experts in this field believe that primary soul mates, once found, never leave each other because the energy is so powerful and the longing so great. Personally, I have seen evidence to the contrary.

For a while, each of you may seem able to express your emotions and have your needs met in sync with the energy of your Moons. You and your partner may either stage a soul reunion to satisfy karmic debts incurred during previous lifetimes or to experience avenues of growth based on special conditions that are set up before you incarnate. In "limited duration" unions, clues start appearing when it is time to move on and complete the relationship. In the ideal state, both partners know it and release each other in love. More often, one of the partners is less eager to let go and resists the evidence that unfolds. If the Moons are the inharmonious points of contact, the reticent partner may complain about insensitivity or the proverbial lack of understanding on the other's part. The outer planets (Jupiter, Saturn, Uranus, Neptune, Pluto) may be colluding with natal planets to upset "coasting" patterns. When you ignore the signs, the impact can affect your health, your finances, and your friendships. Everything seems to fall apart at once. Remember you came here to advance and need to connect with other souls who are part of your blueprint.

Honoring Commitments

As you grow in spiritual awareness, you may recognize that you're not in union with your primary soul mate. An often-asked question is "What happens if I am in a relationship and I have the profound experience of meeting my soul mate?" Surely the benevolent universe knows how much you have longed for this meeting. But if you have some karma on the debit ledger with the person you are now in relationship, you cannot go quietly into the night without accumulating additional debts.

Karma is the accumulation of credits and debits from the ledger of past experiences. Karma may have been instrumental in connecting you with your current partner, and you may still have some loose ends to tie up before you move into a new relationship. If you act prematurely, your life may fall apart. Even when it appears to go smoothly by reuniting you with your soul flame, you may not have done the necessary work to embrace this new relationship with ease. Then you and your twin have new baggage to unpack and another cycle of karma unfolds. By deserting your current partner, you and your flame have involved a third party who is hurting from the shock. The person you believe to be your soul mate may also need help in honoring the commitments of a binding relationship.

At a recent soul mate workshop, a mesmerized participant stated that she had recently met her soul mate and that he was married. She objected to the idea that soul mates don't drop everything and run into each other's arms. The woman asked me if I was saying that she could not have this person and if this was the case, she found it incredulous. I suggested that no one could stop the two parties from getting together if that is what they chose, but they needed to take accountability for any consequences. You complicate the relationship and add years to the cycle of rebirth by plunging into a relationship where another is hurt.

The walking wounded from current commitments are souls with feelings. Side effects mushroom into feelings of rejection, loss of self-esteem, anger, and ultimately revenge that frequently spill over into courtroom battles and generate monetary setbacks. Financial problems often emerge when relationships are out of balance. What could push your life more out of kilter than a demand visit from the karma accountants?

You can't pull in your soul mate just by wishing for one. You have inner work to do on yourself. First you complete all the work you agreed to do with your current mate and bring your soul to a state of readiness through healing. Relationships leave scars. Remember those emotional wounds your Moon brings to the surface? They need to be replaced with self-love so you have a state of wholeness to bring to future partnerships. Give yourself some space between partnerships so you can enjoy your own company and learn who you really are. When you're ready to socialize again, use the guidelines that follow.

Releasing Techniques

1. Create a quiet, meditative environment where you won't be interrupted for at least one hour.

2. If you have had an astrology chart constructed, take a look at it. Locate your natal Moon. Note the degree and minute and the house placement of your Moon. Tune in to the Moon's energy. Do you understand how your Moon helps you sense and reflect not only yours, but others' moods and needs?

3. When you make the decision to find your soul mate, you'll want to purge the remaining anger, negative feelings, misgivings, guilt, and martyr complexes that may be left from other relationships.

4. Check your self-talk. Do you tend to be stuck in the past or future-oriented instead of living in the moment?

5. Make a list of all the things you enjoy and that you would like to manifest in your life.

6. In a separate exercise, perhaps in your journal, list all of the characteristics and qualities you like in a mate. Be sure to ask for a partner who is unencumbered. Visualize yourself being romanced by your dream person. What do you want from your mate?

7. Set meaningful goals for your life and your partnership. Don't be afraid to ask for what you want. Develop affirmations and use visualization techniques to imprint them on your subconscious.

8. Change your routines. Do something new each week. Get off the couch. When invitations come in that you would normally turn down because you are "too tired," accept. You'll be surprised at your surge in energy. No copouts! If you don't get out of the rut you're in, you are probably not serious about wanting to meet new people.

You may not know whether the person you are about to draw into your life is your twin soul or a secondary soul mate. The internal and external work you are doing is vital before you can seriously begin your quest. If you follow these steps and don't meet new or suitable partners, you may have a worthiness block. Go back to the Moon. Is there something that suggests past life karmic patterns are surfacing in this incarnation? The Moon is not rigid—it represents change—so study the natal aspects and look at current planetary transits to see if they are triggering blocks.

Since the soul recognizes when meaningful people are coming into your life, it is possible to block out possibilities and ignore evidence, particularly if previous encounters with the soul flame have been stressful. In cases where individuals have a series of short marriages or relationships with the mate because early death parts them, the soul comes reluctantly into the encounter fearing the old abandonment pattern. If you are wondering what to look for when your soul mate is near, here are a few indicators.

- ☽ You meet a new person and it is love at first sight. Individuals report a feeling of intense joy and love. The sky lights up; the room they are in lights up; they know when they see the person across a crowded room that destiny has stepped in; some see images and symbols.

- ☽ You meet a new person and feel you have been together before; some say the newcomer's eyes or mannerisms seem familiar.

- ☽ Dreams indicate someone is coming into your life. The person you meet matches your picture of what you want in a relationship and has the qualities you have been dreaming about.

- ☽ Sometimes you have intuitive flashes and see parts of the person's face or body as a clue. When you meet the individual, you are able to understand the foreshadowing information.

- ☽ The new person you meet seems to understand you completely and you are not a bit self-conscious.

- ☽ You experience a destiny-making moment and sense this person is going to be a major force in your life in the years ahead.

- ☽ You get tongue-tied from receiving the force of the soul mate's energy and can't figure out why you are so unbalanced. Once you do, you feel empowered to explore the new relationship.

- ☽ Your soul mate reads your mind and acts on what you are thinking without a word from you, and you love it!

- ☽ You sense that some greater force is directing you to bring you what you truly want.

- ☽ You can honestly say, "My life changed in a day."

Things happen fast! To the aisle! Although many of these indicators are present, and the person you meet seems very special, it is not uncommon to think this individual is your soul mate only to have the relationship fall apart. Sometimes you don't know how to assimilate the clues that are in front of you. Or perhaps you or the new person may not be able to handle the energy or frequency shift.

When you are in attunement, you receive messages immediately from the individual and don't need to be anywhere near the person to catch their drift or sense they want to communicate with you. You can't bear to be apart, yet feel at one regardless of physical distance. You want to know everything about this magnificent soul, your other half. Once you have attracted a powerful presence in your life, it is important to check in with your astrologer to examine your chart for connections and for greater clarification of roles and purpose.

Astrological Insight

Your astrology chart tells a lot about the relationships you are likely to encounter in this lifetime. Be sure to have it examined routinely to look at trends in areas of your life for which you need spiritual and psychological guidance. If you meet a new person, have your charts compared for compatibility in body, mind, spirit, and emotion. When you are curious about the timing for your soul mate quest, have your chart examined for a range of dates that are compatible for planning or attending social events. Here are a few pointers for looking at two charts for potential relationships and compatibility:

1. Look at the Ascendant to see if the other has planets that are conjunct (within 10 degrees of the Ascendant's degree).

2. List the degree of the Descendant (Seventh House cusp) which is very sensitive in relationship matters. Look for planets in the natal First, Fifth, and Seventh Houses. What are their rulers (planets that govern the cusp or door to each house) and where are they located?

3. Look for Venus and Mars and where they are placed.

4. Write down the degree and sign of your natal love planets, the Sun, Moon, Venus, and Mars. See if these planets are in compatible signs with each other: Fire signs (Aries, Leo, Sagittarius) with Air signs (Gemini, Libra, Aquarius) or Water signs (Cancer, Scorpio, Pisces) with Earth signs (Taurus, Virgo, Capricorn).

5. How many planets are in the zone of relationships (Fifth through Eighth Houses)?

6. Has an eclipse made the conjunct aspect with any of the love planets, particularly the Moon? Did it occur in either the Fifth or Seventh House? If so, you could be making a love connection.

7. Will the New Moon enter the Fifth or Seventh House of your chart? A new love may enter your life.

Since the Moon represents your desire to be nurtured and express your feelings, let's take a brief look at the needs reflected by the Moon in each of the signs.

Ardent Aries

If you were born with the Moon in this sign, you're a flaming arrow in the passion department and want someone who keeps love and affection on the front burner. A prerequisite for you is a partner who listens when you need to brainstorm and fills your head with compliments when your big deals pay off. You value independent thinking and expect trust and latitude in making routine decisions on your own. "Love me, respect my ego and initiative" are prerequisites for harmony. You can handle a mate who is a little feisty because you like to kiss and make up when the battles are over.

Tantalizing Taurus

Attraction is your game and you don't feel a chase is necessary when pursuing the object of your affection. Once you fall in love, you want to keep your partner for life. Love burns slowly and steadily. Your fondest wish is to be admired for your loyalty, predictability, and good taste. A quiet evening at home means a leisurely soak in the hot tub with candles, aromatherapy, and a romantic CD setting the mood. It's music to your ears to hear your mate say, "I know a soothing backrub is just what you need." You feel balanced with a practical, financially secure partner who understands your need for sharing experiences and checkbooks.

Genial Gemini

The Moon in Gemini's emotional barometer attracts a twin who is witty, talkative, and flexible, and doesn't mind being the last to leave the party. You learn by osmosis and crave rubbing elbows with intelligent, artistic people. The truth is you don't care to spend many weekends at home. When you are not out cruising the neighborhood, you spend your leisure time reading and solving crossword puzzles. A potential partner must understand that the politically correct thing to do to win your hand is to join you in a game of Scrabble every now and then. Once you validate your feelings about the game of love, you endearingly write love letters or poetry to capture your soul flame's heart. "I'm affable, amiable, and aware—and I'm free next weekend."

Captivating Cancer

You Cancer Moons put the "feelers" out to balance emotions. What you pick up with your tenacious little claws may go straight to your heart or into your oven. Moons in Cancer are in love with ovens and the rest of the household. Your measuring spoons hold a pinch of mothering, a dash of adoration, a dollop of protection, and a bushel of love. You desire demonstrative affection in large portions. To keep your nest stable, you need to stock your pantry with the sensitive adoration of your soul mate. A partner who seasons your palate with devotion to your birth family receives your benevolent approval for all eternity. By selecting suitors from a spiritually balanced menu, you taste the tantalizing options that bring you the greatest infusion of soul growth for this lifetime. In sync with your caring Cancer nature you can truly say, "I'm cookin'!"

Love Machine Leo

Leo Moons were born to love in a dramatic, passionate way. Your relationship prerequisite is total commitment. You expect hero worship and prove you can handle the adulation by doing everything perfectly—and the one who loves you says so, several times a day. Although members of your Moon sign detour a lot in your quest for your perfect mate, the experience leads to greater understanding in relationships. You personalize TLC (touching, listening, and caressing) to show your subject that love is forever when you're serious about adoring your mate. Fun, games, and getaways are part of your imperial touch. You understand how visualization helps you manifest what you want in a relationship. Your treasure map includes: a royal seat beside an adoring mate who honors and serves your emotional needs; the crown jewels of enthusiasm, generosity, and affection reinforced daily; and a crested platter filled with joy for living and a sunny personality.

Vigilant Virgo

For years you told the universe you were too busy to find love because everyone you met had to pass your microscope test. You criticize and analyze, yet underneath you really want to find your soul mate. It's just that you Virgo Moons want to make sure the character of your loved one is solid as a rock before you show your emotions this time around. On some level, you think your twin flame needs the kind of reality check only you can provide—a detailed inventory of all past life encounters and where each of you is on the balance wheel. If your mate is unequally yoked this time around, you'll jump at the opportunity to shape him up. Yet in your journey toward spiritual perfection you find that getting everything right is not

so important as getting in touch with deep feelings, compassion, and kii
ness. Once you figure out that it's OK to act on your emotions instead
merely thinking about them, life leads to love and soul-to-soul contact.

Lovable Libra

Libra Moons are here to find balance with partners. You thrive in re
tionships based on diplomacy, compromise, and romance. Since you're
lover of all things beautiful and harmonious, you enjoy socializing ai
have many friends. Before you cement spiritual bonds, you need time
evaluate all the competitors who are vying for your time. Most of the
think you're indecisive when you table commitment decisions. You a
very touchy about their criticism because your spirit craves appreciatio:
adulation, and approval. You're one of the signs that may know your so:
mate for years without recognizing the individual in that role. Many a L
bra Moon draws a partner with a considerable age difference, yet lov
grows unconditionally based on cherished qualities of trust and respec
and ultimately, satisfaction with yourselves.

Scintillating Scorpio

Finding your soul mate is an exercise in regeneration for you, Scorpic
You know what it means to have the karma cleaners come to town. You
hide your true nature under a smoldering facade until you are sure you rec
ognize the flickering essence of your spiritual partner. Since you play ar
intriguing game, you need a sensitive mate who fleshes out your interna
secrets and discovers the truth about feeling, caring, passionate, sensua
you. A water sign partner seems most appropriate for understanding your
sizzling brand of emotional intensity. Venture forward to crack your ancient soul code and experience the cornucopia of blessings released
through the process of relationship rebirth.

Savvy Sagittarius

Moon in Sagittarius gets in touch with the higher planes of love by taking to the road. You whip around the planet reconnecting with soul
mates in foreign countries to finish up old business or start something
new. Your vagabond Moon searches for the company of upbeat, optimistic, friendly mates who thrive on adventure or all-night gabfests. You
need opportunities for soul-searching philosophy and telling the absolute
truth. While many of your sign are wizards with words, some too-frank
comments may leave you flirting with disaster. As you head for the hills

to do damage control, know that soul reunions create conditions for opening your heart to love.

Calculating Capricorn

Capricorn Moons understand the law of karma. Many of you think you are here to shape up the world. Since you're an accountability expert and assess facts quickly, you have special kinship with the debit and credit ledger from previous incarnations. You whip out your spiritual checkbook expecting to pay back whomever you owe and choose challenging relationships to bring home the goal. Karmic completions with soul mates may include exhausting encounters with family members, friends, and teachers, yet the stamina of your symbolic goat keeps you going upward into the light. You desire balance in love partnerships and may attract your opposite sign, Cancer, to give you a much-needed infusion of love and affection.

Altruistic Aquarius

With an Aquarius Moon you intuitively understand Spirit's deepest message to free yourself from the bonds of rebirth on the earthly plane. To carry out your mission, you are blessed with potent charisma that draws intelligent, inventive companions into your circle. The motto for your humanitarian goals might be "Do all the good you can by all the means you can." You express it by making friends, organizations, and charities the beneficiaries of your good will and precious time. You need a soul mate who loves your creative mind and charming disposition and doesn't mind sharing you with the rest of the world. A loving partner is just what you need to be less abstract and more connected to your deep emotions and touching romantic expression.

Perceptive Pisces

Pisces, you have a very deep need to be intimately loved, cherished, and adored, and a sense that fulfillment awaits you. Before you can manifest the ideal relationship to satisfy your wishes, you have to dissolve illusions and unload emotional baggage that has accumulated over many lifetimes. To facilitate your desires, the messenger from the cosmos reveals past life secrets to you in your dreams. When you make the conscious decision to reconnect with your soul you embark on a journey of releasing. Inspired by the symbolic richness in your dreams, you tap your subconscious wellspring and focus on your true emotional needs. Your deeply sensitive Pisces Moon creates dramas that reunite you with old souls.

Your Psychic Potential

By Estelle Daniels

There is little written in the astrological literature that addresses psychic talent. While some texts concentrate on the outer planets, Uranus, Neptune, and Pluto, there are two more "mundane" planets that can show psychic aptitude.

The Moon is the swiftest planet in a horoscope. It symbolizes emotion, intuition, feelings, impressions, instinct, routine, and things that you do that are patterned and require little conscious thought. It rules the sign Cancer and the Fourth House of an astrological chart. Where the Moon is in your chart by sign and house can show what you need to do to be happy and emotionally satisfied.

Mercury is the next swiftest planet. It has a dual or multiple nature. It rules thought, mind, mentality, commerce, language, communication, everyday life, transactions, and contacts that a person makes in the course of a day. Mercury also rules the five senses, and so rules over visualization and information gathering in general. Mercury rules the signs Gemini and Virgo and the Third and Sixth Houses in the astrological chart. Where you find Mercury in your chart by sign and house is where you need to be heard or communicate.

So what happens when you combine emotion and mind, instinct and communication, intuition and thought? You get what people term psychic power, that ability to go beyond logic to get information.

Aspects

The most basic way the Moon and Mercury can interact in a chart is by aspect, or angles between the planets. When talking about aspects, the question of orbs always comes up. Orbs are the maximum amount of "slop" or "fudge space" an astrologer allows between the planets involved in the aspect to be considered still to be within the influence of the aspect. For this article we will be middle of the road. If an aspect is within 6 degrees of being exact, it is within orb. For example, a perfect square aspect is 90 degrees. If we are allowing a 6 degree orb, any aspect within 6 degrees of 90 degrees is considered a square.

Conjunction

The first and most powerful aspect is the conjunction (two planets in the same degree or sign). This aspect fuses the natures and activities of the two bodies. They are forever yoked in the person's life. A Moon-Mercury conjunction can be the most psychic position, though it can also be most difficult to work with as there is no way to turn off the feelings and impressions streaming into the conscious mind. What sign the conjunction occurs in then colors the type of abilities manifest, and the house the conjunction occurs in shows the area of life where these abilities come forth most strongly.

Sextile

The next aspect is the sextile (two planets 60 degrees or two signs apart). This aspect is one of communication, contact, networking, and opportunity. With a Moon-Mercury sextile, there will be psychic ability, but it will not be always present without practice and work. This placement may indicate an ability to communicate with others either by telepathy or mediumship. Again, the signs will show how the abilities will manifest, and the houses where the planets are will show what areas of life will be best suited for the possible communications.

Square

The square (two planets 90 degrees or three signs apart) is considered a difficult aspect, one of friction, conflict, and a call to action. There would be psychic ability but it would not be easily controlled, certainly not to be relied upon or manifest at will. This psychic might be someone who gets sudden impressions that are jarring or upsetting, or sometimes cannot be turned off. There is a strong need for discipline or work to get the abilities harnessed, or perhaps even turned off so as to get peace of mind. As the person ages, the challenge of this aspect can start to pay off in rewards for the work put into control and mastery.

Trine

The trine (two planets 120 degrees or four signs apart) is an easy or lucky aspect. It can bring great gifts (in this case psychic gifts), but those gifts are in danger of being taken for granted. Trines bring talents that are easy for the possessor, but may not be easy or even possible for those not so blessed. Trines can also make a person lazy. Things come easily so there is no need to work at honing or polishing skills. With a Moon-Mercury trine there is probably a great native psychic talent, but unless worked with and honed,

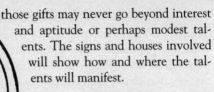

those gifts may never go beyond interest and aptitude or perhaps modest talents. The signs and houses involved will show how and where the talents will manifest.

Opposition

The opposition (two planets 180 degrees or six signs apart) is an aspect of tension and/or balance, and magnifies the properties of each planet. With a Moon-Mercury opposition there may be psychic talents, but also psychic blocks. As with the square, work and discipline will help the talents become more reliable and steady. The person can be either totally psychic or totally in the material world. The key is to achieve a balance between the psychic and material worlds. Keep a balance between purely psychic impressions and material rationality. The signs and houses involved will show types and areas of ability and application.

The Moon in the Signs

Even though a person may have no aspect between their Moon and Mercury, each planet is in one of the twelve signs of the zodiac, and so psychic ability can be gauged through placement alone, though it is heightened by an aspect. Below are delineations of the Moon and Mercury in the twelve signs. These are "pure" interpretations and may be modified by aspects to other placements. For example, a Moon in Taurus that is opposite a Neptune in Scorpio will be more impressionable, suggestible, and psychic than would a Moon in Taurus not in aspect to Neptune at all. However, interpretations have to start somewhere, and the signs show how the energies of the planets will manifest in the person. The house the planet is in shows in what areas of life these energies will play the biggest part, though the house that planet rules will also be strongly tied in.

Moon in Aries

Moon in Aries makes for someone who likes to play with fire, literally or figuratively. Energy work is a possibility for this person, as is being a psychic warrior. This is a placement that tends toward emotions geared more to the self than others. There is a certain naive courage displayed. There is a lot of emotional energy displayed, sometimes more than others can easily handle for long periods. There is a pioneering spirit and a wish to be first, foremost, or in front of the crowd. There is an abundance of good ideas, but the attention span can be quite short, and projects can be abandoned as soon as something new and interesting comes along.

Moon in Taurus

Moon in Taurus is the Moon's exaltation sign, and the Moon is extremely strong and beneficial in this sign. It is solid, comfortable, and very secure. Sometimes it is so secure that there can be a reluctance to move or leave the comfortable environment. Psychic abilities are possible, though more in terms of a good intuition or good practical ideas. Music and song may be strong interests. This placement would work well with crystals, rocks, or other things of the earth. This might be a natural gardener. This can indicate someone who will stick to most anything, and can be excessively stubborn if pushed or rushed. This can also indicate an "Earth Mother" type. This person can have very good natural shields.

Moon in Gemini

Moon in Gemini can indicate many abilities in many areas. It is a sort of "jack of all trades, and master of none." This can also indicate a short attention span, though how interesting the subject is will determine how long the attention is focused upon it. There is a certain amount of verbal ability, and the person may be able to talk their way into or out of most anything. Reading, writing, talking, and communicating are strong aptitudes. There might be a good ability to visualize and there may be an ability for telepathy, with or without words. This placement may also confer the ability to know who is on the phone before you pick it up, or to be able to know what someone is going to say before they actually say it. This can also give the person the ability to get an accurate first impression of people irrespective of what sort of face they may be showing to the world. Reading cards can be effective, but care should be taken to not read into the cards what might be wished for when the psychic abilities aren't working on demand.

Moon in Cancer

The Moon in Cancer is in the sign it rules and is at its strongest. It can make for very strong emotions and psychic impressions. The need is to learn to control and shield from unpleasant or unwanted influences, otherwise this person can pick up on the emotions of others like a sponge. They make good psychic barometers and natural mediums. Those with this placement need time alone and also a special place away from the world to rest and recharge their batteries. This can be the placement of an excellent cook or one who really enjoys food. This person can understand the magic in food and how good food and a congenial eating environment can help restore the soul. This can also be the placement of a natural empath, one who can sense or project emotions. If you can engage this person's sympathy they will do most anything for you. They will sometimes overextend or let others take advantage of their good nature.

Moon in Leo

Moon in Leo is one who can shine if they are secure and happy. Otherwise the emotional need is for adulation and recognition. This person can also be an energy worker, and they can create more permanent energy structures than some of the other signs. This person likes the grand gesture. They also communicate well with children, though they may not have any of their own. They may have a certain amount of native luck, which might be honed to getting better odds than may naturally be expected. They work well in crowds and places where there are lots of people, especially if they feel in control in some way. Working with cards, dice, and other objects for divination can be effective.

Moon in Virgo

Moon in Virgo can be a craftsperson, one who creates with their hands things that are magically useful. This can be the placement of the herb worker, and also one who understands the medicinal qualities of plants, foods, stones and other things. This placement can indicate one who is a natural healer, though this will usually manifest through using things, rather than pure laying on of hands. The interest will be in practical uses for psychic abilities. This person needs to understand what or why before their psychic talents may manifest. This is the esoteric rulership of the Moon, so the Moon's strong emotional and psychic nature is tempered by the practical and analytical nature of Virgo. This placement also works better at night, for the night is the Moon's natural time.

Moon in Libra

Moon in Libra can be a gardener of beautiful and decorative plants. They may be helpful and beneficial plants, but they have to be beautiful also. People with this placement can use their psychic skills to make life beautiful or harmonious or in balance. This can be a placement of a psychic warrior or peacemaker. They will prefer peace, but will resort to war if it is necessary. They will prefer that emotions be in balance. The use of jewelry, color, feng shui, and other aesthetic disciplines in psychic settings are beneficial for this placement of the Moon. This Moon is happiest when things are pleasant, pretty, and in order. Care should be taken that the strong emotional desire to please is not sacrificing of telling the whole truth, or glossing over things that might be upsetting or unpleasant.

Moon in Scorpio

Moon in Scorpio is in its fall, a placement that can make the emotions strong but not necessarily beneficial. There is great psychic ability, but it can also bring upset and discord. People with this placement tend to seek extremes of emotional experience. It can also lead to paranoia and the need to know everyone else's secrets without divulging any of their own. There can be a talent in communicating with the dead. This placement can have very strong psychic impressions, and needs to learn to be diplomatic in divulging what was discovered. Sometimes the insights can be into the more unpleasant sides of life, and that can be difficult to deal with. There is a great need for solitude in the life, and mistrust can cause this person to shut down faster than anything. The higher nature should be cultivated. Sex is of endless fascination and sexual disciplines can produce psychic results. This is also the Moon of the true occult researcher, delving into "those things that humans were not meant to know."

Moon in Sagittarius

Moon in Sagittarius can be fun-loving and active. There is a love of the great outdoors, and of learning and discourse. This can incline the person to religion and its outward expression. There is a love of other cultures and a possible facility for language. This can also lead to a bit of a know-it-all streak in the personality. Psychic archaeology and dealing with other cultures (especially long-lost ones) can manifest. Work with the Akashic records and other planes of higher learning are possible. Ethics are a topic of interest. Working with and discovering universal laws is another possible area for study. Esoteric philosophy and the comparison of various disciplines are interests that might be explored.

Moon in Capricorn

Moon in Capricorn is in its detriment, which chills and represses the emotions. There may be psychic ability but it usually isn't developed or used as there is little "real world" value in it. Psychometry is a possible talent. This is the ruthless Moon, and can cause the person to act in ways that might seem expedient or practical, yet range from insensitive to actively heartless. There is a strong business sense, and if psychic ability can be disguised as a business hunch, then it will be used and developed. There may be an inclination toward ceremonial systems, and the person may collect psychic credentials. There will be an ability to shield naturally that if developed can become formidable.

Moon in Aquarius

Moon in Aquarius is the least emotional and most detached of all Moons. It is rational and logical, yet also subject to sudden emotional insights and surprises. This Moon loves people. It's just the individuals it has trouble coping with. There is a facility for working with groups and organizations. Telepathy can manifest, but it might be dismissed as mere intuition or co-incidence. There is a knack for networking and organizing people into groups, and people with this Moon may end up being the founders of groups dedicated to psychic study. Certainly there is an inclination to working with others rather than solo. This can also be the Moon of the wild-eyed eccentric, and the ability to predict the future may be strong, though not always reliably accurate. There is also an ability to tell when another is telling the truth or lying that can be uncannily accurate.

Moon in Pisces

Moon in Pisces is extremely psychic, sometimes to the point of being unable to turn it off or to operate effectively in the non-psychic world. The need to learn to shield is strong, and if this cannot be learned, then it might be better to turn the psychic faculties off than to be subjected to constant outside influences. This person is also an excellent psychic barometer and possible empath. A natural healing ability, up to and including the laying on of hands, can manifest. This person is extremely sympathetic and understanding, sometimes being unable to detach from the problems and concerns of others. Most any psychic skill is possible for this person, but they need to learn discipline and control or they can become overwhelmed with impressions. Solitude is naturally sought by these people, but care should be taken to not cut oneself off from others totally. Small groups are the best medium for socializing rather than large crowds.

Mercury in the Signs

Mercury in Aries

Mercury in Aries is the esoteric rulership of Aries. This makes for a fast mind, one that can leap to conclusions, sometimes wrong. There is a temper often expressed verbally, sometimes with foul language. There is a facility for using and directing energy, and work in an active art is helpful, such as martial arts, Reiki, rolfing, etc. There is great physical energy that can manifest as clumsiness unless channeled. The mind is always active, and cannot easily rest. Learning meditation can be rewarding but can also be frustrating. There is a need to learn to think and plan before speaking or acting—much more gets accomplished that way. There is a great facility for starting things and little stamina for seeing them through.

Mercury in Taurus

Mercury in Taurus makes for a slow and deliberate but solid and practical mentality. The person might not learn as quickly as Aries or the air signs, but they have excellent retention of what they have learned. The voice can be melodious, musical, or occasionally silent. Movement is more slow and deliberate. Tai chi is something well suited to these people. Music will be an interest. There may be a need to create with the hands, especially with rocks or clay. This is a practical mind, one that might be inclined to disbelieve in psychic things, for they cannot be seen, felt or touched by one's "natural" senses.

Mercury in Gemini

Mercury in Gemini is in one of the signs it rules and quite strong. It makes for a quick facile mind, but also a short attention span. This is an exquisitely verbal Mercury, it can make for a writer, gossip, or thief. This person can say most anything and make you believe it. The hands like to stay busy and knitting or whittling can be helpful. Telepathy is possible, though the concentration may have to be cultivated. This Mercury is also good at visualization. There is a facility for justification and semantics, so ethics should be cultivated. This can be the perpetual motion Mercury and quiet meditation is difficult. Meditation while moving (jogging, bicycling etc.) is much better for the body is engaged so the mind can drift free. There are excellent reflexes and unless afflicted, good eye-hand coordination.

Mercury in Cancer

Mercury in Cancer filters the mind through the feelings and impressions. This person has a hard time hiding their feelings. Feelings are apparent whenever they speak. There is an especially acute "intuition" that when heeded can save the person from future harm. Just paying close attention to first impressions upon meeting people can be found to be uncannily accurate down the road. People with this Mercury can easily develop empathy, but must also learn to separate their own feelings from those of others. This is another psychic barometer position. Sometimes there is an inability to separate the thoughts from the emotions, i.e. all impressions are colored by the present emotional state. There is an interest in history and the past. This makes for a good researcher or family historian.

Mercury in Leo

Mercury in Leo is in one of the signs of its fall, where it doesn't operate as well. It makes for a broad open mentality that likes to see the big picture, and possibly ignore the details (take care of the big stuff and the small stuff will sort itself out). The voice can be hale and hearty and they like to make a big verbal impression. There can be a tendency to boast or exaggerate. Psychically this person should be careful not to blast others, as their enthusiasm can translate into power if not controlled. Learning control and discipline techniques can make this Mercury much more effective, otherwise there is danger of burnout. Sometimes this Mercury can be clumsy, but that comes from trying to take too big steps or do too much at once.

Mercury in Virgo

Mercury in Virgo is in one of the signs it rules and of exaltation and is quite strong. It has a meticulous mentality that pays close attention to the details and minutiae, and can miss the forest for the trees. There is a love of working with the hands. There is a very good coordination, and this can translate to martial arts, moving with speed, precision, and control. The senses are highly developed, and some can be so acute they may be "turned off" so as to allow mental peace, though this is usually due to an affliction. There is a love of crafts and creating with the hands (especially pottery). This Mercury is also very good at spotting details and inconsistencies that others might miss. They are disinclined to believe in things that are not tangible, though are convinced by results.

Mercury in Libra

Mercury in Libra is desirous of peace and balance. This is the "devil's advocate" Mercury. It just cannot stand some viewpoint or side being unrepresented. The voice can be soft and melodious and there may be a love of music and dance. This is the placement of the psychic judge who can listen to both sides and determine who is right or wrong. This placement can make for a cosmic peacemaker and diplomat, one who can find a compromise and persuade others to work within it. This person works well with a close partner, someone who compliments their skills and abilities. This person also has a good people sense as in who might get along well with whom, and works to get them together.

Mercury in Scorpio

Mercury in Scorpio can seem to be eternally suspicious and wary. Trust is not easily earned. There is an incredible eye for detail and the ability to notice inconsistencies and catch people in lies. This person can also be a consummate liar if necessary. This person can be an incredible researcher. This is the Mercury of the alchemists and occultists of old who labored long to uncover that knowledge that humans were not meant to know. Sometimes this constant "need to know" can get the person in trouble, but they would rather know and suffer than be blissful in ignorance. They also don't want anyone else to be able to discover their secrets. This placement can produce a psychic warrior, or a psychic cop who tries to keep everyone else honest in their psychic dealings and is not afraid to call the violators on their bad behavior.

Mercury in Sagittarius

Mercury in Sagittarius is the sign of detriment and is disadvantaged. This person is one who talks a lot, loves to expound their ideas, thoughts, philosophies, knowledge, and whatever else they can think of, sometimes non stop. This Mercury can be pompous, overbearing, and just a blowhard if they don't watch their tendency to talk. They love knowledge and learning and want to share it with everyone, no matter who or when, even when the other person isn't interested or is actually bored. This can also be the placement of someone who has an eidetic memory. The mind is broad and all-encompassing, and sometimes the person becomes a perpetual student because they don't want to limit their field to just one specialty. They can work well with astral travel, dream work, and other higher plane visitations. They can also just blurt out whatever they are thinking without regard to circumstances or the feelings of others.

Mercury in Capricorn

Mercury in Capricorn's emphasis is on practical get-ahead strategies in life, and there may be little time for psychic endeavors unless you show them what's in it for them. Once convinced there is a benefit from the study and work, this person will dive into the work with abandon. This person likes to create on the physical plane, because they want things that are useful, and to have an end product to show for their labors. This Mercury is probably good at grounding and shielding. Telekinesis is an aptitude that might be developed. Psychokinesis is also possible with some training. They will be impressed with titles and degrees, and may be more comfortable and satisfied working in a hierarchical environment. This is a sure-footed Mercury who walks cautiously but with seemingly endless stamina.

Mercury in Aquarius

Mercury in Aquarius is in one sign of exaltation and operates very well. This is the genius who can take seemingly unrelated facts and weave them into a comprehensible whole. This is the magus who can draw power from above, shape it, control it, and direct it with pure will. They are able to discern whether a person is telling the truth or not, or how much truth they may be withholding. This person prefers to work with like-minded people in groups, or absolutely alone. There is little middle ground. This person also likes to say shocking or unexpected things and watch how others react. Sometimes there is a need to be a rebel or act contrary just because it's different. This person may try new and unusual things just to see what they are.

Mercury in Pisces

Mercury in Pisces is in the sign of its fall and at a disadvantage. This person is no less able or intelligent, it's just that they are bombarded with sensory input from other planes and extrasensory perception so that they have trouble sometimes relating to the here-and-now world of everyday life. This person may appear spaced out, daydreamy, or perhaps just like they don't get it, but they are actually considering things you haven't dreamt of. The trick is to be able to tap into all that wonderful universal stuff and still operate effectively in the here and now. This person may communicate better through non-verbal means—art, music or dance. This person can be an excellent medium, but they must take care to avoid possession. The person may be somewhat uncoordinated, due to not concentrating totally on what they are doing. When responding to their muse (and they all have one) they can be amazing in what they can accomplish. Most any psychic ability is available to this person. It's just a matter of work, discipline, and concentration to get solid results.

Aspects to the Moon

By Kim Rogers-Gallagher

When astrologers look at a chart, many of us first consider the "big three"—the Sun, the Ascendant (rising sign), and the Moon. These are typically thought of as the three most important factors in determining the personality of the chart owner because between them, they describe the outside, the inside, and the "front door" of a person. The Sun is the outside. It's all about what you'll really want to do with your life, and the way you'll take off after what gives you joy. The Ascendant is the "front door" of your chart. It's how you act and seem to be—your physical appearance, your body, and the way you dress. The Moon is the inside of you. She doesn't act, as the Sun does, and she doesn't determine your appearance, as the Ascendant does. She describes how you'll react emotionally to what the world tosses at you. She's your soft underbelly, the piece of you that feels. She's the head of the department of feelings, and the bringer of moods—a great Moon word.

Now, the Moon has a very important job to do. She's in charge of your instinct, your emotions, your memories, and your need to express your feelings. She's got an awful lot to do with your mom, and the incredible connection you share with her. As such, the Moon is the part of you that points both to how you were nurtured and how you'll nurture others. She's the side of you who decides what's safe and what's not, the side that shows how you'll cope when you're hurt.

Needless to say, although she's a rather silent energy, she's not to be ignored. Any planets that are connected to her in your chart—by aspect, that is—are contributors to the way you'll express her energy. But what does that mean, exactly? Well, it's like this.

So What's an Aspect?

As the planets move along on their circular journey through the heavens, they often form angles to one another. No matter when we freeze-frame the universe to create a birth chart, some of the planets—but not all of them—will show up in an angular relationship to each other. Planets in this type of relationship are "hotwired" to one another—connected in a very powerful way. Planets in aspect are "up" on what's happening with each other at all times, as if they're having a nonstop conversation. The particular angle that separates any two planets describes the nature of that conversation. There are seven angles astrologers consider most often, each of which produces a different type of relationship or conversation between the planets they connect. Let's go over the meaning of each of the seven major aspects.

The Conjunction
Planets within 0–8 degrees of each other; 10 degrees with the Sun or Moon

When we say that two things are operating "in conjunction" with one another, it means they're operating together—as one. This holds true with the planets, as well. Two (or more) planets conjoined are inseparable—an eternal team. They're bound together, cosmically fused so that one or the other doesn't ever act alone. Think of two people, dressed in the same costumes (if the two planets are in the same sign, that is), telling the same story in the same language and tone of voice.

Now, some planets, of course, will do better with this arrangement than others—because some "pair up" more easily than others. Venus and the Moon, for example, do pretty well in conjunction, since both are feminine and receptive. The Sun and Mars, both pretty feisty by nature, also take well to this type of bond.

The thing to remember about planets in conjunction is that they "live together"—usually even in the same room, or house in your chart—so it's especially important to give them activities to pursue that will allow them to act together.

The Semi-Sextile
Planets 30 degrees apart

Think of the semi-sextile as the kind of aspect that connects two planets in such a way so that they're having a quiet conversation. Planets in semi-sextile are in signs that are right next to each other—they're neighbors. Although they don't have anything in common—that is, they're not of the same element, quality, or gender—they've still come to know each other pretty well by virtue of that closeness. The strength of this aspect is not monumental, and it seems to indicate that the two energies it links affect each other indirectly or that the connection between these two planets needs to be consciously created, rather than automatically done. Now, there are two ways a semi-sextile ordinarily becomes noticed by its owner. First off, if other planets join in by forming a major aspect to one or both planets involved in the semi-sextile, these two will really notice their relationship a lot more—like neighbors who find out how much they might have in common through a mutual acquaintance. Secondly, if a planet moving through the sky (a transiting planet) makes an aspect to one planet in the semi-sextile, it will make an aspect to both, which will set off the energy of the relationship—big time—and turn that quiet chat into a full-fledged conversation between neighbors.

The Semi-Square and the Sesquiquadrate
Planets 45 degrees and 135 degrees apart respectively

Both of these aspects are really cousins to the square, another aspect. In fact, one of my very first astrology teachers used to refer to these aspects as "sneaky squares," and I've never heard a more apt description of them. Divide a square in half, and you've got a semi-square. Add three semi-squares, and you've got a sesquiquadrate. Subtract either of them from an opposition and you've got the other. If the aspects are conversations, then, these two are arguments that sneak up on you, or rumblings of arguments yet to come. Since the square inspires action by irritating you into movement, these two can also provide similarly provocative experiences.

The Sextile
Planets 60 degrees apart

Signs that are two doors down from each other on either side show up as happy couples. That is, since the sextile links planets in compatible elements, these planets are either in fire/air or earth/water. Since these pairings of elements get along so splendidly, so do planets "wearing" them. This aspect encourages an active exchange between the two planets involved, so these pieces of you will be stimulated by each other—eager and anxious to get to work together. Sextiles also support each other's needs—much as fire needs air to burn, and earth needs water to keep it alive. Think of your planets in sextile as friends who just can't wait to see each other.

The Square
Planets 90 degrees apart

Just as you might expect, planets in this sign relationship are at cross-purposes, or rubbing each other the wrong way. In essence, they're having a nonstop argument. Think of it this way: if you rub two sticks together at a right angle, you're creating a square between them, and practicing the age-old technique of conjuring fire. Now, astrologically speaking, you can learn an awful lot about the nature of the relationship of two planets in a square aspect if you pay close attention to just exactly what happens when we start our fire with those two sticks. The friction causes sparks, and the sparks create flames. Well, that's how squares work. There's a friction between the two planets that won't go away, and that keeps them in constant motion. Now, although they're uncomfortable at times, and even aggravating, your squares point to places where tremendous growth is possible. They require constant movement to burn up that energy, however.

The Trine
Planets 120 degrees apart

Trines are traditionally thought of as favorable aspects. They're formed between planets in signs of the same element, so they're kindred spirits. As far as the type of conversation they're having goes—well, chitchat is just about unneccessary for the two of them. They understand each other so well they can finish each other's sentences. They show an ease of communication not found in any of the other aspects, and they're traditionally thought of as "easy." Of course, as with all else, there is a downside to trines. The problem is that sometimes they get so comfy they bore each other and neither of them ever really does anything. Planets in trine show urges or needs that automatically get where each other is coming from. The catch is that you've got to get them up off the couch to get them operating.

The Quincunx
Planets 150 degrees apart

This aspect is a tough one, in several ways. First off, like the semi-sextile it joins planets in two signs that are completely different—they don't share a quality, an element, or a gender, so they have absolutely nothing in common. Needless to say, it's very difficult, but not impossible, for them to communicate with each other. It's as if two strangers who don't speak each other's language are put in a noisy room and told to tell each other a story. For that reason, this aspect has always been considered to insist on adjustment in the way the two planets are used. Now, they can still communicate if they use other methods, like drawing or gesturing, or pulling in a third party to interpret, perhaps. Because they do often need someone to interpret, however, planets in quincunx relationship can often feel pushed, forced, or obligated to perform. They also seem to correspond with health issues or disease.

The Opposition
Planets 180 degrees apart

Two forces in opposition are working against each other. That's the situation with planets in opposition to one another. Although they have the same mission—the same goal, that is, because they're in compatible elements—their techniques are very different. It's as if the two are politicians from opposing parties, standing across from one another with their arms folded, involved in a verbal debate, neither willing to concede an inch. They can only break out of their stand-off by first becoming aware of one another, and then only by compromising. This aspect is the least difficult of the traditionally known "hard" aspects because planets at odds with one another still have a middle point to come to.

What's It Like For the Moon to Be in Aspect to a Planet?

When the Moon is "hooked up" by an aspect to another planet, you've got two things to consider that will help you to figure out how that relationship will act in your life. First, consider the nature of the aspect the two are sharing. That's what describes the nature of the conversation the Moon is having with the other planet. Planets in square to your Moon are arguing with her—which can manifest either as an inner tension that emerges whenever you try to express your feelings, or a provocative push toward finding a way to make those feelings known.

Second, consider the energy of the planet that's connected to the Moon. Is it adding to or taking away from her ability to emote? For example, if it's Saturn in an opposition to your Moon, you may find that authority figures (Saturn) seem to oppose you (opposition) when you try to let the world know how you feel, and that the only solution is to become a combination nurturer-authority figure. Here's a nutshell description of how each of the aspects another planet makes to your Moon make you feel.

Squares to the Moon

Squares (or semi-squares, or sesquiquadrates) to the Moon can point to arguments or conflicts with women, but they can also mean that whenever you take steps to nurture others or allow them to nurture or take care of you, there's an inner argument going on inside about what you really need. Again, remember that these aspects also show how you'll be pushed toward growth by feeling forced to find a new way to handle a situation, so although they might feel difficult, these are often the aspects that signify a personality that's a mover and a shaker. These aspects can

also point to a bit of tension in our lives, too, with regard to the issues presented by the other planet, since that's the dynamic of the square. When the Moon is in a difficult aspect to another planet, you may have to do battle with the world to get your deepest needs met.

Oppositions to the Moon

The opposition, on the other hand, although another traditionally difficult aspect, isn't usually experienced so internally. Planets opposing the Moon often show up as if you're involved in a tug of war with them—a symbolic debate. You may feel as if others deliberately try to stop you from nurturing, or that you can't accept sympathy or protection—as if someone is standing in the way. In reality, this is a debate you're having with yourself—you've just hired out one side of the opposition to someone else to help you see it. In truth, since the opposition is, above all else, symbolic of awareness, this aspect really presents us with the opportunity to see a part of ourselves we wouldn't ordinarily see. Remember, you own both of these planets, so whatever you're seeing in the other that you're not fond of might be a projected part of your own personality that you need to own.

Trines and Sextiles to the Moon

Moon trines and sextiles are just dandy—they're like presents from the universe, in fact. Your emotions come out easily and appropriately. Others are protective and respectful of your feelings. This is especially true of the trine, but you might not notice this gift so much because things ordinarily go along so well you've learned to take for granted that everything will always work out just fine. Again, trines can also be a bit on the lazy side, so you may have to consciously push yourself to express what's going on inside, but the results will be good. Now, with the sextiles, the planet that's hooked up to your Moon will provide opportunities to let your emotions out. You may find that someone is always there to give you a hug, or that you've got what it takes to cope with any situation. Now let's look at how each of the planets meshes with the Moon's energy.

Planetary Pairings

Sun/Moon

When the Sun aspects the Moon in your chart, your personal spotlight is on your home, your family, your mom, your women friends, and your feelings. Now, on an emotional level, depending on the aspect between the two, this can mean that you're a bit on the moody side, because when these two are hooked up, what you feel is what you send out. With the conjunction, it's hard to say how you'll act out what you feel, but it's a given that you won't make a secret of it. The Sun is an agent on patrol for stars, and your Moon has just taken the stage.

Since the Sun often brings dealings with yang or male individuals into our lives, the cause of your emotionality may always seem to be men or authority figures. With the squares or other hard aspects you may feel an inner tension but not quite be able to put your finger on the reason for it, or feel that authority figures are out to upset you or deprive you. Family members or the women in your life may seem to be a bit on the testy side, too. You might also experience the challenging aspects quite literally as emotional challenges sent your way by the universe periodically to make you aware of how you're feeling about a certain issue. The easy aspects, like trines or sextiles, represent a happy, sociable personality, with an inner harmony between what you love and how you express emotions that will reflect in your dealings with the world, especially with your family and your women friends. Regardless of the aspect, when the Sun and Moon shine together, you'll know yourself a little better.

That same need to shine means that you'll necessarily need to bring your Sun—along with any planets that aspect it—into your career, too. So with the Sun in aspect to the Moon, your career choice may be something that deals with kids, moms, women, or homes. You may even work out of your own home.

Moon/Mercury

Your motto is always going to be "talk about it"—and whatever "it" is won't matter. When Mercury whispers in the Moon's ear, feelings tumble out of our mouths, unfiltered. If you know you've got this mechanism at work inside you, take a moment to reflect on how best to express those feelings, and don't be surprised to hear yourself say, "But what about my needs?" now and then. Don't feel bad about it, either—it's okay to talk about your needs. Just be very sure that no matter what you say or to whom you say it, you let them know that these are your feelings, and you're not blaming, condemning, or congratulating anyone. Remember, Mercury is the messenger of the gods. When the Moon is hooked up to him, the gods have determined that emotional issues in your life are there to be discussed.

"Tough" Moon/Mercury contacts can mean that you'll amaze even yourself at how self-absorbed you sound at times. Your thinking—and all your communications—will be colored by what others may say are irrational impulses. Well, nobody ever said the Moon had to be rational, of course, but Mercury's supposed to be. With these harder contacts, the more emotional you are, the more irrational you may appear to others. You may be faced with others who don't seem to be paying attention to how you feel, or, with the opposition, you may feel as if putting your feelings into words doesn't accomplish anything, or that it actually alienates you from others. On the other hand, easy Moon/Mercury aspects are the inspiration behind heart-to-heart chats, softly spoken promises, and offers to help. Moon/Mercury connections are tailor-made for teaching children, talking to women about feminine issues, and writing or teaching in your home or in a place that's a home or nest for women or children.

In a nutshell, no matter which aspect Mercury makes to the Moon, expect your feelings and your instinct to color your judgment, your navigation skills, and your ability to learn.

Moon/Venus

These two planets are astrological girlfriends. As the two prime representatives of the feminine among the personal planets, they back each other up, hug each other when they need it, and watch each other's pets when one of them is on vacation. This is the type of combination that produces an urge to embrace, hold, and take care of your precious ones—animal, vegetable, or mineral—since Venus shows who and what you love, and how you'll love it. Now, the Moon shows how you'll cope when you're hurt and how you'll express your joy when you're delighted. When she's touched by Venus, the Moon experiences emotional issues with the loved ones in your life that will mirror how you're feeling about yourself, and what you feel you deserve, another Venus issue. The Moon's aspects to Venus can also point to a personality that's especially emotional about its possessions. Under the tougher Moon/Venus aspects, the worst you can expect is to occasionally feel as if your feelings aren't reciprocated. In other words, you may often feel as if you're pining over someone or something you don't feel belongs to you. This is another of the "sighing" aspects, by the way, and another of the dreamy, wistful, romantic aspects, too—regardless of the aspect involved. Now, with easy Moon aspects, you'll ordinarily feel safe, loved, and satisfied—as if life has provided an emotional safety net for you via your family, your mom, and the women in your life. You may find that no matter what happens, you're surrounded by everyone and everything you care about—and life is generally pretty good.

Moon/Mars

I like to think of Mars as your own personal Rambo, the planet in your chart who'll show what will get you riled up, ticked off, and inspired to take action—and how you'll act when that happens. Of course, he's also a good indicator of how you'll react when you're challenged and of how you'll defend yourself when you feel it's necessary. When the emotion-toting Moon is in aspect to Mars, there's a couple of things that can happen. First off, Moon/Mars aspects, in general, point to someone who can be quite literally "guarded"emotionally. Now, that doesn't mean that you'll never emote, only that when you're hurt, you may find yourself expressing it through anger. Similarly, when you're angry, you may just cry. Either way, asserting yourself on behalf of yourself is something that will always emerge in most emotional fashion. You won't hold back on any of the other emotional theatrics these two planets can conjure when they're excited about something.

See, "excitement" is usually the operative phrase here. The Moon and Mars both represent some pretty darned trigger-happy urges inside us humans: anger and feelings. Both of those urges rear up before we know it, albeit for different reasons. When the excitement is of the pleasant kind—which might be as simple as a really good time out with friends—your energy level in general is high, you're instinctively keyed into everyone there, and a great, great time is had by all. When you're born with these two in an easy aspect, no matter what happens, if it touches you emotionally, you're going to be quite charged. It will always be easy for you to initiate action, then, as long as you care about what happens. Mars and the Moon in an easy partnership can also mean that you're surrounded by energetic, "go getter" women friends—and regardless of the aspect, it's a good bet your mom was a force to be reckoned with. If the aspect is a tough one, on the other hand, you might see the women in your life as contentious or argumentative. Internally, you may feel that there's always a battle to face when you try to get your needs met or express your anger. You may find that whenever you assert yourself, it's at the risk of shutting yourself off from the love of others. Then, too, since neither the Moon

nor Mars has ever been accused of being very rational, you may also tend to be a bit over-defensive at times. All of this simply points to the fact that you've always felt as if your only defender was you—so the high side of the tougher aspects is that you're going to be quite self-sufficient.

Moon/Jupiter

Sometimes your heart is just plain happy, for no apparent reason. There's a warm, full buzz that comes along with those moments that some of us might put on a par with the halfway point of that first margarita. Euphoria, some call it. At any rate, it's good—and it's how you'll feel most of the time if you're lucky enough to have Jupiter connected to the Moon by an easy aspect in your chart. See, Jupiter is where you keep your real-good-feel-good stash. When he's touching the Moon comfortably, that feel-good is hooked up to your emotions, and the end result of any feeling is a good, warm glow. Now, when you're feeling this good, you'll tend to give it out to others. Since whatever you give out to the world is what you'll get back from it, this aspect can be a super one to own. On the other hand, both the conjunction and the traditionally hard aspects can point to overdoing it. In that case, you may find that it's easy for you to become over-emotional about something, or that you often wonder if maybe you haven't taken something personally that wasn't intended so. You may find that it's easy for you to become emotionally involved with someone very quickly—and that when you're involved, you tend to overdo what you do for them so that they'll love you back. See, Jupiter's specialty, for better or worse, is blowing things way out of proportion. When it's the Moon he's aspecting, and when that aspect is a difficult one, it's tough to feel anything a little bit.

Now, since the Moon is the planet we associate with home, and since Jupiter is a long-distance kinda guy, any of the aspects may point to a personality who's more at home on the road—free of any emotional commitments, that is. You'll probably end up living a long distance from your birthplace, then, or moving long-distance several times throughout your life. Since the Moon rules children and families, you may also often feel the urge to expand by adding to the family periodically. This could mean that you came from a large family, or that you're in the process of creating one, or both. As with all the difficult aspects from Jupiter, the pitfall is that you can get carried away in the Moon department—and have too many kids, too many pets, or a house so big that you can't afford it. Regardless of the aspect, then, keep yourself as free as possible, and try to make your nest in a wide open space. Remember, too, that you've been born with a heart the size of a watermelon, and make sure you don't overextend to folks who'll take advantage of your generous personality.

Moon/Saturn

Saturn is your supply of dutiful, responsible, and unemotional energy. He's where you're an expert at stifling your emotions in the name of duty, where you're quite skilled at just saying no and just following orders, regardless of how you feel. Needless to say, when Mr. Serious visits the Moon, look out. This is a combination that's made of two distinctly opposite energies, and there's a couple of ways it will play out in your life.

First of all, Saturn doesn't like to feel. Saturn's usual reaction to a connection with the Moon is to turn her nurturing impulse into an opportunity to complete a duty of some kind. In other words, if you've got these two hooked together in your chart, you may not be much of a bearhugger, but you're going to be wonderful at taking care of whomever or whatever you feel is dependent on you by doing the right thing for them. You'll never miss a chance to do a family-oriented chore or task, something responsible, to let them know you care. In short, your responsibilities to your family and children will always be first and foremost on your mind. You may have learned all this by being raised in a military family, by the way—literally or figuratively speaking.

Now, if you've got an easy aspect between the two, you'll also be an expert at initiating heart-to-heart talks—not emotional displays, you understand—but factual, realistic meetings. You'll be the rock your friends turn to when they're distressed, the family historian, and the child your mom will lean on most as she grows older. You'll have a disciplined way of expressing your emotions, too, so if you are upset about something, it may not show at all until the time is right. Chances are you'll also be extremely self-sufficient, and that you'll have learned very early on how to take care of your own needs quite matter-of-factly. If you've got a tough aspect between the two, this emotional discipline can go a bit too far at times, and you may often feel as if you just can't let your feelings out, or that it would be weak of you to express yourself. Tough aspects often point to a personality that's not much on the warm and fuzzy side, because that's not what you learned in childhood. Remember, Saturn contracts. When he's in a difficult aspect to the Moon, you can also expect to be a bit on the pessimistic side, too. Saturn would always rather expect too little from life than too much. Regardless of the aspect Saturn makes to your Moon, you're going to be a rather solitary creature—since solitude, after all, is Saturn's favorite state.

Moon/Uranus

Uranus is the spot in your chart where you're at your most unpredictable, where anything can change at a moment's notice. He's the symbolic impulse behind all last-minute reversals and abrupt changes of heart. Uranus is like an on/off switch. If you've got him hooked up to your Moon, well, then, whenever you feel anything, you may become a bit nervous, or restless—as if stability is the one thing that makes you wonder when the other shoe is going to drop. As a result, you may find that whenever you're settled, you're uncomfortable—or that nesting means that you're trapped somehow. When that caged feeling happens, don't be surprised if you react by either starting or stopping something suddenly to get free. All that goes for any and all situations of the heart, too. Remember, Uranus is your radical, rebellious self. When he's connected to the Moon, any feeling will set him off.

Now, if the aspect between the two is a conjunction, you may not express you needs or emotions much at all, but when you do, it's going to be through an outburst or a sudden shift in life direction that will shock and amaze the masses. You may also find that those you care about often stop you in your tracks and surprise you, too.

The best of Moon/Uranus connections point to a personality who's quite at home with change—sudden change. You may also be the one who's different in your family—the one who's here to break the old traditions and start new ones. If you're a parent, your way of parenting is going to be quite different, too. You'll probably be quite adamant about letting your children express themselves, and you may push them to develop their own personalities without what you see as your interference.

The harder Moon/Uranus contacts can mean that you automatically retreat behind an icy shell whenever you're hurt, wounded, or frightened. Others may see you as cold, but you're really not. It's just that you've learned that not showing any emotions at all is the safest way to get through upsets. Your way of coping with tough emotional situations may be to get away quickly, too, so don't be surprised if you feel the need to leave the room—or the state—after an argument. Uranus is cold, clear mind energy. When your Moon is connected to him by a tough aspect, separating from an emotional situation to think things over rationally is your best bet. Just make sure you explain it to your others, so they won't think you've left for good.

Moon/Neptune

If your Moon is aspected by Neptune, the most intuitive lady out there, you've got a super antenna—and when they engage, you're a regular psychic sponge, feeling everything that's happening around you, for better or worse. That includes the anger that's bouncing off of the argument currently being waged in the corner, as well as the infatuation those two high-school kids are bouncing off of each other in the booth behind you.

Now, your Neptune is also the place where you're idealistic, dreamy, and romantic. Regardless of the aspect she makes to the Moon, you'll need to find a place to hide out every now and then, like a movie theater, a steam bath, or a room with all of the shades pulled down. In fact, with these two in any aspect, you'll always need periods of total alone-time to draw back and regroup from the emotionally exhausting world.

If you were born with the conjunction, you're often going to be struck by a feeling of unconditional love for someone or something. Although the Moon represents personal emotions, when she's visited by Neptune, the creator of the "we are all one" theory, you'll be quite aware of the connection we share with all living creatures. It may also be tough for you to separate your emotions from their emotions—because, after all, Neptune dissolves the boundaries. Under the easier aspects, you'll possess a wonderful gift—the realistic possibility of falling in love with the "right one." You may send off letters to Robert Redford, too—or another celebrity you see as the perfect lover—only half believing he or she won't answer. See, this is a team that's all about dreaming, and convincing yourself that your dreams are real. It's also a team that's tailor-made for charity work or hopping in and helping a stranger.

Under the tougher Moon to Neptune aspects, you may often feel emotionally confused, or unsure of where to turn when you're hurt. You may also feel vaguely worried about something at times, or, at worst, a bit paranoid—without quite knowing what the problem is. Neptune does represent fears, remember, since she's where you're very aware of not having any boundaries to separate what's out there from you. It's also possible to experience physical problems stemming from that lack o' boundary—such as bad effects from drugs or alcohol, for example, or allergies that kick up suddenly and then disappear just as suddenly, before they can even be diagnosed.

Moon/Pluto

The subject is emotional control—and the arena is your closest relationships. Pluto, of course, is the spot in your chart where you're a ruthless, power-hungry little dictator and/or where you're equal parts detective, analyst, and assassin. Pluto is the symbolic king of perception, in other words—he's equally able to plant clues or skillfully interpret them. If he's connected to the Moon in your chart, then, you're going to be amazingly aware of little things that may not be noticeable to others, but mean a lot to you. Being that good at picking up subtleties, of course, also means that you're going to be able to send equally subtle signals back out into your world. When the Moon is connected to Pluto, you're also going to be able to either bend and manipulate emotional situations, or be manipulated by them.

Now, manipulation is a word with a heavy reputation. Somewhere along the way, it became distinctly uncool to use Pluto to turn a life scenario to our liking. This is where the matter of personal integrity comes in. If you know you've got this power, use your Pluto to change over a situation than needs changing—to sell someone on a positive, helpful idea. Convince them that they really can stand on their own two feet, without an abusive spouse, or end a habit that's destroying their health. The Moon and Pluto are an amazingly persuasive team—she lends her instinct to Pluto and changes the detective into a mother figure of sorts. With easy Moon/Pluto aspects, you can be a force for positive change in someone's life, and you'll also be a well of emotional endurance. This is one of the aspects that just about guarantees that no matter what happens, you'll see the deeper meaning in it and land on your feet. If you've got one of the tougher Moon/Pluto aspects, your relationships may take on a quality of intensity that often turns into emotional power struggles. You may often obsess on someone (or something), becoming quite wrapped up in it emotionally. Regardless of the aspect Pluto makes to the Moon, remember that she's an emotional creature—when Pluto adds his intensity to those emotions, they're going to be amplified, funneled, and focused to the "nth" degree. Use these aspects well—direct your energy into an honest, worthwhile cause.

Business & Legal Ventures

How to Choose the Best Dates

When starting a new business or any type of new venture, check to make sure that the Moon is in the first or second quarter. This will help it get off to a better start. If there is a deadlock or anxiety, it will often be broken during the Full Moon.

You should also check the aspects of the Moon to the planet that rules the type of venture with which you are becoming involved. Look for positive aspects to the planet that rules the activity in the Lunar Aspectarian (pages 28–51), and avoid any dates marked Q or O.

Planetary Business Rulerships

Listed below are the planets and the business activities that they rule. If you follow the guidelines given above and apply them to the occupations of activities listed for each planet, you should have excellent results in your new business ventures. Even if it is not a new venture, check the aspects to the ruler of the activity before making moves in your business.

Sun: Advertising, executive positions, banking, finance, government, jewelry, law, and public relations.

Mercury: Accounting, brokerage, clerical, disc jockey, doctor, editor, inspector, librarian, linguist, medical technician, scientist, teacher, writer, publishing, communication, and mass media.

Venus: Architect, art and artist, beautician, dancer, designer, fashion and marketing, musician, poet, and chiropractor.

Mars: Barber, butcher, carpenter, chemist, construction, dentist, metal worker, surgeon, and soldier.

Jupiter: Counseling, horse training, judge, lawyer, legislator, minister, pharmacist, psychologist, public analyst, social clubs, research, and self-improvement.

Saturn: Agronomy, math, mining, plumbing, real estate, repair person, printer, paper-making, and working with older people.

Uranus: Aeronautics, broadcasting, electrician, inventing, lecturing, radiology, and computers.

Neptune: Photography, investigator, institutions, shipping, pets, movies, wine merchant, health foods, resorts, travel by water, and welfare.

Pluto: Acrobatics, athletic manager, atomic energy, research, speculation, sports, stockbroker, and any purely personal endeavors.

Business Activities

Advertising, General

Write advertisements when it is a favorable day for your Sun sign and Mercury or Jupiter is conjunct, sextile, or trine the Moon. Mars and Saturn should not be aspecting the Moon by square, opposition, or conjunction. Advertising campaigns are best begun when the Moon is in Taurus, Cancer, Sagittarius, or Aquarius, and well aspected. Advertise to give away pets when the Moon is in Sagittarius or Pisces.

Adverstising, Newspaper

The Moon should be conjunct, sextile, or trine (C, X, or T) Mercury or Jupiter.

Advertising, Television, Radio, or Internet

The Moon should be in the first or second quarter in the signs of Gemini, Sagittarius, or Aquarius. The Moon should be conjunct, sextile or trine (C, X or T) Uranus, and Uranus should be sextile or trine (X or T) Jupiter.

Business, Education

When you begin training, see that your lunar cycle is favorable that day and that the planet ruling your occupation is marked C or T.

Business, Opening

The Moon should be in Taurus, Virgo, or Capricorn and in the first or second quarter. It should also be sextile or trine (X or T) Jupiter or Saturn.

Business, Remodeling

The Moon should be conjunct, trine, or sextile (C, T, or X) Jupiter, and sextile (X) or trine (t) Saturn, and Pluto.

Business, Starting

In starting a business of your own, see that the Moon is free of afflictions and that the planet ruling the business is marked C or T.

Buying

Buy during the third quarter, when the Moon is in Taurus for quality, or in a mutable sign (Gemini, Virgo, Sagittarius, or Pisces) for savings.

Good aspects from Venus or the Sun are desirable. If you are buying for yourself, it is good if the day is favorable to your Sun sign.

Buying Clothing

See that the Moon is sextile or trine to the Sun, and that the Moon is in the first or second quarters. When the Moon is in Taurus, buying clothes will bring pleasure and satisfaction. Do not buy clothing or jewelry or wear them for the first time when the Moon is in Scorpio or Aries. Buying clothes on a favorable day for your Sun sign and when Venus or Mercury are well aspected is best, but avoid aspects to Mars and Saturn.

Buying Furniture

Follow the rules for machinery and appliances but buy when the Moon is in Libra as well. Buy antique furniture when the Moon is in Cancer, Scorpio, or Capricorn.

Buying Machinery, Appliances, or Tools

Tools, machinery, and other implements should be bought on days when your lunar cycle is favorable and when Mars and Uranus are trine (T), sextile (X), or conjunct (C) the Moon. Any quarter of the Moon is suitable. When buying gas or electrical appliances, the Moon should be in Aquarius.

Buying Stock

The Moon should be in Taurus or Capricorn, and should be sextile or trine (X or T) Jupiter and Saturn.

Collections

Try to make collections on days when your Sun is well aspected. Avoid days when Mars or Saturn are aspected. If possible, the Moon should be in a cardinal sign: Aries, Cancer, Libra, or Capricorn. It is more difficult to collect when the Moon is in Taurus or Scorpio.

Consultants, Work With

The Moon should be conjunct (C), sextile (X) or trine (T) Mercury or Jupiter.

Contracts

To make contracts, see that the Moon is in a fixed sign and sextile (X), trine (T), or conjunct (C) Mercury.

Contracts, Bid On

The Moon should be in the sign of Libra, and either the Moon or Mercury should be conjunct, sextile or trine (C, X, or T) Jupiter.

Copyrights/Patents, Apply For

The Moon should be conjunct, trine, or sextile (C, T, or X) Mercury or Jupiter.

Electronics, Buying

When buying electronics, choose a day when the Moon is in an air sign (Gemini, Libra, or Aquarius) and well aspected by Mercury and/or Uranus.

Electronics, Repair

The Moon should be sextile or trine (X or T) Mars or Uranus, and be in one of the following signs: Taurus, Leo, Scorpio, or Aquarius.

Legal Matters

In general, a good aspect between the Moon and Jupiter is the best influence for a favorable decision. If you are starting a lawsuit to gain damages, begin during the increase of the Moon. If you are seeking to avoid payment, get a court date when the Moon is decreasing. A good Moon-Sun aspect strengthens your chance of success. In divorce cases, a favorable Moon-Venus aspect may produce a more amicable settlement. Moon in Cancer or Leo and well aspected by the Sun brings the best results in custody cases.

Loans

Moon in the first and second quarters favors the lender, in the third and fourth favors the borrower. Good aspects of Jupiter and Venus to the Moon are favorable to both, as is the Moon in Leo, Sagittarius, Aquarius, or Pisces.

Mailing

For best results, send mail on favorable days for your Sun sign. The Moon in Gemini is good, as are Virgo, Sagittarius, and Pisces.

Mining

Saturn rules drilling and mining. Begin this work on a day when Saturn is marked C, T, or X. If mining for gold, pick a day in which the Sun is also marked C, T, or X. Mercury rules quicksilver, Venus rules copper, Jupiter rules tin, Saturn rules lead and coal, Uranus rules radioactive elements, Neptune rules oil, and the Moon rules water. Choose a day when the planet ruling whatever is being drilled for is marked C, T, or X.

New Job, Beginning

When you take a new job, Jupiter and Venus should be sextile, trine, or conjunct the Moon.

News

The handling of news is related to Uranus, Mercury, and all of the air signs. When Uranus is aspected, there is always an increase in the spectacular side of the news. Collection of news is related to Saturn.

Photography, Radio, TV, Film, and Video

For all these activities it is best to have Neptune, Venus, and Mercury well aspected, that is, trine (T), sextile (X), or conjunct (C) the Moon. The act of photographing is not dependent on any particular phase of the Moon, but Neptune rules photography, while Venus is related to beauty in line, form, and color.

Promotions

Choose a day when your Sun sign is favorable. Mercury should be marked C, T, or X. Avoid days when Mars or Saturn is aspected.

Selling or Canvassing

Contacts for these activities will be better during a day favorable to your Sun sign. Otherwise, make strong efforts to sell on days when Jupiter, Mercury, or Mars is trine, sextile, or conjunct the Moon. Avoid days when Saturn is square or opposite the Moon.

Signing Papers

Sign contracts or agreements when the Moon is increasing in a fruitful sign, and on a day when Moon-Mercury aspects are operating. Avoid days when Mars, Saturn, or Neptune are square or opposite the Moon.

Staff, Fire

The Moon should be in the third or fourth quarter, but not Full. There should be no squares (Q) to the Moon.

Staff, Hire

The Moon should be in the first or second quarter and should be conjunct, trine, or sextile (C, T, or X) Mercury or Jupiter.

Travel

See the travel listing in the Leisure & Recreation section.

Writing

Writing for pleasure or publication is best done when the Moon is in Gemini. Mercury should be direct. Favorable aspects to Mercury, Uranus, and Neptune promote ingenuity.

Lunar Financial Forecast

By Barbara Koval

Historically the stock market performs poorly as Jupiter and Saturn move toward their conjunction. 1999 sees Jupiter and Saturn enter the same sign to start the economic transformation that culminates next year. The best we can expect is a flat market that trades in a range. The worst we can expect is an extended decline. A flat market means you make money from dividends and interest. Corporate America has been extraordinarily stingy with dividends the past twenty years or so. This is the year to look for a good return on your investment, i.e. money earned by dividends, not a good return on speculation, a rise in the price of stocks.

Lunar Tides

The Moon has two main tides. The one we are all familiar with is the lunation cycle. We see her move from a thin crescent after her conjunction with the Sun to a blazing circle of light at the Full Moon, the opposition to the Sun. The second tide is declination, the distance above or below the Earth's equator. What we see is a Moon that travels from a position high above the horizon to one that is low. While the range is generally one in which we also view the Sun and planets, the Moon does not define the upper and lower limits. In some years she rises much higher than the Sun and planets. In some she stays below them, and 1999 is such a year. While a lower declination range does not equate to low stock prices, it does suggest that the monthly regulating force of the Moon is weakened. The lowest lunar declinations were in 1996 and 1997. Those years saw an extremely volatile market. 1987 was a year of extremely high declination. Each month the Moon pulled higher than usual. The market topped and crashed.

The lunar declination cycle suggests the market is slowly on the rise. The mutation cycle is pulling the market down. The Venus/Mars cycle is pulling up. This should keep us from any serious prolonged market decline. It could also set us up for some very severe corrections once the Jupiter/Saturn and Venus/Mars cycles turn in mid-year 2000. Play it cautious this year. Buy value. Look for dividends and interest, not speculative gains.

January

The tidal chart is very lopsided as it always is when the planets cluster in one area of the zodiac. Lunar energy is weak the first half of the month. It gets increasingly strong the second half. The Sun, Mercury, and Venus are all in their lowest declinations as the year opens, so we can presume prices will stay relatively low.

Full Moon

January 1, 8:45 pm. Wall Street Ascendant 1:01 Virgo, Midheaven 25:48 Taurus. The month opens on a potential high. While speculation is emphasized with the Sun and Venus in the Fifth House, we find Jupiter close to the Eighth House cusp and Pluto angular in the Fourth House. Bonds and interest rates dominate the action. Mars in Libra is weak for bonds. Rising interest rates could keep the market moving down.

New Moon

January 17, 10:30 am. Wall Street Ascendant 8 degrees 44 minutes Aries. Midheaven 4 degrees 40 minutes Capricorn. While speculators and investors may be of two minds with Aries in the First House and Mars in the Seventh House, we could see a flurry of short-term buying and selling over the next two weeks. Venus, Uranus, and Neptune in the Eleventh House are likely to bring people back into the market. The potential for rising prices is marked by Mercury and the lunation in the Tenth House. The significant transit of this lunation period is Saturn and Mars in hard aspect to the United States' natal Pluto. This aspect could be good news for a declining budget deficit or debt. Optimistically, it could mean a cut in interest rates.

Lunar Eclipse

January 31, 11:04 am. Wall Street Ascendant 13 degrees 56 minutes Taurus. Midheaven 25 degrees 25 minutes Capricorn. Eclipse charts continue to have life until the next pair of eclipses, in this case July and August. Although Capricorn maintains control of the Tenth House, its hold is somewhat weakened by ruling Saturn's position in Aries, a sign of weakness. The stellium across the Tenth and Eleventh Houses with both Venus and Jupiter in Pisces, a sign of strength for each, suggests a rising market in this period. As always, be cautious with eclipses. A lunar eclipse can be either a low or a high in terms of price. Much money is flowing into the market on this chart. Whether this chart means the top or the start of the flow is difficult to say. Saturn and Jupiter hit 27 degrees this month, an extremely strong degree for stock market activity. Uranus is in a harmonic, too. The vote goes

January 1999 Lunar Tide Table

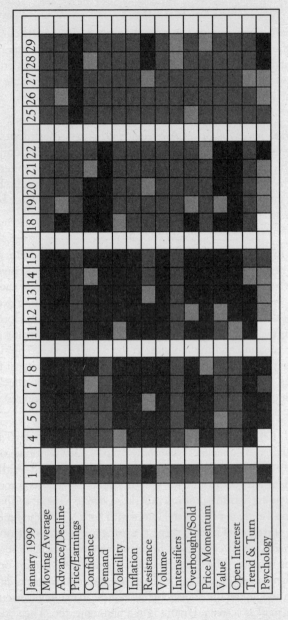

Light spaces indicate an "up" market with rising price pressure. This is a tidal "heavy pressure" period.
Dark spaces indicate a "down" market with falling price pressure. This is a tidal "light pressure" period.
Read chart down columns like a gauge. Missing dates are weekends, when the market is not open.

to a top that could carry over for a few more days. Neptune and Mars are in degrees that affect the dollar. Look for volatile moves both ways.

February

Solar Eclipse

February 16, 1:30 am. Wall Street Ascendant 2 degrees 36 minutes Sagittarius. Midheaven 18 degrees 16 minutes Virgo. This eclipse takes place in the Third House of the United States chart to highlight exports, domestic trade, and travel. The 27 degree area appears again this time in the eclipse itself and exactly on the United States Moon, the population, and the ruler of the Eleventh House of debt and taxes. Look for an announcement that could have great impact on homes, the elderly, and tax policy. Note that Jupiter moves into Aries this month to start a period where youth and enterprise is favored. Mars in the Twelfth House may bring bad news for social security recipients, a change in retirement policies, and problems with hospitalization funding.

Though both this eclipse chart and the tidal chart (not shown) point to a potential low here, one can never count on eclipses. Most likely the market will make a significant turn at this time or in the next few days. Venus and Mercury are moving into north declination, which is positive for prices. Though many indicators are negative in the first quarter, they are not so bad as to produce serious disasters.

March

Full Moon

March 2, 1:17 am EST. Wall Street Ascendant 23 degrees 56 minutes Sagittarius. Midheaven 16 degrees 05 minutes Libra. The ruler of the Tenth House of price, very weakly placed at the bottom of the chart, could make this normal topping off rather weak. Saturn moved into Taurus just prior to this lunation, which correlates to a shrinking of personal assets in general and job opportunities specific to the United States.

There is a strong potential for depleting market energy and market price during the second week. Mercury retrograde reinforces a decline. March looks lackluster at best.

New Moon

March 17, 3:09 pm. Wall Street Ascendant 23 degrees 00 minutes. Leo Midheaven 15 degrees 43 minutes Taurus. The placement of this lunation in the House of death, debt, and taxes puts the focus on interest rates and bonds.

Saturn is moving toward the Tenth House and its ruler, Venus, in a sign of weakness, suggest falling prices. Mars is also making a station in the harmonic of the eclipses. Be prepared for very volatile moves, more likely to the downside. Bonds could be especially affected. The tidal chart shows a strong upward bent the latter half of the month, which coincides with the passage of the Sun into north declination, a rising price placement.

Full Moon

March 31, 4:08 pm. Wall Street Ascendant 15 degrees 28 minutes Virgo. Midheaven 13 degrees 09 minutes Gemini. The lunation lies across the Second and Eighth Houses with the added bonus of the Sun conjunct Jupiter. The strength this month is likely to be determined by an influx of global money, particularly if foreign markets were badly hit at the eclipses in prior months. Mars is also very close to the New York mutation at this lunation, so Wall Street could take some hits. Look for a top and drop on or about March 31.

April

New Moon

April 16, 12:52 am EDT. Wall Street Ascendant 1 degree 10 minutes Capricorn. Midheaven 24 degrees 40 minutes Libra. Except for a debilitated Venus, ruler of the Tenth House, which signals falling prices, this chart is not particularly informative about the state of the stock market. It does remind us that Mars is retrograding in the First House of the New York and United States Mutation charts, the Twelfth House of the United States chart, and the Third House of the Stock Market Chart. Lots of money will be changing hands. It could be a field day for short sellers. The tidal chart suggests a low somewhere between April 7 and 16, but as the lunar cycles spread apart the trends become less well defined.

Full Moon

April 30, 11:14 am EDT. Wall Street Ascendant 28 degrees 47 minutes Cancer. Midheaven 13 degrees 36 minutes Aries. Price potential is very high here with Sun, Saturn, Jupiter, and Mercury in the Tenth House. Venus is also moving toward her highest declination, enhancing the possibility of a six month high. The separating Moon/Mars conjunction in the Fourth House is pulling in the opposite direction, so we should see a top and topple here, reinforced by the simultaneous Saturn conjunction to the Sun.

April 1999 Lunar Tide Table

April 1999	1	2		5	6	7	8	9		12	13	14	15	16		19	20	21	22	23		26	27	28	29	30
Moving Average																										
Advance/Decline																										
Price/Earnings																										
Confidence																										
Demand																										
Volatility																										
Inflation																										
Resistance																										
Volume																										
Intensifiers																										
Overbought/Sold																										
Price Momentum																										
Value																										
Open Interest																										
Trend & Turn																										
Psychology																										

Light spaces indicate an "up" market with rising price pressure. This is a tidal "heavy pressure" period.

Dark spaces indicate a "down" market with falling price pressure. This is a tidal "light pressure" period.

Read chart down columns like a gauge. Missing dates are weekends, when the market is not open.

May

New Moon

May 15, 7:04 am EDT. Wall Street Ascendant 16 degrees 43 minutes Gemini. Midheaven 22 degrees 21 minutes Aquarius. The Nodes across the Fourth/Tenth House axis could signal an important price turn this month. Mars is in the degree of the prior solar eclipse, so we could see a jolt and/or a bottom at this lunation. Mars transiting the Fifth House of speculation is in the Eleventh United States House of the market participants and mutual funds, and square the United States' Pluto. Look for some negative interest rate news. The tidal charts (not shown) suggest a possible low mid-month, in line with the New Moon timing. However, any rise thereafter may be slight or slow.

Full Moon

May 30, 3:16 am EDT. Wall Street Ascendant 20 degrees 57 minutes Aries. Midheaven 11 degrees 22 minutes Capricorn. Jupiter rising adds confidence to investors and speculators. Because the Moon is applying to a conjunction of Pluto this could well be a signal of a top and turn down.

June

New Moon

June 13, 4:02 pm EDT. Wall Street Ascendant 00 degrees 15 minutes Scorpio. Midheaven 5 degrees 46 minutes Leo. Venus conjunct the Midheaven and Jupiter in a harmonic of the prior eclipses could start another rise. Although the tidal pressures suggest a down trend, astrology works forward and backward. If the market does not correct down the first two weeks, then anticipate that this New Moon will hover in the middle price range and maintain a continued rise. We are approaching the natural high of the year at the Cancer ingress, so this timing is likely to be distorted by other factors, especially Mercury's reaching its highest declination early in the month. The fly in the ointment is Pluto in 8 degrees. The market is preparing for a serious fall, so be prepared for moves either way in this very contradictory month.

Full Moon

June 28, 4:29 pm EDT. Wall Street Ascendant 17 degrees 06 minutes Scorpio Midheaven 27 degrees 25 minutes Leo. The combination of Venus just past the Midheaven and Saturn just past the Decendant signals an important turn down. Add in the decline potential of Sun's turning down in its declination path to forecast a decline the closing week, if not slightly earlier. Although declination factors may be keeping the market from a serious decline, prices often hold off a truly strong move until all the aspects are in place. Once this Full Moon is past there is very little to hold the market up.

July

New Moon

July 12, 10:53 pm EDT. Wall Street Ascendant 12 degrees 28 minutes Pisces. Midheaven 20 degrees 33 minutes Sagittarius. The very negative Pluto in 8 degrees in the sign of the Midheaven and fairly close to a square of the Ascendant suggests falling prices. The retrograde Mercury reinforces the potential for a decline. Look for a low in the vicinity of this lunation and a rise the second half of the month.

Lunar Eclipse

July 28, 8:54 am EDT. Wall Street Ascendant 10 degrees 13 minutes Virgo. Midheaven 6 degrees 57 minutes Gemini. Venus rising on the Ascendant makes happy campers of speculators and investors, but its separating aspect, combined with an applying aspect of Pluto to the IC, is likely to mark a top and turn. Add in a Sun/Neptune opposition, another top and turn signal, to end any developing rise. This eclipse is in 5 degrees Leo/Aquarius which is very significant for gold prices. Look for a major turn in precious metals either here (more likely silver) or at the solar eclipse in August. The tidal charts (not shown) suggest a low and turn up, but we may simply be seeing a rise followed by another rise or exactly the reverse. The stock market could reach a significant low between these eclipses. The trend for the subsequent two week period is difficult to call.

August

Solar Eclipse

August 11, 5:32 am EDT. Wall Street Ascendant 11 degrees 19 minutes Leo. Midheaven 00 degrees 29 minutes Taurus. The Nodes' placement across the Ascendant of this chart signals an important price level and a significant turn. Because this chart could have a strong impact on precious metals it may coincide with an important turn for those commodities as well as for the stock market. Uranus in a silver harmonic makes the price very volatile and could give a spiky boost.

The Nodes are in a market harmonic, Jupiter is conjunct the Midheaven, and the eclipse is separating from a square to Mars, which looks like an important reversal. If this chart represents a bottom, the market will rise. If it reverses the trend, as would appear from the tidal charts, we could see a top. It is always best to stay out of the markets at eclipses. While we know eclipses mark turns, the direction is not predictable in advance. In this case Jupiter on the Midheaven looks wonderful, but it is applying to the conjunction of Saturn, which is not so hot. In addition, retrograde Venus also coincides with serious market dislocations. Be prepared for strong moves as Venus revisits the price levels she held last month.

Full Moon

August 26, 6:54 am EDT. Wall Street Ascendant 18 degrees 12 minutes Aquarius. Midheaven 6 degrees 01 minute Sagittarius. Pluto sits right on the Midheaven of this chart, which is bad news. It is also forming an applying square to the Sun and Moon, which is also bad news. Uranus on the Ascendant signals an important change of heart among the buying public. There is a bit of good news. Venus becomes visible coincidentally with this Full Moon and moves to a conjunction of Mercury, a syzygy, which often signals the top of a major move up. The combination could delay the correction for several days.

September

New Moon

September 9, 6:52 pm EDT. Wall Street Ascendant 8 degrees 59 minutes Pisces. Midheaven 18 degrees 36 minutes Sagittarius. The lunation in the Seventh House attracts foreign investors into the New York markets. Jupiter in the Second House is mildly favorable. The lunar tides are mostly even through the month, so we could see the start of a rise, however slow. Venus direct will help boost prices.

Full Moon

September 25, 8:27 am EDT. Wall Street Ascendant 21 degrees 08 minutes Libra. Midheaven 24 degrees 40 minutes Cancer. Jupiter in the Seventh House continues to attract foreign funds. Saturn's move to the cusp of the Eighth House creates more caution and less of an inclination toward leverage, which may be negative for bond prices.

October

October always shakes up the players in the stock market, because it has a dreadful history of performance in this and subsequent months. This October carries similar indicators of earlier disasters.

September 1999 Lunar Tide Table

September 1999	1	2	3	6	7	8	9	10	13	14	15	16	17	20	21	22	23	24	27	28	29	30
Moving Average																						
Advance/Decline																						
Price/Earnings																						
Confidence																						
Demand																						
Volatility																						
Inflation																						
Resistance																						
Volume																						
Intensifiers																						
Overbought/Sold																						
Price Momentum																						
Value																						
Open Interest																						
Trend & Turn																						
Psychology																						

Light spaces indicate an "up" market with rising price pressure. This is a tidal "heavy pressure" period.

Dark spaces indicate a "down" market with falling price pressure. This is a tidal "light pressure" period.

Read chart down columns like a gauge. Missing dates are weekends, when the market is not open.

New Moon

October 9, 5:48 am EDT. Wall Street Ascendant 00 degrees 22 minutes Libra. Midheaven 00 degrees 25 minutes Cancer. The autumnal equinox degree on the Ascendant warns of a possible major adjustment in the stock market. This New Moon is also on the Saturn of the United States Chart, which is not a good omen for money and banks. Saturn and Jupiter in the Eighth House can increase taxes and decrease revenue simultaneously or increase indebtedness and decrease payment. The major concern of the population will be money and taxes. This configuration does not lend itself to feeling safe. The tides (not shown) support the possibility of a major reversal to the downside the middle of the month. Pluto in 8 degrees usually has a very bad effect on price.

Full Moon

October 24, 4:26 pm EDT. Wall Street Ascendant 21 degrees 00 minutes Pisces. Midheaven 25 degrees 38 minutes Sagittarius. Mars in the Tenth House supports a turn down. Pluto, still in 8 degrees, and the lunation just past the Sun/Jupiter opposition, could mark a top and serious decline. If the market is going to go into any kind of free fall it should happen in the days surrounding this Full Moon.

November

New Moon

November 7, 10:55 pm EST. Wall Street Ascendant 13 degrees 53 minutes Leo. Midheaven 3 degrees 54 minutes Taurus. Saturn atop the chart suggests a continued slide in price and a possible bottom. Uranus opposite the Ascendant gives hope for a major reversal and an influx of foreign money or mutual funds. Mercury retrograde is also pulling for a low. The tidal chart is down heavily the first part of the month, so any rise is likely to be lackluster or short-lived.

Full Moon

November 23, 3:15 am EST. Wall Street Ascendant 17 degrees 10 minutes Libra. Midheaven 19 degrees 56 minutes Cancer. Both Venus and Jupiter in the angles presage a return of confidence and a possible influx of money, which should make Thanksgiving a bit more palatable for all. The placement in Gemini/Sagittarius also promises a major turn of events. The rise may continue beyond the Full Moon, but look for a decline the final week.

November 1999 Lunar Tide Table

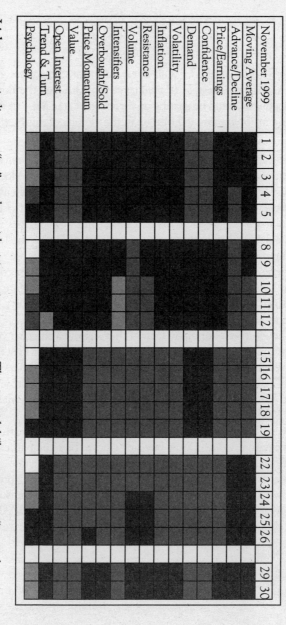

November 1999	1	2	3	4	5	8	9	10	11	12	15	16	17	18	19	22	23	24	25	26	29	30
Moving Average																						
Advance/Decline																						
Price/Earnings																						
Confidence																						
Demand																						
Volatility																						
Inflation																						
Resistance																						
Volume																						
Intensifiers																						
Overbought/Sold																						
Price Momentum																						
Value																						
Open Interest																						
Trend & Turn																						
Psychology																						

Light spaces indicate an "up" market with rising price pressure. This is a tidal "heavy pressure" period.

Dark spaces indicate a "down" market with falling price pressure. This is a tidal "light pressure" period.

Read chart down columns like a gauge. Missing dates are weekends, when the market is not open.

December

New Moon

December 7, 6:51 pm EST. Wall Street Ascendant 18 degrees 48 minutes Cancer. Midheaven 0 degrees 10 minutes Aries. Although the Bond market looks choppy, we could be gearing up for something of a rise in stocks. We could see a major bottom and turn up in the vicinity of this New Moon.

Full Moon

December 22, 12:21 pm EST. Wall Street Ascendant 12 degrees 18 minutes Aries. Midheaven 6 degrees 35 minutes Capricorn. This Full Moon falls almost exactly on the winter solstice and across the Midheaven/Imum Coeli of the lunation chart. If the market bottom did not occur at the New Moon we could see it happen here. Sun at 0 degrees Capricorn marks the default low of the stock market year and starts the long rise to the summer solstice in June of the following year.

Because this is a Full Moon rather than a New Moon it could represent one last decline to the next lunation in January, before the stock market starts to pull up, driven by the Mars, Venus, Mercury, Sun conjunction in May of 2000.

Although there are many factors that suggest a sluggish year in the economy and in the financial markets, it is unlikely we will see anything like the serious declines of the late seventies and late thirties. A lesser mutation in Taurus does not create as serious a downturn as those in Capricorn and Virgo. The quadruple conjunction of Sun, Venus, Mercury, and Mars in 2000 could even keep the overall move up.

Nevertheless, be cautious in your investments. Buy intrinsic rather than speculative value. Don't buy hot stocks. Buy companies that will outlast financial crises and pay good dividends. Buy income-generating real estate, as Saturn in Taurus and the Nodes in Cancer/Capricorn edge prices toward a major bottom and turn. This is a year for caution. It need not be a year of loss. Whatever the performance this year, 2000 may well provide a staging for another long term rise.

Electional Astrology

By Bruce Scofield

One of the oldest branches of astrology is the one called electional astrology. No, it's not about choosing a president, but it is about making choices. It's about choosing the right time to set sail, to make a change, or to write a book. It's about dancing in step to the rhythms of the cosmic environment. While electional astrology can be quite complex, there are a few things that everybody should know about. Let's look at a few simple techniques that can make your life run more smoothly.

Everybody knows that when the Sun passes through the Vernal Equinox on the first day of spring we are heading toward summer. This is when we plant our seeds, at least in the northern hemisphere. We know that growing conditions will be improving as spring wears on and summer arrives. This is electional astrology. We go with the natural cycles of nature that, in this case, are driven by the Sun's cycle which is the cycle of the year. We don't sow our seeds in November. That would be disastrous (dis=apart from, aster=the stars).

Crops are planted according to the Sun, but mammals go through fertility cycles according to the Moon. The most obvious case is the human female menstrual cycle, which is the same length as the lunar cycle of twenty-seven to twenty-nine days. Under natural conditions, women living together will tend to fall into the same fertility cycle, which follows the Moon. In our age of bright lights at night, television, and other unnatural surroundings, this feminine attunement is often distorted. If a woman knows how her cycle follows the Moon, then she will know about when she will be fertile. The cycle of the Moon can then be used to begin a pregnancy. This is another example of electional astrology.

The cycle of the Moon affects many living things. Fish bite at the New and Full Moons, and also at the quarters. If you choose to fish according to the Moon, you are doing electional astrology.

In traditional electional astrology the cycle of the Sun and Moon is important no matter what you want to do. It is the classic cycle against which everything else must be judged. This is the cycle of New Moon, second quarter, Full Moon, and last (fourth) quarter—a cycle that is crucial when doing electional astrology. Memorize the following sequence and its meaning. Imagine that an action or idea is born at the New Moon, a time of formless potential. The first quarter is a time of crisis as the emerging form struggles to find itself. The Full Moon reveals what has been developing. The action or idea that was hatched at the New Moon takes on its fully developed form and becomes visible and apparent. At the fourth quarter another crisis is reached, a crisis of usefulness and purpose. The cycle is over as the new Moon is reached again. Knowing this cycle enables one to employ electional astrology in a most fundamental way.

Let's look at an example. Suppose you want to build a house and you are able to choose when to start. First, you consider the cycle of the Sun— the season and its weather. Second, you consider the Moon's cycle. It makes sense to start building somewhere after the New Moon, the point in the cycle where the new idea or action is born. While starting after the Full Moon, during the second half of the cycle, might not result in total failure, it is just not the natural time to begin the project. Beginning during the second half of the lunar cycle may result in more problems during construction, and even afterward, than one would expect. In fact, this is what the old astrology books, some over 2,000 years old, say. Start at the New Moon and finish at the Full.

Now suppose you want to begin a renovation of an existing home. The home is an established reality—its form has been realized. The changes you want to make will not alter the home significantly. Probably the best time to begin this building project would be near or after the Full Moon. Again, this is keeping in step with nature.

Suppose you want to reach an agreement with someone. Schedule a meeting at the Full Moon, a time when each person's ideas or opinions will be fully revealed. If you reach agreement, great. If you don't, at least you know why you can't and you wouldn't have wasted any time.

The above rules will work for nearly anything you want to do. If it's new, start at the New Moon. Open up a new business at the New Moon. If it's a change to something that already exists, or you need to reach an agreement with someone, start at the Full. Merge your business with another at the Full Moon.

One other rule is worth heeding: stay away from doing things at the quarters, which represent crisis conditions. In most cases, when you exercise choice astrologically, you don't want to make things worse. All this information can be found in the Moon Tables on pages 28–51.

The aspects (anglular relationships) the Moon makes to the other planets are important. When the Moon favorably aspects Jupiter, Venus, Mercury, and the Sun, things tend to go well. It's better to do things when the aspect is moving toward completion, not afterward. When the Moon makes stressful aspects to Mars, Saturn, Uranus, Neptune, or Pluto, exercise caution as these are not good times to begin things. You'll find these aspects listed in the Lunar Aspectarian tables on pages 28–51.

After the Moon completes its last aspect within the sign it's in, it is said to be void-of-course until it enters the next sign. Actions taken during this period tend to fizzle out or evolve into something other than what was originally intended. For most elections, the Moon should not be void-of-course. It should be moving toward a favorable aspect. If you absolutely must do something when the Moon is void-of-course, have a flexible game plan and be ready to accept a range of outcomes. Doing things under a void-of-course Moon doesn't necessarily imply failure, just that the outcome is less predictable. These periods are good for processing information without the intention of reaching a conclusion. Things like therapy, discussions about closure and endings, meditations, and free-form jam sessions are appropriate during a void-of-course Moon. Check the void-of-course tables on page 55.

After checking out the Moon, check out Mercury. This second fastest mover in the sky (only the Moon is faster) does a circular dance three times a year, from the perspective of the Earth. As it makes its loops in the sky its direction shifts from forward to reverse to forward again. The reverse section of this loop is better known as its retrograde period. When Mercury is moving retrograde, which totals about nine weeks each year, conditions favor activities that replicate the backward movement of the planet. For example, r-writing a book or refurnishing an office are appropriate things to do under Mercury retrograde.

When Mercury is retrograde I buy things that are add-ons or completions to things I already own, or I buy a duplicate of something I already have. In other words, don't break new ground when Mercury is retrograde. This is especially true for those things that come under the symbolism of Mercury: communications (like talk, writing, phones, computers, radio, TV, and paperwork) and transportation (cars, bikes, planes, trains, skates, and skis). Notice that what these two themes share is the idea of connection or linkage between two or more people or places. If you want to do something that involves communication or transportation, and you want to achieve a specific outcome, don't elect to do it when Mercury is retrograde. The dates when Mercury is retrograde can be found on page 54.

Here are a few more tips about this crazy planet. When Mercury turns retrograde, and also when it turns forward again, it pivots in space. It's virtually motionless for a day or two at these points, called *stations*. On these days all sorts of complications can arise in the world. Just read the news on these days and you'll see what I mean. Go to an airport on the day Mercury stations and check out the chaos. Here's a tip: don't fly on the day, or within a few days, of when Mercury stations. If you want to start something that comes under the influence of Mercury and you want it to move along quickly, do it when Mercury is moving quickly. Mercury is at full speed between its retrograde periods, and this turns out to be most of the time.

Although electional astrology is a complex study in itself, using only the Moon and Mercury can make a big difference. I encourage readers to look at the choices and initiatives that they, and their friends and family, have made and think about the outcomes. Then correlate this information with the Moon and Mercury's astrological situation at the time choices were made or the actions initiated. If you notice a pattern, and you should, try using the Moon and Mercury at your next election.

Astrology is the conscious road map of life. Electional astrology is about using our free will in the world. The difference between electional astrology and the use of free will, as it is normally thought about in the dominant culture, is an important one. The dominant culture (Western civilization) does not admit that human life is affected by the cosmic environment. From this unnatural perspective, free will is simply doing what we choose to do. Electional astrology is based on the knowledge that human life is influenced by the rhythms of the cosmic environment. Electional astrology seeks out appropriate, or best, times to exercise free will. In this sense, electional astrology is a kind of environmental consciousness. Astrology helps us attune ourselves to the world around us. The dominant culture, whose values are based on Western religious mythologies, believes humanity has a god-given right to dominate nature. This is why astrology is not taken seriously by the majority of people. Astrology takes humanity out of the power seat and into a more realistic perspective—one in which we are simply conscious players in a much larger world, a world that reaches to the sky.

Yard Sales by the Moon

By Louise Riotte

Whether you are having a yard or garage sale (or a "jumble sale" as they call it in England), advertising items for sale in the paper, or planning an estate sale or auction, timing your sale by the Moon works to your advantage.

Planning by the Moon

Here is the general rule: sell on days when Jupiter, Mercury, or Mars are trine, sextile, or conjunct (T, X, C) the Moon, and avoid days when Saturn is square or opposite (Q or O) the Moon. Look in the Moon Tables section under the Lunar Aspectarian for this information. Find a date when as many of these aspects as possible are in effect and when your Sun sign is favorable. If there are no good dates with all of these factors, the most important ones to look for are the sextile or trine to Jupiter, with no square or opposition to Saturn. Jupiter is the planet of good fortune, so aspects to it will bring more money and people to your sale. When advertising specific items in your newspaper, you will have a little more flexibility because you can choose the date the ad will appear.

If you are selling kitchen or dining room furniture or appliances, having the Moon in Libra or Taurus will probably bring more calls as these signs have to do with fine dining, the senses, and other such things that go along with cooking and entertaining. Libra is also a good sign for the Moon to be in when selling art, books, expensive and designer goods, and any fine jewelry.

If you are selling antiques, the best signs are Scorpio, Cancer, and Capricorn. Taurus is also a good alternative. When the Moon is in one of these signs and the above instructions are followed, you will have a good turnout at your auction or estate sale. You will be flooded with calls from your ad. People like to buy things when the Moon is in one of these signs. To sell a car, choose a date when the Moon is in Taurus, Leo, Scorpio, or Aquarius. Sporting goods seem to sell quickly in Virgo, Sagittarius, Gemini, and Capricorn. Leo is a good alternative. Virgo is a health-conscious sign, and people are more inclined to buy exercise equipment at that time.

Whatever you are selling, try to time it according to the sign that rules the activity associated with the item. You will have better luck and will not have to reduce your price.

Advertising

If this is your first sale, watch the papers a week or so ahead of time and you will get an idea of how to place your ad. If you have some especially choice items, mention them, but do not give the price. If you have a nice collection of costume jewelry, glassware, or the current fad in boxes or bottles, mention these. Sometimes I have a profusion of give-away items. I once had 300 feet of iris on a terrace about six feet wide. That is a *lot* of iris. Iris keeps well out of the ground if properly stored, and I would save rhizomes (some very choice) as I divided my plants and put them away in one of my outbuildings. When I held a sale I would advertise free iris. Some plants like dill produce profuse seeds, as do garlic and walking onions. I made up small packets for give-away. Sometimes, if I had nothing else, I would advertise free cookies for children. These inexpensive items will really get your ad noticed.

There are other ways of advertising your sale besides the newspaper. Put up lots of signs. Hang bold posters at work, church, day care, senior centers, and entrances to your neighborhood. Be sure to get permission. Most people love garage sales and permission is usually given.

Preparing for the Sale

Going through the house, straightening and cleaning as we go, a large part of the work can be done at the same time as preparation for the holiday season. Take it easy! If you are working outside the home, try to do one room a week. Begin planning around the first of September, and let the kids help in the decision making if they're old enough. They can try on clothing to be discarded because it will soon be too small, or they can go through their toys and thin out those that they no longer use.

If you are an inexperienced garage saler it may help you also to begin pricing the items that you wish to sell while you are cleaning, rather than waiting and pricing in a hurry the day before the sale. Obey the rule of price setting: begin with one-fourth the original price for furniture and electronics in good condition. Some glass items can run from twenty-five to fifty cents, sheets two dollars, paperbacks fifty cents, and a dollar for a hardcover book. Videos are great sale items at three to four dollars each. People get weary of seeing their own movies and are always ready for a change.

Don't be timid about putting out broken or defective items (always, of course, with a note attached explaining the break or defect). Lots of people like to tinker with clocks, radios, fans, and other items. The same is true of lids with no bowls and bowls with no lids—I have purchased many of these myself. Wash and mend clothing if possible, but a piece otherwise good, with a rip or stain will often go for a small price. Applique can cover a stain, and a rip can be mended. Wash and display good dishes and appliances and price them accordingly.

Save boxes for the larger items if possible. Sometimes they are stacked up in the back of a grocery store and you can get permission to take them. Ask your friends to help you save paper sacks and plastic bags.

Tag each item separately if they are fairly valuable, or price them as a group. Group pricing for other things goes well. I once bought a huge bag of clean frayed bath towels and washcloths for a dollar, and have been using these as cleaning cloths ever since. Put a group of clean but really shabby clothing or broken toys in a box and sell it for a small price. You will be happily surprised at just what unusual things people will buy, including broken antiques or collectibles. Using different colored price tags for some items sometimes helps both you and the customers keep track.

It is a good idea to talk to your neighbors in advance and get their cooperation in securing parking places. They may want to include an item or two in your sale. If they have a lot of items, you could form a temporary partnership. This would help you both with breaks for telephoning, luncheon, bathroom, picking up your kids from school, or whatever. Items belonging to each of you can be tagged in different colors. Make sure your neighbor understands the pricing rules, including what happens if you sell something of hers while she is out for a break, if she is willing to let people haggle over prices, or if she wants to be present when her things are sold. It's a nuisance if you must keep a customer waiting while you try to phone her or wait until she returns. Work these things out in advance.

You may also need to get a city permit to hold your sale. Find out the rules for your city: where the sale can be held, length of time, and how often. If you live on a corner lot you might do as a friend of mine did. She had a sale on one street one week and another on the other street later!

The Day of the Sale

Yard sale shoppers tend to be early birds, so you might start your sale at 7:00 or 8:00 AM and close at 4:00 or 5:00 PM. Be sure to be ready at the time you have advertised. Prepare to spend the previous day getting everything ready, with each item tagged and taped with the price legible. Get up early and have breakfast, because you're going to have a day to remember. Be ready to greet the first customer with a smile. People do not like to be asked to come back, and often do not return. There may be other sales that day in addition to yours, and they may be better organized.

What About Leftover Items?

You may wish to keep good items that do not sell readily as holdovers for another sale. If you have items you really wish to part with, do. Experienced garage salers say to start dropping prices around noon. Some people deliberately come late in the day to take advantage of this. Experience will guide you in how low to go. Goodwill and the Salvation Army are another alternative, and will accept good or repairable items. They will give you a receipt that comes in mighty handy at tax time.

Books and magazines, like *Readers' Digest,* can give a lot of pleasure to those in veterans' or nursing homes or a nearby hospital. Nursery schools and child care centers may welcome nursery catalogs with colorful pictures of flowers and plants for children to cut out with blunt scissors, greeting cards, or good toys that your children have outgrown.

Some Dos and Don'ts

I will try to save you some of the grief of learning the hard way!

1. Don't hold items for customers without a partial payment. They might not come back.

2. Don't offer to deliver large items.

3. Don't hesitate to use salesmanship. Tell the customer the virtues of a particular item and its many uses.

4. Don't bother with people who want something for nothing, but if an item has been a hard sell and a reasonable offer has been made, use your own best judgment as to whether to accept it or not.

5. Don't mark prices directly on articles where ink can cause damage. Use masking tape or stickers.

6. Never leave the cash box unattended.

7. Don't hang around after your sale is over. Plan an evening out to celebrate, and spend some of that hard-earned cash on a good dinner. Look forward to the holidays with a clean house, money to spend on presents, and peace of mind.

Farm, Garden, & Weather

How to Choose the Best Dates

Animals and Animal Breeding

Animals are easiest to handle when the Moon is in Taurus, Cancer, Libra, or Pisces. Avoid the Full Moon. Buy animals during the first quarter or New Moon in all signs except Scorpio or Pisces. Castrate animals in Gemini, Cancer, Capricorn, or Aquarius. Slaughter for food in the first three days after the Full Moon in any sign except Leo.

Eggs should be set and animals mated so that the young will be born when the Moon is increasing and in Taurus, Cancer, Pisces, or Libra. Young born in these signs are generally healthier, mature faster and make better breeding stock. Those born during a semi-fruitful sign (Taurus and Capricorn) will generally mature quickly, but will produce leaner meat. The sign of Libra yields beautiful, graceful animals for showing and racing.

To determine the best date to mate animals or set eggs, subtract the number of days given for incubation or gestation from the fruitful dates given in the following tables. (Tables on pages 250–1.) For example, cats and dogs are mated sixty-three days previous to the desired birth date.

Garden Activities

Cultivating

Cultivate when the Moon is in a barren sign and waning, ideally the fourth quarter in Aries, Gemini, Leo, Virgo, or Aquarius. The sign of Sagittarius and the third quarter also work.

Cutting Timber

Cut timber during the third and fourth quarters while the Moon is not in a water sign.

Fertilizing and Composting

Fertilize when the Moon is in a fruitful sign (Cancer, Scorpio, Pisces). Organic fertilizers are best used when the Moon is in the third or fourth quarter. Chemical fertilizers are best used in the first or second quarter. Start compost when the Moon is in the fourth quarter in a water sign.

Grafting

Graft during first or second quarter Capricorn, Cancer, or Scorpio.

Harvesting and Drying Crops

Harvest root crops when the Moon is in a dry sign (Aries, Leo, Sagittarius, Gemini, or Aquarius) and in the third or fourth quarter. Harvest root crops intended for seed during the Full Moon. Harvest grain for storage just after the Full Moon, avoiding the water signs (Cancer, Scorpio, Pisces). Fire signs are best for cutting down on water content. Harvest fruits in the third and fourth quarters in the dry signs. Dry crops in the third quarter when the Moon is in a fire sign.

Irrigation

Irrigate when the Moon is in a water sign.

Lawn Mowing

Mow in the first and second quarters to increase growth and lushness, and in the third and fourth quarters to decrease growth.

Picking Mushrooms

Gather mushrooms at the Full Moon.

Planting

For complete instructions on planting by the phases and signs of the Moon, see Gardening by the Moon on page 247, A Guide to Planting Using Sign and Phase Rulerships on page 253, and Companion Planting on page 271.

Pruning

Prune during the third and fourth quarters in Scorpio to retard growth and to promote better fruit, and in Capricorn to promote better healing.

Spraying and Weeding

Destroy pests and weeds during the fourth quarter when the Moon is in Aries, Gemini, Leo, Virgo, Sagittarius, or Aquarius. Weed during a waning Moon in a barren sign. For the best days to kill weeds and pests, see page 267.

Transplanting

Transplant when the Moon is increasing and preferably in Cancer, Scorpio, or Pisces.

Weather

For complete weather forecasts for your zone for this year, see page 274.

Gardening by the Moon

Today, we still find those who reject the notion of Moon gardening. The usual non-believer is not the scientist, but the city dweller who has never had any real contact with nature and no experience of natural rhythms.

Camille Flammarian, the French astronomer, testifies to Moon planting. "Cucumbers increase at Full Moon, as well as radishes, turnips, leeks, lilies, horseradish, and saffron; onions, on the contrary, are much larger and better nourished during the decline and old age of the Moon than at its increase, during its youth and fullness, which is the reason the Egyptians abstained from onions, on account of their antipathy to the Moon. Herbs gathered while the Moon increases are of great efficiency. If the vines are trimmed at night when the Moon is in the sign of the Lion, Sagittarius, the Scorpion, or the Bull, it will save them from field rats, moles, snails, flies, and other animals."

Dr. Clark Timmins is one of the few modern scientists to have conducted tests in Moon planting. Following is a summary of his experiments:

Beets: When sown with the Moon in Scorpio, the germination rate was 71 percent; when sown in Sagittarius, the germination rate was 58 percent.

Scotch marigold: When sown with the Moon in Cancer, the germination rate was 90 percent; when sown in Leo, the rate was 32 percent.

Carrots: When sown with the Moon in Scorpio, the germination rate was 64 percent; when sown in Sagittarius, the germination rate was 47 percent.

Tomatoes: When sown with the Moon in Cancer, the germination rate was 90 percent; when sown in Leo, the germination rate was 58 percent.

Two things should be emphasized. First, remember that this is only a summary of the results of the experiments; the experiments themselves were conducted in a scientific manner to eliminate any variation in soil, temperature, moisture, etc., so that only the Moon's sign varied. Second, note that these astonishing results were obtained without regard to the phase of the Moon—the other factor we use in Moon planting, and which presumably would have increased the differential in germination rates.

Further experiments by Dr. Timmins involved transplanting Cancer and Leo-planted tomato seedlings while the Moon was increasing and in Cancer. The result was 100 percent survival. When transplanting was done with the Moon decreasing and in Sagittarius, there was 0 percent survival.

The results of Dr. Timmins' tests show that the Cancer-planted tomatoes had first blossoms twelve days earlier than those planted under Leo; the Cancer-planted tomatoes had an average height of twenty inches at the same age when the Leo plants were only fifteen inches high; the first ripe tomatoes were gathered from the Cancer plantings eleven days ahead of the Leo plantings; and finally, a count of the hanging fruit and comparison of size and weight shows an advantage to the Cancer plants over the Leo plants of 45 percent.

Dr. Timmins also observed that there have been similar tests that did not indicate results favorable to the Moon planting theory. As a scientist, he asked why one set of experiments indicated a positive verification of Moon planting, and others did not. He checked these other tests and found that the experimenters had not followed the geocentric system for determining the Moon sign positions, but the heliocentric. When the times used in these other tests were converted to the geocentric system, the dates chosen often were found to be in barren, rather than fertile, signs. Without going into the technical explanations, it is sufficient to point out that geocentric and heliocentric positions often vary by as much as four days. This is a large enough differential to place the Moon in Cancer, for example, in the heliocentric system, and at the same time in Leo by the geocentric system.

Most almanacs and calendars show the Moon's signs heliocentrically—and thus incorrectly for Moon planting—while the *Moon Sign Book* is calculated correctly for planting purposes, using the geocentric system.

Some readers are also confused because the *Moon Sign Book* talks of first, second, third, and fourth quarters, while some almanacs refer to these same divisions as New Moon, first quarter, Full Moon, and last quarter. Thus, the almanacs say first quarter when the *Moon Sign Book* says second quarter. (Refer to "A Note about Almanacs," page 10.)

There is nothing complicated about using astrology in agriculture and horticulture in order to increase both pleasure and profit, but there is one very important rule that is often neglected—use common sense! Of course this is one rule that should be remembered in every activity we undertake, but in the case of gardening and farming by the Moon it is not always possible to use the best dates for planting or harvesting, and we must select the next best and just try to do the best we can.

This brings up the matter of the other factors to consider in your gardening work. The dates we give as best for a certain activity apply to the entire country (with slight time correction), but in your section of the country you may be buried under three feet of snow on a date we say is a good day to plant your flowers. So we have factors of weather, season, temperature and moisture variations, soil conditions, your own available time and opportunity, and so forth. Some astrologers like to think it is all a matter of science, but gardening is also an art. In art you develop an instinctive identification with your work so that you influence it with your feelings and visualization of what you want to accomplish.

The *Moon Sign Book* gives you the place of the Moon for every day of the year so that you can select the best times once you have become familiar with the rules and practices of lunar agriculture. We try to give you specific, easy-to-follow directions so that you can get right down to work.

We give you the best dates for planting, and also for various related activities, including cultivation, fertilizing, harvesting, irrigation, and getting rid of weeds and pests. But we cannot just tell you when it's good to plant at the time. Many of these rules were learned by observation and experience, but as our body of experience grew, we could see various patterns emerging that allowed us to make judgments about new things. Then we tested the new possible applications and learned still more. That's what you should do, too. After you have worked with lunar agriculture for a while and have gained a working background of knowledge, you will probably begin to try new things—and we hope you will share your experiments and findings with us. That's how the science grows.

Here's an example of what we mean. Years ago, Llewellyn George suggested that we try to combine our bits of knowledge about what to expect in planting under each of the Moon signs in order to benefit with several such lunar factors in one plant. From this came our rule for developing "thoroughbred seed." To develop thoroughbred seed, save the seed for three successive years from plants grown by the correct Moon sign and phase. You can plant in the first quarter phase and in the sign of Cancer for fruitfulness; the second year, plant seeds from the first year plants in Libra for beauty; and in the third year, plant the seeds from the second year plants in Taurus to produce hardiness. In a similar manner you can combine the fruitfulness of Cancer, the good root growth of Pisces, and the sturdiness and good vine growth of Scorpio. And don't forget the characteristics of Capricorn: hardy like Taurus, but drier and perhaps more resistant to drought and disease.

Unlike common almanacs, we consider both the Moon's phase and the Moon's sign in making our calculations for the proper timing of our work within nature's rhythm. It is perhaps a little easier to understand this if we remind you that we are all living in the center of a vast electromagnetic field that is the Earth and its environment in space. Everything that occurs within this electromagnetic field has an effect on everything else within the same field, but since we are living on the Earth we must relate these happenings and effects to our own health and happiness. The Moon and the Sun are the most important and dynamic of the rhythmically changing factors affecting the life of the Earth, and it is their relative positions to the Earth that we project for each day of the coming year.

Many people claim that not only do they achieve larger crops gardening by the Moon, but that their fruits and vegetables are much tastier.

A number of organic gardeners have also become lunar gardeners using the natural growing methods within the natural rhythm of life forces that we experience through the relative movements of the Sun and Moon.

We provide a few basic rules and then give you month-by-month and day-by-day guidance for your farming and gardening work. You will be able to choose the best dates to meet your own needs and opportunities.

Planting by the Moon's Phases

During the increasing light (from New Moon to Full Moon), plant annuals that produce their yield above the ground. (An annual is a plant that completes its entire life cycle within one growing season and has to be seeded each year.)

During the decreasing light (from Full Moon to New Moon), plant biennials, perennials, bulb and root plants. (Biennials include crops that are planted one season to winter over and produce crops the next, such as winter wheat. Perennials and bulb and root plants include all plants that grow from the same root year after year.)

A simple, though less accurate, rule is to plant crops that produce above the ground during the increase of the Moon, and to plant crops that produce below the ground during the decrease of the Moon. This is the source of the old adage, "Plant potatoes during the dark of the Moon."

Llewellyn George went a step further and divided the lunar month into quarters. He called the first two from New Moon to Full Moon the first and second quarters, and the last two from Full Moon to New Moon the third and fourth quarters. Using these divisions, we can increase our accuracy in timing our efforts to coincide with natural forces.

First Quarter (Increasing)

Plant annuals producing their yield above the ground, which are generally of the leafy kind that produce their seed outside the fruit. Examples are asparagus, broccoli, Brussels sprouts, cabbage, cauliflower, celery, cress, endive, kohlrabi, lettuce, parsley, spinach, etc. Cucumbers are an exception, as they do best in the first quarter rather than the second, even though the seeds are inside the fruit. Also plant cereals and grains.

Second Quarter (Increasing)

Plant annuals producing their yield above the ground, which are generally of the viney kind that produce their seed inside the fruit. Examples include beans, eggplant, melons, peas, peppers, pumpkins, squash, tomatoes, etc. These are not hard and fast divisions. If you can't plant during the first quarter, plant during the second, and vice versa. There are many plants that seem to do equally well planted in either quarter, such as watermelon, hay, and cereals and grains.

Third Quarter (Decreasing)

Plant biennials, perennials, and bulb and root plants. Also plant trees, shrubs, berries, beets, carrots, onions, parsnips, peanuts, potatoes, radishes, rhubarb, rutabagas, strawberries, turnips, winter wheat, grapes, etc.

Fourth Quarter (Decreasing)

This is the best time to cultivate, turn sod, pull weeds, and destroy pests of all kinds, especially when the Moon is in the barren signs of Aries, Leo, Virgo, Gemini, Aquarius, and Sagittarius.

Planting by Moon Sign

Moon in Aries

Barren and dry, fiery and masculine. Used for destroying noxious growths, weeds, pests, etc., and for cultivating.

Moon in Taurus

Productive and moist, earthy and feminine. Used for planting many crops, particularly potatoes and root crops, and when hardiness is important. Also used for lettuce, cabbage, and similar leafy vegetables.

Moon in Gemini

Barren and dry, airy and masculine. Used for destroying noxious growths, weeds and pests, and for cultivation.

Moon in Cancer

Very fruitful and moist, watery and feminine. This is the most productive sign, used extensively for planting and irrigation.

Moon in Leo

Barren and dry, fiery and masculine. This is the most barren sign, used only for killing weeds and for cultivation.

Moon in Virgo

Barren and moist, earthy and feminine. Good for cultivation and destroying weeds and pests.

Moon in Libra

Semi-fruitful and moist, airy and masculine. Used for planting many crops and producing good pulp growth and roots. A very good sign for flowers and vines. Also used for seeding hay, corn fodder, etc.

Moon in Scorpio

Very fruitful and moist, watery and feminine. Nearly as productive as Cancer; used for the same purposes. Especially good for vine growth and sturdiness.

Moon in Sagittarius

Barren and dry, fiery and masculine. Used for planting onions, seeding hay, and for cultivation.

Moon in Capricorn

Productive and dry, earthy and feminine. Used for planting potatoes, tubers, etc.

Moon in Aquarius

Barren and dry, airy and masculine. Used for cultivation and destroying noxious growths, weeds, and pests.

Moon in Pisces

Very fruitful and moist, watery and feminine. Used along with Cancer and Scorpio, especially good for root growth.

A Guide to Planting
Using Phase & Sign Rulerships

Plant	Phase/Quarter	Sign
Annuals	1st or 2nd	
Apple trees	2nd or 3rd	Cancer, Pisces, Taurus, Virgo
Artichokes	1st	Cancer, Pisces
Asparagus	1st	Cancer, Scorpio, Pisces
Asters	1st or 2nd	Virgo, Libra
Barley	1st or 2nd	Cancer, Pisces, Libra, Capricorn, Virgo
Beans (bush & pole)	2nd	Cancer, Taurus, Pisces, Libra
Beans (kidney, white, & navy)	1st or 2nd	Cancer, Pisces
Beech Trees	2nd or 3rd	Virgo, Taurus
Beets	3rd	Cancer, Capricorn, Pisces, Libra
Biennials	3rd or 4th	
Broccoli	1st	Cancer, Pisces, Libra, Scorpio
Brussels Sprouts	1st	Cancer, Scorpio, Pisces, Libra
Buckwheat	1st or 2nd	Capricorn
Bulbs	3rd	Cancer, Scorpio, Pisces
Bulbs for Seed	2nd or 3rd	
Cabbage	1st	Cancer, Scorpio, Pisces, Libra, Taurus

Plant	Phase/Quarter	Sign
Cactus		Taurus, Capricorn
Canes (raspberries, black-berries, and gooseberries)	2nd	Cancer, Scorpio, Pisces
Cantaloupes	1st or 2nd	Cancer, Scorpio, Pisces, Libra, Taurus
Carrots	3rd	Taurus, Cancer, Scorpio, Pisces, Libra
Cauliflower	1st	Cancer, Scorpio, Pisces, Libra
Celeriac	3rd	Cancer, Scorpio, Pisces
Celery	1st	Cancer, Scorpio, Pisces
Cereals	1st or 2nd	Cancer, Scorpio, Pisces, Libra
Chard	1st or 2nd	Cancer, Scorpio, Pisces
Chicory	2nd, 3rd	Cancer, Scorpio, Pisces
Chrysanthemums	1st or 2nd	Virgo
Clover	1st or 2nd	Cancer, Scorpio, Pisces
Corn	1st	Cancer, Scorpio, Pisces
Corn for Fodder	1st or 2nd	Libra
Coryopsis	2nd or 3rd	Libra
Cosmos	2nd or 3rd	Libra
Cress	1st	Cancer, Scorpio, Pisces
Crocus	1st or 2nd	Virgo
Cucumbers	1st	Cancer, Scorpio, Pisces

Plant	Phase/Quarter	Sign
Daffodils	1st or 2nd	Libra, Virgo
Dahlias	1st or 2nd	Libra, Virgo
Deciduous Trees	2nd or 3rd	Cancer, Scorpio, Pisces, Virgo, Taurus
Eggplant	2nd	Cancer, Scorpio, Pisces, Libra
Endive	1st	Cancer, Scorpio, Pisces, Libra
Flowers	1st	Libra, Cancer, Pisces, Virgo, Scorpio, Taurus
Garlic	3rd	Libra, Taurus, Pisces
Gladiola	1st or 2nd	Libra, Virgo
Gourds	1st or 2nd	Cancer, Scorpio, Pisces, Libra
Grapes	2nd or 3rd	Cancer, Scorpio, Pisces, Virgo
Hay	1st or 2nd	Cancer, Scorpio, Pisces, Libra, Taurus
Herbs	1st or 2nd	Cancer, Scorpio, Pisces
Honeysuckle	1st or 2nd	Scorpio, Virgo
Hops	1st or 2nd	Scorpio, Libra
Horseradish	1st or 2nd	Cancer, Scorpio, Pisces
House Plants	1st	Libra, Cancer, Scorpio, Pisces
Hyacinths	3rd	Cancer, Scorpio, Pisces
Iris	1st or 2nd	Cancer, Virgo
Kohlrabi	1st or 2nd	Cancer, Scorpio, Pisces, Libra

Plant	Phase/Quarter	Sign
Leeks	1st or 2nd	Cancer, Pisces
Lettuce	1st	Cancer, Scorpio, Pisces, Libra, Taurus
Lilies	1st or 2nd	Cancer, Scorpio, Pisces
Maple Trees	2nd or 3rd	Virgo, Taurus, Cancer, Pisces
Melons	2nd	Cancer, Scorpio, Pisces
Moon Vine	1st or 2nd	Virgo
Morning Glory	1st or 2nd	Cancer, Scorpio, Pisces, Virgo
Oak Trees	2nd or 3rd	Virgo, Taurus, Cancer, Pisces
Oats	1st or 2nd	Cancer, Scorpio, Pisces, Libra
Okra	1st	Cancer, Scorpio, Pisces, Libra
Onion Seeds	2nd	Scorpio, Cancer, Sagittarius
Onion Sets	3rd or 4th	Libra, Taurus, Pisces, Cancer
Pansies	1st or 2nd	Cancer, Scorpio, Pisces
Parsley	1st	Cancer, Scorpio, Pisces, Libra
Parsnips	3rd	Taurus, Capricorn, Cancer, Scorpio, Capricorn
Peach Trees	2nd or 3rd	Taurus, Libra, Virgo, Cancer
Peanuts	3rd	Cancer, Scorpio, Pisces
Pear Trees	2nd or 3rd	Taurus, Libra, Virgo, Cancer
Peas	2nd	Cancer, Scorpio, Pisces, Libra

Plant	Phase/Quarter	Sign
Peonies	1st or 2nd	Virgo
Peppers	2nd	Cancer, Pisces, Scorpio
Perennials	3rd	
Petunias	1st or 2nd	Libra, Virgo
Plum Trees	2nd or 3rd	Taurus, Virgo, Cancer, Pisces
Poppies	1st or 2nd	Virgo
Portulaca	1st or 2nd	Virgo
Potatoes	3rd	Cancer, Scorpio, Taurus, Libra, Capricorn
Privet	1st or 2nd	Taurus, Libra
Pumpkins	2nd	Cancer, Scorpio, Pisces, Libra
Quinces	1st or 2nd	Capricorn
Radishes	3rd	Cancer, Libra, Taurus, Pisces, Capricorn
Rhubarb	3rd	Cancer, Pisces
Rice	1st or 2nd	Scorpio
Roses	1st or 2nd	Cancer, Virgo
Rutabagas	3rd	Cancer, Scorpio, Pisces, Taurus
Saffron	1st or 2nd	Cancer, Scorpio, Pisces
Sage	3rd	Cancer, Scorpio, Pisces
Salsify	1st or 2nd	Cancer, Scorpio, Pisces

Plant	Phase/Quarter	Sign
Shallots	2nd	Scorpio
Spinach	1st	Cancer, Scorpio, Pisces
Squash	2nd	Cancer, Scorpio, Pisces, Libra
Strawberries	3rd	Cancer, Scorpio, Pisces
String Beans	1st or 2nd	Taurus
Sunflowers	1st or 2nd	Libra, Cancer
Sweet Peas	1st or 2nd	Cancer, Scorpio, Pisces
Tomatoes	2nd	Cancer, Scorpio, Pisces, Capricorn
Shade Trees	3rd	Taurus, Capricorn
Ornamental Trees	2nd	Libra, Taurus
Trumpet Vines	1st or 2nd	Cancer, Scorpio, Pisces
Tubers for Seed	3rd	Cancer, Scorpio, Pisces, Libra
Tulips	1st or 2nd	Libra, Virgo
Turnips	3rd	Cancer, Scorpio, Pisces, Taurus, Capricorn, Libra
Valerian	1st or 2nd	Virgo, Gemini
Watermelons	1st or 2nd	Cancer, Scorpio, Pisces, Libra
Wheat	1st or 2nd	Cancer, Scorpio, Pisces, Libra

1999 Gardening Dates

Dates	Qtr	Sign	Activity
Jan. 1, 3:16 am– Jan. 1, 9:50 pm	2nd	Cancer	Plant grains, leafy annuals. Fertilize (chemical). Graft or bud plants. Irrigate. Trim to increase growth.
Jan. 1, 9:50 pm– Jan. 3, 5:31 am	3rd	Cancer	Plant biennials, perennials, bulbs and roots. Prune. Irrigate. Fertilize (organic).
Jan. 3, 5:31 am– Jan. 5, 10:49 am	3rd	Leo	Cultivate. Destroy weeds and pests. Harvest fruits and root crops for food. Trim to retard growth.
Jan. 5, 10:49 am– Jan. 7, 7:53 pm	3rd	Virgo	Cultivate, especially medicinal plants. Destroy weeds and pests. Trim to retard growth.
Jan. 10, 7:48 am– Jan. 12, 8:23 pm	4th	Scorpio	Plant biennials, perennials, bulbs and roots. Prune. Irrigate. Fertilize (organic).
Jan. 12, 8:23 pm– Jan. 15, 7:29 am	4th	Sagittarius	Cultivate. Destroy weeds and pests. Harvest fruits and root crops for food. Trim to retard growth.
Jan. 15, 7:29 am– Jan. 17, 10:47 am	4th	Capricorn	Plant potatoes and tubers. Trim to retard growth.
Jan. 17, 10:47 am– Jan. 17, 4:12 pm	1st	Capricorn	Graft or bud plants. Trim to increase growth.
Jan. 19, 10:41 pm– Jan. 22, 3:26 am	1st	Pisces	Plant grains, leafy annuals. Fertilize (chemical). Graft or bud plants. Irrigate. Trim to increase growth.
Jan. 24, 6:53 am– Jan. 24, 2:16 pm	1st	Taurus	Plant annuals for hardiness. Trim to increase growth.
Jan. 24, 2:16 pm– Jan. 26, 9:30 am	2nd	Taurus	Plant annuals for hardiness. Trim to increase growth.
Jan. 28, 11:57 am– Jan. 30, 3:16 pm	2nd	Cancer	Plant grains, leafy annuals. Fertilize (chemical). Graft or bud plants. Irrigate. Trim to increase growth.
Jan. 31, 11:07 am– Feb. 1, 8:37 pm	3rd	Leo	Cultivate. Destroy weeds and pests. Harvest fruits and root crops for food. Trim to retard growth.
Feb. 1, 8:37 pm– Feb. 4, 4:55 am	3rd	Virgo	Cultivate, especially medicinal plants. Destroy weeds and pests. Trim to retard growth.
Feb. 6, 4:06 pm– Feb. 8, 6:58 am	3rd	Scorpio	Plant biennials, perennials, bulbs and roots. Prune. Irrigate. Fertilize (organic).
Feb. 8, 6:58 am– Feb. 9, 4:38 am	4th	Scorpio	Plant biennials, perennials, bulbs and roots. Prune. Irrigate. Fertilize (organic).
Feb. 9, 4:38 am– Feb. 11, 4:10 pm	4th	Sagittarius	Cultivate. Destroy weeds and pests. Harvest fruits and root crops for food. Trim to retard growth.
Feb. 11, 4:10 pm– Feb. 14, 12:57 am	4th	Capricorn	Plant potatoes and tubers. Trim to retard growth.
Feb. 14, 12:57 am– Feb. 16, 1:40 am	4th	Aquarius	Cultivate. Destroy weeds and pests. Harvest fruits and root crops for food. Trim to retard growth.

1999 Gardening Dates

Dates	Qtr	Sign	Activity
Feb. 16, 6:40 am– Feb. 18, 10:07 am	1st	Pisces	Plant grains, leafy annuals. Fertilize (chemical). Graft or bud plants. Irrigate. Trim to increase growth.
Feb. 20, 12:29 pm– Feb. 22, 2:54 pm	1st	Taurus	Plant annuals for hardiness. Trim to increase growth.
Feb. 24, 6:09 pm– Feb. 26, 10:44 pm	2nd	Cancer	Plant grains, leafy annuals. Fertilize (chemical). Graft or bud plants. Irrigate. Trim to increase growth.
Mar. 2, 1:59 am– Mar. 3, 1:34 pm	3rd	Virgo	Cultivate, especially medicinal plants. Destroy weeds and pests. Trim to retard growth.
Mar. 6, 12:23 am– Mar. 8, 12:47 pm	3rd	Scorpio	Plant biennials, perennials, bulbs and roots. Prune. Irrigate. Fertilize (organic).
Mar. 8, 12:47 pm– Mar. 10, 3:41 am	3rd	Sagittarius	Cultivate. Destroy weeds and pests. Harvest fruits and root crops for food. Trim to retard growth.
Mar. 10, 3:41 am– Mar. 11, 12:54 am	4th	Sagittarius	Cultivate. Destroy weeds and pests. Harvest fruits and root crops for food. Trim to retard growth.
Mar. 11, 12:54 am– Mar. 13, 10:32 am	4th	Capricorn	Plant potatoes and tubers. Trim to retard growth.
Mar. 13, 10:32 am– Mar. 15, 4:31 pm	4th	Aquarius	Cultivate. Destroy weeds and pests. Harvest fruits and root crops for food. Trim to retard growth.
Mar. 15, 4:31 pm– Mar. 17, 1:48 pm	4th	Pisces	Plant biennials, perennials, bulbs and roots. Prune. Irrigate. Fertilize (organic).
Mar. 17, 1:48 pm– Mar. 17, 7:13 pm	1st	Pisces	Plant grains, leafy annuals. Fertilize (chemical). Graft or bud plants. Irrigate. Trim to increase growth.
Mar. 19, 8:09 pm– Mar. 21, 9:05 pm	1st	Taurus	Plant annuals for hardiness. Trim to increase growth.
Mar. 23, 11:33 pm– Mar. 24, 5:18 am	1st	Cancer	Plant grains, leafy annuals. Fertilize (chemical). Graft or bud plants. Irrigate. Trim to increase growth.
Mar. 24, 5:18 am– Mar. 25, 4:22 am	2nd	Cancer	Plant grains, leafy annuals. Fertilize (chemical). Graft or bud plants. Irrigate. Trim to increase growth.
Mar. 30, 8:50 pm– Mar. 31, 5:50 pm	2nd	Libra	Plant annuals for fragrance and beauty. Trim to increase growth.
Apr. 2, 7:49 am– Apr. 4, 8:08 pm	3rd	Scorpio	Plant biennials, perennials, bulbs and roots. Prune. Irrigate. Fertilize (organic).
Apr. 4, 8:08 pm– Apr. 7, 8:39 am	3rd	Sagittarius	Cultivate. Destroy weeds and pests. Harvest fruits and root crops for food. Trim to retard growth.
Apr. 7, 8:39 am– Apr. 8, 9:51 pm	3rd	Capricorn	Plant potatoes and tubers. Trim to retard growth.
Apr. 8, 9:51 pm– Apr. 9, 7:24 pm	4th	Capricorn	Plant potatoes and tubers. Trim to retard growth.

1999 Gardening Dates

Dates	Qtr	Sign	Activity
Apr. 9, 7:24 pm- Apr. 12, 2:35 am	4th	Aquarius	Cultivate. Destroy weeds and pests. Harvest fruits and root crops for food. Trim to retard growth.
Apr. 12, 2:35 am- Apr. 14, 5:46 am	4th	Pisces	Plant biennials, perennials, bulbs and roots. Prune. Irrigate. Fertilize (organic).
Apr. 14, 5:46 am- Apr. 15, 11:22 pm	4th	Aries	Cultivate. Destroy weeds and pests. Harvest fruits and root crops for food. Trim to retard growth.
Apr. 16, 6:07 am- Apr. 18, 5:39 am	1st	Taurus	Plant annuals for hardiness. Trim to increase growth.
Apr. 20, 6:28 am- Apr. 22, 10:06 am	1st	Cancer	Plant grains, leafy annuals. Fertilize (chemical). Graft or bud plants. Irrigate. Trim to increase growth.
Apr. 27, 2:47 am- Apr. 29, 2:13 pm	2nd	Libra	Plant annuals for fragrance and beauty. Trim to increase growth.
Apr. 29, 2:13 pm- Apr. 30, 9:55 am	2nd	Scorpio	Plant grains, leafy annuals. Fertilize (chemical). Graft or bud plants. Irrigate. Trim to increase growth.
Apr. 30, 9:55 am- May 2, 2:36 am	3rd	Scorpio	Plant biennials, perennials, bulbs and roots. Prune. Irrigate. Fertilize (organic).
May 2, 2:36 am- May 4, 3:12 pm	3rd	Sagittarius	Cultivate. Destroy weeds and pests. Harvest fruits and root crops for food. Trim to retard growth.
May 4, 3:12 pm- May 7, 2:40 am	3rd	Capricorn	Plant potatoes and tubers. Trim to retard growth.
May 7, 2:40 am- May 8, 12:28 pm	3rd	Aquarius	Cultivate. Destroy weeds and pests. Harvest fruits and root crops for food. Trim to retard growth.
May 8, 12:28 pm- May 9, 11:16 am	4th	Aquarius	Cultivate. Destroy weeds and pests. Harvest fruits and root crops for food. Trim to retard growth.
May 9, 11:16 am- May 11, 3:54 pm	4th	Pisces	Plant biennials, perennials, bulbs and roots. Prune. Irrigate. Fertilize (organic).
May 11, 3:54 pm- May 13, 4:57 pm	4th	Aries	Cultivate. Destroy weeds and pests. Harvest fruits and root crops for food. Trim to retard growth.
May 13, 4:57 pm- May 15, 7:06 am	4th	Taurus	Plant potatoes and tubers. Trim to retard growth.
May 15, 7:06 am- May 15, 4:08 pm	1st	Taurus	Plant annuals for hardiness. Trim to increase growth.
May 17, 3:40 pm- May 19, 5:38 pm	1st	Cancer	Plant grains, leafy annuals. Fertilize (chemical). Graft or bud plants. Irrigate. Trim to increase growth.
May 24, 8:29 am- May 26, 8:05 pm	2nd	Libra	Plant annuals for fragrance and beauty. Trim to increase growth.
May 26, 8:05 pm- May 29, 8:37 am	2nd	Scorpio	Plant grains, leafy annuals. Fertilize (chemical). Graft or bud plants. Irrigate. Trim to increase growth.

1999 Gardening Dates

Dates	Qtr	Sign	Activity
May 30, 1:40 am– May 31, 9:06 pm	3rd	Sagittarius	Cultivate. Destroy weeds and pests. Harvest fruits and root crops for food. Trim to retard growth.
May 31, 9:06 pm– Jun. 3, 8:37 am	3rd	Capricorn	Plant potatoes and tubers. Trim to retard growth.
Jun. 3, 8:37 am– Jun. 5, 6:01 pm	3rd	Aquarius	Cultivate. Destroy weeds and pests. Harvest fruits and root crops for food. Trim to retard growth.
Jun. 5, 6:01 pm– Jun. 6, 11:21 pm	3rd	Pisces	Plant biennials, perennials, bulbs and roots. Prune. Irrigate. Fertilize (organic).
Jun. 6, 11:21 pm– Jun. 8, 12:09 am	4th	Pisces	Plant biennials, perennials, bulbs and roots. Prune. Irrigate. Fertilize (organic).
Jun. 10, 2:44 am– Jun. 12, 2:49 am	4th	Taurus	Plant potatoes and tubers. Trim to retard growth.
Jun. 12, 2:49 am– Jun. 13, 2:03 pm	4th	Gemini	Cultivate. Destroy weeds and pests. Harvest fruits and root crops for food. Trim to retard growth.
Jun. 14, 2:14 am– Jun. 16, 3:07 am	1st	Cancer	Plant grains, leafy annuals. Fertilize (chemical). Graft or bud plants. Irrigate. Trim to increase growth.
Jun. 20, 3:10 pm– Jun. 23, 2:18 am	2nd	Libra	Plant annuals for fragrance and beauty. Trim to increase growth.
Jun. 23, 2:18 am– Jun. 25, 2:51 pm	2nd	Scorpio	Plant grains, leafy annuals. Fertilize (chemical). Graft or bud plants. Irrigate. Trim to increase growth.
Jun. 28, 3:12 am– Jun. 28, 4:38 pm	2nd	Capricorn	Graft or bud plants. Trim to increase growth.
Jun. 28, 4:38 pm– Jun. 30, 2:20 pm	3rd	Capricorn	Plant potatoes and tubers. Trim to retard growth.
Jun. 30, 2:20 pm– Jul. 2, 11:35 pm	3rd	Aquarius	Cultivate. Destroy weeds and pests. Harvest fruits and root crops for food. Trim to retard growth.
Jul. 2, 11:35 pm– Jul. 5, 6:22 am	3rd	Pisces	Plant biennials, perennials, bulbs and roots. Prune. Irrigate. Fertilize (organic).
Jul. 5, 6:22 am– Jul. 6, 6:57 am	3rd	Aries	Cultivate. Destroy weeds and pests. Harvest fruits and root crops for food. Trim to retard growth.
Jul. 6, 6:57 am– Jul. 7, 10:22 am	4th	Aries	Cultivate. Destroy weeds and pests. Harvest fruits and root crops for food. Trim to retard growth.
Jul. 7, 10:22 am– Jul. 9, 11:59 am	4th	Taurus	Plant potatoes and tubers. Trim to retard growth.
Jul. 9, 11:59 am– Jul. 11, 12:27 pm	4th	Gemini	Cultivate. Destroy weeds and pests. Harvest fruits and root crops for food. Trim to retard growth.
Jul. 11, 12:27 pm– Jul. 12, 9:24 pm	4th	Cancer	Plant biennials, perennials, bulbs and roots. Prune. Irrigate. Fertilize (organic).

1999 Gardening Dates

Dates	Qtr	Sign	Activity
Jul. 12, 9:24 pm- Jul. 13, 1:25 pm	1st	Cancer	Plant grains, leafy annuals. Fertilize (chemical). Graft or bud plants. Irrigate. Trim to increase growth.
Jul. 17, 11:19 pm- Jul. 20, 4:01 am	1st	Libra	Plant annuals for fragrance and beauty. Trim to increase growth.
Jul. 20, 4:01 am- Jul. 20, 9:30 am	2nd	Libra	Plant annuals for fragrance and beauty. Trim to increase growth.
Jul. 20, 9:30 am- Jul. 22, 9:49 pm	2nd	Scorpio	Plant grains, leafy annuals. Fertilize (chemical). Graft or bud plants. Irrigate. Trim to increase growth.
Jul. 25, 10:09 am- Jul. 27, 8:55 pm	2nd	Capricorn	Graft or bud plants. Trim to increase growth.
Jul. 28, 6:25 am- Jul. 30, 5:27 am	3rd	Aquarius	Cultivate. Destroy weeds and pests. Harvest fruits and root crops for food. Trim to retard growth.
Jul. 30, 5:27 am- Aug. 1, 11:47 am	3rd	Pisces	Plant biennials, perennials, bulbs and roots. Prune. Irrigate. Fertilize (organic).
Aug. 1, 11:47 am- Aug. 3, 4:08 pm	3rd	Aries	Cultivate. Destroy weeds and pests. Harvest fruits and root crops for food. Trim to retard growth.
Aug. 3, 4:08 pm- Aug. 4, 12:26 pm	3rd	Taurus	Plant potatoes and tubers. Trim to retard growth.
Aug. 4, 12:26 pm- Aug. 5, 6:57 pm	4th	Taurus	Plant potatoes and tubers. Trim to retard growth.
Aug. 5, 6:57 pm- Aug. 7, 8:52 pm	4th	Gemini	Cultivate. Destroy weeds and pests. Harvest fruits and root crops for food. Trim to retard growth.
Aug. 7, 8:52 pm- Aug. 9, 10:55 pm	4th	Cancer	Plant biennials, perennials, bulbs and roots. Prune. Irrigate. Fertilize (organic).
Aug. 9, 10:55 pm- Aug. 11, 6:09 am	4th	Leo	Cultivate. Destroy weeds and pests. Harvest fruits and root crops for food. Trim to retard growth.
Aug. 14, 8:25 am- Aug. 16, 5:41 pm	1st	Libra	Plant annuals for fragrance and beauty. Trim to increase growth.
Aug. 16, 5:41 pm- Aug. 18, 8:48 pm	1st	Scorpio	Plant grains, leafy annuals. Fertilize (chemical). Graft or bud plants. Irrigate. Trim to increase growth.
Aug. 18, 8:48 pm- Aug. 19, 5:32 am	2nd	Scorpio	Plant grains, leafy annuals. Fertilize (chemical). Graft or bud plants. Irrigate. Trim to increase growth.
Aug. 21, 5:59 pm- Aug. 23, 4:49 am	2nd	Capricorn	Graft or bud plants. Trim to increase growth.
Aug. 26, 12:49 pm- Aug. 26, 6:48 pm	2nd	Pisces	Plant grains, leafy annuals. Fertilize (chemical). Graft or bud plants. Irrigate. Trim to increase growth.
Aug. 26, 6:48 pm- Aug. 28, 6:09 pm	3rd	Pisces	Plant biennials, perennials, bulbs and roots. Prune. Irrigate. Fertilize (organic).

1999 Gardening Dates

Dates	Qtr	Sign	Activity
Aug. 28, 6:09 pm– Aug. 30, 9:40 pm	3rd	Aries	Cultivate. Destroy weeds and pests. Harvest fruits and root crops for food. Trim to retard growth.
Aug. 30, 9:40 pm– Sep. 2, 12:25 am	3rd	Taurus	Plant potatoes and tubers. Trim to retard growth.
Sep. 2, 12:25 am– Sep. 2, 5:18 pm	3rd	Gemini	Cultivate. Destroy weeds and pests. Harvest fruits and root crops for food. Trim to retard growth.
Sep. 2, 5:18 pm– Sep. 3, 3:10 am	4th	Gemini	Cultivate. Destroy weeds and pests. Harvest fruits and root crops for food. Trim to retard growth.
Sep. 3, 3:10 am– Sep. 6, 6:29 am	4th	Cancer	Plant biennials, perennials, bulbs and roots. Prune. Irrigate. Fertilize (organic).
Sep. 6, 6:29 am– Sep. 8, 10:57 am	4th	Leo	Cultivate. Destroy weeds and pests. Harvest fruits and root crops for food. Trim to retard growth.
Sep. 8, 10:57 am– Sep. 9, 5:03 pm	4th	Virgo	Cultivate, especially medicinal plants. Destroy weeds and pests. Trim to retard growth.
Sep. 10, 5:16 pm– Sep. 13, 2:09 am	1st	Libra	Plant annuals for fragrance and beauty. Trim to increase growth.
Sep. 13, 2:09 am– Sep. 15, 1:35 pm	1st	Scorpio	Plant grains, leafy annuals. Fertilize (chemical). Graft or bud plants. Irrigate. Trim to increase growth.
Sep. 18, 2:13 am– Sep. 20, 1:38 pm	2nd	Capricorn	Graft or bud plants. Trim to increase growth.
Sep. 22, 9:51 pm– Sep. 25, 2:34 am	2nd	Pisces	Plant grains, leafy annuals. Fertilize (chemical). Graft or bud plants. Irrigate. Trim to increase growth.
Sep. 25, 5:51 am– Sep. 27, 4:51 am	3rd	Aries	Cultivate. Destroy weeds and pests. Harvest fruits and root crops for food. Trim to retard growth.
Sep. 27, 4:51 am– Sep. 29, 6:21 am	3rd	Taurus	Plant potatoes and tubers. Trim to retard growth.
Sep. 29, 6:21 am– Oct. 1, 8:32 am	3rd	Gemini	Cultivate. Destroy weeds and pests. Harvest fruits and root crops for food. Trim to retard growth.
Oct. 1, 8:32 am– Oct. 1, 11:03 pm	3rd	Cancer	Plant biennials, perennials, bulbs and roots. Prune. Irrigate. Fertilize (organic).
Oct. 1, 11:03 pm– Oct. 3, 12:14 pm	4th	Cancer	Plant biennials, perennials, bulbs and roots. Prune. Irrigate. Fertilize (organic).
Oct. 3, 12:14 pm– Oct. 5, 5:40 pm	4th	Leo	Cultivate. Destroy weeds and pests. Harvest fruits and root crops for food. Trim to retard growth.
Oct. 5, 5:40 pm– Oct. 8, 12:52 am	4th	Virgo	Cultivate, especially medicinal plants. Destroy weeds and pests. Trim to retard growth.
Oct. 9, 6:34 am– Oct. 10, 10:01 am	1st	Libra	Plant annuals for fragrance and beauty. Trim to increase growth.

1999 Gardening Dates

Dates	Qtr	Sign	Activity
Oct. 10, 10:01 am– Oct. 12, 9:18 pm	1st	Scorpio	Plant grains, leafy annuals. Fertilize (chemical). Graft or bud plants. Irrigate. Trim to increase growth.
Oct. 15, 10:03 am– Oct. 17, 9:59 am	1st	Capricorn	Graft or bud plants. Trim to increase growth.
Oct. 17, 9:59 am– Oct. 17, 10:17 pm	2nd	Capricorn	Graft or bud plants. Trim to increase growth.
Oct. 20, 7:33 am– Oct. 22, 12:42 pm	2nd	Pisces	Plant grains, leafy annuals. Fertilize (chemical). Graft or bud plants. Irrigate. Trim to increase growth.
Oct. 24, 2:26 pm– Oct. 24, 4:03 pm	2nd	Taurus	Plant annuals for hardiness. Trim to increase growth.
Oct. 24, 4:03 pm– Oct. 26, 2:34 pm	3rd	Taurus	Plant potatoes and tubers. Trim to retard growth.
Oct. 26, 2:34 pm– Oct. 28, 3:09 pm	3rd	Gemini	Cultivate. Destroy weeds and pests. Harvest fruits and root crops for food. Trim to retard growth.
Oct. 28, 3:09 pm– Oct. 30, 5:47 pm	3rd	Cancer	Plant biennials, perennials, bulbs and roots. Prune. Irrigate. Fertilize (organic).
Oct. 30, 5:47 pm– Oct. 31, 7:04 am	3rd	Leo	Cultivate. Destroy weeds and pests. Harvest fruits and root crops for food. Trim to retard growth.
Oct. 31, 7:04 am– Nov. 1, 11:07 pm	4th	Leo	Cultivate. Destroy weeds and pests. Harvest fruits and root crops for food. Trim to retard growth.
Nov. 1, 11:07 pm– Nov. 4, 6:56 am	4th	Virgo	Cultivate, especially medicinal plants. Destroy weeds and pests. Trim to retard growth.
Nov. 6, 4:45 pm– Nov. 7, 10:53 pm	4th	Scorpio	Plant biennials, perennials, bulbs and roots. Prune. Irrigate. Fertilize (organic).
Nov. 7, 10:53 pm– Nov. 9, 4:15 am	1st	Scorpio	Plant grains, leafy annuals. Fertilize (chemical). Graft or bud plants. Irrigate. Trim to increase growth.
Nov. 11, 5:00 pm– Nov. 14, 5:46 am	1st	Capricorn	Graft or bud plants. Trim to increase growth.
Nov. 16, 4:21 pm– Nov. 18, 10:58 pm	2nd	Pisces	Plant grains, leafy annuals. Fertilize (chemical). Graft or bud plants. Irrigate. Trim to increase growth.
Nov. 21, 1:26 am– Nov. 23, 1:14 am	2nd	Taurus	Plant annuals for hardiness. Trim to increase growth.
Nov. 23, 2:04 am– Nov. 25, 12:29 am	3rd	Gemini	Cultivate. Destroy weeds and pests. Harvest fruits and root crops for food. Trim to retard growth.
Nov. 25, 12:29 am– Nov. 27, 1:18 am	3rd	Cancer	Plant biennials, perennials, bulbs and roots. Prune. Irrigate. Fertilize (organic).
Nov. 27, 1:18 am– Nov. 29, 5:11 am	3rd	Leo	Cultivate. Destroy weeds and pests. Harvest fruits and root crops for food. Trim to retard growth.

1999 Gardening Dates

Dates	Qtr	Sign	Activity
Nov. 29, 5:11 am- Nov. 29, 6:19 pm	3rd	Virgo	Cultivate, especially medicinal plants. Destroy weeds and pests. Trim to retard growth.
Nov. 29, 6:19 pm- Dec. 1, 12:29 pm	4th	Virgo	Cultivate, especially medicinal plants. Destroy weeds and pests. Trim to retard growth.
Dec. 3, 10:36 pm- Dec. 6, 10:28 am	4th	Scorpio	Plant biennials, perennials, bulbs and roots. Prune. Irrigate. Fertilize (organic).
Dec. 6, 10:28 am- Dec. 7, 5:32 pm	4th	Sagittarius	Cultivate. Destroy weeds and pests. Harvest fruits and root crops for food. Trim to retard growth.
Dec. 8, 11:14 pm- Dec. 11, 11:59 am	1st	Capricorn	Graft or bud plants. Trim to increase growth.
Dec. 13, 11:18 pm- Dec. 15, 7:50 pm	1st	Pisces	Plant grains, leafy annuals. Fertilize (chemical). Graft or bud plants. Irrigate. Trim to increase growth.
Dec. 15, 7:50 pm- Dec. 16, 7:30 am	2nd	Pisces	Plant grains, leafy annuals. Fertilize (chemical). Graft or bud plants. Irrigate. Trim to increase growth.
Dec. 18, 11:45 am- Dec. 20, 12:39 pm	2nd	Taurus	Plant annuals for hardiness. Trim to increase growth.
Dec. 22, 11:52 am- Dec. 22, 12:31 pm	2nd	Cancer	Plant grains, leafy annuals. Fertilize (chemical). Graft or bud plants. Irrigate. Trim to increase growth.
Dec. 22, 12:31 pm- Dec. 24, 11:32 am	3rd	Cancer	Plant biennials, perennials, bulbs and roots. Prune. Irrigate. Fertilize (organic).
Dec. 24, 11:32 am- Dec. 26, 1:34 pm	3rd	Leo	Cultivate. Destroy weeds and pests. Harvest fruits and root crops for food. Trim to retard growth.
Dec. 26, 1:34 pm- Dec. 28, 7:15 pm	3rd	Virgo	Cultivate, especially medicinal plants. Destroy weeds and pests. Trim to retard growth.

Dates to Destroy Weeds & Pests

From		To		Sign	Quarter
Jan. 3	5:31 am	Jan. 5	10:49 am	Leo	3rd
Jan. 5	10:49 am	Jan. 7	7:53 pm	Virgo	3rd
Jan. 12	8:23 pm	Jan. 15	7:29 am	Sagittarius	4th
Jan. 31	11:07 am	Feb. 1	8:37 pm	Leo	3rd
Feb. 1	8:37 pm	Feb. 4	4:55 am	Virgo	3rd
Feb. 9	4:38 am	Feb. 11	4:10 pm	Sagittarius	4th
Feb. 14	12:57 am	Feb. 16	1:40 am	Aquarius	4th
Mar. 2	1:59 am	Mar. 3	1:34 pm	Virgo	3rd
Mar. 8	12:47 pm	Mar. 10	3:41 am	Sagittarius	3rd
Mar. 10	3:41 am	Mar. 11	12:54 am	Sagittarius	4th
Mar. 13	10:32 am	Mar. 15	4:31 pm	Aquarius	4th
Apr. 4	8:08 pm	Apr. 7	8:39 am	Sagittarius	3rd
Apr. 9	7:24 pm	Apr. 12	2:35 am	Aquarius	4th
Apr. 14	5:46 am	Apr. 15	11:22 pm	Aries	4th
May 2	2:36 am	May 4	3:12 pm	Sagittarius	3rd
May 7	2:40 am	May 8	12:28 pm	Aquarius	3rd
May 8	12:28 pm	May 9	11:16 am	Aquarius	4th
May 11	3:54 pm	May 13	4:57 pm	Aries	4th
May 30	1:40 am	May 31	9:06 pm	Sagittarius	3rd
Jun. 3	8:37 am	Jun. 5	6:01 pm	Aquarius	3rd
Jun. 12	2:49 am	Jun. 13	2:03 pm	Gemini	4th
Jul. 30	2:20 pm	Jul. 2	11:35 pm	Aquarius	3rd
Jul. 5	6:22 am	Jul. 6	6:57 am	Aries	3rd
Jul. 6	6:57 am	Jul. 7	10:22 am	Aries	4th
Jul. 9	11:59 am	Jul. 11	12:27 pm	Gemini	4th
Jul. 28	6:25 am	Jul. 30	5:27 am	Aquarius	3rd
Aug. 1	11:47 am	Aug. 3	4:08 pm	Aries	3rd

Dates to Destroy Weeds & Pests

From		To		Sign	Quarter
Aug. 5	6:57 pm	Aug. 7	8:52 pm	Gemini	4th
Aug. 9	10:55 pm	Aug. 11	6:09 am	Leo	4th
Aug. 28	6:09 pm	Aug. 30	9:40 pm	Aries	3rd
Sep. 2	12:25 am	Sep. 2	5:18 pm	Gemini	3rd
Sep. 2	5:18 pm	Sep. 3	3:10 am	Gemini	4th
Sep. 6	6:29 am	Sep. 8	10:57 am	Leo	4th
Sep. 8	10:57 am	Sep. 9	5:03 pm	Virgo	4th
Sep. 25	5:51 am	Sep. 27	4:51 am	Aries	3rd
Sep. 29	6:21 am	Oct. 1	8:32 am	Gemini	3rd
Oct. 3	12:14 pm	Oct. 5	5:40 pm	Leo	4th
Oct. 5	5:40 pm	Oct. 8	12:52 am	Virgo	4th
Oct. 26	2:34 pm	Oct. 28	3:09 pm	Gemini	3rd
Oct. 30	5:47 pm	Oct. 31	7:04 am	Leo	3rd
Oct. 31	7:04 am	Nov. 1	11:07 pm	Leo	4th
Nov. 1	11:07 pm	Nov. 4	6:56 am	Virgo	4th
Nov. 23	2:04 am	Nov. 25	12:29 am	Gemini	3rd
Nov. 27	1:18 am	Nov. 29	5:11 am	Leo	3rd
Nov. 29	5:11 am	Nov. 29	6:19 pm	Virgo	3rd
Nov. 29	6:19 pm	Dec. 1	12:29 pm	Virgo	4th
Dec. 6	10:28 am	Dec. 7	5:32 pm	Sagittarius	4th
Dec. 24	11:32 am	Dec. 26	1:34 pm	Leo	3rd
Dec. 26	1:34 pm	Dec. 28	7:15 pm	Virgo	3rd

Gestation & Incubation

Animal	Young/Eggs	Gestation/Incubation
Horse	1	346 days
Cow	1	283 days
Monkey	1	164 days
Goat	1–2	151 days
Sheep	1–2	150 days
Pig	10	112 days
Chinchilla	2	110 days
Fox	5–8	63 days
Dog	6–8	63 days
Cat	4–6	63 days
Guinea Pig	2–6	62 days
Ferret	6–9	40 days
Rabbit	4–8	30 days
Rat	10	22 days
Mouse	10	22 days
Turkey	1–15	26-30 days
Guinea	15–18	25-26 days
Pea Hen	10	28-30 days
Duck	9–12	25-32 days
Goose	15–18	27-33 days
Hen	12–15	19-24 days
Pigeon	2	16-20 days
Canary	3–4	13-14 days

Dates to be Born	Sign	Qtr.	Set Eggs
Jan. 1, 3:16 am–Jan. 1, 9:50 pm	Cancer	2nd	Dec. 11, 1998
Jan. 19, 10:41 pm–Jan. 22, 3:26 am	Pisces	1st	Dec. 29–Jan. 1
Jan. 24, 6:53 am–Jan. 24, 2:16 pm	Taurus	1st	Jan. 3
Jan. 28, 11:57 am–Jan. 30, 3:16 pm	Cancer	2nd	Jan. 7–Jan. 9
Feb. 16, 6:40 am–Feb. 18, 10:07 am	Pisces	1st	Jan. 26–Jan. 28
Feb. 20, 12:29 pm–Feb. 22, 2:54 pm	Taurus	1st	Jan. 30–Feb. 1
Feb. 24, 6:09 pm–Feb. 26, 10:44 pm	Cancer	2nd	Feb. 3–Feb. 5
Mar. 17, 1:48 pm–Mar. 17, 7:13 pm	Pisces	1st	Feb. 24
Mar. 19, 8:09 pm–Mar. 21, 9:05 pm	Taurus	1st	Feb. 26–Feb. 28
Mar. 23, 11:33 pm–Mar. 24, 5:18 am	Cancer	1st	Mar. 2–Mar. 3
Mar. 30, 8:50 pm–Mar. 31, 5:50 pm	Libra	2nd	Mar. 9–Mar. 10
Apr. 16, 6:07 am–Apr. 18, 5:39 am	Taurus	1st	Mar. 26–Mar. 28
Apr. 20, 6:28 am–Apr. 22, 10:06 am	Cancer	1st	Mar. 30–Apr. 1
Apr. 27, 2:47 am–Apr. 29, 2:13 pm	Libra	2nd	Apr. 6–Apr. 8
May 15, 7:06 am–May 15, 4:08 pm	Taurus	1st	Apr. 24
May 17, 3:40 pm–May 19, 5:38 pm	Cancer	1st	Apr. 26–Apr. 28
May 24, 8:29 am–May 26, 8:05 pm	Libra	2nd	May 3–May 5
Jun. 14, 2:14 am–Jun. 16, 3:07 am	Cancer	1st	May 24–May 26
Jun. 20, 3:10 pm–Jun. 23, 2:18 am	Libra	2nd	May 30–Jun. 2
Jul. 12, 9:24 am–Jul. 13, 1:25 pm	Cancer	1st	Jun. 21–Jun. 22
Jul. 17, 11:19 pm–Jul. 20, 4:01 am	Libra	1st	Jun. 26–Jun. 29
Aug. 14, 8:25 am–Aug. 16, 5:41 pm	Libra	1st	Jul. 24–Jul. 26
Aug. 26, 12:49 pm–Aug. 26, 6:48 pm	Pisces	2nd	Aug. 5
Sep. 10, 5:16 pm–Sep. 13, 2:09 am	Libra	1st	Aug. 20–Aug. 23
Sep. 22, 9:51 pm–Sep. 25, 2:34 am	Pisces	2nd	Sep. 1–Sep. 4
Oct. 9, 6:34 am–Oct. 10, 10:01 am	Libra	1st	Sep. 18–Sep. 19
Oct. 20, 7:33 am–Oct. 22, 12:42 pm	Pisces	2nd	Sep. 29–Oct. 1
Oct. 24, 2:26 pm–Oct. 24, 4:03 pm	Taurus	2nd	Oct. 3
Nov. 16, 4:21 pm–Nov. 18, 10:58 pm	Pisces	2nd	Oct. 26–Oct. 28
Nov. 21, 1:26 am–Nov. 23, 1:14 am	Taurus	2nd	Oct. 31–Nov. 2
Dec. 13, 11:18 pm–Dec. 15, 7:50 pm	Pisces	1st	Nov. 22–Nov. 24
Dec. 18, 11:45 am–Dec. 20, 12:39 pm	Taurus	2nd	Nov. 27–Nov. 29
Dec. 22, 11:52 am–Dec. 22, 12:31 pm	Cancer	2nd	Dec. 1

Companion Planting

Plant Helpers and Hinderers

Plant	Helped By	Hindered By
Asparagus	Tomatoes, Parsley, Basil	
Beans	Carrots, Cucumbers, Cabbage, Beets, Corn	Onions, Gladiola
Bush Beans	Cucumbers, Cabbage, Strawberries	Fennel, Onions
Beets	Onions, Cabbage, Lettuce	Pale Beans
Cabbage	Beets, Potatoes, Onions, Celery	Strawberries, Tomatoes
Carrots	Peas, Lettuce, Chives, Radishes, Leeks, Onions	Dill
Celery	Leeks, Bush Beans	
Chives	Beans	
Corn	Potatoes, Beans, Peas, Melons, Squash, Pumpkins, Cucumbers	
Cucumbers	Beans, Cabbage, Radishes, Sunflowers, Lettuce	Potatoes, Aromatic Herbs
Eggplant	Beans	
Lettuce	Strawberries, Carrots	
Melons	Morning glories	
Onions, Leeks	Beets, Chamomile, Carrots, Lettuce	Peas, Beans
Garlic	Summer Savory	
Peas	Radishes, Carrots, Corn, Cucumbers, Beans, Turnips	Onions
Potatoes	Beans, Corn, Peas, Cabbage, Hemp, Cucumbers	Sunflowers

Plant	Helped By	Hindered By
Radishes	Peas, Lettuce, Nasturtium, Cucumbers	Hyssop
Spinach	Strawberries	
Squash, Pumpkins	Nasturtium, Corn	Potatoes
Tomatoes	Asparagus, Parsley, Chives, Onions, Carrots, Marigold, Nasturtium	Dill, Cabbage, Fennel
Turnips	Peas, Beans	

Plant Companions and Uses

Plant	Companions and Uses
Anise	Coriander
Basil	Tomatoes; dislikes rue; repels flies and mosquitos
Borage	Tomatoes and squash
Buttercup	Clover; hinders delphiniums, peonies, monkshood, columbines
Chamomile	Helps peppermint, wheat, onions and cabbage; large amounts destructive
Catnip	Repels flea beetles
Chervil	Radishes
Chives	Carrots; prone to apple scab and powdery mildew
Coriander	Hinders seed formation in fennel
Cosmos	Repels corn earworm
Dill	Cabbage; hinders carrots and tomatoes
Fennel	Disliked by all garden plants
Garlic	Aids vetch and roses; hinders peas and beans
Hemp	Beneficial as a neighbor to most plants
Horseradish	Repels potato bugs

Plant	Companions and Uses
Horsetail	Makes fungicide spray
Hyssop	Attracts cabbage fly away from cabbages; harmful to radishes
Lovage	Improves hardiness and flavor of neighbor plants
Marigold	Pest repellent; use against Mexican bean beetles and nematodes
Mint	Repels ants, flea beetles and cabbage worm butterflies
Morning glory	Corn; helps melon germination
Nasturtium	Cabbage, cucumbers; deters aphids, squash bugs and pumpkin beetles
Nettles	Increase oil content in neighbors
Parsley	Tomatoes, asparagus
Purslane	Good ground cover
Rosemary	Repels cabbage moths, bean beetles, and carrot flies
Sage	Repels cabbage moths and carrot flies
Savory	Deters bean beetles
Sunflower	Hinders potatoes; improves soil
Tansy	Deters Japanese beetles, striped cucumber beetles, and squash bugs
Thyme	Repels cabbage worm
Yarrow	Increases essential oils of neighbors

Editor's note: Companion planting, or placing plants that "help" each other together, can greatly enhance your garden when used in conjunction with organic gardening methods. This table is a general guide to companion planting, and is not meant to be comprehensive.

1999 Weather Predictions

By Nancy Soller

January 1999

Zone One: A severe winter is predicted in the extreme north with much snow and low temperatures. Most of this zone, however, will have below-average temperatures with little precipitation. Watch for winds in the extreme south. Watch for precipitation January 12, 13, and 17; January 23 in the extreme north, January 27, 29, and 31. Watch for winds January 15, 23, 26, 27, 29, and 31.

Zone Two: Very cold weather is predicted for this zone this month. Little precipitation is forecast east, but a dumping of precipitation is possible west. Winds are likely to be strong throughout much of this zone. Watch for precipitation January 4, 12, 13, 17, 26, and 31. Winds are likely January 4, 12, 13, 15, and 23, and January 31 east.

Zone Three: A severe winter is forecast for the Plains. There will be much precipitation and some very low temperatures. Watch for snowfall January 4, 11, 12, 13, 16, 17, 26, and 31. Watch for winds January 4, 11, 12, 13, 15, 16, 26, and 30. Snowfall farther west may come this far east January 2, 5, 8, 20, 23, 24, and 25.

Zone Four: A warm January is predicted for this zone. There will be both snowfall and chill, but the weather will be milder than usual. Watch for precipitation January 4, 11, 12, 13, 16, 17, 26, and 31. Snowfall may also reach this area January 2, 5, 8, 20, 23, 24, and 25. Watch for winds January 4, 9, 11, 12, 13, 15, 16, 26, and 30.

Zone Five: January weather will be seasonable with temperatures likely to be more mild than usual. Watch for precipitation January 1, 4, 5, 8, and 12; also January 19, 22, 23, 24, 26, and 30. January's weather patterns should continue into the month of February.

Zone Six: January weather will be chill and windy on the Alaskan Panhandle, but warmer than usual and relatively dry in the interior of the state. Hawaii should have a normal month. Watch for precipitation January 1, 4, 5, 8, 12, 13, and 17; also January 19, 22, 24, 26, 27, 29, and 31.

6
Alaska
Hawaii

Map of Weather Zones

Dates to Watch

Precipitation: January 1, 3, 4, 5, 8, 11, 12, 13, 16, 17, 19, 22, 23, 24, 26, 27, 29, and 31. **Winds:** January *1*, *2*, 4, *12*, *13*, *15*, *16*, *19*, 23, *24*, 26, 27, 29, *30*, and *31*. (*Italicized dates are strong winds.*)

February 1999

Zone One: Severe weather in the extreme north and chill, dry and windy weather in the extreme south is the forecast for this zone this month. Watch for precipitation February 1, 2, 8, 11, the 16 south; also February 17, 24, and 26. Winds are due February 1, 2, 3, February 4 south, February 5, 10, 11, and 14; also February 15, 16, and 18.

Zone Two: Chill, windy weather is forecast for most of this zone in February. Areas near the Mississippi may see a dumping of precipitation. Watch for snowfall or freezing rain February 1, 2, 4, 5, and 8; also February 17, 23, 24, and 26. Winds are likely February 1, 2, 3, 4, 5, and 10; also February 14, 15, 16, 17, 18, and 21. February's weather patterns should continue in March.

Zone Three: A severe February with low temperatures and much precipitation is forecast for most of this zone. Some areas near the Mississippi may miss the extremely low temperatures. Watch for snowfall February 2, 8, 11, 16, 17 east, February 23, 24, and 26. Winds are likely February 2, 3, 4, 5, 10, 11, and 21. February weather patterns should continue into March.

Zone Four: January's normal weather patterns should continue throughout February for most of this zone, although areas in the extreme east may see some very low temperatures and extremely heavy precipitation. Watch for snowfall February 2, the 4 east, February 5, 8, 11, 16, and 24. Watch for winds February 1, 2, 5, 11, and 18.

Zone Five: A mild month is forecast for this zone in February. It should also be relatively dry. Precipitation will be most likely February 2, 5, and 22. Watch for winds February 1, 2, 3, 5, and also February 14, 16, and 17. Warmer-than-normal temperature patterns should continue into the month of March, but the spring will be chill here.

Zone Six: Chill, windy and relatively dry weather is forecast for the Alaskan Panhandle; the central part of the state should see mild temperatures and less precipitation than usual. Hawaiian weather should be normal for the season. Watch for precipitation February 1–3, February 5, 8, and 11, February 16, and 17; also the 22, 24, and 26. Winds will be frequent and very chill on the Panhandle.

Dates to Watch

Precipitation: February 1, 2, 5, 8, 11, 16, 17, 22, 23, 24, and 26. **Winds:** February *1*, *2*, *3*, *4*, *5*, *10*, 11, *14*, *15*, 16, *17*, *18*, and *21*.

March 1999

Zone One: Most of the month will have chill weather with much precipitation in the extreme north and very cold, chill temperatures in the south. Watch for precipitation north March 2. Watch for more precipitation March 7, 12, 14, 19, 21, 24, 27, and 31. Watch for winds March 2 north, March 7, 12, 20, 23, 27, and 31. Spring weather will be wet throughout the entire zone.

Zone Two: A chill, dry and windy month is the forecast for this zone, but the last week of the month will see much rainfall. Watch for precipitation March 7, 12, 14, 19, 21, 24, 27, and 31. Winds are likely March 7, 12, 20, 23, 27, and 31. Wet weather will come the last week of the month in the east.

Zone Three: A chill month with much precipitation is forecast for this zone in March. Watch for precipitation March 2, 5, 7, 19, 21, and 24. Watch for winds March 1, 5, 7, 20, 23, 29, and 31. Dry weather may be found in western portions of this zone at the end of this month.

Zone Four: Wet weather east and dry, mild weather west is the forecast for this zone in March. The last week of the month should usher in dry weather over the entire zone and this should last throughout the entire spring. Precipitation will be most likely March 2, 5, 7, 19, 21, and 24. Watch for winds March 1, 5, 7 20, 23, 29, and 31.

Zone Five: A dry month is predicted for this zone in March. Temperatures will be mild the first part of the month, but the last week of the month should be more chill and also windy. Best chances for precipitation occur March 2, 5, 10, 12, and 17. Winds are likely March 1, 2, 5, 19, and 31. Chill, dry and windy weather should continue throughout the spring.

Zone Six: A dry month with mild temperatures is predicted for the Alaskan Panhandle. The interior of the state could see some extremely cold weather with much precipitation. Hawaii should have normal weather, but the last week of the month should be cooler than normal. Precipitation is most likely March 1, 5, 7, 10, 12, 17, 19, 21, 24, 27, and 31.

Dates to Watch

Precipitation: March 3, 5, 7, 10, 12, 14, 17, 19, 21, 24, 27, and 31. **Winds:** March 1, 2, 5, 7, 12, 19, 20, 23, 27, 29, and 31.

April 1999

Zone One: generous precipitation is forecast for this zone during the month of April. Watch for heavy rainfall April 4, 6, 15, 24, and 26. Other dates are also likely to result in rain. Winds are likely April 4, 5, and 23. Generous rainfall in this zone this month should continue setting a pattern for the entire spring season. Summer should be wet north.

Zone Two: Generous rainfall is forecast for this zone during the month of April. Watch for very heavy rain April 4, 6, 15, 24, and 26. Other dates should result in more rain. Watch for wind April 4, 5, and 23. Rainfall patterns set this month should continue throughout the entire spring season. A wet summer is predicted for most of this zone.

Zone Three: Normal temperatures and precipitation patterns are forecast for this zone in April, but areas in the extreme west will see some dry weather. Watch for rainfall east April 4 and 15; watch for more rainfall April 19, 22, 24, 26, and 27. Winds are likely April 19, 24, 25, 26, and 30. Weather patterns established here this month will set the pattern for the entire spring.

Zone Four: Dry weather is forecast for this zone in April. Temperatures will be mild. Watch for precipitation April 4 east; also April 15, 19, 22, 26, and 27. Watch for winds April 19, 24, 25, 26, and 30. Weather patterns established this month are likely to continue throughout the entire spring. Summer weather will be normal for the season in most of this zone.

Zone Five: Dry, cool weather is predicted for this zone in April. Winds are likely to be prominent. Precipitation will be most likely April 8, 15, 20, 21, 22, 23, and 27. Winds are likely April 5, 21, 23, 25, and 30. The cool, dry weather patterns established this month will be likely to continue throughout the entire spring. Summer weather should return to normal.

Zone Six: The Alaskan Panhandle will have less precipitation than normal and temperatures will be high this month. Seasonal weather is predicted for the rest of the state. Hawaii will see weather drier and cooler than normal. Watch for rainfall April 4, 6, 8, 15, and 20; also April 21, 22, 23, 24, 26, and 30. Winds will be frequent in Alaska.

Dates to Watch

Precipitation: April 4, 6, 8, 15, 19, 20, 21, 22, 23, 24, 26, and 27. **Winds:** April 4, 5, 19, 21, 23, 24, 25, 26, and 30.

May 1999

Zone One: Wet weather with seasonable temperatures is forecast for this zone in May. Watch for very heavy rainfall May 13, 16, 21, 22, 25, 30, and 31. Other rains are likely May 8, 12, and 15. Winds are due May 1, 7, 12, 13, 17, and 18; also May 21, 24, 30, and 31. Wet weather should continue into the month of June in this zone.

Zone Two: Wet weather is predicted for the easternmost portions of this zone; normal precipitation is forecast for the rest of this area. Temperatures should be seasonable. Watch for rainfall May 8, 12, 13, 15, and 16; also May 21, 22, 25, 30 and 31. Winds are likely May 1, 24, 30, and 31. June's weather should be a continuation of May weather.

Zone Three: Eastern portions of this zone should see seasonable precipitation and temperatures; to the west it should be very dry. Rainfall will be most likely May 8, 12, 13, 15, 22, 25, and 31. Winds are likely May 18, 24, 25, 30, and 31. May's weather patterns should extend well into the month of June. Summer should be dry east.

Zone Four: Dry weather is forecast for this zone in May. Temperatures should be seasonable. Dates most likely to result in rain include May 8, 12, 13, 15, 22, 25, and 31. Winds are forecast May 7, 8, 12, 13, and 17; also May 18, 24, 25, 30, and 31. Weather patterns in effect this month in this zone should extend well into the month of June.

Zone Five: Dry weather and cool temperatures are forecast for this zone in May. Best chances for precipitation should occur on May 7, 9, 11, 15, 16, 21, 25, and 30. Winds are likely May 4, 7, 9, 11, 12 and 18; also May 21, 25, 27, 29, 30, and 31. June should bring more dry weather, but more normal precipitation is likely to return in the summer.

Zone Six: The Alaskan Panhandle should be drier than normal this month; Central Alaska should see seasonable weather. Hawaii should be relatively dry and cooler than normal. Watch for precipitation May 7, 9, 11, 13, 15, and 16; also May 21, 22, 25, 30, and 31. Watch for winds throughout the entire month. A dry summer is forecast for most of this zone.

Dates to Watch

Precipitation May 1, 7, 8, 9, 11, 12, 13, 15, 16, 21, 22, 25, 30, and 31.
Winds May *1, 4, 7, 8, 9,* 11, *12, 13, 17, 18, 21, 24, 25, 27, 29, 30,* and *31.*

June 1999

Zone One: A wet month is forecast for this zone in June. Temperatures should be seasonable. Watch for some especially heavy downpours June 5, 6, 14, 19, and 23. Winds are due June 4, 7, 10, 14, and 23. June's wet weather should continue into the months of July and August.

Zone Two: Wet weather east and normal precipitation west is the forecast for this zone in June. Temperatures will be seasonable. Watch for rainfall June 5, 6, 14, 19, and 23. Winds will be likely June 4, 7, 10, 14, and 23. Wet weather in this zone this month is likely to continue throughout the entire summer in most of this zone. Areas near the Mississippi, however, will be dry.

Zone Three: Normal precipitation is forecast for much of this zone in June, but in western portions of this zone it will be dry. Watch for heavy precipitation east June 13, 20, and 30. Watch for winds June 4, 10, 13, 19, 23, 26, and 30. The last week of the month will be relatively dry with the exception of rain on June 30. A dry summer is forecast.

Zone Four: Dry weather is forecast for this zone this month. Precipitation will be most likely June 5, 13 and 30. Watch for winds June 4, 10, 13, 19, 23, 26, and 30. Super-dry weather should exit at the end of the month and the summer should bring more normal precipitation patterns to this zone. Temperatures in the summer should be seasonable.

Zone Five: Dry weather is forecast for this zone in June. Temperatures could be a little below normal. Best chances for rain come June 5, 9, 13, and 14; also June 18–20, 25, 28, and 30. Winds are likely June 4, 7, 13, 14, and 16; also June 19, 25, 26, and 30. More normal precipitation patterns should come in at the end of the month and continue throughout the summer.

Zone Six: Weather drier than normal is forecast for the Alaskan Panhandle; the rest of the state should see weather wetter and cooler than normal. Hawaii should see drier-than-normal weather the first three weeks of the month. Watch for rainfall June 5, 6, 9, 13, and 14; also June 18–20, 23, 25, 28, and 30. Winds should be frequent in this zone this month.

Dates to Watch

Precipitation June 5, 6, 9, 13, 14, 19, 20, 23, 25, 29, and 30. **Winds** June 4, 7, 10, 13, 14, 16, 19, 23, 25, 26, and 30.

July 1999

Zone One: Wet weather is forecast for this zone in July. Temperatures should be seasonal. Watch for heavy precipitation July 6, 11, 14, 18, 20, 25, and 26. Winds are likely July 7, 14, 17, 25, 26, and 31. Wet weather will continue into August and September. A dry, cool fall is forecast here.

Zone Two: Wet weather and dry, cooler-than-normal weather near the Mississippi is the forecast for this zone in July. Watch for heavy precipitation July 6, 11, 14, 18, 20, 25, and 26. Watch for winds July 7, 14, 17, 25, 26, and 31. The weather patterns established this month in this zone should continue into the months of August and September.

Zone Three: Dry weather with cooler-than-normal temperatures is the forecast east. More normal July weather is forecast from about Dodge City west. Best chances for precipitation come July 6, 7, 11, 14, 18, 25, and 26. Winds are likely July 7, 9, 14, 16 21, 25, and 26. July weather patterns should repeat in August and throughout most of September.

Zone Four: Normal precipitation and seasonable temperatures are forecast for this zone in July. Watch for rainfall July 6, 7, 11, 14, and 18; also July 25 and 26. Winds are likely July 7, 9, 14, and 16; also July 21, 25, and 26. These patterns should carry over into August and September.

Zone Five: Normal Precipitation and seasonable temperatures should prevail in this zone this month. Watch for rainfall July 2, 6, 7, 12, 14, 16, and 17; also July 21, and 27. Winds are likely July 6, 14, 16, 17, 18, 21, and 26. July's weather patterns should continue into August and September.

Zone Six: Dry weather is forecast for the eastern half of Alaska this month; western portions of the state should see much more precipitation. Hawaii should have a normal month with normal rainfall and seasonable temperatures. Watch for rainfall July 2, 6, 7, 12, 14, 16, 17, 21, and 25–27.

Dates to Watch

Precipitation: July 2, 6, 7, 11, 12, 14, 16, 17, 18, 20, 21, 25, 26, 27, and 29. **Winds:** July 6, 7, 9, 14, 16, 17, 18, 21, 25, 26, and 31.

August 1999

Zone One: A wet month is forecast for this zone in August. Temperatures should be seasonal. Watch for very generous rainfall August 4, 13, 16, 24, 26 south and August 28. Winds are likely August 2, 4, 5, 7, 16, 22, 24, 28, 30, and 31. August's wet weather should continue well into September, but dry, cool weather is forecast for most of the fall.

Zone Two: Wet weather is predicted for most of this zone in August, but areas near the Mississippi will be dry. Temperatures will be seasonal for most of this zone, but it should be cooler than normal west. Watch for very generous rainfall August 4, 13, 16, 24, 26, and 28. Winds are likely August 2, 4, 5, 7, and 16; also August 22, 24, 28, 30, and 31.

Zone Three: Dry weather is predicted for much of this zone in August, but areas west will have a more normal precipitation pattern. Temperatures may be a little below normal. Best chances for precipitation should come on August 4, 11, 20, 24, 26, and 28. Watch for winds August 4, 5, 7, 11, 16, and 18; also August 20, 22, 24, and 26.

Zone Four: Normal precipitation and seasonable temperatures are predicted for this zone in the month of August. Rainfall will be most likely August 4, 11, 20, 24, 26, and 28. Watch for winds August 4, 5, 7, 11, 16, and 18; also August 20, 22, 24, and 26. Weather patterns in effect this month in this zone should continue into the month of September.

Zone Five: Seasonal temperatures and normal amounts of precipitation are forecast for this zone in August. Watch for rainfall August 5, 9, 14, 18, and 27; watch for winds August 5, 7, 14, 16, 18, 23, 26, and 27. August's weather patterns should continue well into the month of September.

Zone Six: Dry weather east and either very wet or very dry weather in the central part of Alaska is the forecast for August. Hawaiian weather is likely to be very wet. Watch for rainfall August 4, 5, 9, 13, 14, 16, and 18; also August 24, 26, 27, and 28. Watch for winds August 2, 4, 5, 7, 14, 16, 18, 22, 23, 24, 26, 27, 28, 30, and 31.

Dates to Watch

Precipitation: August 4, 5, 9, 11, 13, 14, 16, 18, 20, 24, 27, and 28. **Winds:** August 2, 4, 5, 7, 11, 14, 16, 18, 22, 23, 24, 26, 27, 28, 30, and 31.

September 1999

Zone One: A wet month is forecast for this zone in September, but the very end of the month may be dry and chill. Watch for rainfall September

2, 3, 9, September 10 south, September 17 and possibly 24, 26, and 30. Winds are due September 2, 4, 8, 17, 19, 21, and 22. Weather patterns in effect the end of the month should continue into October and November.

Zone Two: Wet weather east and dry, cool weather in the west is the forecast for this zone in September. Watch for rainfall September 2, 3, 9, 10, 17, 24, 26, and 30. Winds are likely September 2, 4, 8, and 17; also September 19, 21, and 22. The end of the month should see seasonable temperatures throughout this zone setting a pattern for the fall.

Zone Three: A dry, cool month is forecast for this zone in September, but the last week of the month may have some unseasonably hot weather. Best chances for rain come September 3, 5, 9, 10, 24, and 30. Winds are likely September 2, 4, 5, and 9; also September 22, 24, 25, and 30. A warm, dry fall is predicted for the entire zone.

Zone Four: Seasonal temperatures and normal amounts of precipitation are forecast for this zone in September. Watch for rainfall September 3, 5, 9, 10, 24, 25, and 30. Watch for winds September 2, 4, 5, and 9; also September 22, 24, 25, and 30. A very dry and very warm fall is predicted for this zone and rainfall the last week of September may be sparse.

Zone Five: A drier-than-normal month with seasonable temperatures is the forecast for this zone in September. Watch for precipitation September 7, 10, and 17. Watch for winds September 2, 4, 7, and 15; also September 21, 24, 25, and 30. There may be more precipitation than usual.

Zone Six: A normal month is forecast for Central Alaska and Hawaii, but the Alaskan Panhandle should be drier than normal. Temperatures on the Panhandle should be above normal. Watch for precipitation September 2, 3, 7, 9, 10, 17, 24, 25, and 30. Winds will be likely September 2, 4, 7, 8, 15, 17, 19, 21, 22, 24, 25, and 30.

Dates to Watch

Precipitation: September 2, 3, 5, 7, 9, 10, 17, 24, 26, and 30. **Winds:** September 2, 4, 5, 7, 8, 9, 12, 15, 17, 19, 21, 22, 24, 25, and 30.

October 1999

Zone One: A dry, cool month is forecast for this zone in October. Best chances for precipitation come October 1, 7, 9, 14, 17, 18, 23, 24, and 29. Watch for winds October 1, 2, 6, 7, 14, 17, 18, and 20. October's dry weather and chill temperatures should continue on into the month of November and December throughout this zone.

Zone Two: Normal temperatures and normal precipitation are forecast for most of this zone in October, but the north and east are likely to be dry and cool. Watch for precipitation October 1, 7, 9, 14, 17, and 18; also October 23, 24, and 29. Winds are likely October 1, 2, 6, and 7; also October 14, 17, 18, and 20. October's weather patterns should continue into November.

Zone Three: A dry, warm month is forecast for this zone in October. Best chances for rain will come October 1, 9, 11, 18, 25, 29, and 31. Watch for winds October 1, 14, and 18. October weather patterns should continue into the months of November and December. The entire fall should be unusually warm and unusually dry.

Zone Four: Warm and dry is the forecast for most of this zone in October. In the extreme west there could be an excess of moisture. Best dates for precipitation include October 1, 9, 11, and 18; also October 25, 29, and 31. Winds would be likely October 1, 14, and 18. Weather patterns in effect this month in this zone should continue the rest of the fall season.

Zone Five: The weather in this zone this month could have either an excess of moisture or be very dry. Temperatures should be seasonal. Dates most likely to result in rain include October 6, 7, 14, 16, and 17; also October 18 and 24. Watch for winds October 2, 6, 7, and 18. October's weather patterns are likely to extend into the months of November and December.

Zone Six: A dry month is forecast for Central Alaska, but some areas on the Panhandle may see an excess of moisture. Hawaii should have relatively dry weather with temperatures a little below normal. Watch for rainfall October 1, 6, 7, 9, 14, 16, 17, and 18; also October 23, 24, and 29.

Dates to Watch

Precipitation: October 1, 6, 7, 9, 11, 14, 16, 17, 18, 24, 25, 29, and 31.
Winds: October 1, 2, 6, 7, 14, 16, 17, 18, and 20.

November 1999

Zone One: Dry and chill is the forecast for this zone in November. Most likely dates for precipitation include November 4, 7, 13, 14, 16, 17, 24, and 29. Winds are likely November 4, 11, 14, 16, 17, 21, and 28. The day before Thanksgiving should bring precipitation to this zone, but it is unlikely to interrupt travel. November's dry weather should continue into September.

Zone Two: Northeastern portions of this zone should be dry and chill, but normal weather patterns should prevail in the rest of this zone this month. Watch for precipitation November 4, 7, 13, 14, 16, and 17; also November

24 and 29. Winds are likely November 4, 11, 14, 16, and 17; also November 21 and 28.

Zone Three: Dry weather is predicted for this zone in November. Temperatures should be above normal. Dates most likely to result in precipitation include November 9, 23, 28, and 29. Winds are likely November 5, 9, 11, 15, 16, and 21; also November 28. Notice that Thanksgiving is likely to be nice. November's weather patterns should continue into December.

Zone Four: Dry weather with temperatures above normal is the forecast for this zone this November. Dates most likely to result in precipitation include November 9, 23, 28, and 29. Watch for winds November 5, 9, 11, 15, 16, 21, and 28. November's dry weather is likely to continue into and throughout most of December.

Zone Five: There will be either an excess of precipitation in this zone in November or it will be very dry. Dates most likely to result in precipitation include November 6, 9, 10, 16, 17, 19, 21, and 24. Winds are due November 5, 9, 14, 16, 17, and 21. November's weather patterns should continue well into the month of December. The day before Thanksgiving could see some precipitation.

Zone Six: Most of Alaska will be dry this month, but some areas on the Panhandle could be very wet with very low temperatures. Hawaii should be a little drier than usual with some temperatures a little below normal. Dates for precipitation include November 4, 6, 7, 9, and 10; also November 16, 17, 19, 21, and 24. November 29 could also result in precipitation.

Dates to Watch

Precipitation November 4, 6, 7, 9, 10, 13, 14, 16, 17, 19, 21, 23, 24, 28, and 29. **Winds** November 4, 5, 9, 10, *11, 13, 14, 15, 16,* 17, *21,* and 28.

December 1999

Zone One: Dry, chill weather is forecast for this zone in December. Dates most likely to result in precipitation include December 7, 10, 15, 23, and 27. Winds are likely December 6, 7, 9, 10, and 12; also December 23, 27, and 28. Notice that precipitation is likely to come both before and after Christmas, but Christmas Day itself is likely to be clear.

Zone Two: Normal precipitation and normal temperatures are forecast for this zone in December, although some areas north and east may be dry and chill. Watch for snow north and rain south December 7, 10, 15, 23, and

27. Watch for winds December 6, 7, 9, 10, and 12; also December 23, 27, and 28. Note that Christmas Day is likely to be clear.

Zone Three: December should be dry and warmer than usual in this zone. Best chances for precipitation come on December 1, 7, 10, 12, 14, and 15; also December 22 and 23. Watch for winds December 7, 10, 12, and 16; also December 20, 23, 25, and 27. Note that Christmas Day is likely to be windy but clear. The new year, however, is likely to begin with snowfall.

Zone Four: Dry weather with temperatures above normal is forecast for this zone in December. Dates most likely to result in precipitation include December 1, 7, 10, 12, 14, and 15; also December 22 and 23. Winds are likely December 7, 10, 12, and 16; also December 20, 23, 25, and 27. The new year is likely to come in with long-lasting precipitation.

Zone Five: Either an excess or a lack of precipitation is likely in this zone in December. Dates most likely to result in precipitation include December 3, 10, 15, 17, 23, 27, and 28. Winds are due December 2, 6, 10, 14, 17, and 18; also December 20, 23, 25, 27, and 28. Notice that Christmas Day is likely to be clear and windy.

Zone Six: Dry weather and relatively mild temperatures are forecast for this zone in December. The Alaskan Panhandle, however, could see a deluge and temperatures in Hawaii could be a little below normal. Dates most likely to result in precipitation include December 3, 7, 10, 15, and 17; also December 23, 27, and 28. Winds should be frequent.

Dates to Watch

Precipitation: December 1, 3, 7, 10, 12, 14, 15, 22, 23, 27, and 28. **Winds:** December 2, 6, 7, 9, 10, 12, 14, 16, 18, 20, 23, 25, 27, and 28.

1999 Earthquake Predictions

By Nancy Soller

A nn E. Parker of Skokie, Illinois, has revolutionized earthquake predictions. Ann notes the location of solar and lunar eclipses in the ecliptic. Then she notes that when the sign and degree of an eclipse corresponds with the sign and degree of the geodetic ascendant, geodetic mid-heaven or geodetic vertex of a location on Earth, a large, destructive quake is likely when Mars forms a hard angle to the eclipse point. The hard angles involved are the conjunction, square, opposition, semisquare, and sesquiquadrate. Such a quake can occur up to eighteen months before or after the eclipse.

An eclipse that could trigger a big, destructive quake in 1999 is the *February 26, 1998 solar eclipse at 8 degrees of Pisces*. This quake could affect Texas, Colorado, New Mexico, the Azores and Mexico. Danger dates include January 9 and 10, April 22 and 3, July 1 and 2, September 16, 18, and 19, November 17 and 18, and November 29 and 30.

The March 13, 1998 lunar eclipse at 22 degrees of Virgo could trigger a quake that would affect West Texas, Colorado, New Mexico, Oklahoma, Western Nebraska, Fiji, New Zealand, American Somoa, the New Hebrides, the Marshall Islands, Peru, and Ecuador. Danger dates include January 22 and 23, February 16–18, April 14–16, May 1 and 2, July 23–25, July 27 and 28, October 6 and 7, October 10 and 11, December 6, and December 21 and 22.

The August 8, 1998 lunar eclipse at 15 degrees of Aquarius could trigger a big, destructive quake at many locations in California, in Nevada, Montana, and Brazil. Danger dates include February 10, May 18 and 19, August 9, October 18, October 23 and 24, and December 16 and 17.

The August 22, 1998 eclipse at 28 degrees of Leo could trigger volcanic action in Hawaii or quakes in the Marianas, New Guinea, Tokyo or other locations in Japan or locations in Iran. Dates that could be critical include March 11 and 12, May 19 and 20, August 31, September 1 and 2, November 4 and 5, and November 13 and 14.

The September 6, 1998 lunar eclipse at 13 degrees of Pisces could result in big, disastrous quakes in Texas, Oklahoma, Mexico, or the Caroline Islands, or it could result in volcanic activity in Iceland. Danger dates include January 2–4, January 22–24, April 12 and 13, May 9–11, June 29–July 1, July 10 and 11, September 23 and 24, September 26 and 27, November 23 and 24, and December 6 and 7.

The January 31, 1999 lunar eclipse at 11 degrees of Leo could result in a quake in Alaska, Turkey, Iraq, Ethiopia, Bulgaria, Greece, or Poland. Dates when such a quake could be triggered include February 1 and 2, March 25–April 1, May 9 and 10, August 1–4, October 11 and 12, October 17 and 18, December 10 and 11, and December 27 and 28.

The February 16, 1999 solar eclipse at 27 degrees of Aquarius could result in a disastrous quake in California, Arizona, or Utah. Danger dates include March 8–10, June 10 and 11, August 29–31, November 2 and 3, and November 11 and 12.

The July 28, 1999 lunar eclipse at 5 degrees of Aquarius could result in a large quake in Newfoundland, California, Oregon, Avuncular, Paraguay, Pakistan, or Brazil, and could also result in volcanic activity at Mount St. Helen. Dates when such events could occur include January 17–20, February 9–11, April 20–22, April 25 and 26, July 18–20, July 22–24, October 2–4, October 7 and 8, December 2–4, and December 17–19.

The August 11, 1999 solar eclipse at 18 degrees of Leo could result in a big quake in Alaska, Indonesia, the Caroline Islands, Iraq, Turkey, or Poland. Danger dates include February 3–5, March 13–24, May 11 and 12, August 2–4, August 4–6, October 13 and 14, October 18–20, December 12 and 13, and December 28–30.

The January 21, 2000 lunar eclipse at 0 degrees of Leo could result in a big, disastrous quake in Alaska, the Philippines, China, Japan, Kenya, Italy, Hungary, or locations in the old Yugoslavia. Danger dates include January 6–8, January 27 and 28, April 16–18, May 4 and 5, July 6–8, July 14 and 15, September 26 and 27, September 29 and 30, November 26 and 27, and December 9–11.

The February 5, 2000 solar eclipse at 16 degrees of Aquarius could result in a big quake in California, Montana, or locations in Brazil. Dates when a disastrous quake could occur include February 12 and 13, May 20 and 21, August 10–13, October 18 and 19, October 24–26, and December 17 and 18.

The July 1, 2000 solar eclipse at 10 degrees of Cancer could result in a big, disastrous quake in Indonesia, China, Sumatra, Algeria, Morocco, or the Rukuyu Islands. Dates that could result in such a quake include March 4–6, June 6 and 7, August 25–28, November 8 and 9, and December 28 and 29

The July 16, 2000 lunar eclipse at 24 degrees of Capricorn could result in a big quake in New England, New Brunswick, St. Vincent Island, the Virgin Islands, Bolivia, the Dominican Republic, Puerto Rico, Chile, Brazil, or the American Northwest. It could mean volcanic activity at Mount St. Helen. Danger dates include January 14 and 15, April 3–5, May 27–June 1, June 2–4, September 17 and 18, September 19–20, November 18 and 19, November 30, and December 1.

The July 31, 2000 solar eclipse at 8 degrees of Leo could result in a disastrous quake in Alaska, the Philippines, China, Ethiopia, Kenya, Bulgaria, Greece, Poland, Hungary, and parts of the old Yugoslavia. Critical dates include January 22–26, February 19–22, April 11–13, May 3 and 4, July 25–27, July 28 and 29, October 7 and 8, October 12 and 13, and December 23 and 24.

The December 25, 2000 solar eclipse at 4 degrees of Capricorn could affect the New Madrid Fault, Nicaragua, British Honduras, El Salvador, the Fiji Islands, Iran, Turkey, Southeastern Europe, or Paraguay. Critical dates include February 19 and 20, May 26 and 27, July 16 and 18, August 17 and 18, October 22 and 23, October 29–31 and December 21–23.

The January 9, 2001 lunar eclipse at 19 degrees of Cancer could result in a big, destructive earthquake in Indonesia, China, or the Philippines. Dates that would be critical include January 2–4, March 23–25, June 23–25, September 9 and 10, September 12–13, November 12 and 13, and November 22 and 23.

The June 21, 2001 solar eclipse at zero degrees of Cancer could result in a big quake in Sumatra or Northern Ireland. Danger dates include February 9–11, May 17–19, August 8–11, October 23 and 24, and December 15–17.

Soil Fertility

By Jim Sluyter and Marilyn Meller

"You are what you eat" is a well-known phrase and one good reason for eating your own organically grown vegetables. It is useful in the garden to think of your plants in much the same way: they are what they eat. Feed them organic matter and rock powders rich in nutrients, and you have veggies full of goodness. Feed them chemicals, and, well....

On Five Springs Farm, a community-supported farm in northern Michigan, we feed our plants manure, compost, rock powders, and organic fertilizers that we mix ourselves. Mixing your own fertilizer is easy, rewarding, and best of all, the plants love it!

Plants grow and produce because they want to. Fertile soil is the basis of organic agriculture and compost is one key to fertile soil. Learn how to make and use compost from your kitchen scraps, garden residues, and those of your friends. Compost grass clippings (or mulch with them) as long as you know that there were no fertilizers or weed killers used on the lawn. Of course, manure, if you can get it, is a great addition to any garden. All of these materials enhance the fertility of the soil by increasing humus and adding nutrients. After years of this treatment with inconsistent results in our gardens, however, we tried a balanced natural fertilizer with spectacular improvements in yield, quality, and consistency. The next logical step was to blend our own fertilizers. Why and how to do that is the point of this article.

What Does Your Garden Need?

There are several ways of looking at your fertilizer needs. You might replace the nutrients that your previous crop has taken out. You might put in what you think your next planting needs. A fixed amount of fertilizer could be added to your soil each year. The recommendations from a lab performing a soil test can be followed, or, based on experience with your soil and growing conditions, you might use your gardener's intuition as a guide. Each approach has its problems and its appeal. We do a bit of each, and are willing to change from year to year and within the growing season.

In a way it was easy for us to start. We intensively cultivated just under a half acre of what was best described as "blow sand" before we started. We began by adding anything organic we could find: pond dredgings, manure, rotted sawdust, and growing "green manures." These are all effective in sandy soil like ours. If your soil tends toward clay it may also be useful to add sand. In any event, for optimal plant growth, any soil will need a high organic content. Most of this is humus, and the same activities that encourage the development of humus will improve the structure and texture of your soil.

Your plants have many nutrient needs that may not be contained in the humus you have built up. These can be viewed in two major categories. First are the main nutrients, of which nitrogen, phosphorous, and potash (or potassium) are the most well known. Second, and often ignored, are the micronutrients.

The Big Three

If you buy a bag of commercially made fertilizer it will usually have three numbers. A common synthetic formula is 10-10-10, and a natural fertilizer may be rated 5-3-4. These numbers refer to the amount, by percentage, the enclosed product contains of nitrogen (N), phosphorous (P), and potash or potassium (K). Nitrogen, often deficient in soil, provides green growth and is important for plant vigor. Phosphorous is important for root growth, disease resistance, and is critical for proper fruiting, blooming, and seed production, that is, proper maturation of the plant. Potash regulates the metabolic activities of the plant, promotes strong stems and roots, and increases disease resistance.

Secondary Nutrients

Calcium, magnesium, and sulfur are often neglected in gardening books, though they still qualify as main nutrients, but look at what they do and decide how important they are. Calcium builds cell walls and is needed in the growing points of roots. Magnesium is a component of chlorophyll and is important in the metabolism of phosphorus. Sulfur is an essential ingredient in some amino acids, and amino acids that contain sulfur are necessary for all proteins. Ignore these minerals at your peril!

Micronutrients or Trace Minerals?

Exceedingly small amounts of many other nutrients are necessary to plant health. Note well that they are necessary. We are convinced that our dramatic improvements in the garden can be traced to the "traces." Six of these trace minerals are widely recognized: boron, copper, iron, manganese, molybdenum, and zinc. They are sometimes added to commercial fertilizers. Seaweed and many land plants contain these and at least forty more elements than have yet been mentioned. Little is known about the role of even those that are recognized, and it can be expected that many more are essential or beneficial to plant growth and health. Furthermore, several elements have little known effect on plant health but are essential for human health. Now it is time to review our opening phrase: you are what you eat. Your plants are what they eat.

Most trace elements are important in metabolic processes within the plant. While they are essential in small quantities, poor judgment in their application could result in excesses, which can be toxic to plants. Inclusion of seaweed as a meal or liquid is our primary strategy in provision of trace elements. They are also present in varying amounts in other parts of our soil building program.

Armed with some understanding of what is required for your plants' health, you can better assess the ability of your fertilizer, whether commercial, organic, or homemade, to provide the right stuff. We use lots of horse manure, make compost in as large a quantity as possible, compost leaves for a year (then add them to the gardens as mulch), and mulch with straw. I recommend doing as much as possible with local materials, like leaves, composted kitchen and garden scraps (this is SO good for your garden that it cannot be emphasized too much), or what have you. Beyond this, we add fertilizer to the soil every year. Here are the elements of our mixture:

Alfalfa pellets (NPK: 2.7-0.5-2.8) are widely available at any outlet that sells feed, including pet food. This is a good source of nitrogen and potash in a slow release form that is easy on the soil and plants alike.

Bone meal (NPK: 4-12-0) is used mainly for its phosphorus content. It is quickly available to the plants. Generally available at your garden center.

Rock phosphate (NPK: 0-18-0). We use soft rock phosphate because that is what is available here. Hard rock phosphate is used the same way but has nearly twice the phosphorus per pound. Use half our recommendation if this is what you find where you shop. This is a very slow release product and needs to be in the soil for at least a season before it is available to plants. It lasts in the soil for several years. Purchase at most garden centers.

Greens (NPK: 0-1.5-5.5). For potash needs this is our choice, though crushed granite can be used instead. Both are slow-release materials that persist in the soil for several years and provide trace minerals as well. Your garden center will generally have this in stock.

Kelp. Even if you don't make your own fertilizer, you will do well to add kelp to your soil. Though kelp (a form of seaweed) contains some major nutrients, the value of kelp is really in the concentrations of trace minerals and growth stimulants. As a soil additive kelp should be used sparingly (no more than one pound per one hundred square feet) as the growth hormones can become too potent at higher rates. Kelp as a meal may have to be ordered by your garden center or purchased from a mail order supplier.

Wood ash (NPK: 0-0-5). We burn wood for heat, so we always have a source of ashes for a potash supplement. We use them sparingly, as they are highly alkaline and can easily upset the pH balance of your soil if used indiscriminately. We substitute it for greens when we use it. It also repels root maggots, so we sprinkle it sparingly around the stems of radishes and turnips.

Here is our basic formula for 100 square feet of garden: Five pounds alfalfa pellets, a quarter pound bone meal, a half pound greensand, a half pound soft rock phosphate, and a quarter pound kelp. I measure everything but the alfalfa pellets into a pail and hand broadcast it as evenly as possible. Then I go back and do the same with the alfalfa.

These amounts are very small. You will find recommendations for up to five pounds of bone meal per hundred square feet, and ten pounds each for phosphate and greensand. My approach has been to build the soil fertility slowly over a period of years. A timed approach with slow release material is much less likely to create nutrient imbalances and allows me to use the same formula year after year with little fear of creating excesses of any nutrient.

No discussion of soil fertility is complete without a word on pH. Most vegetable plants and desirable soil organisms are happiest at near-neutral acid/alkaline conditions, of which pH is a measure. A very slight acid pH of 6.5 to 6.8 is ideal, though any value from 6.0 to 7.5 is considered acceptable. I have read that when adequate organic matter is present, crops will tolerate a wider range. This is perhaps our salvation, as our attention to pH has been less than most guides recommend. A soil test, either with a kit (low accuracy) or from a lab, is required to establish pH. Corrective actions include lime to raise the pH or sulfur to lower it.

We operate a community-supported farm on very little ground, so it is very important to us that plants grow quickly and that the soil can support constant and intensive cultivation. For the home garden these qualities are important, too. Plants that grow rapidly and well tend to be more vigorous, taste better, and repel or outgrow insect pests. We do several things throughout the season to help things along.

Side dressing long season crops and "heavy feeders" with composted manure or compost once or twice during the season is very helpful. Some crops really like to be mulched. Potatoes are mulched with six to twelve inches of straw, and onions, strawberries, and peppers like either straw or year-old leaves. Mulch helps keep weeds down and adds nutrients as it breaks down and is incorporated into the soil.

We have found that a boron boost helps our beets. A very fine sprinkling of Borax around young plants works wonders (too much can be toxic to plants, so be gentle). Epsom salts (a source of magnesium) sprinkled around tomatoes and peppers (about a teaspoon per plant) will get them blooming and setting fruit if they seem reluctant.

Finally, we use foliar feeds. Every couple of weeks we spray liquid kelp on most of the garden, and early in the season we spray fish emulsion. These sprays give an extra boost of energy and nutrition directly to the plant.

I hope that the quick reference in the last paragraph to insect control caught your eye. It has often been said that insects are attracted to poorly growing plants and that when plants are in optimal health there will be little or no trouble with bugs. I was skeptical about this for many years, but as our gardens become more and more fertile, our insect pests seem less and less troublesome. Prevention of a problem is always better than the fix, and soil fertility is a piece of the solution to insect problems.

We are less diligent about watching Moon signs when fertilizing than when planting seeds or seedlings. Why is this? I really don't know, but we are usually fertilizing as we plant, and we are careful to plant during fruitful signs, which works out well for fertilizing too. Organic fertilizers are best spread when the Moon is in the third or fourth quarter. The best signs are Cancer, Scorpio, and Pisces. Use Taurus or Capricorn if necessary. These are the best signs for starting your compost as well, when the Moon is in the fourth quarter.

Soil fertility can be a complex issue. If you start to research the fine points, it becomes downright scary, with the possibility of imbalances in nutrients causing all sorts of problems. Most of these problems tend to come from high-nutrient, fast-release chemical fertilizers. When you use a combination of organic matter, organic fertilizer, and rock powders, the nutrients enter the system slowly and in forms that plants are best able to use. Just keep in mind that if you tend your soil well your plants will eat well. And if your plants eat well, so will you.

The Bio-Dynamic Garden

By Leslie Nielsen

The philosophy of bio-dynamic agriculture was introduced by Rudolph Steiner in 1913. The work of bio-dynamics is to be in harmony with nature and the cosmos and to counteract the unbalanced state of farming and gardening.

Steiner was born on February 27, 1861, in Austria. His family recognized that their son was truly gifted and saw that his education was more complete than that of some of the other boys in their village. Steiner received degrees in mathematics, physics, and chemistry, and later wrote a philosophical thesis for a doctorate. He was an avid reader of the scientific writings of Goethe, who was born a century before, and whose approach was based on the intensified and selfless observation of nature. Annie Besant and the Theosophy movement had great influence on his thinking as well.

A versatile and creative man, Steiner put his energies into a broad scope of activities that he felt would be for the betterment of humanity. Through his extensive writings (there are over 800 Steiner volumes cataloged at the Library of Congress) and through his energetic lecturing, he was able to touch people in education, agriculture, hospitals, and those in the medical practices, artists, architects, banks, and businesses. While his life spanned the last part of the nineteenth century and the early part of the twentieth, his inspirations are unequaled and are proving to carry us well in the twenty-first century.

Like his father, Steiner was every bit a free thinker. In 1894 he published *The Philosophy of Spiritual Activity*, which he felt was his most important philosophical work. Though it was poorly received, it proved to be a turning point in his life. He believed that a healthy social order is created by true and deep insights not only into the material world but also the soul and spiritual nature of human beings. This seemed to be the foundation on which all of his work was built.

The Rise of Bio-dynamics

By the end of World War I much of Europe was in shambles. It had been the first war to use chemicals, and, after the war, the manufacturers of these chemicals were looking for new markets for their products. By 1924 Steiner was approached by German and Austrian farmers who were worried about the serious degeneration of their animals and plant life. Their seed stock had become virtually worthless and their land was nearly dead. Synthetic chemicals that were supposed to help the land had virtually killed it.

It was because of this situation that Steiner developed the bio-dynamic system. Bio-dynamics is the oldest organic approach to farming and gardening using crop rotation, lunar and planetary rhythms, composting, soil cultivation, homeopathic formulas, and special bio-dynamic preparations, each of which is specific and numbered.

The Bio-Dynamic System

Steiner felt that understanding and using lunar and planetary rhythms could not only stimulate fruit and vegetable growth, but also enhance the development of livestock. His belief was that the whole Earth is but a reflection of what takes place in the cosmos. Keeping very precise records, he analyzed the structure of plants, and through rigorous experimentation, developed formulas for strengthening not only the various parts of the plant but also the many varieties of plant life.

Quite simply, in the bio-dynamic system the parts of a plant are associated with the four elements of the zodiac. The earth signs, Taurus, Virgo, and Capricorn, influence the development of a plant's root system. Likewise, the water signs, Cancer, Scorpio, and Pisces, enhance the development of the green and leafy portion of the plant; the air signs, Gemini, Libra, and Aquarius, assist in developing the flowering part of the plant; and the fire signs, Aries, Leo, and Sagittarius, influence the development of the seed. In addition, it was found that the planets traveling close to the Earth (between the Earth and the Sun: Moon, Mercury, and Venus) were most helpful in developing the root nature of the plant. The more distant planets, Mars, Jupiter, and Saturn, made for a sturdier upper portion of the plant. It was also found that when the Sun, Moon, and even the planets were in conjunction, trine (120 degrees apart) or opposition (180 degrees apart), the life forces of the plant were strengthened.

Harvesting and Bio-Dynamics

By very careful and time-consuming experiments and by using the strictest scientific methodology, Steiner determined that the effects of the Sun, Moon, and planets were not only helpful in developing charts for sowing seed, but were also useful in harvesting crops. The practitioners of bio-dynamics found that certain times of day can be important in the harvesting process. The upper parts of the plant seem to be more vital and life-supporting in the early morning to mid-day, while the lower root system is stronger during the later part of the day. That is, in the morning the sap rises, and in the evening, as the Sun is setting, the sap lowers to strengthen the lower part of the plant. The plant has a cyclic rhythm much like the daylight (or active/rest) cycle of the human being.

Composting

The philosophy of bio-dynamics is that of a perfectly self-sufficient farm or garden. This can include the introduction of composting to enrich the soil as well as the use of natural fertilizers. Many compost recipes are available and may be helpful; however, the original bio-dynamic formula was quite simple and produced a great quantity of compost. It included digging a trench five feet wide, six feet long and eight inches deep. For most purposes a much smaller trench can be dug as a very small amount of this compost will be sufficient for garden use. The trench should be dug in an area that is well drained and also has partial shade. The compost is built in layers, with the bottom layer consisting of small twigs that assist in drainage. The next layer, which is fairly thick, should contain hay, fresh garden debris, and even tall weeds or corn stalks. If this material is too tall or bulky it should be chopped, as this will speed up the process of fermentation. The next layer should be any type of manure that is available. A small layer of soil is added on top of this and topped with leaves or grass that have not been treated with chemicals. Added next are any coffee grounds, vegetable scraps, blood meal, and bone meal. This compost pile can be layered up as high as workable, keeping in mind that a little bit of the mixture can go a long way. In true bio-dynamic composting, holes are punched through the mixture and it is inoculated with one of the bio-dynamic preparations. The compost pile should be kept moist at all times so the cooking process can take place. It should also have been constructed to allow for air circulation. The pile can be turned as necessary to keep it from getting too hot or too cold. The ideal heat is about 150 degrees, but will be considerably hotter if too much manure has been added. If it gets too hot, then it's time to turn it. A good quantity of earthworms shows that the compost is doing just fine, and when they disappear the compost should be ready.

Bio-Dynamic Preparations

Many bio-dynamic preparations are used to enhance the soil, which stimulates root growth, enriching the seeds and keeping weeds and fungus from multiplying to stunt the growth of the plants. These preparations, with very precise formulas, are labeled from BD500 to BD507 and can be used for creating a healthy and nutritious garden.

Other parts of the philosophy for the bio-dynamic garden include the use of quartz crystals, which were ground and became part of some the bio-dynamic formulas. The herbs dandelion, valerian, and yarrow were also used in the formulas.

Crop Rotation

Crop rotation was important in the picture of a healthy garden. It borrows from the idea that a total rotation takes about four years (or as many years as the parts of the living plant) to complete. For example, the first year a root crop is planted and harvested, then the second year a leafy and green plant is sown in the space that the root crop had occupied the year before, and the third year a flowering crop is planted, and the fourth year a seedling plant is grown.

When bio-dynamic agriculture came to the United States in the late 1930s, it was also being recognized worldwide. The people's acceptance of the bio-dynamic movement has grown and you may find individuals, if not groups, that can be helpful to you in giving information about this work. To get more information and order preparations, you can contact Bio-dynamic Preparation, Box 133, Woolwine, VA, 24185. Catalogs and books that are helpful can be ordered from Antroposphic Press, RR4, Box 94-A1, Hudson, New York, 12534. Their telephone number is (518)851-2054. You can also contact the Anthroposophical Society at 529 Grant Place, Chicago, IL 60614, telephone number (312)248-5606. For those who are interested in obtaining organic seeds, contact Seeds of Change, 621 Old Santa Fe Trail, Suite 10, Santa Fe, NM 87504, telephone (505)983-8956.

Rudolph Steiner was a carrier of new thought. In his early work he wrote, "Nutrition as it is today does not supply the strength necessary for manifesting the spirit in physical life. A bridge can no longer be built from thinking to will to action. Food plants no longer contain the forces people need for this." Steiner himself may well have been the bridge that he thought was missing.

Fertilizer Teas

By Penny Kelly

The first tea I ever made to bring a sickly plant back to health was Lipton. I had a small Wandering Jew plant that was thin and stringy and fading fast on my kitchen window ledge. I loved tea with cream and sugar in it, and one day, while relaxing with my tea, I contemplated the sad looking plant, wondering what was wrong with it. On the spur of the moment, wishing it could feel better, I offered it a drink of my tea. A few days later I thought it looked somehow a little brighter. I offered it another drink, and when it perked up even more, I began to make a small cup for it once a week, leaving out the cream and sugar. The plant came back to life and thrived!

Other experiments followed. Eventually I became involved in biodynamic gardening, and I now have a small medicine chest of fertilizers and teas that I have used, as well as a whole list of things I want to try.

Making Fertilizer Teas

If you grow vegetables, flowers, small fruits, or even houseplants, try some of the following to perk up your soil or your plants. Most teas are made in one of two ways. Heat a gallon of water in a stock pot on the stove and when it begins to boil, turn it off, add two to three cups of fresh herb (or one cup dried herb), cover, and steep until the water is cool. Strain out the herb using cheesecloth or a large strainer, add enough water to make three gallons, and go spray using a three-gallon pump-up sprayer. If you don't have a sprayer, you can simply sprinkle it onto a plant using a paintbrush, or even put it in a watering can, then pour it over and around the plant into the soil.

The other method of steeping tea is to get a five-gallon pail and put three gallons of water in it. If you can collect some of it as rainwater, so much the better. Put in two to three cups of fresh herb (or one cup dried herb), cover it with a couple of boards or something heavy to help cut down on evaporation, and allow it to sit in the Sun for at least a few days. Strain out the herbs, putting their remains in the compost, and spray, sprinkle, or pour around your plants.

Most of these teas do not store for long periods of time. Sometimes they will get moldy in just a few days. This does not mean they are ruined or useless. It's just that lots of people don't like working with moldy stuff. The fact is, your tea will have become more potent. We call this "fermented tea," and in the bio-dynamic system of gardening you frequently allow your tea to ferment for three weeks. Just strain out the moldy growth on top when you strain out the herb.

Compost Tea

Of all the teas that you might want to try, the one that is the most useful, versatile, fast-acting, and powerful is compost tea. Fill a five-gallon pail about three-fourths full of water. Make a cloth bag about one foot square out of cotton or cheesecloth, designing in a drawstring-type closing for the top of the bag. Fill the bag about half full with compost and then suspend the bag from a heavy stick or a two-by-four laid across the top of the bucket. Let it steep for at least a week and it's ready. You can use it full strength on your vegetables, or cut it to half strength to soak seeds and water your seedlings. It is food, fertilizer, and medicine all in one.

Manure Tea

The other tea that has a multitude of uses is manure tea. It's made the same way, a five-gallon pail with a half bag of chicken, cow, goat, or sheep manure suspended in it. The difference is that it's much stronger, and if used too strong, can burn your plants, especially if it's made with chicken manure. The best way to use it is to put two cups (one pint) of the tea into a two-gallon watering can, fill the watering can, and water along the base of your plants every two weeks. Observe your plants carefully, and if they show signs of burn, with dried-out edges along the leaves, dilute the manure tea using three gallons of water per pint of tea.

Once you've got some compost or manure tea going, it's not likely you'll run into many problems with disease, pests, or mildews simply because plants do extremely well on this kind of diet, and healthy plants don't seem to be as susceptible to these troubles.

One excellent way to prepare your soil in the spring is to make a bucket of manure tea, put it in your sprayer full strength, and walk around your garden spraying a light to medium mist as evenly as possible. Spray early in the morning or late in the evening, then turn over or till your soil within a day or two. Let the garden sit for two weeks and then spray again lightly a day or two before you plan to plant your seeds and seedlings.

Problem-Solving Teas

Dandelion Tea

If a problem crops up later on, there are all sorts of teas that can help remedy the situation. Dandelion tea made in a stockpot with one gallon of water for each two to three cups of dandelion flower heads, or one gallon of flower heads soaked in a five-gallon pail of water for a week or two, can be used full strength. Poured along the base of your vegetables, it will help your plants absorb and utilize whatever nutrients are in the soil they happened to be planted in, especially if the soil does not seem to be healthy or well balanced. If you have soil that is too sandy, or is mostly clay, you might want to alternate doses of compost or manure tea to feed your plants and dandelion tea to help them take in what you fed them.

Horsetail Tea

We regularly use the fermented form of horsetail tea both in the garden and in our vineyards. Not only does it help to control and even cure mildew problems, it helps give fruits and vegetables superior flavor, smell, and taste. Our recipe for horsetail tea calls for two to three cups of dried horsetail mixed into three to four gallons of water that has been placed in a large stockpot or canner. Bring to a boil, turn down immediately, and simmer for twenty minutes. Remove from heat and allow to cool. Move to a dark, cool place and allow the covered stock pot of tea to sit undisturbed for three weeks. Put one quart of the tea in a three-gallon pump-up hand sprayer and move along your vegetables and fruits, spraying lightly. For serious mildew or black rot kinds of problems, repeat the spraying three days in a row, preferably in the morning after the dew has dried for the day. Otherwise, as a health maintenance program, spray every ten to fourteen days, simply dipping tea from the pot you made early in the season, which should be enough to last the entire growing season.

Valerian Tea

Another great tea to have on hand is valerian tea, made from the crushed flowers and leaves of the valerian plant. Steep two to three cups of the herb in one gallon of hot, but not boiling, water, and allow to sit, covered, for twenty-four hours. When you've put your beloved tomatoes, peppers, cucumbers, and cantaloupe plants out into the garden and a frost is threatening to end their delicate existence, put one gallon of valerian tea in a three-gallon sprayer and fill it with water. Spray the plants lightly in the evening before the dew develops on the night of the expected frost. Spray for the next four nights as well, and your plants should be able to bounce back from some pretty serious frosts. If you get up the next morning and discover they have keeled over and covered with frost, don't touch them! Let the Sun come up and warm them naturally and the chances are very good that they will bounce back by the afternoon. If freezing temperatures are predicted for several nights in a row and you want to give them an extra layer of protection, spray first, and when the plants are dry, lay a piece of floating row cover over them. Don't touch the row cover until noon or so of the next day in case the plants have been frozen over the night. Plants will often recover from some pretty cold temperatures if you don't disturb them while they are trying to get back on their feet. Our lettuces and tomatoes regularly survive repeated freezing, with temperatures down to 24 degrees and even lower.

Chamomile and Oak Bark Teas

Two other teas that have remarkable effects on plant growth are chamomile tea and oak bark tea. Both help produce a profusion of leaves and flowers on stems and stalks that are sturdy and well developed. Both are made using the hot water and steeping method, and the oak bark has turned out to be even more powerful for healing than the chamomile. Oak bark can also be used for all varieties of mildew or rot, and helps to restore order and healthy processes in many kinds of plants, whether flowers, fruit, vegetables, herbs, or trees. Used early in the season it gives wonderful form to roses, brings shape and strength to flowers and trees, and a natural resistance to disease. It creates an inner structure in almost any plant that predisposes it to drought resistance, balanced growth during rainy periods, and a strong seed product with a good germ of life in the seed at harvest time.

Nettle Tea

Nettle tea is another miracle worker. I cut a half-dozen stinging nettles just as they begin to flower, crush them to the best of my ability, and put them into a five-gallon pail of water. A week or two later, holding my nose to avoid the awful smell, I dip out a gallon, put it in my watering can, add 1 gallon of water, and pour around anything that seems to be growing slowly, has pale leaves, is stunted, or seems sickly for no obvious reason. In short order the tree or plant begins to grow and the leaves become thick and shiny. Nettle tea has a marvelous effect on the soil, rather than the plant, and seems to get the soil to make all kinds of chemical adjustments that end up nurturing the plant. Thus, I think of nettle tea as the mother tea, a nurturing drink that feeds her plants and flowers.

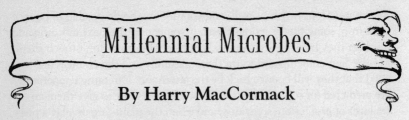

Millennial Microbes

By Harry MacCormack

I can think of no better way to celebrate the changing millennium than to dedicate ourselves to a focus on the thing that actually allows life to exist on this planet. Without living soils humans would never have come to be. How much do we know about their mystery? The processes of mineral and organic decomposition and transmutation that feed us are generally not taught. While we promote computer literacy, we condone basic soil process ignorance. Who is it that inhabits our soils? How do they survive? How do humans hinder or help their existence?

Characters in the Earthly Drama

Dr. Alan Kapuler adapted the terminology of Margulis and Schwartz and began writing about our common ancestors as belonging to five kingdoms. We are most familiar with some ten million animal species and around 300,000 plant species. Some people are familiar with some of the 100,000 species of fungi. There our knowledge of who we live with often ends.

Scientists have revealed that about 700 million years ago, in the twenty-seven known phyla of protoctists, some 50,000 species came into being. Their habits are critical to earth biology as we know it. A few of these creatures you will recognize: red algae, spirogyra, slime molds, sea-weeds, other algaes, diatoms, and water molds. You get the picture because we can *see* most of these life forms.

Somewhere in this vast period of creation, protozoa, which are closer to algae than animals and are very important to soil life, came into being. They are known as the rodents of the protoctistan world, eating bacteria and themselves being a staple in the diet of worms.

It is bacteria, of the monera kindom, who have been around over four billion years. There are sixteen phyla, 5,000 described species, and perhaps a million or more non-described species of bacteria about which we know very little. It is these bacteria that are the basis of soil life. We know the names of some: bacillus, lactobacillus, rhizobia, cyanobacters, etc. These are all classed as eubacteria, and are found in the upper layers of living soil and around and on other life. Deeper in earth are archaebacteria, methanogens, halophiles, and thermoplasma, all critical to the transformation of inner earth "fire" into basic life forms.

When I'm gardening I like to think of all the visible creatures of the animal kingdom five (which include ctenophores, mollusks, arthropods, and a host of familiar soil animals such as ants, spiders, beetles, slugs, and worms) as interacting with the invisible kingdom two, the algaes; three, the fungi; four, the exudates of plants; and the bacteria of kindom one. I refer to these invisible creatures as the microherd. I do this because as gardeners we are shepherds responsible for caring for and feeding this microherd.

In soils that are actively gardened, the most important and fragile population of microherd activity is the bacteria. Bacteria are critical to the decomposition of plant and animal wastes. They are also the life forms that will ultimately save the planet from the residue of human synthetic pesticides. Certain bacteria, namely rhizobia, can transform gaseous nitrogen gleaned from Earth's atmosphere into useable plant food nitrogen compounds. Some actinomycetes are root symbionts with roses and also fix atmospheric nitrogen. Some bacteria are known to fix nitrogen on perennial corns and other grains grown by indigenous peoples. The reason human garden systems can thrive is that we have stumbled upon ways to encourage bacterial growth. Most bacteria function in a narrow range of pH 6–7. Outside this range of acidity bacteria multiply more slowly, and soil is less fertile. Bacteria also function in a narrow temperature range, generally in soils that are above 59 degrees Fahrenheit but less than 90 degrees Fahrenheit. Greenhouses, hoophouses, and floating row covers all raise soil temperatures to stimulate bacterial growth.

Bacteria produce soil enzymes critical to decomposition and soil building. In the dynamics of soil life fungi (kingdom three) generate the largest amount of micro protoplasm if the soil is properly aerated (one reason for tillage). Fungi populations are determined by the amounts of oxidizable carbon containing substrates and useful organic materials. Fungi are more durable than bacteria in terms of acidity and other chemical conditions. Some fungi can grow in a pH as low as 2; some like alkaline conditions of pH 9. Fungi in any of these acid ranges can act on a wide range of organic and inorganic compounds. Sometimes soil fungi achieve unbalanced population levels, such as when fusarium and verticillium wilts infect soils at uncontrolled levels.

Actinomycetes are a fungus-like bacteria. They can constitute up to 50 percent of a microbial soil population. They increase in number and kind in alkaline areas, functioning best in a pH of 6.5–8.0. After bacteria and some of the fungi have grown, actinomycetes increase in the soil. These soil characters have a narrow range of nutritional requirements. Among other effects, actinomycetes create classes of unique biomolecules, including many antibiotics.

Visible and invisible algae (kingdom two) convert carbon dioxide to larger carbon-containing materials, making organic matter from gases and inorganic substances. Specific algaes grow in the top six inches of soil when there is sufficient light. Algaes make polysaccharides, which increase the water-binding capability of soil, giving it texture, making it more permeable and spongy, and giving soil tilth.

Feeding the Microherd

Most human agriculture relies on forms of cultivation. If our ancestors (or we) chose perennial plantings, then annual rituals of preparing seed beds would not need to occur so often. Annual cultivation of soils is one of the best ways to stimulate aerobic microbial populations. Through cultivation with tools tailored to loosen and stir variant soil types, enough air or oxygen is retained in soils to allow high level microherd decomposition activity. Compaction and an overabundance of water tend to cool soils and make a site more suitable to anaerobic microbes, many of which are not helpful in agricultural systems.

Cultivation is a dangerous practice. Whole civilizations have lost fertility because of reckless opening of soils. Deserts have resulted from not replenishing and rejuvenating food-growing areas. Generally speaking, we must consider cultivation in light of feeding the microherd. Cultivation is where we give back breath to our soils, so, we need to use tools like chisels or Dutch gardening forks to loosen the soil a foot to sixteen inches deep without turning over the surface six inches and burying it. We also need to use tillers or other stirring tools to mix in surface organic matter. Always think of tillage not as digging dirt, but as feeding micro life.

The members of the microherd are digesters. They are voracious, eating all kinds of organic matter, feeding on each other, and feeding on the root exudates in plant zones. We can greatly stimulate these processes, thereby building high levels of fertility. We can do this through the addition of all kinds of animal manures and through the growth and incorporation of green manures (legumes and grains grown for soil food and incorporated through tillage while they are lush and green). I like to think of such feeding as inoculation. Putting composts into soil is perhaps the best way to quickly bring to life bacteria, fungi, algae, and other soil characters who may be in low population numbers. Composts are themselves replete with high populations of all kinds of microbial life, usually in balanced form. Raw manures or partially composted manures and raw green manures act as foods for soils with good levels of microheard populations, causing a flush of eating activity when they are incorporated. In fact, there is so much microbial activity when non-composted materials are added to soil that you do not want to plant in these soils until that activity has slowed. Otherwise, the microherd will devour seeds, seedlings, and roots of more mature transplants. If the season is warm and the moisture and air levels are balanced, this flush of decomposition activity can be accomplished in several weeks. I highly recommend such sheet composting, especially of plants grown for their nitrogen-placing characteristics, their allopathic (natural herbicide) effects, and their variant sugar/protein contents.

When we incorporate plant and animal residues into soil they are broken down by enzymes made by bacteria. These enzymes break down the bodies and cells into simpler molecules that include amino acids, precursors to nucleic acids, five- and six-carbon sugars, vitamins, and fatty acids, and they release minerals. These molecules are taken up by the bacteria, who reproduce the most rapidly of all kindoms. We are talking millions of bacteria per handful of soil, reproducing in matters of minutes. Then the fungi, who grow more slowly than bacteria, take over in the next stage of fermentation of the microbial brew. All this activity ends up producing what we call soil organic matter.

Organic matter is the developmental decomposition process of building of soil biological tissue. This process is taking carbon dioxide, water, sugar, and some minerals, and generating proteins, polysaccharides, nucleic acids, and vitamins. In this brewing, microbial-enzymatic decomposition products are excreted into the top six inches of soil, which is the root zone for future plants. There the decomposition products accumulate and are further metabolized by microherd characters. Molecules that become stable, are resistant to breakdown, have both acid and base properties, and contain positive or negative electrical type charges are built. Many of these compounds contain benzene ring compounds, which have an odor. These compounds bind many useful soil nutrients and water and are a reservoir for all that is required by growing cells. Organic matter is visible, somewhat, but it is more an ongoing microbial process. When we speak of high levels of organic matter in gardening as a requirement for fertile soil, we are speaking about the success of our microbial feeding.

Longevity: Millennial Microbes

A colleague at Oregon State University, Dr. Richard P. Dick, has done some of his most interesting research at sites in Colca Valley, Peru, where gardens are at least 1,500 years old. At these sites he found that levels of organic matter, nitrogen, and phosphorus were greater than in the surrounding uncultivated soils. In *Soil Enzyme Activities After 1500 Years of Terrace Agriculture in the Colca Valley, Peru, Agriculture, Ecosystems and Environment*, He states, "Maintenance of enzyme activities over hundreds of years in agricultural soils is partly attributed to traditional management practices including rotations with legumes, additions of animal manures, and minimum tillage." As an example, in the terraces potatoes and beans were grown after several years of alfalfa. These results are only amazing because modern gardening and farming practices worldwide have been damaging the soil resource at a rapid rate. Most heavily cropped soils have lost organic matter because of excessive tillage, therefore oxidation of compounds involved in decomposition processes. Many soils have been damaged by excessive chemical fertilization and the use of both herbicides and insecticides. What was even more interesting in Dick's study was his comparison of gardens in continual use with those that have been abandoned for 400 years. Even in these soils, which were once cultivated using traditional soil building practices, micro flora (organisms) remained relatively high, their stimulation from long ago affecting the soil biology even today. As Dick points out: "This is consistent with a report by Jenkinson and Johnson (1977) who found residual effects on total N (nitrogen) content 123 years after animal manure inputs had ceased." The indicator enzymes amidase and phosphatase are at high levels in these ancient garden areas because of management practices.

A critical note in this study is that climate at Colca Valley is semi-arid. You would not ordinarily expect the results Dr. Dick found. But, this climate also provides stable seasonal soil temperatures. Like well-ventilated greenhouses, soil biological activity is likely in almost continual process production mode, and soil enzymes indicating active microbial bacteria are the clue. Dr. Dick's study is one more important piece of information aimed at convincing the unconvinced that healthy soils are alive and will remain alive over the millennia.

Work by Dr. Elaine Ingram and her colleagues at Oregon State University suggests that the kinds of foods fed to the microherd affect the relationship between specific plants and soil ecology. We know that certain plants are acid-loving: blueberries, strawberries, and rhododendrons. If you grow these plants in areas that are fertilized for plants like corn or broccoli, they do not do as well as they do when they are fertilized to be more like a woody forest floor. Dr. Ingram finds that different kinds of microherd characters are involved in the decomposition process in these disparate planting zones. The work of J. Macura and V. Vancora from Czechoslovak Academy of Science (*Plant Microbe Relationships*) shows that the oozings and tricklings of specific species of plants into the rhizosphere (root zone) attract different bacteria, from pseudomonades to actinomycetes as well as fungi. Specific species of plant exudates accelerate microbial enzyme interactions of specific bacterial species. The zones between roots show less activity. Furthermore, we know that some of these exudates, particularly when a plant is in the seedling stage, are toxic to specific fungi while being primary food for specific bacteria.

It is these long-term plant-microbe interactions that are and should be the basis for traditional agricultural management systems that include green manuring, the use of plants as allopathic suppressants of other plants (that we call weeds), and companion planting.

Most importantly, we need to be aware of residual effects of any of our agricultural management practices. Some of these effects that are microherd-based last for hundreds of years.

Timing and Other Considerations

I have mentioned throughout this article that our Sun is primary as we consider microbial soil management. The warming of soils seasonally or artificially is critical to bacterial activity. Climate is therefore a crucial factor in what crops can be easily grown. Some crops require very high levels of fertility, while others can get by with lower levels but must be involved in longer rotations that include nitrogen-fixing legumes, etc. Short seasons of low light levels make some crops impossible for some climates. Equatorial heat continuously makes it difficult to grow cool climate crops.

What I wonder about is the relationship of Moon cycles to microbial activity. Traditional gardeners worldwide do incorporation of green manures at specific periods of the Moon. We also find that if we harvest when the Moon is in the fourth quarter most crops keep better. Could this reflect microbial activity? Are soil microbes more active during the second and third quarter? And, what is the relationship of apparent heightened protein levels as a result of planting in the proper quarter of the Moon and microbial activity? There are whole areas of potential research!

Growing Great Potatoes

By Carly Wall, C.A.

I magine growing potatoes with no mud, no mess, and no back-breaking tilling or digging. "Impossible," you say, but it's not impossible with the no-trouble method that I use, based on the famous gardener Ruth Stout's year-around permanent mulch gardening system. I learned of this method when I came across her book, *The Ruth Stout No-Work Garden Book*, with Richard Clemence, Rodale Press, 1971. Over the years I've tried her tips, found some of my own, and enjoyed great bounties of enormous and delicious potatoes.

First of all, I'd like to say that before any consideration for planting is done, I consult the phase of the Moon. To me, gardening by the Moon is all-important. If someone tells you Moon planting is a load of bunk, you can be sure that that person has no experience in gardening. For potatoes, it is said that the best time to plant is during the decreasing light of the Moon: from Full Moon to New Moon. More accurately, it is said to be best to plant the spuds in the third quarter as the Full Moon declines and grows old.

Whatever you believe, plan on setting your potato seeds as early in the spring as you can. The best tubers are obtained when plants have daytime air temperature of 60–65 degrees Farenheit and night temperatures of about 50–55 degrees Farenheit. Some varieties have been developed for warmer climes and these are usually planted as a late winter or fall crop. You can usually safely sow these about two to four weeks before the last frost-free date.

Potatoes are classed by size, shape, and their skin color (red or white). The sweet potato is another article altogether, as are the buttery-tasting varieties like Yukon Gold. For now, we will concentrate on the two most popular potatoes, the red and white. The white potato wins hands down as it is used every day in all kinds of recipes, and by itself either steamed, baked, fried, or boiled. Most varieties mature at around 100–110 days. The Irish Cobbler is an old-fashioned favorite, with oval tubers of medium size and deep-set eyes. Superior is another early white that doesn't discolor after cooking. Kennebec is a large tuber with fine flavor and high yields.

The red varieties make especially nice new potatoes (tiny potatoes harvested early) when boiled and added to creamed peas fresh from the garden (heaven!). Red potatoes can usually be harvested after about 115 days, and varieties include Norland (thick with smooth skin, good yields), Red Pontiac (oblong and a good winter keeper) and Viking (drought resistant).

The Mulch Method of Growing

Through the years, I've grown all varieties of potatoes and I've gotten excellent results in a weed-free patch without turning the soil once. Here's how you can do it too.

First, locate a nice, sunny spot. It can be grassy or barren. Just make sure that your plot isn't marshy and that it does get good Sun exposure. Potatoes can't take standing in water (they'll rot).

Next, you'll need some seed potatoes. Up to twenty pounds of potatoes will grow in a square yard of space, to give you some idea of how big a plot you'll want. Gather up as much newspaper as you can. Discard the funnies and ads since they may contain harmful chemicals in the colored inks. You'll also need some spoiled hay, straw, or grass clippings (enough to cover your plot completely, twelve inches deep total). To help bulk up your mulch you can add ground corncobs, compost, chopped leaves, or any sort of mulching material.

Spread the newspapers down over your chosen area, laying the paper double thickness with overlapping edges so that no grass peeks through (otherwise you'll have a weedy mess later). On top of the newspapers, lay at least six inches of your choice of mulch. It helps to lay down one section of newspaper, then top with six inches of mulch, then lay down the next section of newspaper, then top with the mulch and so on. That way, the wind won't conspire against you. When you have finished with the entire area in this manner, then evenly distribute your seed potatoes and cover them with at least six more inches of mulch.

If you are used to the conventional methods of gardening, you may question my sanity, but this no-till method does work. Let me explain.

When you covered the sod with newspaper, you started a decomposition process. Without light, the grass dies and breaks down into more nutrients for the soil. By the time the grass is gone, the newspaper breaks down too, taking with it all the weed seeds. The heavy mulch keeps things nice and moist while temperatures stay even. This means it's a great environment for growing potatoes and it attracts earthworms.

After the planting is done, you can really forget about the potatoes until harvest. Then just take your pitchfork and uncover the mulch to reveal your potato booty—relatively clean and easy to pick up.

Harvesting

To make use of fresh potatoes, you can lift up the mulch cover carefully after the plant begins to bloom. Pick out one or two spuds in each spot, and carefully replace the mulch cover. These can be used as new potatoes in your best-tasting dishes. Fresh potatoes don't keep very well, so use them quickly, within one or two weeks. Your cured crop is ready to pick up one to two weeks after the plant has turned brown and withered. If the plants die back before a frost, suspect a late blight. Otherwise, harvest soon after the frost when plants are well dried, because if the potatoes freeze they become like mush. The cured potatoes should keep well for many months under the proper conditions. When ready for harvest, take a wheelbarrow and fill it with your bounty of potatoes. Be gentle with the spuds, as blackening problems during storage stem from a rough harvest. Spread the spuds out to dry for several hours, then store for winter use. It's as easy as that. Even easier, you can leave the shriveled plants and mulch right where it lies. Let it winter over and all you need do is lay out next year's crop of seed potatoes in the spring and cover it with the six-inch layer of spoiled hay on top.

Of course, once you start this method of gardening, you may wonder if you might do all your gardening in this manner. The answer is yes, with a few changes. Tender seeds shouldn't be covered under such a thick mulch. Lay out the garden as before, but with a good eight-inch layer of mulch. Now make rows where you want to plant, heaping the mulch up on both sides. Sow your seed almost on the newspaper, covering with a sprinkling of the mulch. As the plants grow, simply pull the mulch cover around them to keep the weeds at bay. For plants, wait until the newspaper begins to disintegrate, dig a hole, plant, then surround with the mulch, tightly tucking the plant in.

Storage

When I first started out, one of my problems was storage of my crop of potatoes. Potatoes can be stored a variety of ways and everyone is sure to find a method to suit them. Root crops like potatoes love it best in cold, moist air; preferably between 40 and 45 degrees Farenheit. Here are a few methods that have worked for others. Pick the method that appeals to you.

Root Cellars

There are root cellars and then there are root cellars. My dream is to have a deluxe root cellar. First, it would be an eight by ten-foot structure separate from the house, with soil banked along three walls and a wood-lined room with a hatch to get in. An air vent would provide circulation. Three inches of gravel on the floor sprinkled with water occasionally should provide enough humidity. There would also be plenty of shelving so I could easily line up my baskets of potatoes and any other produce (canned items as well as other root crops, cabbage or fruits).

If you have an empty storage shed, you can improvise a root cellar if you insulate it well. Also, it should be placed a foot off the ground so that plenty of air flows underneath.

Some people may have space in a basement window well. This can be used as a mini root cellar. Box the window in with a lift-up wooden door. This helps keep the area cool and keeps mice from stealing. Place a bushel basket of potatoes within the box. When temperatures drop below freezing, open the wooden side of the door a few inches to keep the area cool but not freezing. When temperatures rise above seventy, open the basement window a bit to let the heat out and encourage circulation of air.

An outdoor basement entrance is an excellent substitute for potato storage. Install a door at the bottom of the steps to block off house heat. Store the potatoes at the top steps where temperatures stay coolest.

Hay Storage

In a pinch, you can use bales of hay to store your crops. Lay out bales in a rectangle with a central opening. This central opening is your storage area. Line this opening with straw and stack your produce, covering each layer with more straw. Next, lay two two-by-fours across the opening and place bales of straw on top. These two-by-fours act as ventilation and can be removed during severe weather to seal the opening.

Barrel Method

Last, you can choose the barrel method of over-wintering your potato crop. Dig a space for the barrel in a well-drained area. Lay down a layer of leaves or straw and place the barrel on top. Slant the open end down so any moisture will run out. Place a board over the opening, using a rock to hold it in place. Cover the sides and upper end of the barrel with about eighteen inches of soil. The lower end should have only three inches covering it. Cover the whole thing with straw and place boards or bales of straw on top to hold it all in place.

Growing Fruit

By Roslyn Reid

Images of fruit occupied a prominent position in the old religions. The Greeks told tales of Eris and her golden apple, Persephone and her pomegranate, and Dionysus and his grapes, to name just a few examples. According to Barbara Walker, peaches were considered the ambrosia of life in ancient China, and who could forget the story of the encounter between Eve and the apple in the Garden of Eden?

Myths about Growing Fruit

Considering this rich heritage, why is it that people seem to grow lots of herbs and vegetables, but not much fruit? Well, it could be due to common misperceptions about the resources needed to grow fruit. For instance, many people think that a lot of room is required to grow fruit. This is because when we think about growing fruit these days, we tend to think about trees—*big* trees, in big orchards. It doesn't seem to occur to us that trees are not the only way to grow fruit.

Actually, there are four forms of plants that produce the edibles we call fruit: trees, vines, bushes, and canes. There are also unusual forms, such as strawberries, that don't fit quite neatly into any of these four categories. Such forms are usually ambiguously referred to as "plants."

As for space requirements, a friend of mine once stated that if you have enough room to grow a zucchini, you have enough room to grow a melon! In fact, I grow kiwi vines tied to trellises that are placed along one side of my garage. This type of vertical growing saves a lot of space and can make use of odd little plots of land that might otherwise go to waste.

Another misperception about growing fruit is that it requires more of an effort from the gardener than growing either vegetables or herbs. True, herbs are some of the easiest plants to grow, but certain fruits can be even easier to grow than herbs are. For example, check out wild blueberries, which seem to do best when they are growing in the cracks of rocks under pine trees in northern climates! One would be hard pressed to find worse growing conditions than this, and it's certainly not the kind of situation you would find in a typical garden.

What about objections to all that spraying that we seem to think fruit trees require? Well, depending on the type of tree and the pests or diseases around the area in which it grows, some types of fruit trees may do better if they are sprayed. Certainly we all know that commercial growers spray their trees—but they have lots of trees to worry about, and spraying fattens the bottom line. However, we are not discussing commercial growers here—I have a friend who has never sprayed his peach trees, and his family is blessed with a large crop of juicy peaches every year.

The Real Drawbacks

Of course, growing fruit is not entirely a bed of roses, so to speak. Pruning is an inescapable part of fruit horticulture. Although all forms of fruiting plants benefit from pruning, trees, because of their size, can be more difficult to cut back than other forms of fruit. Apple trees provide a good example of the benefits of pruning. I've seen at least one straggly tree, over half a century old, revive beautifully and bear several grocery bags full of apples after gardeners cut off nearly a third of its branches! So yes, if you don't know how to prune, don't want to take the time or trouble to learn, and can't afford to hire someone to do proper pruning, trees might not be the best form of fruit for you to grow.

Speaking of room—some fruiting plants are gendered! This means they take both a male and a female form, like holly trees. Before you acquire any fruiting plant, be sure to find out whether it requires another plant of the same species for cross-fertilization! For instance, my female kiwi vines need a male vine to cross-fertilize them or they will be unable to bear fruit. This situation is more common than you may think and you need to plan ahead for it: gendered forms of fruit require twice as much property, because you must plant two of them.

Probably the biggest real disadvantage to growing fruit is that you may have to wait a long time for the plants to actually bear fruit. The kiwi vines I previously mentioned typically take seven years to bear! Fruit trees usually don't produce anything during the first year of their lives, either. On the other hand, berries usually do bear fruit during their first year; so if you're the impatient type, you might prefer berries.

Some types of fruit have drawbacks that differ from the ones mentioned above. For instance, strawberry plants must be uprooted and thrown away or burned (not composted) every three years because they are prone to a certain virus. On the other hand, new strawberry plants can be grown from "runners," a vinelike shoot the established plant sends out;

so buying new strawberry plants may not be necessary if the runners can be properly rooted in the garden.

There's also a monetary disadvantage to growing fruit. Startup can be expensive, especially with trees. Unless you are attempting to grow a peach or avocado tree from a pit (and I should have such patience), you will need to buy saplings from a nursery. Trees can also be started from cuttings; but this isn't much faster than using a pit. The larger the tree, the more expensive it is, although it's probably money well spent—nursery trees that are at least two years old have reached a size that gives them a better chance of survival, and they will bear fruit sooner. Depending on the type, variety, size, and number of fruit trees you want to grow, buying from even discount mail-order nurseries can run into quite a bit of money. On the other hand, berry bushes or canes can be cheaper to buy, or even had for free, if you don't mind digging them up!

So What Does It Take to Grow Fruit?

Now we'll take a closer look at the four forms of fruiting plants and see what the basic needs are for growing each kind. At my place, I grow all four types—trees, vines, canes, and bushes. Most of them have done pretty well over the years, although I'm still waiting for those kiwis to bear fruit!

Keep in mind that this article is only an overview and is not intended to turn your yard into an organic version of ConAgra. Those of you who wish to pursue fruit growing at a more intensive level can consult the resources listed at the end of this article to help with any further questions you may have.

Trees

Despite what I previously said about not needing a lot of room, if trees are your choice of form for growing fruit, you will need a wee bit more space than you would for, say, lettuce, but not more than you would for corn! If you have the room to grow six cornstalks (each stalk taking up one square foot of space), then you have enough room to plant a dwarf fruit tree.

Dwarf fruit trees are the greatest thing since sliced apples. They can bear almost as much fruit as full-sized trees, but in much less space. Because dwarfs are smaller than regular trees, they require less pruning, fertilizing, and watering.

Best of all, almost any kind of fruit tree is now available in a dwarf variety. (Figs seem to be a notable exception; but because agricultural research is an ongoing process, dwarf figs might yet be available some day.)

Growing in my yard right now is a grove of six dwarf fruit trees that occupy a space twenty feet long by ten feet wide.

Another good thing about fruit trees is that they don't require as much sunlight as most other plants do. So don't worry about shading out your dwarf fruit trees if you can only find your favorite apple variety in a full-size tree—plant it anyway!

When buying your tree at the nursery, it's a good idea to find out whether it's been "pre-pruned" before you take it home. This will save you the trouble of pruning it after planting. If it hasn't been, you might ask the nursery to prune it for you at the time of purchase. Usually they will do this for free.

After bringing your new sapling home, soak its roots in a bucket of water for at least an hour before planting. (Make sure its roots are never allowed to dry out at this time!) While the tree is soaking, dig a hole big enough so you can spread out all its roots. There is an old saying that one should dig a "ten-dollar hole for a five-dollar tree." This means that fruit tree roots need a lot of space, so be sure to provide it. When planting a tree, you should observe these three important rules.

1. Be sure to space trees far enough apart from each other—usually ten feet for dwarf varieties. Remember, the roots will need room for future growth, and it's almost impossible to move trees later!

2. Other than compost or peat, do not put any fertilizer into the freshly dug hole before the tree goes in.

3. "Heel in" the dirt around the tree roots while filling in the hole (i.e., pack the loose dirt firmly down with your foot). Do this again around the base of the tree after you finish planting it.

The reasoning behind the first rule should be obvious; but it's a good idea to double-check acceptable distances, because they may vary with each type of tree. If you look up the distances and find two different numbers, use the larger one. (Figs are a good example of trees that need a great deal of room for their roots to expand—they should never be placed near any water or sewer lines because fig tree roots are notorious for clogging them!) Furthermore, there is always the chance that you might like your new fruit trees so much that you may want to plant more of them in the future, so be sure to leave enough room for expansion.

Putting commercial fertilizer into the hole before the tree goes in (rule two) sounds like a good idea, but it is not. A strong, non-organic fertilizer will overwhelm the tree and you stand a good chance of killing your new tree if you apply some at this time. If you feel you really must fertilize the tree when planting it, a nice organic compost never hurts. Build a pyramid of soil and compost in the bottom of the hole and spread the roots of the tree in all directions over this pyramid. Then start refilling the hole as described above.

Rule three, although simple, is crucial. Air pockets around the roots of a newly planted tree can encourage invasion by insects or diseases. While it's not necessary to go as far as jumping up and down on the tree base, do make sure the soil around the roots is firmly tamped down.

After tamping, scrape out a shallow round depression in the soil around the base of the tree. Fill it with water, let the water soak into the ground, then refill the depression with more water. Now place about six inches of mulch (rotted leaves, hay, grass clippings—anything that will prevent weeds) on and around the base of the tree.

Finally, don't forget to water the tree every day. You don't have to worry about fertilizer right now, but studies indicate that people overwater indoor plants and underwater outdoor plants! If you feel you have this problem, you might want to invest in a drip hose, which makes the job easier. A drip hose also saves water, which is a significant advantage if you have a water bill to pay.

If it looks like the tree will need to be sprayed for insects or disease during the following year, check out organic sprays such as sulfur dust or dormant oil. Sulfur dust is used on some kinds of apple tree diseases, such as scab. Dormant oil, which is a very old pesticide, has had several other names, but I refer to it as dormant oil because it is sprayed on while the tree is still dormant in the spring. This treatment prevents certain boring pests from even getting a toehold (assuming they have toes). You can find these organic pesticides at almost any nursery.

Vines

Believe it or not, vines can require more growing room than trees do! Fruiting vines should be planted about the same distance apart as you would plant dwarf fruit trees. Don't forget to prune vines back mercilessly—I can't emphasize enough how quickly vines can get out of control and take over the yard before you even realize it. Vine pruning differs from tree pruning in that vines are pruned according to their age. If you choose to grow this form of fruit, make sure you have enough time to prune.

Vines must also be trained to grow along sturdy supports, or they will climb up the nearest structure—trees, the wall of the garage, your car—

vines are not fussy. Suitable supports can be bought, or you can make them from almost anything of sufficient strength. A good gardening book such as the *Reader's Digest Illustrated Guide to Gardening* can give you specifics on how to prune, train, and support whatever fruiting vine you wish to grow. It's probably a good idea to read up on this form of fruit before you try growing it to get a better idea of the level of commitment required.

Planting vines differs from planting trees in that you should not tamp down the ground on top of the vine's roots. You can firm the soil around them with your hands, but do not pack it hard—give the roots plenty of room. However, make sure to water vines just as well as you would trees. Compost is usually all the fertilizer your vines will ever need.

Unlike trees, vines do require weeding because their roots are shallow and weeds can interfere with their growing. (Weeding isn't too bad, however, because some of the weeds you pull out are probably edible or medicinal; but that's another article!) Deep mulch is probably the best way for preventing weed growth.

Bushes

Bushes are a nice controlled way to grow fruit. The catch is that not many fruits grow on bushes. Blueberries and cranberries come to mind. Both of these might be considered more of a shrub due to their low-growing form, although there are larger-growing blueberry bushes that can be grouped into a hedge. Cranberries, on the other hand, are a good choice for ground cover because they can be mowed when they spread out too far!

Fruit bushes are grown in much the same way as any other bush, although fruits prefer a more acidic soil than most other plants. Therefore, fruit bushes are a good choice to plant where you've had no luck growing anything else—under oak, pine, or beech trees, for example. They can be planted in the same manner described above for vines.

Like vines, the roots of fruit bushes are shallow; so again, deep mulching is better for weed control than cultivation with tools. Fruit bushes don't require much pruning, either; and whatever pruning they do need can be done easily with a hedge clipper, just as you would prune any other bush. If you like berries but are short on the time or energy it takes to care for your plants, fruit bushes might be a good choice for you.

Canes

Fruiting canes are quite common. Unfortunately, because their fruit is a diet delight to many species and because many of these plants grow in the wild, it is also quite common for fruiting canes to have large thorns! Osage orange is an outstanding example. Its thorns are so big that long hedges of osage orange are used at some U.S. government locations in Washington, D.C. as a deterrent to trespassers. Not only is this landscaping method cheaper, easier, and much more effective than erecting the usual fence; it's also been discovered recently that the fruit of the osage orange repels cockroaches.

Just like roses, thornless varieties of fruiting canes do exist; however, these varieties must be purchased from a nursery. On the other hand, many thorny canes such as blackberry can be obtained for free from along the roadside, near wooded areas, or from neighbors. The situation seems to be a choice between living with thorns or paying money. If you want to try transplanting the thorny wild varieties, wear heavy leather gloves when you dig them up, and be careful!

There are three ways of raising canes. (Get it? Sorry, I can't help myself.) One method is to let the canes grow into huge hedgerows as they do in the wild. This is not a recommended growing form for the thorny varieties because it's very difficult to get past the thorns to pick the berries, as you probably discovered if you dug up those wild canes for transplanting.

The other two ways of training canes involve wires. The one-wire method, as its name implies, requires tying each individual cane to a single wire that has been stretched between posts situated at both ends of the row of canes. The two-wire technique also uses posts located in the same place; but this method requires crossbars placed across the tops of the posts, making them look like giant Ts. A wire is then run along each side of the row of canes, from the end of the crossbar on one post to the end of the crossbar on the other. The canes are trained to grow between these two wires.

Unless wire is really expensive in your area, there appears to be no advantage of one method over the other. I prefer the two-wire method because I think tying each cane to a wire seems like more work than I'm willing to do!

Whichever method you choose to use, the preparation for planting is the same: dig a trench about six inches deep and whatever length you wish your row of canes to be. Canes need a lot of room because not only do they grow prodigiously, but the ends of any canes that come in contact with the ground will take root. (This is why they grow in such large tangles in the wild.) Therefore, plants should be placed at least three feet apart.

After digging the trench, line it with compost and plant the canes. Firmly press the soil down around them with your hands, but do not tamp it in with your feet. Like vines, the roots of canes need lots of room too. Water your new cane row, and you're done for the day.

After the canes have borne their yearly crop, cut down to ground level any canes that had fruit on them. The rest of the canes can be left alone until late fall, when you should cut them down to about three feet high. Make the cut above a bud. Don't worry about pruning too much off. Believe me, when spring comes, you'll be glad you didn't spare the shears!

Container Growing

You've probably seen lots of fruit trees growing in huge containers in hotel lobbies and other such places, but taken no special notice of them at the time. After all, the containers in those places are well hidden to give the illusion of a naturally growing forest. (In a lobby. Sure!) Of necessity, most fruit trees that are grown in home-sized containers are very small, so either they don't bear fruit, or their fruit is inedible. Vines would be unwieldy in a container unless they are well trained and kept meticulously pruned.

On the other hand, strawberries are perfect for containers, and are frequently grown in them. There are even special containers manufactured just for growing strawberries. Oddly enough, they are usually known as "strawberry jars." These are large jars made with openings all around the sides that look like tiny balconies. After the jar is filled with a growing medium such as soil, one strawberry plant is placed into each "balcony." Water the jar every day, and soon you will have a nice crop, right on your own porch or patio!

Other than strawberries, bushes are probably the best choice for growing edible fruit in containers. Make sure to get a large container—four gallons or more. You might want to look for one made of fiberglass so it won't be too heavy, or buy a wheeled dolly to go underneath it so you can move it conveniently.

Advantages of Growing Fruit

And what does all this hard work get you? Healthy, organic, perennial food that is ready to eat right out of the garden. If you've chosen to plant trees, you'll have shade in the summer and perhaps even a place to hang a swing! If you have annoying neighbors, a hedgerow of thorny canes can serve as an amiable fence between you and them.

There's also another benefit most folks don't consider. Perhaps your fruit crop will turn out to be so successful that you'll find yourself with a surplus. Why not sell your extra fruit at a farmers' market, or erect a small produce stand in front of your house? Fruit sales bring in more money than the sale of vegetables, and you can earn back your initial investment in fruiting plants many times over. Or, if you don't wish to sell your extra fruit, you can help your community by donating it to a local food bank.

No matter what form of fruit you choose to plant, you'll have edible landscaping, singing birds, and perhaps even beautiful and fragrant flowers in the spring.

Resources

Books and Magazines

Country Journal. 4 High Ridge Park, Stamford, CT 06905. Published bimonthly. Subscriptions are $21. Call 1-800-829-3340 (U.S. and Canada). Their e-mail address is cntryjrnl@aol.com.

Llewellyn's Organic Gardening Almanac (back issues only) and *Llewellyn's Magical Almanac.* Subscribe or order back issues by calling 1-800-THE-MOON; or checking Llewellyn's web site at http://www.llewellyn.com.

Reader's Digest Illustrated Guide to Gardening. Pleasantville, NY: Reader's Digest Association, 1978.

Internet Web Sites

City Farmer's Urban Agriculture Notes, http://www.cityfarmer.org.

Dwarf Apple Trees web page, http://www.mes.umn.edu/Documents/D/G/Dg1109.html.

Edible Landscaping, http://www.rawspace.com/edible.

Garden Web, http://www.gardenweb.com.

Horticultural Web, http://www/horticulture.com. You can look up your nearest Cooperative Extension Agent in the list here.

"Plants for a Future," Ground Cover Plants web page, http://www.scs.leeds.ac.uk/pfaf/grdcover.html.

County Extension Agents

Your cooperative extension agent is there to help with your agricultural questions. Agents can give advice for growing plants in your specific area. If you can't access the Internet listings of them, you will be able to look up the nearest agent in the blue pages of your phone book. The exact listing varies with each phone book, but your agent can be typically listed under "County Government—Agriculture Agent" for each individual county in your area.

Harvesting at the Peak

By Penny Kelly

I watched a friend of mine plant a large garden for five years in a row and harvest hardly anything from it. When I asked her why she got so little for her efforts, she said, "I think my garden produces a lot. I just never know when stuff is ready to harvest." Another friend, raised in an automated world of mass production and just-in-time-deliveries, kept waiting for everything to ripen at once so she could march out to the garden, pick it clean, and be done with it!

A relative beginner in my neighborhood got little reward for his efforts because he put his entire stock of seeds and plants in the ground at the same time in late May. The radishes were ready before anything else, but since he didn't really like radishes when eaten alone, he ignored them until mid-July when the lettuce was ready. By that time the radishes had gone to seed and the lettuce was bitter. His cucumbers had mostly collapsed because he had not covered them during a late cold snap. The cantaloupe and watermelon didn't have time to ripen because they went in as seeds instead of three-week old seedlings, and wandering around the garden only once a week made him the beneficiary of zucchini that were big enough to feed a tyrannosaurus rex.

There's no point in going to all the trouble of putting in a garden if you aren't really going to get a decent harvest for all that work. The first thing you need to know about getting great harvests is when to plant a particular veggie. For instance, in Michigan you can't plant a fifty-day leaf lettuce in May and expect a decent harvest in July. The heat will make the lettuce so bitter you won't be able to eat it.

The second thing is how to feed, water, and nurture what you've planted. For example, potatoes need sufficient water in the first three weeks of sprouting or the potatoes will be the size of marbles. Peas don't like hot weather, and tomatoes need cages and warm nights to ripen into their best.

The third thing to know is that there are lots of little harvests to be picked every day or two. You do have to patrol the garden regularly or your beans will be tough, dry, and lumpy, the cabbages wormy, the radishes and beets woody, and the broccoli bolted. Once you get these three things down, the rest is relatively easy. Just pick and eat.

Cool-Weather Crops

In very early spring we plant cool weather crops such as snow peas, shell peas, and snap peas, lettuces, spinach, early cabbage, broccoli, radishes, kohlrabi, and potatoes.

Peas

All peas thrive in cool, wet weather and need to be harvested every other day. Snow peas can be harvested when the pods are still small, only one and a half inches long and quite flat. They can go to about four inches long but there is a very tough string that develops along each edge of the pod when they do. The string should be removed before steaming or tossing into a raw salad, which makes preparation more time-consuming, but the peas will still be tasty.

If you have traditional shell peas that need to be removed from the pod before steaming or freezing, wait until peas are full and round, but not until the outer pod begins to dry out or turn brown. The peas inside will be tough and less flavorful.

If you have some form of a sugar snap, the peas can be a little more rounded than for snow peas, but smaller than for shell peas. The pods are delicious and the string still has to be removed, but these peas are like candy and well worth the harvest effort.

Lettuce

When it comes to lettuce, we seed in February, plant in March, and harvest is over by the end of June. We don't harvest the whole lettuce plant even if it's head lettuce. We just harvest the large outer leaves continuously, taking one or two off of every other plant about every other day.

Spinach

Spinach is definitely a spring or fall crop and won't even germinate in hot, dry weather. Once it's up and has six to eight leaves, you can begin harvesting single leaves from each plant. Later, just before the weather gets hot, the whole plant can be harvested.

Cabbage

Red or green heads of cabbage can be harvested any time after the heads get three to four inches across. Watch them closely, though, as they grow quite slowly and then, when it begins to get hot and rainy, they will suddenly split open in their effort to grow too quickly and absorb too much water. If you have small heads about four inches in diameter and it rains for a week, you should go out and give the whole plant a good, swift twist to break or at least disturb the outer root zone and prevent the plants from drinking too much then splitting. If they do split you can still pick them immediately and eat them, but they always seem less appetizing once they're split.

Broccoli

Broccoli first grows a head, which will usually be about three inches across, in the center of the plant. This head should be cut when the buds are still closed tight. If the weather gets hot, keep an eye on it and harvest sooner if necessary or the whole thing will bolt to bright yellow flowers and seeds. If it does bolt, cut the center head off and allow the smaller side heads to develop so you can still enjoy an extended harvest. If the plant bolts in mid-July, seed another batch immediately, and transplant around August 1.

Potatoes

Everyone has heard the old joke about the gardener who couldn't harvest his potatoes because the plants all died. Of course the joke is that potatoes of any variety (except sweet potatoes) are ready to be dug up when the plant turns brown and dies. Potatoes won't get any larger at that point, and they can get wormy, so dig them up with a garden fork. Let them dry in the shade for a few hours, then knock the dirt off carefully so as not to break the skin. Eat a few immediately so you can enjoy the incredible taste experience of fresh potatoes, and store the rest in a cool, dry, dark place. Do not wash them, either, or you'll remove the beneficial bacteria that eat the destructive bacteria. In fact, here in the upper Midwest, potatoes can be planted almost any time from April to August, and planting a small amount several times guarantees that you won't have too much at once, and what you do have will be fresh. If you do end up with a lot of potatoes and can't eat them all over the winter, save them, even if they're all shrunken and spongy, and use them as seed potatoes in next year's garden.

Hot-Weather Crops

About the same time that the potatoes go in the ground, we start our hot weather vegetables and fruits in the greenhouse. These include cantaloupe, watermelon, zucchini, green and yellow beans as well as shell beans, beets, carrots, corn, cucumbers, squash, tomatoes, peppers, and sweet potatoes.

Cantaloupe

If you like cantaloupe and would like to get a little taste of heaven, plant your seeds indoors in small pots three or four weeks before you plan to transplant them into the garden. Feed them with liquid seaweed, or side-dress them with ample amounts of compost in late June and again in mid-July. Pick them when the netting and the surface areas in between the netting are a rich, creamy tan color without hints of green. When the fruit is really ready, the stem will separate easily from the plant, sometimes before you even get around to picking it. A cantaloupe lying there unattached to its mother plant is trying to tell you it is past time to pick it!

Watermelon

Watermelon is another delicacy that must be started indoors early, and nurtured with compost or seaweed. If you plant the green and white striped variety, it is ready to harvest when the white stripes are rich and cream-colored. As a second test for ripeness, turn the watermelon over and look at the part touching the ground. It should also be a creamy white, not greenish-tinged. A third test is to rap smartly on the middle of its belly. If you hear a sharp, hollow ring, it is ready. If you hear a dull thud-thud, it's likely to be overripe and mealy. Good, healthy watermelon picked at the right moment lasts a long time when kept cold. We regularly enjoy watermelon in January that was picked, ripe and sweet, in September.

Zucchini

Be careful in deciding how many zucchini plants to put in. To say they are prolific is a gross understatement. We easily get by with one or two plants. Once they begin producing you can almost sit down in the garden and watch the zucchini grow. Check every day, maybe two or three times a day, or you will end up with monstrous fruits that lack taste, juice, and tenderness. The best size is about five to six inches long, although three to four inches is considered a very tender delicacy. If you miss one and it gets to be ten to twelve inches long, dice it up and put it in a vegetable soup. As for the giants that are five inches in diameter and over a foot and a half long, I shred them and make numerous loaves of zucchini bread, putting them in the freezer and giving them away as Christmas gifts. In this form, zucchini is never refused!

String Beans

Green and yellow beans need to be picked every other day and will keep producing as long as you keep picking. Sometimes they will slow down after about six weeks of production, but if picked, a whole new generation of flowers will appear with a new supply of beans shortly after. They are best about a quarter inch in diameter and about six to eight inches long.

Shell Beans

If you plant shell beans such as soldier beans, black beans, or kidney beans, you can pick and eat a few of these when they're green and slim, but generally you leave them alone until after the first frost or two when the entire plant will be dry and brown. Don't let them stay out in the garden through too many cold, rainy autumn days or the beans will get moldy in their dry pods. Harvest whole plants on a warm, sunny day and let them dry for several days on a few old window screens in the utility room. Then shell them and let them air dry for another few days on a cookie sheet before putting them in Mason jars for storage. If they're too damp when put in the jar, they'll get moldy or mildewed. Sometimes a few hours in a food dehydrator is a good idea to make sure they're dry enough. If you plan to use some of them as seed for next year, separate these from the ones that will go in the bean pot and let next year's seeds dry naturally.

Beets

I don't know many people who like beets, but they are so good for your liver you should grow at least a small patch. Harvest them when they are small and tender, about one to three inches in diameter, and most juicy. Shred them into fresh green salads and they are wonderful. After three inches in diameter or really cold weather, they get tough and more fibrous but can still be diced and steamed. If they're harvested at peak taste and texture and kept in a cold, damp environment, they keep a very long time. As I write this I am still using beets I grew a year and a half ago!

Carrots

Carrots are also most tender when small—about two to four inches in length—but not only do they taste "soapy" to me at this stage, they are so much work to plant, keep weeded and cultivated that I tend to leave most of them in the ground until they are nearly two inches in diameter and a foot long. That way I get the most payback for my efforts. If your soil is bad you may not be able to do this because they'll get wormy. Just before fall frosts I harvest them all, put half in our large storage refrigerator for juicing and fresh use in salads, then dice, slice, and freeze the rest to be used in soups and casseroles over the winter. It seems that no matter how many I grow, we never have enough to last until the next season.

Corn

Corn on the cob is ready to pick when the silk sticking out of the ear turns dry and brown. Sometimes birds or insects will eat the silks off the end. Try not to pull the husks down just to see if the kernels are full enough as this is an invitation to pests, corn smut, corn borers, and bacteria. Instead grasp the ear and run your hand along it, trying to feel the fullness of the kernels inside. When you're learning, you may pick one or two ears that aren't ready, but you'll quickly learn to tell which are ready to pick, which are over-ready, and which need another week before going into the steamer and on to your dinner plate.

Cucumbers

My absolute favorite cucumber is the Suyo Long variety because it is so crisp, has exquisite taste, is never bitter, never seedy, and keeps for two or three weeks in the refrigerator. In my book, everything else is second rate by comparison, thus I may not be a good one to decide when to pick the more conventional cucumbers. Suyo Longs are best at one and a half inches in diameter and about eighteen inches long. We usually plant two or three other varieties, which seem to be okay at about six to eight inches in length and still slim. Harvest before they begin to get yellowed or too rounded and seedy, otherwise they're much too bitter to enjoy.

Winter Squash

Squash, whether acorn, butternut, spaghetti, or another of the winter varieties, should be harvested before fall frosts begin. Acorn squash should be a rich black color and not starting to turn orangey in spots. Butternut should be a rich, nutty, light brown or tan color without streaks of green along the sides, or a yellowish cast to the skin. Spaghetti squash should be a beautiful yellow, however, and not cream-colored or greenish. Cut the stems with heavy shears or a very sharp knife, then set the squash in dry, dappled shade to cure for two or three days. Store in a dark, dry place where the temperature is not too cold, about 44 to 55 degrees, and you can enjoy squash all winter.

Tomatoes

Here in Michigan I have grown tomatoes that we feasted on right up to Christmas. Of course, it was because they were from extremely healthy plants, which doesn't happen every single year, although we try. To get a good harvest from tomatoes, they really need to be kept off the ground or they get moldy as fast as they ripen. Tomatoes come in all sizes and colors, so pay attention to what were the general expectations for the seeds or plants you put in your garden. One year I experimented with a variety that was different. They were a sort of small, pinkish red variety, and half of them rotted because I kept waiting for them to get bigger and turn a richer looking red. If you bought red tomato plants, pick them when they are a deep red color and still firm to the touch. The same goes for yellow, pink, purple, or whatever color they're supposed to be. If your fingers easily make indentation in the tomato, the skins are already loosening, or there are cracks in the top whose edges are turning brown, you waited too long.

Peppers

Peppers, whether of the sweet bell or hot variety, are fairly simple. If it's a green sweet bell, you can pick when the peppers are good sized, firm, and dark green in color. If you miss them at this point and leave them on the plant, they will start to turn red, which is still okay but changes the flavor slightly, some people say for the better, some say for the worse. You'll know you left the pepper on the plant too long when the pepper starts to get wrinkled skin and feels spongy.

Sweet Potatoes

Sweet potatoes, which are relatively easy to grow, should be dug up with a garden fork immediately after the first hard frost when the plant has gone down because of the cold. Don't leave them in the ground too long though, or they change flavor, lose sweetness, and get tough if the temperature of the soil drops much below 50 degrees. Once they're dug, leave them to dry and cure in the Sun from a couple of hours to a couple of days, then knock off any remaining soil, and store in a dark, dry, not-too-cold environment of about 55 degrees.

Gardening has become a nearly year-round activity for us simply because we are committed to growing our own food in order to get superior nutrition. As the seasons change, so does our diet, and seasonal eating has proven to be very good for our general health. Even if you work at a corporate job from nine to five every day, you can enjoy the results of a small garden or greenhouse much more if you think of harvest as a half-hour chore that happens every evening, much like stopping at the grocery store after work, rather than a monstrous, weekly chore in a big garden that leaves you with too much produce to deal with. Plan something small, tend it conscientiously, and harvest it continuously. You will be amazed at the amount of good food you'll get.

Wildcrafting Tips

By Carly Wall, C.A.

Many people who are interested in herbs and who use them frequently come to a point in their lives when they would like to enjoy the bounties of nature by gathering their plants directly from the wild, an activity that is called wildcrafting. However, to wildcraft, you have to have a little know-how. Here, we'll go over some tips and hints on how you can begin the adventure of wildcrafting safely and successfully.

Foraging Safely

Before you even start, safety must be the main concern. "You have to absolutely know that the plant you are harvesting is the plant you want to harvest. You have to be a hundred percent sure in your identifications, because otherwise you may get hold of something that is poisonous or deadly," says master herbalist Jude Williams, author of *Jude's Herbal Home Remedies*. She adds, "Before you even think about wildcrafting, invest in a good identification book with pictures, such as one of the books in *The Audubon Society Field Guide* Series. I often use their *Guide to North American Wildflowers*, as well as the one for mushrooms, or trees."

Other ways to find out about wild plants is by reading such books as *Stalking the Wild Asparagus* by Euell Gibbons, *A Field Guide to Edible Wild Plants* by Lee Peterson, or *Wild Foods Cookbook and Field Guide* by Billy Jo Tatums. You might also consider taking various classes or walks offered by local nature centers, garden clubs, or Audubon Centers. Keep your eye out for such notices or call and ask to be placed on a mailing list if the coming calendar has something that interests you.

The Modern Wildcrafter

Another thing to remember is that in today's world, there aren't many places left that are wild. On top of that, many plants left in the few wild spaces are becoming endangered or extinct. Wildcrafting as we once knew it may be out as statistics reveal that over 28,000 plant species are lost per year worldwide. Goldenseal has become extinct in twenty-eight states, and as each plant is lost, we also lose four to eight insects and two to three animals because of dependence on that plant species. The best thing to do would be to leave wild areas alone.

Does this mean wildcrafting is a lost art? No. It just means that we must change the way we do things. "We have to remember to honor the Earth. It is our job now more than ever," says Williams. "Spread the word. Never gather more than what you need. Learn to give back. Make it your purpose to seed certain plants or trees in your yard, or your friends' yards."

If you are going to become a wildcrafter, be responsible. Today's modern wildcrafter doesn't have to go far afield to harvest wild plants. Many are growing right in your own back yard, like wild violets, dandelions, or plantain. You can create a wild patch in your back yard specifically for your own use for plants that are rare or can't be found. In this way, you can purchase your seed and watch as the plant grows, getting to know it intimately. Eventually, the plant will go wild on its own in your yard and you'll have plenty to use over the coming years. Williams was quick to add that as you think about cultivating your own wild area, you think of what you want to use these herbs for. "When you harvest plants growing in the area in which you live, these plants are best for your bodies for they often contain minerals and vitamins that you specifically need, in a form you can assimilate easily," adds Williams. "At one time, wildcrafters lived in the wild, and they merely used what was around them. By creating your own wild spot in your yard, you are merely re-creating your own wilderness."

Looking Around You

You may have an uncultivated yard, a woodland, or field, or know someone who has something similar for you to use. Make sure that whatever spot you choose, it is a place that hasn't been sprayed with weed-killers, pesticides, or fertilizers, and that it is not near any heavily trafficked areas that can contain pollution. Once your site has been chosen, you can take your identification book with you and begin to look around for plants you can harvest that may already be growing around you. Remember these tips: When eating wild foods, go slowly. Mix greens in with regular foods so your body will become easily adjusted. Again, be very careful with your identification and with how the plants should be used. Last, be conservative so that the plant colony can grow on and multiply.

Here is a list of the most commonly used plants that you might find nearby: poke (*Phytolacca americana*); plantain (*Plantago major* and *Plantago lancelote*); mullein (*Verbascum thapsus*); dock (*Rumex crispus*); common burdock (*Arctium minus* or *lappa*); milkweed (*Asclepias syriaca*); Indian turnip, also called jack-in-the-pulpit (*Arisaema triphyllum*); mayapple (*Padophyllum peltatum*); catnip (*Nepeta cataria*); chamomile (*Anthemis nobilis*); safflower (*Carthamus tinctoria*); ginseng (*Panax quinquefolium*); and wild ginger (*Asarum canadensis*)

The easiest way to begin is to collect wild spring greens to add to cooking. These are perhaps the easiest plants to identify. This has been a traditional activity of pioneers and peasants because these tender greens were the first fresh fare after a long winter, a welcome treat after long months of pickled and wrinkled dried vegetables from the root cellar. These herbs were important for health and well-being, and were deemed good tonics and cleansers. Common spring greens should be gathered at the first sign of new growth in the spring. Clean them by soaking and swishing in cold water. Mix the greens fresh in salads or boiled or steamed as you would kale or spinach.

Here are some common spring greens that can easily be found: dandelion leaves, flowers, buds, and roots; poke shoots and leaf tips; common plantain leaves; chickweed; wild onion bulb and greens (make sure it has onion smell); clover leaves and blossoms; violet leaves and flowers; field cress leaves and stems; lamb's quarter leaves; sheep's sorrel leaves and stems; purslane; wild mustard leaves; strawberry leaves; blackberry and raspberry leaves; catnip leaves; cattail shoots; daylily shoots; wild asparagus shoots; and fiddle heads shoots.

Harvesting by the Moon

The belief is that these wild plants we call weeds have greater healing qualities, especially when gathered according to certain Moon phases. This belief has been passed on to us since ancient times. The Moon was believed to affect every aspect of life on this planet, and plants were no exception. It is believed that the herbs are much more powerful when gathered during the Full Moon, though you don't have to harvest at night. If you want to dry your crops of wild-harvested herbs, it is best to pick them during the phase of the Moon when it is in a dry sign such as Aries, Gemini, Sagittarius, or Aquarius, since the plants will have less water content.

Pick your plants to seed, learn about their habits and appearance, and harvest your wild crops according to the Moon's proper phase, and you will be rewarded not only with powerful medicinal herbs, but useful herbs to brighten up recipes.

The Organic Pest Patrol

By Penny Kelly

There is nothing as satisfying as planting a garden, and nothing as aggravating as losing most of it to the rabbits, deer, worms, or insects that also find your garden exquisitely satisfying. Every gardener eventually learns to share some of that precious produce with the multitude of creatures that inhabit the garden, but what do you do when they are taking more than their share and leaving you the stems and stalks? Dousing the plants with conventional poisons quickly undoes the very reason you want to have a garden in the first place—to enjoy safe, healthy, delicious food. So how do you get from here to harvest without doing serious damage to yourself, the soil, the plants, and the environment?

The first thing to understand about pest control when deciding to have an organic garden is that the condition of your soil should be your number one concern. Why the soil? Because healthy, living soil will make it possible for your plants to extract all the minerals, sugars, and compounds they need, thus ensuring not only disease- and pest-resistance, but the ability to produce fruits and vegetables with superior nutrition in them.

Healthy, living soil is chock full of bacteria, fungi, various microorganisms, and humic compounds made of decomposing plant and animal life, as well as earthworms, beetles, centipedes, slugs, and a host of other living critters. Plants living in this kind of healthy soil will not only be more drought and mildew tolerant, they will emit an electromagnetic (E-M) field with a full spectrum of frequencies. These frequencies determine both the form of the plant and its functions, including the health and energy it utilizes to create its fruit and seed.

Plants living in poor or deficient soil will emit weak, partial, or off-color E-M fields. Insects flying or crawling around the garden then use their antennae to pick up E-M signals from plants that are weak, diseased, or deficient. Since insects are Mother Nature's trash collectors, they search for, and immediately go to work on, sickly plants, finishing them off in short order. Thus plants that are healthy and emit a full E-M spectrum are, for all intents and purposes, effectively protected from marauding insects simply by the fact of their own health.

In addition, healthy plants will produce an extraordinary amount of natural carbohydrates in their leaves. This sugary substance is so high in a healthy plant that a bug deciding to have lunch on its leaves will quickly get a stomach ache and be unable to keep feeding on the plant. After relatively little damage, it goes off to look for other, less sweet-laden leaves.

Thus, the first rule of organic pest control is actually to build the healthiest soil you can. Old leaves, kitchen wastes, animal manures (except for cats; kitty manure has too many parasites), manure tea, herbal teas, grass clippings, and anything that will break down into its component parts releasing those components back to your vegetables is useful for creating the silky black soil that plants will thrive on.

Types of Organic Pest Control

There are two common forms of organic pest control. One consists of physical or mechanical barriers, and the second consists of a group of organic insecticides you can apply. There is a third means of control via use of beneficial predator bugs—insects that prey on the bugs and worms that do damage in your garden, but this is an area of pest control that is just coming into its own and requires careful study of what kinds of pests you have, what their density is per acre or square foot, and what varieties of predators might best handle the problem. I have heard of good results with beneficial predators, but if you want to try this, I'd recommend finding an integrated pest management consultant to advise you.

Barrier Methods

Returning to the more common kinds of organic pest control, one form of physical defense is to literally pick bugs or worms off your produce, drop them on the ground and step on them. Obviously, if you have a one-acre garden with two hundred tomato plants and a variety of other vegetables, this may be too large to be able to hand-pick bugs or worms, but if you only have five or six tomato plants, you could easily watch them for hornworms, picking them off and squashing them (carefully—they squirt).

Cutworms are another matter. Nothing is more discouraging than planting a dozen broccoli and cabbage one afternoon, only to come out the next morning and discover that seven of them are lying shriveled on the ground, their stems neatly severed by a cutworm in the night. The best defense here is to get a dozen Styrofoam cups, cut the bottoms off, and slide the bottomless cup over the stem of each plant, then push the cup down into the ground until it's anchored in the soil, maybe a half inch or so. For some reason, cutworms aren't smart enough to climb up and over it to get to the stem. Either that, or they simply prefer to crawl along at their leisure, stop at the base of a cabbage, then reach up an inch or so and nibble right through the stem.

Rabbits, deer, and other furry four-leggeds are another problem. In my experience, the simplest and most effective pest control for them is chicken wire. A fifty-foot roll of chicken wire that's twenty-four inches wide costs around twenty dollars. Unroll the entire length and then fold it in half lengthwise. Lay this folded wire alongside your row of cabbages, broccoli, and tomatoes and cut off the amount you need, adding an extra foot or two at each end of the row. Now stand the chicken wire over your row, tent-fashion, anchoring the sides about every ten or twelve feet with stones, stakes, or whatever is handy. You now have a wire tunnel about one foot high protecting the entire row. To keep small animals out of the tunnel, at each end fold the "raw edges" of the wire toward one another, bending the cut-off wires and hooking them over one another to "seal" the ends.

You now have a triangular tent of chicken wire protecting your plants that can stay in place until the plants begin to poke leaves through it. If you want protection for a longer period, you can do the same thing with a four-foot wide roll, and you'll have a two-foot high tent that you can leave on longer. The only difference is that you might have to pound a couple of two-foot tall stakes in the ground amidst the cabbage plants to help support the tent.

Another excellent pest control is a floating row cover. After the plants are well established and the weather is quite warm, I remove my chicken wire tent and cover the row with a five-foot wide length of row cover, which costs around thirty or forty cents per linear foot. It keeps flying pests off, lets in light, rain, and air, and the only thing that bothers me is the reduced visibility as far as visually checking my plants is concerned. There is also a certain amount of pleasure in just looking at the garden that is lost, as well as the possibility that you will fail to look under the row cover and not respond to other problems like mildews or attacks from ground insects. Worse, you might not notice that your vegetables are ready for picking! Other than that, row covers do a wonderful job of protecting your plants.

Organic Insecticides

As the weather warms up, most insects become extremely active and chances are you may be overwhelmed by them. If you need an organic insecticide, in most cases a very light application or two, early on, is better than heavy doses later. Typically there are two or three generations of an insect over the growing season. The first one will emerge, eat, mature, and lay the eggs for the next generation. If you interrupt this cycle early enough, you will have less "insect pressure" to contend with.

Any insecticide, whether conventional or organic, is poisonous. The differences between conventional pesticides and the organic ones are numerous. Conventional poisons are synthetic, much stronger, and pose serious risks to the humans using them. They are usually meant to kill, seldom to deter, and they kill indiscriminately, including the living organisms in the soil and beneficial predator insects. Worst of all, they don't break down quickly or well. Their residues end up in the soil for months, sometimes years, as well as in the vegetables. From there the pesticides get into humans, where the damaging effects from the E-M fields of their molecules cause subtle derangements within the human energy system.

Organic insecticides are made from plants and trees found in nature. There are simple deterrents as well as poisonous substances, and although they can kill, the innate intelligence that is Mother Nature seems to know how to handle and bounce back better from organic insecticides than she does from synthetic ones. The greatest advantage in using organic or botanical pest controls is that they are often target-specific and they break down quickly, sometimes within two or three hours, the rays of the Sun turning them into harmless natural materials. Thus there are fewer long-term effects for the soil, the beneficial insects, and the humans.

The most common organic insecticides are made from pyrethrin, neem, rotenone, or *Bacillus thuringiensis*.

Pyrethrin

Pyrethrin is a combination of two oils and a soft resin extracted from a member of the chrysanthemum family, *Chrysanthemum cineraiifolium*. Technically, it is called a "botanical" control since it is plant-derived, and it's completely inactive only twenty-four hours after application. Although it is very powerful against many kinds of worms, beetles, aphids, moths, caterpillars, mites, leafhoppers, and thrips, it is relatively non-toxic to bees and ladybugs—if you don't mix and spray too heavy a dose! It also works on ordinary houseflies, fruit flies, fleas, ticks, lice, silverfish, and ants.

Pyrethrin is best used on adult populations of cabbage and tomato worms, rather than those in the larval stages. It works by paralyzing the gastrointestinal tract, and it works best when sprayed late in the day so the Sun's rays are going down. Sometimes you will find a pyrethrin-based insecticide to which piperonyl butoxide has been added. Be careful of this combination as it is not only much stronger, but the piperonyl butoxide may adversely affect the mammal liver, and that includes you!

The Safer Company makes several kinds of pyrethrin-based insecticides, many of which are available through seed catalogs and better garden centers. Or you can make your own by grinding up a half dozen chrysanthemum heads, soaking them in a gallon of water for several days, then pouring it through cheesecloth to filter out the flower debris. Add a teaspoon of dish soap to improve consistency, and you are ready to spray. If you keep it tightly covered in a cool, dark place, it will last several years.

Neem

Neem is another botanical insecticide extracted from the seeds of the neem tree, *Azadirachta indica,* of Africa, Asia, and Australia. It works both as a repellent and an insecticide, does not harm many beneficial insects, and works for two to seven days on average. All sorts of worms and caterpillars, beetles, aphids, whiteflies, weevils, leaf miners, leaflloppers, psyllids, and gypsy moths are controlled without building up any resistance to neem, and it works by interrupting the insect's growth cycle. When larvae ingest neem, they stop feeding and die within several days. It's best to spray neem either in the early morning or late in the afternoon when insects feed heavily.

Rotenone

Rotenone comes as either a dust or a wettable powder, and like pyrethrin, is a very powerful botanical. It is obtained from the roots of several kinds of tropical plants, as well as a native weed called Devil's Shoestring, *Tephrasis virginiana.* This plant was used by the American Indians to kill fish, which were then used as fertilizers in their gardens. It is safe for use on almost all vegetables, fruits, flowers, and trees, but kills many kinds of insects, including beneficial ones, as well as several kinds of external parasites that can bother or infest animals. It is especially toxic to fish; so if you use it in dust form or put a spray on too heavily, you might have to watch for the possibility of run-off into ponds or creeks. Although it comes in 1 percent, 3 percent, and 5 percent strengths, we have used the 3 percent dust form and found it is plenty powerful enough.

Rotenone offers a short period of protection, from three days to a week, and you should read labels when shopping for rotenone-based pest controls because it is sometimes combined with synthetic chemicals that are dangerous to a whole range of birds and mammals. California no longer considers rotenone to be an acceptable organic insecticide and has banned it on those farms seeking organic certification, but most other states see it as an acceptable botanical control *if used appropriately*.

Bacillus Thuringiensis

Bacillus thuringiensis, commonly called BT, is a bacterial pathogen used to control all sorts of worms and their larvae. Technically, it is a biological control and it quickly loses strength in the Sun. It can be used on all sorts of vegetables from artichokes and broccoli to cucumbers and cabbage, celery, lettuce, and melons, to potatoes, squash, apples, and strawberries. Its most common target is the worm or caterpillar that emerges from almost any kind of moth. BT works when insects or their larva eat the bacteria that has been sprayed on the leaf. Once inside the body, the bacteria multiply and the insect becomes sluggish, loses its appetite, and gets diarrhea, which leads it to dry up and die. Dipel, Safer's Soap, and Safer Dust are all made from *Bacillus thuringiensis*.

Old-Time Remedies

There are a few old-time organic recipes that have considerable pest control ability. One is a cayenne pepper, garlic, and dish soap mixture sprayed on plants. Mix one cup of water with a quarter cup of cayenne pepper and set aside. Then put another cup of water in the blender, add ten cloves of fresh garlic, and blend well. Let both mixtures sit for two days then filter each through cheesecloth. Add the pepper water to the garlic water, mix well, and store in a glass jar with a tight lid and clear label. When it is time to spray, add a half cup of the pepper-garlic water to a half gallon of tap water and you're ready to go to work. Use it as a serious pest deterrent on plants that have at least six to eight leaves, never on very young seedlings. If plants falter or show burn, add more water, up to an additional half gallon.

Another homemade potion that does far more than deter insects can be made by soaking a half cup of minced garlic in one cup of mineral oil for several days. In the meantime, get a bar of Fels Naptha or Palmolive hand soap, chip off about one-third cup, and put this in one quart of tap water to dissolve. When the garlic is done soaking in the mineral oil, strain out the garlic through cheesecloth and then put two tablespoons of this oil into the quart of water and dissolved soap. Store this garlic oil and soap mixture in a glass jar with a tight lid and clear label. To spray, mix a quarter cup of the garlic oil and soap mixture in one quart of water, shake to mix, and spray lightly. Gone will be all manner of moths and miscellaneous worms, potato, bean, asparagus, and Japanese beetles, grasshoppers, flies, June bugs, squash bugs, mosquitos, slugs, earwigs, and even cockroaches.

Winging It by Moonlight

By Carly Wall, C.A.

G rowing up, I lived on a farm at the top of a hill. The farm consisted of three levels; at the bottom were the woods and creek, the second level contained the fields and pond, and at the very top was the house. One of my fondest memories was the warm evenings when we kids would create our bat show!

Now, we didn't have VCRs back then, or even cable. The television was kind of small, and our parents mostly watched the evening news on it, so it really didn't hold our attention. That meant that we had to come up with our own entertainment. Sometimes we would put on plays, or make up games, or even take a moonlight swim, but on some nights the bat show was the biggest hit around. What is a bat show? Well, it came into being when we noticed one evening, just at dusk, that there were some crazy birds swooping around overhead. When we asked our parents what kind of birds these were, we were told they were bats and that they were swooping about to catch insects.

Putting our imaginations together, my brother, sisters, and I decided to make some fun of it. We spread out a quilt at the edge of the hill where a night light shone brightly, attracting loads of insects and bats. We gathered handfuls of pebbles and brought them back to the quilt to wait for twilight to descend. When it came, we would crane our necks up to watch for the swooping bats. When the mood struck us, we'd throw up a pebble and watch the bats swoop for it. The trick was to get the pebble high enough for the bat to go for it, yet positioned over the head of someone else, and low enough to scare the dickens out of that other person. Heads would be ducking pebbles would be flying, and bat wings would be flapping.

The Wings of Night

Back then, I didn't think much about bats, except that they were great fun to play with. They had an air of mystery. I knew all about the connection between bats and vampires, and the stories about how you had to be careful because bats loved to get tangled in your hair and fed on human blood to survive, or how bats had some supernatural power to shape-shift. I'd seen all the horror movies, after all. It was only much later that I learned that all that was merely myth, and that bats are very useful not only to us, but to our environment.

Today, researchers race to save the bat from extinction. Pollution and loss of habitat contribute to their struggle, but their usefulness has gone unrecognized to the general public, and the supernatural myths, as well as other fears that they carry disease or are dirty, contribute to the problem. Captive breeding programs have been established in the Philippines and the Convention on International Trade in Endangered Species bans traffic in fruit bats in the Pacific, where they are considered a main dish. Many individuals are helping by placing bat houses in back yards with the same fervor as bird houses.

They may look like a cross between a rat and a bird, but actually, bats are mammals, and on top of that, their closest cousins are the primates (which puts us in pretty close quarters with the bat in the whole scheme of things). In fact, they are the only known group of flying mammals, ranging in size from Thailand's tiny bumblebee bat to Indonesia's giant flying fox with a six-foot wing span. Most bats live in large colonies in caves or trees, but some make their home in spider webs or make their own tents out of leaves. The problem comes when they have nowhere to roost. Then they can become pests by finding homes in people's attics or nesting in barns. Creating places for them to roost will solve the problem, keeping them out of your domain, but still giving them room to breathe.

Why Bats Are Good to Have Around

Bats, of which there are nearly 1,000 different species (forty-four of which live in North America) feed on insects, fruit, nectar, and pollen. A few do feed on fish, frogs, rodents, or blood, but for the most part these are a small number, and the vampire bat in Latin America only drinks the blood of cattle and horses, not humans.

That means that gardeners can delight in the increased crops! The bats eat many varieties of hungry insects and can keep insect populations under control, saving precious plants. Researchers estimate that the Mexican free-tailed bats in Texas consume over 250 tons of insects every time they take to the night skies from spring to fall! Individual bats can catch hundreds of insects by the hour, and large colonies can eat tons of beetles and moths nightly that could otherwise cost farmers and foresters a fortune. For example, cucumber beetle larvae cost growers a billion dollars annually. Just one colony of 150 big brown bats can protect crops from 18 million of the beetle offspring. The bats that prefer flowers and fruit work in the same way as the bees in pollinating and spreading seeds. The long-nosed bats of North America pollinate more than sixty species of agave. Even if you don't garden, you should know that just one little brown bat will consume over 600 mosquitoes in an hour—enough to keep you mosquito-free for your backyard barbecues, or to just sit out and enjoy the moonlight. This is like the answer to our dreams—a bug-zapper that doesn't cost a cent, never needs to be tended to (just a bat house or two tucked away somewhere), and as a byproduct, our gardens will flourish without sprays or powders!

All About the Bat

Bats are creatures of the night. They spend the daytime grooming, resting, or sleeping. Night is when they search the skies for food, and mostly it is the early part of the night that they are most active, since that is when the insects are out and about. Around 70 percent of all bats happen to be insect-eaters, and these are the type normally found in the United States. Many people think of bats as being blind, but this is merely another myth. Many bats actually have good vision, but most don't depend upon their sight to guide them in their search for food. For that, they have a special talent. They use a remarkable ability similar to radar called echolocation. In this manner, they emit sounds that strike objects and these sounds come back as echoes. Their highly developed senses can then determine exact location, and how fast something is moving.

Since bats are very sensitive to pollution, if you have bats around, you can usually be assured that your environment is pretty clean. Bats can live up to thirty years and hibernate during the winter in cold climes, while in warmer areas they have the same basic patterns of daytime rest and nighttime feeding.

Some of the types of bats you are apt to see in North America are the pocketed free-tailed bats, which fly the Southwest deserts on narrow wingspans, the red bats, which mate in flight and are found throughout the area, the spotted bat, which cools itself from the desert heat with its giant ears, silver-haired bats who live in tree cavities and migrate between Canada and the southern United States, gray bats, who are fond of caves and are endangered, or the ghost-faced bats with eyes almost in their ears and strange mouth flaps. There's also the common brown bat.

Most of the flower-visiting or fruit-eating bats are in tropical areas. Bat-attracting flowers typically bloom at night, and have a white or cream color, along with a strong odor. These types of bats rely more on scent than sound. Tropical trees that are night-blooming are often pollinated by the bats, and usually have an unpleasant odor. The exception is the ylang-ylang tree (*Cananga odorata*), which grows in the Philippines. This very fragrant blossoming tree is much loved by humans, and the scent is used in expensive perfume, including the perfume Chanel No. 5.

In the past, bats have been feared for being carriers of rabies, but in fact, they are no more subject to this disease than other mammals. Statistics show that in the last thirty years, only ten people died of the disease from bats. Often the trouble comes when someone ventures to pick up a sick bat. If you see a bat lying on the ground, or out in the open, it is most likely sick and shouldn't be handled. There is no evidence that bats carry any other major disease, and they have been found to be very particular in their grooming habits. However, the old fears remain and many seek to destroy bats whenever they are seen. In some parts of the United States, entrances to caves have been dynamited, while others are disturbed from human visitors and vandals. The destruction of just one cave can spell doom and deprive millions of bats of winter shelter. Because we are just beginning to understand the bat, we can now see the loss we face as the bat population teeters on the brink of extinction. Efforts are being made to save them, though.

There's a heart-warming bat story from Texas. It seems that in Austin in the early 1980s the people were horrified to see that hundreds of thousands of Mexican freetail bats had found the ideal resting spot under their newly renovated Congress Avenue Bridge. Today, the city calls itself the "Bat Capital of America," boasting the largest urban bat colony in North America with over 1.5 million bats. Now, when Austinites want a little enjoyment, at dusk they take a blanket out to the bridge and join tourists as all scan the moonlit skies to see the bats emerge. Sounds a little like my childhood bat show, doesn't it?

In the meantime, there's an organization founded by Merlin Tuttle called Bat Conservation International that has been organized to protect bats worldwide. They publish plans for bat houses that can house bats for the summer and attract them to your yard.

If you would like to populate your area with bats, you can purchase bat houses now at most places that sell birdhouses. You can also build your own with the help of the publication put out by BCI, *Bat House Builder's Handbook,* for a small fee. Contact: Bat Conservation International, P.O. Box 162603, Austin, Texas 78716, or call them at (512) 327-9721.

Tools for the Garden

By Penny Kelly

I could rightfully be disqualified from any attempt to advise others on the basic tools needed to garden because I long ago decided that John Deere tractors and Troy-Bilt tillers were absolute necessities. Still, if the world rolled over tomorrow and I had to go back to basics, there are a few items I would not want to be without. The first is a good, heavy duty shovel for turning over the soil, digging holes to plant potatoes, or prying out large stones. The second is a four-prong, long-handled hand cultivator for weeding, loosening the soil, or mixing in compost. The third is a sturdy wheelbarrow for carrying tools, seedlings, produce, compost, and a thousand other things out to the garden and back. The fourth is a short-hand trowel with inch markings for use in transplanting. The fifth is a swan-necked hoe for hilling potatoes or quickly digging narrow, shallow trenches. The sixth is a rake for removing debris and shaping up vegetable beds. The seventh is a solid, tempered-steel garden fork for digging potatoes, onions, carrots, and other root crops in a manner that allows the soil to fall away as the veggie is lifted from its bed. The eighth is a good pair of gloves that can get wet, don't shrink, don't turn to cardboard, and are infinitely flexible. These are my basic eight.

You can go quite a distance with these eight tools, but if you fall in love with the soil, seeds, plants, good food, and the freedom of working in the Sun, you'll quickly want other things that add to the success of your garden and subtract from the sweat. Unfortunately, they also subtract from the pocketbook, so consult your budget before you go shopping.

Tool Shopping

Once you get to the store, think twice before buying. Nowhere is it more obvious than in the world of tools that you get what you pay for. Therefore, think before buying the cheapest version of what you're looking for. My own rule of thumb is: When all else is considered, stick to the basics and buy the best.

A good shovel can cost forty dollars and the blade remains firm, sharp and even. A shovel whose edge bends and folds when it hits a rock not only doesn't work well, it can become impossible to get it to slide through the soil at all, or the handle breaks when put under any kind of pressure, sometimes wrenching your back.

Twenty-nine-dollar garden carts with cheap bicycle-type wheels that bog down in loose, sandy soil, or that bend and torque out of shape when carrying a load of stones, are useless. A hand trowel that was a bargain at four dollars but bends in half when you're transplanting in cold, heavy ground is a real nuisance, and a four-prong cultivator for six dollars whose "teeth" bend and twist in every direction can uproot your plants.

Investing in a really good set of basic tools will probably cost you somewhere between two hundred fifty and three hundred dollars. However, once you have the basic eight, you're going to realize there is another important group of "must-have" items that are suddenly demanded by your accessory inventory, or have landed on your luxury list.

The Luxury List

Important accessories include at least one good three-gallon pump-up sprayer for fertilizers, manure teas, herbal sprays, or pest control, and a garden hose with a spray wand for watering during dry spells. Be sure you have enough hose to reach from the outside faucet to the garden, and if it's a big garden, you'll probably want a reliable sprinkler, which is a considerable timesaver compared to hand watering.

For a cheap and easy way of marking where your rows begin and end, you can use a large stone or two at each end, or perhaps twigs. Some people cut heavy garden stakes out of one by two lumber that can be reused for a few years.

During planting, a couple of movable wooden stakes are needed with a length of three-ply twine (the same length as the row) strung between them, as well as a hammer for pounding the stakes into the ground. One stake is pounded in at the beginning of the row, the other at the end, and the twine provides a reasonably straight line to guide your planting.

A pea and pole bean fence—or at least something to climb on—is necessary if you plant either of these veggies; and if you're going to have any kind of fence, you're going to need fence posts. Dealing with fence posts used to bring on an instant headache for me until one day my husband took a three-foot length of heavy pipe that was about three and a half inches in diameter, and welded a small square plate of quarter-inch steel over one end. Voila! I had a tool for easily pounding fence posts into the ground! Then I went to Quality Farm and Fleet and bought a small bundle of five-foot steel fence posts. Back home in the garden I pushed the bottom of one of those steel posts into the ground where I wanted it to stand. Then I slipped the three-foot length of pipe (with its welded cap) over the upper end of the steel post, and let the heavy pipe drop noisily, which pushed the post into the ground several inches. By lifting and dropping the heavy pipe a half dozen times, the fence post was pounded into the ground and stood there straight and firm, all of which took only a few minutes of time and a minimum of effort.

Other essential accessories include a watering can, which is useful during transplanting or when you need to mix up and deliver a special brew to sickly plants. Floating row covers are great for both frost and insect protection; and a pair of easy-on-easy-off waterproof boots, especially Wellington-style pull-on, are wonderful when you've watered one spot too long and need to walk out to the sprinkler to move it!

Some bushel baskets for harvesting, a couple of two and a half-gallon plastic pails, one five-gallon pail, a fifty-foot carpenter's ruler, a straw hat, and a plentiful supply of sunscreen complete the list of necessary accessories. Now you're ready to garden—as soon as you get your seeds, that is.

Big Ticket Items

Once you start, if gardening does become the love affair you've been waiting for, it won't be long before you'll want some of the big-ticket luxuries that save untold hours and much back-breaking labor. I'm referring here to gas-powered rototillers. Ten years ago my husband came home with what looked like an ancient pile of rolling metal and bolts. It was a used TroyBilt tiller for which he'd paid five hundred dollars. I didn't know if I was more upset at the price or the condition of the machine.

"But it's all rebuilt, and it uses plain gas, no oil mixture," he explained as he turned it over to me. I could barely pull the rope to get it started, but once I got used to this little mechanical luxury, I couldn't even conceive of gardening without it. Ancient-looking or not, the darn thing is still running a decade later! I use it to prepare the soil for planting, to loosen the topsoil after days of rain, which helps keep the deeper moisture from wicking upward, to keep the weeds down, to mix in compost, to turn spent crops under, and whatever else might seem useful. If this one ever dies, I might have to face a fifteen-hundred dollar price tag for a new one, but I have to say, it's really worth it.

The other luxury that I went without for a long time was an Earthway-type seed planter. For years I planted on my hands and knees, slowly and carefully shaking carrot seeds from the seed envelope, or pushing bean or pea seeds into the ground at carefully estimated intervals. Then one day a neighbor offered to loan me his seed planter. A hundred-foot row of corn that would normally take thirty to thirty-five minutes to trench, put the seeds in, cover with soil, and tamp firmly, was all done in less than three minutes. Same with the carrots, the peas, and the beans. I was astounded. The price was around eighty-nine dollars, and in my mind it is another of those things that is more than worth it.

Storing the Tools

Keep in mind that as you collect tools, and the tools get bigger, you'll probably need a garden shed to hold them all. We finally broke down and built one for five hundred dollars, but when a greenhouse became one of my essentials, the garden tools moved to the greenhouse, itself a four thousand dollar affair.

The Want List

There are three items still on my "want list" and I'm working hard to get them before I get to old age. One is an automatic watering system, which would cost about five thousand dollars. The second is a system of composting bins that I could use to make special recipes of compost and would be relatively cheap in terms of dollars, but would cost several weekends of my husband's time.

The last is one of those lovely English garden benches that you put in a romantic spot in your flower garden so you have an excuse to sit down and enjoy the roses. Years ago I would never have considered such an extravagance at all. But lately, as my relationship with the soil and the earth has grown and deepened, I find that more and more it seems important that my garden be a place to relax and rest in, as well as work in. For two years now I have planted my vegetable garden leaving a spot for mythical, mystical contemplation that I keep hoping will be mysteriously filled by a graceful bench that just appears. When it does, I'm promising myself I'll sit on it at least once a week to enjoy the work of art in progress that is my garden year after year.

A Bee Garden

By Caroline Moss

Gardening, however solitary the gardener, is not a lone pursuit. One is tied inextricably to the wider world, and to the flora and fauna that, regardless of our most formal plantings, are at work in the garden unbidden, sometimes unwelcome, but, in their place, vital. Some, such as bind weed and nettle, may frustrate us when cropping up uninvited in our prize flowers, but all have their function. Nettles attract useful predatory insects and provide a valuable food source in spring.

Herbs are especially useful in attracting some of the more welcome visitors to the garden, and the joy of a small mixed herb garden is greatly enhanced in high summer by the constant hum of bees visiting each small pot of nectar. These bees may come from your own or a neighbor's hive, or they may be wild bees. These industrious creatures will travel a number of miles in search of food, and wherever you are gardening, be it in rural acres or with a window box in a city high rise, rest assured that with the right plants the bees will come. Some plants attract by color (such as bee balm, *Monarda didyma*) or scent (lavender), and others even have a tiny path drawn out for the bees (foxglove). It is a pleasant and useful diversion to plan out and plant a garden with the specific purpose of attracting bees and other insect life.

Apart from the sheer joy of watching and listening to them, insects help the gardener by fulfilling their role as pollinator and by acting as predators against less welcome aphids, caterpillars, and the like. This is vital in the balance of an organic garden when natural methods of pest control must be harnessed, and along with the bees you will find other useful friends such as the lacewing, wasp, and hoverfly.

On a larger scale, some of the most delectable honey is produced by the bees feeding on a single herb diet. For a real treat seek out the almost gelatinous heather honey, largely from Scotland. Domestic bee keepers may leave luck to chance on what flowers their bees feed from, but commercial bee keepers will place their hives with careful consideration. In Greece, one can find wild thyme honey where bees feed on strongly fragrant hillsides. In the

Czech Republic an almost black, strong forest honey is said to have highly beneficial medicinal qualities. In England, beekeepers are cursing the wholesale planting of vivid yellow oilseed rape, a relatively modern crop in any quantity. It produces a strong, hard-setting honey. Many herbs and flowers are suitable for a bee garden and the herb gardener cannot help but attract bees with these plants. For the best effect follow some simple guidelines to maximize the bees and butterflies visiting your plot. Set things in groups and masses rather than single plants dotted about. Bees prefer single flowers to fancy double varieties as they tend to be more accessible. Do not, of course, use poisonous insecticides on or near an herb garden. Protect the garden from winds where possible.

The following is a selection of herbs that are especially useful in attracting bees. However, plants that sport bee-attracting flowers are too numerous to mention, and this list is certainly not exhaustive. I have included heights to give some idea of whether a plant is suitable for your plot, but check a reputable herb guide for growing details, particularly with regard to your planting zone.

Bergamot (*Monarda didyma*), three feet tall. It is an indigenous American plant with pink, red, or purple blossoms. It is known as Oswego tea since the Oswego Indians showed early settlers how to make a beverage from the plant. The other common name is bee balm, although some say it is more likely to attract hummingbirds if you have these in your area.

Borage (*Borago officinalis*), three feet tall. Borage shows heavenly blue flowers for half the year. The flowers are pink before they are fully mature, and it is attractive to see the pink and blue on the same plant. Marketed in capsule form as star flower, many women have found it beneficial for certain symptoms of menopause and for premenstrual tension.

Bugle (*Ajuga reptans*), six inches tall. Bugle is an excellent ground cover that is useful as it will grow in some shade. The plant spreads vigorously, so take care when positioning it.

Catnip (*Nepeta cataria*), twelve inches. Catnip appears as a mass of soft green and mauve. It is wonderful in large clumps on the edge of walls and steps, where it tumbles over.

Chamomile (*Chaemaemelum nobile*), nine inches tall. For every person who adores the scent of chamomile there are others who do not. Try the non-flowering lawn chamomile planted in a large shallow pot to form a sweet-scented mass. The tea is a mild sedative, and is lovely made with the fresh herb rather than the dried, which tends to be musty.

Comfrey (*Symphytum olastrum*), three feet tall. The gardener's friend, this plant attracts bees for pollinating. The leaves are a valuable source of nutrients in the compost heap, or simply dig them into the ground in autumn if you don't fancy composting. Leaves can also be soaked in water for a liquid feed, but beware, this does have a strong smell! It is normally only suitable for the back of a larger garden. A comfrey ointment is available that has helped arthritis and rheumatism sufferers. Note that comfrey is no longer recommended for internal use.

Elecampane (*Inula helenium*), five feet tall. Elecampane has bright yellow flowers that are highly prized by insects. Only suitable for larger gardens, this plant has medicinal qualities to ease chest complaints. In the past, children's candy was made from the crystallised root and colored pink.

Forget-me-not (*Myosotis scorpoides*), nine inches tall. Often found growing wild, this little plant spreads like mad, but who is not made happier by chancing upon the innocent tiny blue and pink flowers on a sunny day.

Foxglove (*Digitalis purpurea*), four feet tall. These are especially attractive to the large furry bumble bee who is often completely hidden in the long, finger-like flowers. Growing to around four feet tall, this plant is normally only suitable for the larger garden, but smaller varieties, more akin to the original wild species, are available. Although poisonous (take care in planting if children are about), the foxglove has been used in mainstream as well as herbal medicine, including the heart drug Digitalis.

Flowering currant (*Ribes odoratum*), six feet tall. Be sure to get a specimen with good deep pink flowers, because some are too pale. This bush flowers early so it is especially welcomed by insects. Prune it well each autumn to maintain a good shape and strong flowering.

Heather (*Erica*), one foot tall. Only suitable for cooler locations, this plant is useful as it does not die off in winter, and many colors of flower and foliage are available. Although the usual height is one foot, do seek out the more unusual and lovely tree heather, which grows to six feet or more. It provides valuable cool weather food for bees and other insects.

Horsemint (*Monarda punctata*), two and a half feet. Often more attractive to bees than the other Monarda, the bergamot listed above. You might want to plant this in a large container as it can be very invasive, but the flowers are a treat.

Hyssop (*Hyssopus officinalis*), eighteen inches tall. The upright stems of hyssop bear many flower petals and provide lovely design material for a free-form mass or edging. You will find pink, white, and my favorite, the blue/mauve varieties. Alive with bees, this little plant is of limited daily use, but can be added in moderation to fruit salads and the like.

Joe Pye weed (*Eupatorium purpureum*), five feet tall. I love this plant for its stately crimson flower heads at the back of border, for its late flowering season when many other plants are over, and for the legend of the old Indian, Joe Pye, who cured typhus with this plant and is now ever remembered in its name. This is a plant for the bees and for garden design with limited medical applications today.

Lavender (*Lavandula angustifolia*), two feet tall. I am sure that lavender needs no introduction, and this fragrant friend is mandatory in any herb garden, especially where attracting bees is a priority. Although perennial, lavenders get out of hand after a few years, so take regular cuttings to save buying new plants periodically. For variety, try French lavender (*L. stoechas*) with flower heads themselves reminiscent of bees or wasps.

Marjoram (*Origanum onites*), eighteen inches tall. Marjoram is on a par with thyme for the number of bees it attracts. I have listed the pot marjoram, but a look in nurseries and catalogs will reveal many varieties, including dwarfs, more suitable for window boxes and pots. For culinary use, try to get the stronger Greek oregano (*O. vulgare*).

Rosemary (*Rosmarinus officinalis*), three feet tall. Rosemary is a must for the cook, medical herbalist, and florist. This Mediterranean herb will be surrounded by insects on warm summer afternoons. Try using the woody stems as barbecue skewers, or cut a stem to brush oil on to grilled meats and vegetables.

Sage (*Salvia officinalis*) two and a half feet tall. Another insect-attracting Mediterranean emigrant, sage always puts me in mind of hot, dusty days and that most evocative Zane Gray title *Riders of the Purple Sage*. A staple kitchen herb, sage also has medicinal qualities. A strong sage tea is given in many Greek hospitals as a regular tonic for patients, and a gargle with such an infusion is helpful for sore throats.

Thymes (*Thymus*), one foot tall. The varieties of thyme are too many to list, but all give a mass of tiny flowers that will be appreciated by the bees. Get several plants of one type (or plant seeds) to give a good block of color. Fancy varieties are often not displayed with the herbs at nurseries and garden centers, but are to be found in with alpine plants. Creeping thymes are useful to plant at the edge of pots to tumble over or in cracks in pavement where the scent is released when walked on—automatic aromatherapy!

Moon Gardens

By Lynne Sturtevant

People have been planting moonlight gardens and night gardens for centuries. The Moon garden is a combination of the two. The traditional moonlight garden is composed entirely of white or pale flowers and plants with silver or gray foliage. A night garden contains flowers that only bloom at night as well as plants that release their fragrance at dusk or after dark. Plant a Moon garden and create a stunning, beautifully scented nighttime paradise right in your own back yard!

Everyone loves bright, colorful flower beds full of butterflies and bees. In bright sunlight, the Moon garden is pale, subtle, and restrained. It can't compete with red roses, golden marigolds, hot pink impatiens, or orange poppies. But as the daylight fades, so does our color perception. After the Sun sets, the Moon garden shines.

Planning and Layout

Beautiful gardens aren't accidents. They are the result of thoughtful planning. A complete and detailed gardening book is an indispensable asset. Choose a guide that explains landscaping and garden layout concepts in detail and includes lists or charts of individual plants with descriptions of their requirements and growing habits. Other sources of information are local nurseries, garden centers, and county agricultural extension services.

The most critical factors you must consider relate to your climate. What are the average minimum and maximum temperatures, the length of the growing season, and normal rainfall patterns? What type of soil do you have? What type of drainage will your garden plot have? Will it be damp most of the time, or will you need drought-resistant plants? Even plants that bloom only at night must have light to grow. How much sunlight will your garden receive?

It's possible to convert a shady area into a delightful Moon garden. Simply design the garden with shade-loving plants. The features that cause an area to be shady during the day (trees, walls, buildings, etc.) will also shield the garden from moonlight. You may need artificial lighting to fully enjoy a shady Moon garden.

It's easy to find plants that will thrive in the Moon garden. The difficult part is choosing from the dazzling array of possibilities. As you select plants, consider the amount of space they need. You must know how large the plant will be by the end of the season. Many tiny spring seedlings are behemoths by August. Look for interesting variations in size, shape, and texture. Remember the overall effect you're aiming for and pay heed to scale and balance.

The most satisfying gardens begin blooming in early spring and continue until the hard frosts of autumn. This effect is achieved by mixing spring bulbs, summer annuals, and late season perennials. Your Moon garden will provide constant enchantment from softly illuminated snow drops in February to mounds of white chrysanthemums under a brilliant Full Moon in October.

A Moon garden can be as large or as small as you like. Location is much more important than size. Distance vision is reduced at night. You must be close to the garden to appreciate the subtle details, watch the nocturnal flowers open, and enjoy the fragrance. Plant the garden next to your deck or porch. Consider surrounding a patio or terrace. If you have space, add a garden bench or a small table and chairs. Create a winding path through the flowers and shrubs. A Moon garden next to a pool or a pond is particularly alluring. If you live in an apartment, use potted plants and grow a Moon garden on your balcony.

Be realistic about the amount of time and effort you'll devote to your garden. Plants vary greatly in terms of their needs for attention and maintenance. If you are a new gardener or have limited free time, choose geraniums rather than orchids. It's not necessary to spend a fortune on plants. Many of the most common and inexpensive varieties are perfect for the Moon garden. Of course, as anyone who has tackled a landscaping or a home improvement project knows, if you have the financial means, the sky truly is the limit.

After you've selected a location and determined the general types of plants you'll need, you're ready to begin creating a garden for the night.

White and Pale Flowering Plants

The Moon's colors—silver, gray, and white—are the foundation of the Moon garden. Moonlight highlights and enhances the appearance of white flowers and light-colored plants. Subtle color differences that are washed out by strong sunlight are accentuated by the soft light of the Moon. White flowers are not all the same color. Their hues range from pure, bright whites to light pinks and pale yellows. All light, pale colors are visible in moonlight, but the strong, true whites will predominate. This doesn't mean you can't include colored flowers in the Moon garden. In fact, some of the night-fragrant and night-blooming plants described below are not white. If you decide to use colored flowers in your garden, remember the bright colors will fade and disappear at dusk. Shapes, textures, and delicate tints are the stars in the Moon garden.

Gray Plants

Gray foliage plants shimmer and glow in moonlight. Use them to break up large groups of light-colored flowers and to add interesting texture and variation to the garden. They establish a lovely, soft background for the pale flowers and transform empty spaces and bare spots into silvery patches of understated elegance.

Night-Fragrant Plants

Night-fragrant plants add an incredibly sensual element to the garden. The varieties listed below release their perfumes at dusk or after dark. Some have no scent at all during the day. The scent of others, although present during the day, intensifies at night.

Night-Blooming Plants

Nocturnal flowers are strange, fascinating, and exotic. Unfortunately, exotic plants are often difficult to cultivate. Many night-blooming varieties are fragile and expensive. They require constant attention and are highly susceptible to diseases. Frankly, many night-blooming plants are more trouble than they're worth, but there are two notable exceptions. Moonflowers and night-blooming daylilies are surprisingly easy to grow. Even novice gardeners achieve outstanding results. If conditions permit, include both in your Moon garden.

The moonflower is an annual vine. It produces enormous, fragrant, white flowers all summer long. The blossoms open at dusk and resemble large morning glories. The individual flowers are approximately six inches in diameter. The leaves are heart-shaped.

The moonflower must be planted in full Sun or it will not bloom. It grows quickly, easily reaching a length of fifteen to twenty feet within a few months. The moonflower is a climbing vine and needs some type of support such as a trellis, fence, or post. This spectacular plant could be the focal point of your entire Moon garden.

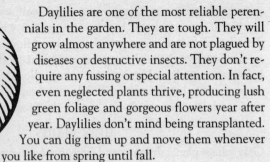

Daylilies are one of the most reliable perennials in the garden. They are tough. They will grow almost anywhere and are not plagued by diseases or destructive insects. They don't require any fussing or special attention. In fact, even neglected plants thrive, producing lush green foliage and gorgeous flowers year after year. Daylilies don't mind being transplanted. You can dig them up and move them whenever you like from spring until fall.

Night-blooming daylilies possess the same wonderful characteristics that make their day-blooming counterparts so popular. There are dozens of night-blooming varieties with colors ranging from soft whites to deep, dark reds. The challenge is finding them. Mail order plant catalogs and garden centers usually don't offer night blooming daylilies. However, there are several books about daylilies that include the names and addresses of specialized mail order nurseries. Visit the library if you don't want to buy a book exclusively about daylilies. This may sound like a lot of trouble, but you'll be well rewarded for your efforts. Daylilies are easy to grow, hard to kill, and multiply so quickly that within a few years, all of your friends and neighbors will have night blooming daylilies too!

Lighting and Decorative Accents

Although it's not absolutely necessary, consider adding artificial lighting to your Moon garden. This is especially important if your garden is in a particularly dark part of the yard, or if the night sky is frequently overcast in your area. Even if the weather is clear most of time, there are nights when the Moon is dark. Outdoor lighting enables you to enjoy the garden every night.

Choose a lighting system that mimics moonlight. It should illuminate the garden with dim, muted light. High-voltage floodlights are too bright and intense for the Moon garden. Low-level path lighting is very effective. Place a small spotlight on the ground and focus it up through a tree's branches. Spotlights can also be used to highlight or draw attention to a particular part of the garden. An old-fashioned carriage lamp on a pole can serve double duty as a support for a moonflower or a clematis vine. Outdoor lighting also creates dramatic and interesting shadows.

Reasonably priced, low-voltage light kits are available in home improvement centers and hardware stores. If you don't have a 120-volt outdoor electrical outlet, you'll need to have one installed. Everything else is included in the kit. If you have never shopped for garden lights, you'll be pleasantly surprised at the wide selection. There are styles and prices to suit every taste and budget.

The Moon garden is the perfect place for outdoor entertaining. Illuminate the area with Japanese lanterns or string miniature white Christmas lights through the bushes and trees. Light garden torches or candles if you don't want to use electricity. The atmosphere of a Moon garden filled with tiny white votive candles is unbelievably romantic.

Decorative accent pieces can be lovely in the garden, if you exercise restraint. Possibilities for the Moon garden include large pieces of quartz, unusual rocks, reproductions of broken classical columns, and statues of gargoyles or ancient Moon goddesses. Add a hint of elegance with a silver Victorian gazing ball on a white pedestal or a pale gray bird bath. Trellises, arbors, and garden benches are decorative as well as functional. Make sure whatever you add is an appropriate size, and remember that in good design, less is more.

The Moon's effect on plants, animals, and people is well known, if not well understood. One thing is certain. The Moon is beautiful. Enjoy your Moon garden. Savor the night smells and listen to the night sounds. Relax, unwind, and let the shimmering moonlight wash away the cares of the day. Surrender to the Moon's mysterious enchantment and celebrate its luminous beauty in the garden of nighttime delights.

Bibliography

Better Homes and Gardens Complete Guide to Gardening. Des Moines, Iowa: Meredith Corporation, 1979.

Coughlin, Roberta M. *The Gardener's Companion*. New York: Harper-Collins Publishers, 1991.

Damrosch, Barbara. *Theme Gardens*. New York: Workman Publishing Company, Inc., 1982.

Hill, Lewis and Nancy. *Daylilies*. Pownal, VT: Storey Communications, Inc., 1991.

Loewer, Peter. *The Evening Garden*. New York: Macmillan Publishing Company, 1993.

Loewer, Peter. *Gardens by Design*. Emmaus, PA: Rodale Press, 1986.

Wirth, Thomas. *The Victory Garden Landscape Guide*. Boston: Little, Brown and Company, 1984.

The Alluring Moonflower

By Carly Wall, C.A.

Often during the summer, I visit various herb gardens, farms, and shops. One place that grows acres of many different and interesting herbs and plants is not too far from my home. It has an enchanting mix of herbal whimsy and is run by a woman who absolutely loves the plants—you can just tell. I discovered her place some years back, but it always sticks in my mind that as I pulled into her drive, the first thing I spied was a gorgeous vine of large, deep-green leaves and giant white blooms. It was tucked at the edge of her porch in a semi-shaded nook. I immediately wanted one of those plants for my own. Surely, I thought, it had to be some rare specimen from some far-off land. Surely it was very hard to grow.

"Oh, that. That's my moonflower," the lady said dismissively. She grabbed a few seeds from a dried flower pod and handed them to me. I cupped them in my hand. "Now come around back to the deck and we'll drink some tea and I'll tell you all about it."

I remember that cool, soft evening with great fondness. That lady introduced me to two loves of my life; one was her raspberry-leaf tea concoction. It was a sweet, yet tangy taste I've never quite been able to match. The other love she introduced me to was a flower that matches no other. Named after the Moon, it has an appropriate title, for the silvery white blooms bob in the night like beacons, and they only open as the Moon's rays begin to shine.

What the Moonflower Offers

There are many things that make this plant a must to add to your flower garden. The first is that it is so unusual, so exotic, yet very easy to obtain and grow. The next and most important is that it is a plant that loves the moonlight, and so can enchant any and all on inky summer nights with its luminescent flowers and exotic, yet entrancing, scent.

It is called *Ipomeoea maxima*, but also *Ipomeosa alba*, *I. Grandiflora*, *I. noctiflora*, *I. bonanox*, and *Calonyction aculeatum*. It is a tropical perennial from South and Central America. We treat it as an annual in northern climes. It blooms the first year from seed for immediate gratification!

Actually, it is a night-blooming cousin to the morning glory. At the first sign of the Sun's rays, as the morning glories are just waking up, the moonflowers are closing their sleepy heads after an all-night orgy of fragrance. Moonflowers open at dusk. You can actually watch them as they slowly pop open. Many a time I have enjoyed seeing the tight buds slowly swirl as the petals unfurl. It takes up to twenty minutes, but it is a sight to see. Fully open, they exude a rich scent some say is reminiscent of magnolias, but that I think is a lemony, musky-sweet scent, and quite intense. That's why it is best to have a plant or two tucked near the house—at an entrance, near the deck, or around a bedroom window—so you can fully enjoy the aromatic treat.

The white flowers outshine all others in an evening garden. They just seem to glow or brighten up at night. Perhaps it is because they are so prolific. The heart-shaped dark green leaves are thick and luxurious. While the plant is covered from midsummer until killing frost with many flowers, each opens only one night, with the plant creating new blossoms for insects and moths to visit each evening. Somehow, the plant knows that evening has come. Perhaps it measures in some way the length of daylight or light intensity, since on cloudy days the blooms may be seen, too.

Growing Your Own Moonflowers

With all that to its merit, you may think that there's a hidden catch somewhere. Honestly, there isn't. The moonflower may grow up to forty feet in tropical areas, but for the colder climates, it will flourish ten feet or more. Make sure that you have something sturdy for this plant to climb on. They can be heavy with all those buds and flowers. It's actually a good flower to cover unsightly areas, and will easily be trained to grow on tall tomato stakes, string, wire, or across arbors.

Don't be fooled by the slow start it takes. As hot weather takes over, the vines will suddenly take off, running up any support in its reach in a thick leafy cover. It can take six to eight weeks from sowing for the vine to begin flowering. In areas with no frost, as the temperatures cool down, the vine will die back. If you are worrying about the heat, don't. These plants love hot weather.

The seeds are encased in a hard, shell-like armor, so you can quicken the germination by soaking them in warm water overnight. You can also use a knife to nick the seedpods. The moonflower grows in most soils, so plant it where you want it (in full Sun or part shade in the south) when the soil temperatures reach 70 degrees Farenheit, and pretty much stay in that temperature range. If insects or moths neglect to pollinate your plant, you can remedy the situation by using cotton swabs to dust the flower's stigma with a bit of pollen.

Night Visitors

Luna moths and other insects find these night flowers by the silver glow (since most of them are white or light in color), or by their intense smell. If you plant night-blooming Moon gardens, you can expect to see all kinds of unusual pollinators.

Moth pollinators go for flowers that are white and heavily perfumed so that they may detect the plant from very far away. During the day, the moths rest hidden under leaves or in nooks and crannies of trees or other hiding places where predators cannot find them. Here are a few of the moths you may find attracted to your new night-blooming planting.

Pink-spotted hawkmoth (*Agrius cingulatus*), with a four-inch wingspan. The caterpillars feed on jimsonweed, pawpaws, sweet potatoes, tomatoes, and many morning glories.

Luna moth (*Actias luna*), a very beautiful, pale green moth that has spots on its four-inch wings that resemble eyes, and a long tail. The caterpillar feeds on willows, cherries, and beeches.

Io Moth (*Automeris io*), another beautiful, yet common species. They are a little smaller, only about three inches, with white-centered, black and blue spots on the hindwings. The caterpillars eat anything within reach and do carry an irritating poison in their spines, so watch out!

Isabella tiger moth (*Pyrrharctia isabella*) is a small moth of about an inch and colored dark orange. The caterpillar may be very familiar to you as they are called the wooly bears, with fuzzy red/brown and black bands. In fall they scurry around looking for a winter hiding spot. They love to eat asters, clover, corn, sunflowers, and maples.

You can see now that the fall of dusk doesn't have to end your enjoyment of your garden.

A Love Garden

By Verna Gates

Love grows in your garden. From love charms to ancient aphrodisiacs, your green friends are standing by to help you attract, keep, and even grow love. With a tiny bit of magic, these garden allies can draw the perfect mate, seal a commitment for faithfulness, and nourish desire. Special flowers can speak the language of love, delivering messages of devotion. Whether you are single, married, or looking for the perfect gift for the newly married, this guide can walk you through the plant world's version of lover's lane.

Preparing for Love

Anise: Start with anise, an ancient cure for those who feel a lack of romance in their lives. In ancient times, it was added to flavor wedding cakes to start the young couple off in the appropriate mood.

Lovage: Whenever there is a potential to meet someone—you are going to a new place or attending a social event—bathe in lovage water. Called the love herb, this plant will inspire romance.

Maiden Hair Fern: At one time, a maiden's hair was considered one of her greatest beauties. Plump up your own womanly beauty and grace by placing maiden hair fern in water. Then either wear it or keep it under your pillow.

Attracting Love

Asters: Asters grown in your garden will attract love. As you place each seed or seedling into the ground, consciously make a wish for love.

Bachelor Buttons: Bachelor buttons naturally attract bachelors. Dare to wear this emblem of masculine resistance and create an irresistible love charm. Pinned to your breast, this flower will attract even the most contented bachelor. It will bloom out or wither, depending on the quality of the match.

Henbane: If a man wants to meet his bride, he needs to plant henbane and let it ripen. Hopefully, he lives in a secluded area, or with late-rising neighbors, because for the magic to work, henbane must be harvested naked, standing on one foot. If this doesn't prove devotion, little will.

Cardinal Flower: Dig up the root of this flaming red flower and touch it to every part of your body. With this love charm, you will attract a mate within seven days. This plant works especially well for old maids.

Lady's Mantle: Lady's mantle grants the lady a potent love charm. Use this herb to cast your love spells and carry it in sachets to draw love.

Rose: Rose is the eternal symbol of love, but only red roses. Yellow roses indicate jealousy, and pink roses mean friendship. Whenever you make a love potion, you should wash your hands in rose water. If you want to go straight to the source, rose petals can magically attract a lover if you remove all of your clothing, including jewelry, and walk through the garden.

Meadowsweet: Place the bride of the meadow, as meadowsweet is often called, freshly picked, on the altar to attract love. The delicate scent of meadowsweet will cheer any heart to love.

Indian Paint Brush: Carried in a sachet, this emblem of the Great Spirit's love for humanity draws love with a powerful tug.

Bay Laurel: Burning the bay leaves not only offers visions of love, but also helps you to attract love. Once you find someone, offer them a bay leaf and break it in half. You keep one half and give them the other. As long as you both have your portion, you'll stay together.

Lemon: To attract a lover, carve out a heart from the lemon peel and carry this emblem in your pocket or purse. Then, once you become intimate, make a tea out of lemon leaves, but be prepared for the results of this "lust-tea." After marriage vows are sealed, serve lemon pie to ensure fidelity.

Leeks: Forget romantic gourmet dinners—serve leeks! When two people share a leek, they fall in love.

Breakups and Reunions

Amaranth: If your romance doesn't work out, carry dried amaranth flowers to mend a broken heart.

Parsley: If your love goes astray and you want to cut your own feelings of love in order to heal the hurt, cut parsley. As you slice the leaves, you cut away your romantic passions.

Lily: If there is someone undesirable pursuing you with love charms, you can break their spell with the lily. Just carry or wear a fresh lily blossom anywhere on the body and you will be protected.

Daisy: To get a lover to return to you, sleep with a daisy root under your pillow. If you give up on your old love and want to attract a new one, wear the daisy in your hair. You can always test his sincerity with "He loves me, he loves me not...."

Forget-Me-Not: Forget-me-not is the eternal symbol of undying love. Many forget-me-not stories relate the sentiments of devoted lovers who experience brief or permanent separations.

Mallow: If your lover leaves you and you want him or her back, use mallow as an attractor. Place a bunch of freshly gathered mallow flowers in a vase. Strategically place the vase outside the door or in the window of your bedroom, wherever your lover could possibly enter. This will bring thoughts of you to your lover, setting the stage for possible return.

Aphrodisiacs

Orchid: The origin of the orchid comes from a fertility god, Orchis, who in a moment of passion tried to rape a bride. Killed by the wedding guests, his dying body was transformed into this flower. The root of the word *orchid* means testicles, which one look at our native orchid, the lady's slipper, will confirm. Orchids are very sexy plants—that's why generations of prom escorts have brought them to blushing maidens.

Orange Blossoms were worn for centuries by hopeful brides to ensure wedded bliss. If you want to attract a good love-making experience, distill water from the flowers for a bath. It will heighten your sensual attractions.

Lavender: One nice hot bath in lavender buds and you see why it's an aphrodisiac. This one is so powerful, it was the chosen fragrance for old world prostitutes. A second benefit is a magical protection against domestic abuse. Rub the fragrant buds on any item associated with love—your body, clothes, pillows, and love letters.

Dill: Dill seeds added to bath water make the bather irresistible. Place dill pickles on the plate to guarantee a night of lustful enchantments. Later, pregnant women won't be able to resist this tangy treat.

Yarrow: Also called "old man's pepper," it was given to older men who married young brides, just in case they needed a pick-me-up, so to speak.

Cattail: A woman low on desire can carry this botanical phallic symbol until she regains her enjoyment of sex.

Thistle: If a man wants to improve his performance, he needs to carry a thistle. The pricks of the thistle will guide him to better lovemaking.

To Keep Love

Cinnamon: The way to a man's heart truly is through his stomach. In a showdown test of perfumes, pumpkin pie won hands down over every perfume brand tested. So, instead of dabbing on expensive scents, dab a little cinnamon behind your ears. Add this savory ingredient to any love potion to attract a mate. *Editor's note: do not put cinnamon essential oil directly on your skin. It burns!*

Marjoram: Marjoram was the green ally of the goddess of love herself, Venus. Mix marjoram into your recipes to bake in stronger feelings of love. If you want to see the face of your true love, take marigold flowers, marjoram, and a pinch of wormwood. Dry and pound into a powder. Mix your powder into honey and vinegar. Rub this mixture on your forehead, neck, and shoulders while you repeat three times, "St. Luke, St. Luke, be kind to me, in dreams let me my true love see."

Caraway: Chew caraway seeds to remain faithful. Toss these seeds instead of bird seed to aid a bride and groom as they navigate the perils of lifelong commitment. There's an added benefit—caraway helps you to keep your possessions, further discouraging divorce.

Myrtle: Plant myrtle on each side of your home to keep peace and love within your walls. Pluck the myrtle leaves to add to sachets. This sachet when carried will keep love vibrant between old lovers. Clasp a circle of leaves on your head to enjoy lovemaking without risking conception.

Basil: Just the scent of basil arouses sympathy between two people. It is an excellent herb to cook with if troubles are brewing in a relationship. For fidelity, sprinkle your entire body with basil powder while your lover sleeps.

Apple: Cut an apple in half and share it with someone you are interested in. If he or she takes a bite, your love will be returned and happiness assured.

Pansy: The pansy, in the language of flowers, says "Think of me, my love." Anytime you see pansies, think about your lover; this act will make love grow. To enrich your attractiveness, carry pansies. For maximum results, pick pansies from a pansy bed planted in the shape of a heart.

Grow in love daily with the beautiful plants put on this earth to delight us. If you plant your garden of life with a full heart, you cannot help but draw the love we all seek on this earthly plane.

Understanding Your Personal Moon Sign

by Gloria Star

It's impossible to deny the continual course of the Moon. Her evolving reflections of light illuminate the night sky; her cycles are reflected in the pull of the ocean's tides.

Since the time of the Sumerians there have been written records linking the Moon's cycles with changes in behavior and alterations in nature. Musings about the Moon and her influences are scattered over time and throughout the literature of human history. But are you aware that you have your personal Moon? It is one of the many features of your astrological chart, and it has a significant meaning in the way you express yourself and your needs.

When calculating your horoscope, an astrologer charts the positions of the Moon, Sun and planets at the exact time of your birth. The detailed picture of your horoscope symbolizes the complex levels of energy which are part of your whole being. You probably know about your Sun sign, which describes the ways you express your drive to be recognized—something easy to see and even easier to show to others. Your Moon tells a more intimate story, because it describes your subconscious nature, and is much more internalized than the energy of the Sun. You *feel* your Moon.

To find your personal Moon Sign, refer to the detailed directions on page 62 of this book. This is a close approximation of your Moon's sign, but if you want to know the exact degree and placement of your Moon you'll need to obtain an astrological chart based on the date, time, and place of your birth. You can visit a competent astrologer or order a chart from Llewellyn Chart Services by calling 1-800-THE MOON.

Even though you may not be familiar with the astrological concepts associated with your Moon, you are well acquainted with the Moon's energy. Whenever you tune into your basic feelings about anything, you're connecting through the Moon. You express the qualities of the Moon through your habits and attitudes. Think of your Moon as a highly impressionable internal recording device, constantly collecting, storing, and assimilating everything you experience and feel. Some of your recorded messages operate automatically, but you can add more information at any time, and you can also make alterations. However, because you hold these impressions at a very deep level, it's not always easy to change or erase an old internal message!

Your Moon's astrological sign provides insights into your inner strengths, but it is also the key to your deepest vulnerabilities. Here you create your feeling of "home." As you learn more about yourself and your needs through experience, you may find that by concentrating on the nature of your Moon sign you can establish an environment that provides comfortable security and safety. Once you're in the flow of the energy of your Moon, you carry your sense of home into every life situation.

Whenever you express nurturing and support, you're sharing your lunar energy, and your Moon's sign indicates the manner in which you express these sentiments. Whether you're male or female, your Moon shows how you "mother" others. Psychologically, your Moon depicts the archetypal feminine quality and represents your relationship with your mother, with women, and with the feminine part of your psyche.

When you probe more deeply into the mystery of your Moon, you uncover your soul. Your Moon represents your most dominant emotional tendencies and needs; it is the part of yourself that has flown to the pinnacle of ecstasy and that also remembers the true emptiness of despair. Your capacity for contentment increases when you strive to fulfill the needs illustrated by your Moon's sign.

This part of the *Moon Sign Book* is designed to help you understand the planetary cycles throughout 1999 that will affect you at an emotional level. Transits to your Moon stimulate change, and you may discover that some of the cycles help you reshape your life, while others stimulate a desire to delve more deeply into the mystery of yourself. Astrology can show you the cycles, but you are the one who determines your responses—and the outcome. By opening to your own needs and responding to the planetary energies in a way that allows you to fulfill your needs, you can experience a renewed sense of self-confirmation and a deepened feeling of personal security.

Aries Moon

Your greatest need centers on your embrace of personal freedom and the expression of your individuality. Driven by the power of your Aries Moon, your life gains momentum when you face an important challenge. You can be an exceptional leader, a champion for the underdog, and an unrelenting warrior. Sometimes your courage may surprise you, but it's not really new to you: as a pioneer for change you're the one who opens the doors, carrying the torch of new possibilities.

Sometimes your impatience gets in your way, especially in relationships. When you find someone who shares your love of excitement and who can nurture a mutually independent and supportive bond, you may feel eternally in love. Because you prefer excitement and passion, any situation that becomes boring or too predictable can quickly lose its luster (including work, by the way). Especially in relationships, if your needs are not being met or if the relationship has ceased to grow, you'll either deal with problems directly or pack your bags and move on.

That part of you always "teasing" may leave the impression that you flirt with disaster (and perhaps you do), but you're simply giving in to your delight at igniting a few fires. This drive keeps you young, but if you carry it too far—leaving the impression that you're willing to follow through when you only wanted to have a little fun—you can hurt others, and may even shortchange yourself in the process. Emotional maturity may sound like a boring solution, but you can be passionate about life and love and still consider the consequences without selling out your need for fiery excitement. You may feel a bit unsettled about choosing the right place to live. You may be most at home if you're in a place that gives you freedom to express yourself. You can be great in a crisis, and you might find gratification by working in crisis-oriented situations like military service, medicine, or counseling. You're the one who's always ready to act, and when others are paralyzed by fear or insecurity, it is your courage that can ignite their own.

The Year at a Glance for Aries Moon

Although there's a little holdover from Saturn finally leaving Aries early this year, you're in for a treat, because Jupiter spends most of its cycle this year in Aries! This means you're trading a feeling of heavier commitment for an experience of increased confidence and optimism.

Whether you're reprioritizing your family commitments, settling into a better home environment, or simply clearing debris from your life, you'll be completing obligations the first quarter of the year. Balance your personal freedom and commitments, and you'll feel much more secure about exploring the new horizons that emerge in the last three quarters of 1999.

Jupiter's powerful transit over your Moon this year brings potential for exceptional growth. This cycle happens only once in twelve years, and you may find that some of the hopes that began to blossom in 1987 now take on more significant proportions. The uplifting qualities of Jupiter stimulate your vision and may also prompt you to reach out to help others. It's important to pay attention to reasonable limitations, however, because you may experience a kind of backlash and overdo it. The difference between exceptional growth and self-indulgence will be determined by the way you handle the stimulus to expand.

The transits of the planets Uranus, Neptune, and Pluto have their long-term influences this year, too. If your Moon is from 0 to 5 degrees Aries, you may feel more drawn to artistic and spiritual pursuits from Neptune's stimulus. But if your Moon is from 6 to 10 degrees Aries, you're ready to assert your need to take charge of changing your life under Pluto's influence. You're feeling the powerful impact of Uranus if your Moon is from 11 to 20 degrees Aries, stimulating your desire to break free and experience an awakening of your potential. If your Moon is from 21 to 29 degrees Aries, you're experiencing the greatest impact from Jupiter's transit—a cycle of courage, hope and opportunity.

Every Aries Moon individual can benefit from the stimulation of renewed aspirations. By listening to the call of your deepest needs, you may feel that you're finally in a place to accept more of the good things life offers. Showing your appreciation to others works like a magical elixir, drawing even more from the cornucopia of abundance.

Affirmation for the Year

*Under Grace and in perfect ways, the Universe provides
for my every need. I am profoundly grateful.*

January

Quiet reflection may sound like a great idea, and it could help ease internal pressures. Releasing and letting go may be more effectively accomplished by taking an active part, like tearing into a project that needs extra attention, or giving in to requirements so you can finally get something off your back! If you're over-obligated, you'll definitely see the origin of the problems near the Full Moon on January 2, but you may not feel that you're out of the woods until after January 17. Creative solutions emerge mid-month, and after January 21 you'll feel much more at ease with your decisions. As you answer to the demands you're feeling from others, keeping your personal boundaries intact works its own magic during the Moon's eclipse on January 31.

February

Although you have every reason to look forward, old obligations can still leave you feeling a bit restrained. Before you give in to the urge to dynamite those barriers standing in your way, consider whether or not they may serve a purpose, or if you might need them for some reason. Careful and deliberate attention to your needs can be quite illuminating, particularly if you've been resentful or hanging onto guilt. Even though you may have thought that the idea of unconditional love is a myth, the true manner in which it operates emerges during the Sun's eclipse on February 16. Give way to the urging of your heart's song and soften your approach after February 21, when you may also feel more romantically inclined.

March

Seeing through the eyes of your soul can be rather clarifying. The sense of connecting to the innermost part of yourself while feeling the energy of everything around you stimulates feelings of passionate creativity. It's like you're alive again—but you're taking it a little easier, because you know the possibilities. Somewhere in time this has been called "wisdom," and the way you utilize it determines whether or not you really have a grasp on its strength. Blending playfulness with your responsibilities requires a little finesse, especially because the playful side is likely to win. Enjoy your natural tendencies but try to remain at least a little realistic about their impact on others. Lending a helping hand feels good now, and your sense of humor lifts your own spirit while bringing smiles to others, too.

April

Your good friends are a treasure, and spending even a little time nurturing your friendships pays handsome dividends this month. But you're also ready to explore new options, and you may even meet new friends whose ideas and insights echo your own needs and desires. This is your period of personal renewal, stimulated by the Aries New Moon on April 15. It is now that you feel you can make a fresh start— at work, in love and with yourself. Establishing new priorities helps you feel more in control of your own destiny, and you may gain insights into your deeper needs by starting a personal journal. Taking a short trip can fulfill your pressing desire to be on the go, and you might also require more variety in your daily routine.

May

Communicating your real feelings sets the stage from May 1 to 8, when you prefer to get to the point instead of playing cat-and-mouse games. Honesty can be brutal, though, and if you are to avoid negative confrontations it's important to keep the flow of energy moving in emotionally charged situations. You're more sensitive to criticism after May 10, but may still feel willing to hang in for the duration if you're seeing progress in personal relationships. You may feel quite confident after May 13, when you're willing to put forth the efforts to get what you want. However, your patience runs thin for the next two months, when the slower pace of advancements may not measure up to your expectations. Take another look at solutions after May 23, when your creative mind is likely to be on fire with new ideas.

June

Forging ahead, you're seeing the culmination of many hopes this month. Celebrate your success with those you love, and use this time to tap into renewed clarity about your future hopes. Partnerships gain momentum, whether emotionally based or business-oriented. You may feel like everything's moving at warp speed, and you need to remain reasonably flexible if you're to flow with some of the surprising developments. The brakes come on after June 18, when obligations can be more difficult than you anticipated, or when someone else you've relied on drops the ball. These apparent setbacks are indicators of the weak points requiring reinforcement. Because you're usually a quick learner, you'll figure out new options while most people are still catching their breath.

July

Before you go out on a limb, make sure you have some idea of how far you could fall. It's entirely too easy to take risks without considering the consequences. Risks certainly do seem to be a large factor, and may be necessary if you're to grow—so don't think you have to lock yourself into "park" while the rest of the world goes zooming along. Listen to your inner voice while weighing the facts, because even the best looking plans may not fit into your life. Even though you realize that there are no guarantees, your sense of what might work seems to be operating okay. Matters of the heart can be confused by mixed signals. If you sense deception, try to determine the truth, because denial can be more heartbreaking than reality. Delicate situations can crumble during the Moon's eclipse on July 28.

August

Despite the surfacing of unreliable information as the month begins, you're capable of maintaining a little objectivity if you work at it. Brewing problems reach their climax and new options arise during the New Moon (and Sun's eclipse) on August 11, allowing you to take a different approach to accomplishing personal fulfillment. While you may still be reconsidering your options in love relationships, you're also thinking about long-term goals that may have little to do with a partner. Individual accomplishment is always important, and giving yourself a chance to shine is crucial now if you're to feel satisfied with your choices. Group projects or shared creative experiences can be quite fulfilling, where your role may be more director than follower, even if you're not aware that others are following your lead.

September

Getting what you want is apt to take longer than you like. The slowdown can be to your benefit if you need to sort through details, and after September 14 you're likely to see signs of progress that leave you smiling. Inflexible attitudes—your own or another's—can be influenced through principles of integrity, but you'll balk if faced with abuse of power and may lose trust in others of questionable honor. Your emotional sensibilities increase as the month moves along, allowing you to stay in touch with your deeper feelings on important matters. The Aries Full Moon on September 25 can stimulate passion and playfulness. But if you're worried, frustrated or concerned about something, the brewing crisis finally reaches its peak. Maybe you're finally ready to pursue the best plan of action!

October

Your excitement carries the emotional momentum from October 1 to 7. Despite a few misunderstandings, you may feel confident about your course of action. If you're facing a challenge during the last half of the month, you're likely to have the best perspective of the situation just after the New Moon on October 9. Your appetite for adventure is fairly strong, but your ability to judge your limitations may be thwarted by your desire to impress someone else. Circumstances filled with misleading starts and stops can leave you feeling rather agitated after October 23, but if you can maintain a fairly resilient attitude you'll get through without too much frustration. Your confidence gets a boost just after the Full Moon on October 24.

November

With Jupiter retrograding back into Aries it will be easier for you to locate your sense of optimism again. But there are a few problems centered on boundaries. Whether you're having trouble keeping your personal boundaries or dealing with someone else who seems too impressionable or weak-willed, you need to continually question the reasons for your actions as you attempt to project their potential effects. You can't afford unnecessary damage, and you will not enjoy putting yourself in harm's way. It's too easy to get in over your head emotionally as the Full Moon nears (November 23), although you might enjoy the rush that accompanies opening your heart. Give yourself time to settle before you do anything rash, but take full advantage of the period of awareness!

December

You're much more easily satisfied now as you feel the power of your convictions gaining intensity. Knowing what you want, you're unlikely to stop until you're certain of success. Releasing your desires during the New Moon on December 7, you're more confident and you can spark a wave of inspiration within others who form a strong support for your needs. Although you don't really like to ask for help, you may find it forthcoming anyway. By taking advantage of the love and care others have to offer, you may also discover a new basis for freedom. Any "strings" that are attached to these supports are fairly visible during the Full Moon on December 22, when you can choose whether or not you're willing to participate. Some obligations have their rewards!

Taurus Moon

Your innate sense of stability, endurance, and your connection to Mother Earth stems from the strength of your Taurus Moon. You know the sweetness of waiting for the fruits of life to ripen to their fullest, and you have an uncanny knack for calming even the most impatient souls. The people and situations that make you feel at home and safe are precious to you, and your heart is filled when you nurture beauty and serenity.

Your characteristic stubbornness is an outgrowth of your sense of commitment—because when you've made a promise to yourself, an idea, a person, or a place, you're in for the duration. Change is not easy for you because you invest so much of yourself in building solid foundations that don't move readily. But you do nourish growth, and you can easily accept changes that promote the ultimate progress. Fearfulness arises when you feel you've lost control or if you sense that your security is being compromised. It is during these times that you must distinguish between stubbornly resisting necessary change and holding your ground through the tough storms of life.

Loving others is the priceless elixir of life, and when you give your heart to the power of love you feel absolutely alive. This love also emanates through your creative artistry and connection to the environment. But you can be possessive and you may have extreme difficulty if a relationship ends or when someone you love grows beyond needing your support. (It's that empty nest syndrome that can be the toughest!) Sometimes letting others make their own mistakes is the most profoundly loving thing you can do. It's all about patience and natural evolutionary change.

The Year at a Glance for Taurus Moon

Even though unexpected changes emerge during 1999, your footing is fairly secure, allowing you to make necessary alterations without compromising your deepest needs. However, it's crucial that you know what you want from your life or you may feel that you're treading on uncertain ground. Rarely has defining your priorities been so interesting or so challenging, but by taking time to explore the inner dimensions of your choices, you may discover things about yourself that add exceptional courage and conviction.

Because Saturn is transiting over your Moon during the next two years, you're experiencing a solid sense of grounding and emotional focus. This cycle happens only once every twenty-eight to thirty years, and the directions you choose now will have long-lasting results. While endings are associated with this cycle, so are solid beginnings. Although some of your commitments may rise from uncertain circumstances, if you're coupling your intuitive sensibilities with your practicality you can make the best of the most unusual occurrences. If you simply cannot bring situations into focus due to changes beyond your control, then this may be a year of transition and experimentation—but you can hold yourself together even if you don't feel quite at home with everything that's going on. Flexibility is not your strong suit, so use your sense of inner calm and maintain your serenity when you deal with the unfamiliar. If your Moon falls between 0 and 20 degrees of Taurus you're experiencing the most intense changes this year; resistance to change now can be self-destructive. If your Moon is from 21 to 29 degrees Taurus, you're clearing the way for the creation of strong foundations as you enter the new millennium. Look for areas that require restoration and repair, and enjoy the work of adding your special touch.

There is a silver lining in what may sound like gloom and doom. (If that's your conclusion, reread the preceding paragraphs and watch your fears.) First, you're highly realistic now, and that can be exceptionally valuable when laying foundations beneath your dreams. Second, you're getting rid of the things you no longer need. Even though that "getting rid of" part sounds a little like losing something, that's not really the case. Think of this as the time of trimming the fat, eliminating attachments that are in your way, and releasing burdens you no longer need to carry. Now, that feels better! But finally, the energy of Jupiter does spend the summer transiting in Taurus, adding confidence and optimism and opening the way for expanding your base of operations a bit. This is a preview of next year's opportunities. Make notes, then clean out those closets and drawers so you have room for the new stuff you're attracting as the century comes to a close.

Affirmation for the Year

I invite a new sense of freedom into my life and bring balance by taking responsibility for my thoughts, words, and deeds.

January

Expanding your outreach and influence feels good, although you may run into a few surprises that require you to regroup before you can move forward. Because the year commences with a Full Moon on January 2, many of the plans and hopes that formed your focus last year are likely to reach their climax as this year begins. It's time to consider your needs and to determine where you want to go from here. Talk over your thoughts and concerns with someone you trust, and set out your foundations during the New Moon on January 17. You may be thinking very long-range, which is fine. But give yourself a few short-range goals, too, so you have something to celebrate along the way. Try to remain flexible in your attitudes after January 21, when changes beyond your control can leave you feeling unsettled.

February

Unreliable actions or attitudes from others can leave you feeling pretty frustrated, and even though you might wish that you could just walk away from something, your sense of commitment wins out. You may be dealing with endings, though, because this is a time of breaking free and releasing your attachments. The New Moon (and the Sun's eclipse) on February 16 initiates a period of vision and a resurgence of creativity, but also marks an excellent period of romantic desire. Blending your need for success in the world with your need for personal satisfaction in your close relationships may be more like a juggling act for a while, especially if you're at odds with someone. Take a careful look at the way you handle aggressive or confrontational acts, because it's easy to overreact and lose power. Try not to show your hand before you state your bid!

March

You may feel like you're in some sort of holding pattern, especially where your needs are concerned. It's like waiting for dinner at a crowded restaurant. Your appetite and hunger can drive you crazy, and your patience is at a low ebb. You may also be tempted to act in an uncharacteristically rash manner if others are pushing your emotional buttons. Perhaps you do need to break out of a rut, and simply resisting change could work against you. Your salvation comes from surrendering to your sense of artistry and indulging your need for something truly beautiful. Whether it's a walk in the woods, spending time in your studio or attending a concert, you need to feel connected to the process of creation. A new relationship is tempting but may require time before you know where it's heading.

April

Second-guessing your feelings only gets you into hot water. Make a realistic and honest assessment of what you need and what you feel. Trouble is, your feet may not be on the ground if you're involved with someone or something new, and that's the core of the problem, because you don't like to drift! Indulge in a few romantic moments to get closer to your sweetheart, but avoid sending anything that could be called a mixed signal, because it will only add to your confusion. If you're happy with your situation, celebrate! If you're dissatisfied, try to get to the core of the issues and release things that are not working. The Full Moon on April 30 amplifies everything, which should help with that "clarity" problem.

May

After a bumpy start, this month offers great promise. It's your turn to take the lead or to set the standards, which feels much better than the series of surprises you've been facing. You may feel that you have a fresh start during the Taurus New Moon on May 15, and this is the perfect time to launch something that's been in the works or to initiate an important change. Because there are fewer confrontations you can also take a deep breath and enjoy the fruits of life instead of continually pressing against deadlines and challenges. You may still be getting rid of a few things, but now it's likely to seem more like it's your choice to eliminate what you no longer need or to let go of what you've outgrown. Drastic changes are less likely than minor adjustments.

June

There are times when your tastes simply do not harmonize with another's, and you may run into a difference of opinion or divergent values. You might be willing to give in on a few minor issues early in the month, but if there's something really important and someone expects that you'll change your mind about your likes and dislikes, you should probably tell him or her now that you're not likely to budge. Holding your ground is a little different from becoming intransigent, though. So do try to listen to reason, and take a careful look at your motivations before you dig any trenches. Your ability to put things into a practical perspective goes a long way toward resolving differences, and after June 20 there's progress and profitability. Do something inspiring during the Full Moon on June 28. You need the break.

July

Even though you usually like a calm pace, you're up for something more active and invigorating to help revitalize you on every level. This is a great time to use physical activity as a means of bringing your mind, body, and emotions into balance. Travel for pleasure can be enjoyable if you keep it simple, but this is not a good period to try to stick with a tight schedule if you're trying to have fun. Artistic pursuits can also be a positive challenge, and you might enjoy getting involved in projects around the house like redecorating, landscaping or gardening. Renovations may not go very smoothly after July 12, and some may be "forced"—like repairs you've been putting off for another day. If you have time to wait, this is a great period to plan, clean up and clear the way for progress.

August

Sudden changes or disagreements with others can feel pretty destabilizing. In many respects, you may be the voice of reason while others seem to be reacting to pressure, but that could be a facade just to give the illusion that you're in control—when you really feel like running for the hills! Strangely enough, your practical sensibilities are actually quite valuable now. The problem can reside in trying to maintain the status quo when there's no reason to try. Before you invest your energy into playing out the role of "Rock of Gibraltar," determine what you need. This is a good time to work creatively with change that will aid progress. Resistance can be emotionally draining unless it's truly necessary for maintaining your personal security and emotional stability. And you may wonder if that's an illusion, too!

September

Getting back into the swing of what feels like a regular schedule brings its own stability into your life this month. You still need to make room for adjustments, especially if you're moving or altering your environment in some way. Your common sense seems to be operating at top capacity—something others grow to rely upon. Move forward with your plans during and after the New Moon on September 9 when you feel more certain of yourself and more secure with your ideas. Support from others helps to absorb some of the stress through September 24, but you may have to ask for help instead of just assuming that someone can tell what you need. Share your plans and dreams with your best friend or partner and determine the more productive course of action.

October

Maintaining a balance between the demands that seem to come from every direction can be a bit tricky unless you have a good handle on your priorities. Even though your responsibilities may seem to be growing, you're also capable of taking on more and after October 8 may feel more confident about delegating a few things that you don't need to do by yourself. If you're trying to keep everyone else happy by carrying the larger load you may be hurting yourself in the long run. Relationships require extra care near the time of the Taurus Full Moon on October 24. If you're unhappy or feel that your needs are being ignored, you're quite likely to show your discontent, unless you're playing the game of denial and codependency. If you're the one who needs to give a little more, this is a good time to start!

November

Satisfaction with your life choices centers on laying a steady foundation this month. You need to see where things are going, and you are willing to do whatever is necessary to stimulate growth and productivity. Even though there can be a few false starts after November 9, your faith in yourself and in the processes you've set in motion can carry you through. As long as you're seeing a little progress, you'll feel okay, but you may get nervous if a situation seems to be going backward. Retracing your steps and delving into unfinished emotional issues can lead to important advancements. But getting stuck in the past or refusing to consider other options can create a real setback. Try to avoid getting caught in another person's unrealistic expectations.

December

You may have a change of heart, and this can alter your plans significantly. Instead of feeling like you have to explain everything to everyone, center on justifying your needs and actions to yourself first. You could also be dealing with unreliable actions on the part of others that make it difficult for you to proceed with your plans. Once again, it seems that your need to be flexible is called into action, and you may even be getting used to unexpected changes. Emotionally it's difficult to remain centered when so many things around you are different. But when you step back and look at your life, you may realize that you are quite different, too. Funny how it happens: you look in the mirror one day and see facets of yourself that seem to have developed overnight. Sometimes it just takes a little time to feel at home with your "new" self!

Gemini Moon

Variety is not only the spice of life for you—it's a main ingredient! The influence of your Gemini Moon drives your hunger to know about things, and your desire to explore the myriad possibilities keeps you forever young. Change is another necessary ingredient for your contentment, and trying new things helps you keep an open mind while feeding your need to know. Sharing your ideas with others is important, and you may be fascinated by others whose lifestyles contrast your own. However, you're not likely to listen carefully to anyone whose ideas are out of date or boring. Your tendency to be easily distracted can lead you to have too many irons in the fire, leaving you with a feeling of frustration if you can't keep up with everything. You prefer to be lighthearted!

Juggling your priorities is much easier when things make sense, but because emotions are frequently illogical, you can be a bit uncomfortable in highly emotional circumstances. However, your objectivity is usually welcome, particularly during trying moments, when you can keep your wits about you quite nicely. And your intuitive ability can be your salvation. Close relationships work for you when you have ample independence and share similar interests—you do, after all, need something to talk about! Your secret desire may center on a need to be revered for your intelligence and wisdom, but it may take some time before you feel fully appreciated. Although you're capable of taking your sense of home with you as you travel the byways of life, you may not feel settled until you embrace the true essence of personal freedom that is an outpouring of your unfettered expression of your mind linked harmoniously to higher principles.

The Year at a Glance for Gemini Moon

There are plenty of reasons to celebrate during 1999, and even though you continue to feel the effects of transformational changes in your life, you may have more confidence in your ability to fulfill your needs. Jupiter's influence to your Moon brings a heightened sense of vision and hope, and may also stimulate a desire to learn that can be translated into improving your skills at work or confidently continuing your education. You may also feel inclined to travel or write. Adjusting your focus can be your primary test, but as long as you stay in touch with your deepest needs you'll be just fine.

Over the next several years you're likely to experience radical changes in your personal priorities. This year, you're creating a foundation based on the principles of universal law: choices centered on cause and effect (karma!) are primary. If your Moon is in early degrees (0 to 10) of Gemini, you're experiencing a powerful upheaval from your past. Things that have been buried in your psyche seem to emerge for your review and release; this is a marvelous time to incorporate your creativity as not only a means of self-expression, but as a means of release of emotional energy. If your Moon is in middle degrees (11 to 20) of Gemini, you're feeling extremely restless, but may not be able to give in to every impulse. You're learning the importance of maintaining your responsibilities as you build bridges toward your future. If your Moon is from 21 to 29 degrees of Gemini, you're experiencing a powerful sense of optimism, confidence and enthusiasm that can be the basis for your success in career and personal relationships.

All Gemini Moon individuals can be more awake, enlivened and satisfied with life choices—but only if those choices fulfill honest needs. This can be a powerful time of self-awareness, and many of the changes you incorporate into your life can alter your long-range direction. Your creative ideas can be part of the leading edge and your ability to trust your intuitive insights, a core element in your effectiveness. Bringing your spirituality into focus is much easier now. The realization that this means transcending the temptations that are harmful helps you choose positive escapes—among them your uplifting wit, strong objectivity and unique manner of keeping things in their proper perspective.

Affirmation for the Year

*I celebrate the new, release that which I no longer need and feel
the true essence of freedom!*

January

Your inventive ideas and novel approach to resolving problems can leave a good impression, and also feel good to you! If you've been hoping for the right time to become more involved with others who share your creative interests, it has arrived; you're also more trusting of your own instincts about people and can solidify important relationships. Changes in your personal environment—from moving to redecorating—can be made more easily, although you may need to watch your budget to avoid overspending. Confining situations are rather uncomfortable now, and if you find that you're distancing from others it could be that this is your response to feeling too restrained. Explore your needs and true feelings about your life path during the Moon's eclipse on January 31.

February

Your affections can change, particularly if you uncover deception or dishonesty. You may also be more realistic than you've been for a while, and are less willing to compromise where your needs are concerned. Even though you may wish you were immune to emotional pain, you're more easily wounded now because your vulnerabilities seem to be exposed. Give yourself ample time to determine what you want from intimate relationships, because rushing into anything can leave you a bit too breathless. The Sun's eclipse on February 16 stimulates a deeper awareness of your most important needs. Listen to your intuitive voice, and allow your objective sensibilities to guide you if you feel uncertain. You may just be in unfamiliar territory!

March

Clarity emerges, although you may feel a bit impatient with everyone else! It's probably a good idea to take advantage of this period of revision and to make amends where necessary. Even though your knee-jerk reaction might be to rush away from a situation, taking time to determine the best course of action may offer alternatives that could lead to more healthy options. Unrealistic situations emerge later in the month (you may think you're just being tempted—probably a good guess!), when you may have fun with your fantasies, but little luck realizing them in real life. Although these are good stimulants for artistic pursuits, there can be obstacles in your path that must be addressed before you'll experience the success you desire. One of those barriers can be poor communication. Are you really listening?

April

If you feel that your life is like a house of cards on an uncertain platform it could be because of the changes in the wind. You're quite capable of finding good solutions to problems at work and at home, even though they may be only temporary. That's okay—you have to get across the bridge! Your emotional sensibilities lend themselves to more harmonious interaction with others after April 13, and you're ready to pursue matters of the heart with greater enthusiasm and confidence. Finding time for entertainment fills an important gap and may lead to a significant relationship. Personal responsibilities may seem to interfere with your romantic or pleasurable activities from April 22 through the Full Moon on April 30. Necessity rules the day during this period.

May

Your needs for independence outweigh some of the obligatory situations you're facing—and giving in to the fact that you're just not happy when someone else is telling you how to live your life helps you put things in perspective. Talking about your needs and concerns with a trusted friend opens the way for better understanding and mutual support from May 1 to 8. But the prevalence of stubborn attitudes from others can be hard to take, prompting you to find a way out of tumultuous circumstances while others fight among themselves. Expectations can run rampant after May 20, so watch a tendency to leave the wrong impression or to fall victim to mixed messages. Making your point is much easier, but you must be clear if you are to be understood during the Full Moon on May 30.

June

Sometimes the Universe is kind—providing confirmation and support just when you need it most. This can be one of those times if you're paying attention to your security concerns and remaining open to solutions that allow you to move ahead. The Gemini New Moon on June 13 stimulates an illuminated understanding of your inner self, and your self-confidence can grow. Spending time with someone you share an understanding with adds stability. Generosity toward others who've helped you and extended true friendship seems quite natural, and you can also be the beneficiary of good will. If you can take a break from the action or spend more time immersed in creative or artistic pursuits you may find a renewed sense of peace that allows you to deal with anything that comes your way.

July

Bringing others together can lead to turmoil if they have different objectives or long-standing problems. However, you may be able to moderate a kind of peace, if that is the goal. Otherwise, this is a good time to step aside instead of getting involved in things that are not your concern. Misunderstandings may seem to run rampant, and if you need to clarify something for yourself, then ironing out those issues is likely to take enough of your time! The Moon's eclipse on July 28 brings events to a crisis, and a once stormy circumstance can become peaceful. With everything in the open, you know what to do, and you're ready to explode all those undermining attitudes and hidden issues.

August

If you feel like you're experiencing déjà vu, don't be surprised! This is a time to deal with issues from the past that require resolution or a deeper understanding. You may finally feel ready to break away from destructive or unhealthy attachments and move toward a new sense of freedom. Breaking old habits, changing your attitudes and clearing out emotional debris feels great, and then you'll be ready to set out on a more fulfilling path after the Sun's eclipse on August 11. Watch for unclear signals from August 12 to 21, when it's just as easy to appear two-faced as it is to misinterpret someone else. Avoid conflict by setting the record straight before the Full Moon on August 26. Otherwise, you may feel like you're sinking in emotional quicksand, and someone else may leap to the inaccurate conclusion that you can fend for yourself.

September

High anxiety can leave you feeling like a nervous wreck, especially if you're being pressured into something you don't want. You may not be able to escape your responsibilities, but you can fight back against unfair circumstances and free yourself from excessive controls. Choose your battles wisely, because you could run into something that goes far beyond your intentions. You need some healthy competition, and setting new goals that push you beyond your comfort zone a little could be the perfect ignition to get your momentum going. Reflecting upon your feelings, needs and concerns can be especially helpful after September 17, when a visit with a counselor could offer the objectivity you desire. Correspondence with a friend can open new doorways to your relationship, and keeping a personal journal can also offer surprising insights.

October

Your patience may finally be gone—especially if you're ready for changes and they're just not arriving at your pace! Take heart, because some unfulfilled opportunities from the spring return for a second chance during the last quarter of this year. Now that you have a different perspective, you may decide that there's a way to make necessary alterations—and now is a good time to accomplish those aims. Take action during the New Moon on October 9, when you can also enlist the aid of others. Listening to their needs and demands is also important, because failure to incorporate these elements can leave you in a lurch in the near future. Watch those distractions, because some of them lead absolutely nowhere.

November

Continuing your current obligations may not be much fun, but your perseverance pays off when the floodgates open on November 9. Despite Mercury's retrograde (from November 4 to 24) you may be sitting in a good position, and can use this time to put the finishing touches on something you've wanted to accomplish. Intimate encounters can be delightful, especially if you can maintain a playful, yet honest, attitude. Cooperative relationships, partnerships, and marriage take center stage during the Gemini Full Moon on November 23, when you may also feel like pouring out the yearnings of your soul.

You're more vulnerable, however, and can only accomplish the closeness you desire if you feel safe. Finding your spiritual link makes all the difference, and this can arise through something as simple as the right gesture in an unforgettable moment.

December

Your compassion toward someone in need can bring healing during the New Moon on December 7. Because your sensitivity to others is intensified early in the month, you may feel that you're tapping into a very special connection. However, awkward moments can arise from December 10 to 14, when inappropriate situations seem to expose your secrets (or those of another). You can be diplomatic, but it's all too easy to blurt out the wrong words or do something unbecoming. Once past this unflattering period, the remainder of the month may be rather quiet, offering a chance to mend fences and move forward. Your courage and conviction can inspire another to trust your promises, particularly if you're committed to your higher self in the process!

Cancer Moon

The rhythm of life pulsates through the core of your being. Through your Cancer Moon you have an innate sense of life's natural cycles and you reflect a quality of nurturing and comfort. You probably learned to trust your intuitive sensibilities when you were a child and you can easily tune into the ebb and flow of human emotion. Home and family may be the central focus of your life, and you may be the keeper of the hearth at home and at work, offering support when necessary and stimulating a sense of connection. Those you love are taken into the fold, and you can weave their energy into the tapestry of family.

Home is more than a place for you. Your personal environment must truly be a haven. You thrive when your nest is safe, secure, and filled with the things and the people you love. Whether raising children, fostering students, or directing a company, your guidance and understanding can be a positive mix of protection and insightful assistance. Letting go when it's time to allow another to fly freely is not easy for you, particularly if you've failed to establish reasonable emotional boundaries. If you're fearful, you may simply be responding to your own feelings of abandonment, instead of celebrating someone else's maturation. Letting go of the past is not always easy for you, either; but you feel more peaceful with these natural changes once you realize the power of the link you've established through your tender care.

Your partner's understanding of the importance of establishing home and family will strengthen your feelings of intimacy, and similar ideals in this regard will add longevity to any close relationship. The continuing cycles of change, which you feel so strongly, will bring a series of alterations over the course of your lifetime. Welcoming these changes adds vibrant confidence to your soul. This sense of contentment shines in your eyes, as you drink in the feeling of peace arising from your awareness of the timeless nature of the essence of life itself.

The Year at a Glance for Cancer Moon

After a year of vacillation between expansive growth and emotional tests, you're ready to solidify your foundations and make long-range plans. You're finally feeling some relief from the pressure to deal with endings and completion, and now you're experiencing more stability. There are still tests, but you may feel more capable of dealing with them—and more confident about your choices.

With Saturn moving away from the frustrating square to your Moon you may feel that the weight of the world is being lifted from your shoulders. For the next two years you're experiencing a bit of assistance from Saturn in supportive aspect to your Moon, helping you focus on your priorities more easily and conferring the determination and strength of commitment to forge a reliable security base. Jupiter's cycle provides a mixture of optimism, a desire for more space, and a sense of long-range vision. The tests from Jupiter center on your awareness of boundaries and limitations, because it's easy to overextend yourself emotionally or to feel frustrated because you want what you cannot easily have!

A continuing feeling of restless discontent, stimulated by the slow-moving outer planets, can leave you feeling dissatisfied. But the essence of these cycles is to shake up your old psychological programming, release old emotional baggage and experiment with new models of personal security. It's like learning to ride a bicycle—in the beginning you may feel a bit insecure about trusting your sense of balance, but after learning the fine-tuned connection between motion and balance, you're spinning along a merry trail. The key concept centered on these cycles is growth and motion. You can't afford to be stuck in old habits, destructive situations, or uselessly supporting people who steal your energy. If your Moon is from 0 to 9 degrees Cancer you're experiencing a powerful urge to allow your dreams and deep desires to play a significant role in transforming your life. If your Moon is from 10 to 19 degrees Cancer you're building strong foundations, but you may feel that you're starting and stopping rather frequently, making room for situations you had not anticipated. And if your Moon is from 20 to 29 degrees Cancer, you're breaking old habits, making room for more choices, and broadening your base of operations.

Affirmation for the Year

I am confident about setting new goals that will confirm my strengths.

January

You may feel that you're stretched beyond your emotional limits, particularly if you're taking up slack for someone else when you'd rather be doing something for yourself. The year begins with the Full Moon in Cancer on January 1, and that can be a good thing if you're willing to take an honest look at your feelings and needs. From this viewpoint you can set realistic goals for yourself, although you may feel a bit vulnerable if you're saying goodbye to familiar but unnecessary supports. The mixture of confidence and sadness is a normal part of growing, because even letting go of something you want to release can result in feelings of loss. Seek peace through your connection to pure love emerging on January 28.

February

You may feel like directing your energy toward romantic or emotionally charged relationships, and you may even allow your fantasies to play a larger role in your life. Breaking away from the tried and true may not be entirely comfortable, though, and even though you may be more experimental than usual, you're not likely to step into something completely foreign to your sensibilities. You may have to deal with something you don't understand or have never before experienced, and if you can balance your sense of caution with your fascination and desire you may actually be pleasantly surprised. You're in safer emotional territory after February 6, and may be most enticed by changes following the Sun's eclipse on February 16.

March

Feeling more assertive; you may run headlong into value differences, prompting you to take a second look at your expectations. Part of the problem could be mixed messages, but it's more likely that you are simply disappointed in responses and that you have to re-evaluate your options. Making room for variations can also expose alternatives not previously considered, and once Mercury enters its retrograde cycle on March 10 you may also have to spend time addressing situations you thought to be resolved or settled. Resistance or stubborn attitudes can bring your dreams crashing to the earth from March 18 to 23, but may also provide a measure of reality that must be considered if you are to build the security you desire.

April

Slow down to take a more careful look at your deeper feelings and needs, and you'll be more confident about your commitments. Although you don't necessarily need to retreat, you may feel that it's essential to pull back just a bit to give yourself time to recover from unexpected changes. Explore your inner self to help balance your emotions. Whether you're keeping a journal, talking with a good friend, or working with a therapist, you can make significant progress in trusting yourself. Pressures in the outside world may leave you feeling cynical, but you can rise above the dampening paralysis of cynicism by focusing on your spirituality and faith. By dedicating some time to forge a strong connection with your higher self during the Full Moon on April 30, you'll gain clarity, resolve and focus.

May

You're not likely to let anything stop you from accomplishing your aims, but your resolve can be tested in the process! Discouraging remarks from others may prompt you to reconsider your decisions from May 8 to 14. However, it's also important to look at your personal boundaries and vulnerabilities, because allowing someone else to exert undue influence on your choices can undermine your self-confidence. You know in your heart what you want and need most, and this can be a test of your faith in yourself. Old resentments need to be released now, because forgiving yourself and others quells your self-doubt. It's easy to make unrealistic promises in an attempt to strengthen your sense of importance.

June

Although you may begin the month feeling that you're out on a limb, you're in a good position to work out solutions to troubling issues. In many respects you're dealing with situations centering on others. Choosing whether or not you should be involved can be your most significant decision. To stay on track with the things important to your personal growth, you may need to let go of some of the burdens you're carrying for others; you may have to move forward while they fend for themselves. Relationships can be complex this month, but you can initiate communications that bring issues into the open so you can deal with them. This is no time to sweep anything under a carpet of denial, particularly during the Full Moon on June 28.

July

Take one last look at emotional issues brought to the forefront in February and April, and you'll see something (or somebody!) with greater clarity. It's still easy to expect more than is possible, but reaching for big changes and accomplishing important goals frequently requires that you push yourself. You have the emotional stamina to maintain your position or to forge ahead, but you need to maintain your flexibility during the New Moon in Cancer on July 12, when compassionate understanding goes a long way toward healing a sensitive wound. Somehow you make sense of it all, and despite Mercury's retrograde cycle (beginning on July 9) you can see signs of progress. Continue to watch your emotional boundaries, because it's easy to let someone take advantage of your sensitivity and desire to help.

August

As a result of your inner changes, you may reconsider your needs and desires in a close, loving relationship. If your relationship is strong enough to incorporate your evolving needs and your partner's changes, you may feel that you're reaching new heights. Yet if you're in a situation that's unhealthy or has run its course, you're likely to feel unsupported by the weaknesses and you may decide that it's time to let go. Some of the changes may be beyond your control, but where you do have some ability to direct the course of events, it's important that you choose growth and progress instead of digging yourself into deeper ruts. Uncovering the spiritual essence of your close relationships produces emotional strength during the Full Moon on August 26.

September

Changes in your routine can leave you feeling a bit out of step, but you can get back in the groove during the New Moon on September 9. If you've eliminated some old habits or shifted your attitudes, you may feel that your resolve is tested during periods of stress. Even so, you're in a great position to confirm your choices if you keep your priorities clearly in mind. A misunderstanding can hurt your feelings near the time of the Full Moon on September 25, and before you react by withdrawing your affection or retreating from your position, determine your options. Letting others know your vulnerabilities does not necessarily weaken your position, particularly if they're your friends! Listening to another's needs may also be an important step toward getting closer and strengthening trust.

October

Dealing with outside pressures can get on your nerves from October 1 to 6, and you may feel that you're in the dark about what someone wants or needs from you during the first ten days of the month. There's a window of opportunity from October 11 to 22 that can be quite helpful if you need to make room for changes or consider the next steps in a relationship, but you're also dealing with a challenge that may be tough to understand. If you're thinking with your heart alone, you may need to let your head in on the action, just to gain some objectivity! By allowing ample time for reflection and periods of singular contemplation around the time of the Full Moon on October 24, you can put things in their proper perspective and determine what you need the most.

November

Supportive actions from someone you trust helps you stabilize long-range plans. Start a more satisfying schedule or change your habits during the New Moon on November 7 for a fresh perspective to your life. You may also find it easier to break away from situations that are finally over. Although you may want to safeguard some traditions, you may also feel that it's time to make a few alterations—but be prepared for a little resistance at first. Excessive indulgence or taking unnecessary risks can leave you feeling quite exposed from November 14 to 26, and it's easy to underestimate what will be required from commitments during this time. Before you make promises, carefully evaluate requirements and take a second look at your obligations—or you may end up burning the candle at both ends!

December

Your generous efforts may go unappreciated if they're misdirected, and trying to make amends or win affections by going overboard may leave you in an emotional lurch early in the month—not to mention the effects on your finances. Careful navigating through emotional waters from December 6 to 18 reveals a change of course, and a relationship that may have been in a stalemate can come back to life if you're ready to forgive and let go of the past. Renewed commitment or exchanging vows with someone you adore can open the way for a sense of rebirth, but you may also be making promises to yourself! The new life you're experiencing during the Cancer Full Moon on December 22 may be centered on a feeling of finally being in control of your own destiny.

Leo Moon

Through your Leo Moon you radiate a warm, vibrant glow that's impossible to miss. You're likely to enjoy being the center of attention and your presence can lend a regal aura to any occasion. When others need a lift, your enthusiasm and faith in their abilities can inspire them. Likewise, you feed on the admiration and respect of those you love and hold in high regard. You may perform your best when challenged to meet high expectations. In your heart of hearts you'll always be something of a child, eager to experience the delight of each moment and embrace life at its fullest.

When you make a promise you mean to fulfill it, and you value the same loyalty from others that you would show to them. Your protective grace, warm hugs, and loving devotion can create a powerful bond with those who are part of the circle of your life. But despite your generosity, if you're feeling insecure you can be intractable, selfish and willful. If you've been hurt, you can feel devastated and you may have difficulty re-establishing trust. Once you fall into the rut of self-absorption you can lose your objectivity, and it is then that your relationships can fall apart. But options that allow you to exercise your creativity and imagination help you reach outside yourself and maintain contact with the world around you. Enhancing your adaptability also strengthens your ability to cope with changes. As a rule, when you initiate changes and feel that you're in charge of your life, you can feel pretty secure. But if unwelcome change disrupts your life, your stubborn streak starts to glow!

These extremes of emotion are part of your sensational approach to life. Your soul is on fire with creativity, yearning to share your expression of love with the world. By fully embracing your inner fire and developing your link with universal power, you can be released from self-focus and become more fully self-expressive. You know that the world is a stage—and you can become the ultimate performer in the drama of life. Just remember that you are always adored, even when you cannot hear the applause.

The Year Ahead for Leo Moon

Continuing your breakthrough changes, this year marks a period of focused intention and a time when moving beyond old limitations can be a positive challenge. You're stimulated to build a solid foundation that will meet your deepest emotional needs, but you also feel the stirring of a desire to open your horizons more fully. Developing patience will aid you immensely this year, because your ideas, creativity, and desire may outdistance the slow-moving pace of change on the physical plane!

With Jupiter transiting in trine aspect to your Moon this year, you're feeling more optimistic about your future. You may have clear and insightful vision about your life direction. After sorting through your priorities during the last two years you may also feel more confident about taking bold steps that will aid your progress toward manifesting your desires and hopes. This is a great year to make improvements on the home front, especially if you're making more room for yourself or opening up your living space in some way. Travel can be a positive enhancement, too, as can education or spiritual searching.

During the first quarter of 1999 Saturn completes its transit in Aries and then moves into Taurus, where it will remain for the next two and a half years. The cycle of Saturn in Taurus tests your attachments and challenges you to honor your true values. This cycle also represents a period of completion and symbolizes a time of taking greater responsibility for fulfilling your needs. Regardless of your age, you'll feel the effects of time and the process of emotional maturation. Although there can be positive associations with these changes, the natural tendency is frequently to first resist—when, in reality, you're simply being challenged to take a more realistic look at yourself and your needs. This is also the time to develop a clear understanding of your drives, motivations, and desires, and to leave behind habits and attitudes that undermine your growth.

If your Moon falls between 0 and 10 degrees Leo, you're experiencing a deeper awareness of your intuitive self, spiritual essence and soul-centered needs. This is also a year of rebirth and emotional healing. But if your Moon is from 11 to 20 degrees Leo you may feel that you're riding an emotional roller coaster, and you may need to adjust your attitudes several times over the course of the year. If your Moon is 21 to 29 degrees Leo you're eager to bring brewing situations to a climax, and you may uncover some unfinished emotional issues that finally free you to live your life on your own terms.

Anyone with a Leo Moon is experiencing heightened insights into self, needs, home and family. This can be an exceptionally empowering year!

Affirmation for the Year
I am honest with myself about my real feelings and needs.

January
You're beginning the year with a series of inspirational and visionary impulses—cycles that can be empowering and mind-altering! Different insights into your needs for intimacy emerge, prompting you to evaluate the nature of your close relationships and to listen to the song of your heart. You may feel that your needs are changing, or that you're on the brink of a breakthrough. Much of what's happening reflects the emerging intensity of the powerful effects of the Full Moon Eclipse in Leo on January 31, which works like a catalyst to bring issues into the open while prompting heightened awareness of your soul-level requirements for growth. These changes can be a bit disorienting at first, but ultimately, as you get your footing, you may find that you feel much more alive.

February
Staying emotionally centered requires concentrated effort, because it's easy to give in to the desire to burn bridges before you cross them. If you're feeling frustrated or angry it could be because your fantasies are out of reach, or that you're facing more unpleasant issues near the time of the Sun's eclipse on February 16. Devoting time to contemplative or meditative practices helps vent some of the emotional tension, but you may also need to be more physically active if

you're going to experience complete release. Your soul may cry out for balance, but accomplishing that task while satisfying everyone else (and yourself) may require more flexibility than you can easily access. Turning to creative or artistic pursuits can be a good solution, particularly after February 22. At least allow time to be entertained.

March

Resist the impulse to lash out against someone or something before you check out the details. It can take a lot of willpower, but by investigating the truth of the matter before you make a decision or close your mind you'll be much happier with the result. In many respects, this can be a productive and insightful month, and you can use any feelings of anger to motivate positive change. Your sense of integrity is operating on overdrive, so it will be difficult for anyone to push you around. Of course, anyone who's tried in the past has probably been sorely disappointed! You may feel a bit cynical about some of your options, particularly if you've just discovered that someone you've admired is not worthy of your respect. Try forgiveness—it works.

April

Creative pursuits absorb much of your emotional vitality, but also add their own positive ingredients to your life now. Everyday matters can be a little confusing, and you may have to deal with a sense of insecurity when some of your old support systems seem to dissolve. Initiate projects or change habits during the New Moon on April 15, when you're feeling greater self-confirmation. Romantic liaisons may not go as planned this month, particularly if you've fallen victim to infatuation. To avoid injury to your pride, clarify your plans, find out what someone else expects, and ask someone you trust for guidance if you're unsure of yourself. And if you sense deception, give yourself time to uncover the truth as you recover your pride.

May

You've heard about red herrings—those undesirable things you don't expect to show up? Sometimes they're people who arrive at the most inconvenient time, and this month you're prone to getting into situations with ample opportunities for the presence of an unwelcome quest! Part of the problem could be those innocent little promises you've made out of the goodness of your heart, only realizing later that you've just given away the family farm. Take time to clarify your motivations to keep from jumping into something you can't handle (you don't have to admit it to anyone else!), and you have good support when you really look for it. Everything is improving after May 22, and you're in a great position to luxuriate in delightful pleasures during the Full Moon on May 29 and 30.

June

Your generosity shows in almost everything you do, and this is an excellent time to let others know how you really feel about them. You can be a bit tentative from June 6 to 19, particularly if there are too many unanswered questions—so trust your intuitive sensibilities to guide you. Dramatic action works best after June 20, when you can not only make your point rather nicely, but when you're comfortable under the spotlight and you can show grace under pressure. This is a good month for matters of the heart—just watch for a tendency to let a beautiful face distract you. Sometimes that, too, can be fun—as long as you can afford the distraction! And pay attention to your tendency to send mixed signals.

July

Your ability to maintain your focus during a crisis comes in handy this month, because you may be surrounded by others in trouble who need your support and leadership. If you can swing it, this is a good time to take a few days away from everyday hassles to give yourself a break and inspire your own objectivity. This is another period of increasing demands from others, and if you're busy with your own priorities you may find that your work takes more time and adds more stress. To avoid losing your focus, you need ample time to let go, rejuvenate and restore your emotional and spiritual vitality. Conflicts with others can rage out of control during the Moon's eclipse on July 28, but you'll see the signs from July 5 to 18 when unrealistic demands can drain your emotional strength.

August

Even though you may begin the month retracing some of your steps or dealing with unresolved issues, you're making significant progress and moving toward greater freedom. The Sun's eclipse in Leo on August 11 (also a New Moon) involves a series of endings and opportunities for new beginnings. But you may feel that some things are happening without your consent or control. When you take another look, you'll probably see that you've been wanting some of the changes or that you've needed to say goodbye to people or situations that you've outgrown. You may also feel pressured by seemingly unfair responsibilities. This is an excellent time to take another look at what you need and want from love relationships and to break away from old habits that stand in the way of filling your heart with pure joy and love.

September

With renewed hope and strong conviction, you're making significant progress toward realizing a long-held dream. Your actions, creative expression, and leadership can inspire others, and their support and respect strengthens your momentum. You may also be dealing with separation or loss that has an emotional impact, although it's unlikely that this will come as a surprise, particularly if it is your choice. Even if you're only altering some old habits that have undermined your sense of security, you'll grieve their loss or have a conscious awareness that you're missing something—it's a natural response! Aroused by loving desire, you're more confident about fulfilling your needs after September 23, and may feel exceptionally romantic during the Full Moon on September 25.

October

You may feel alive with passion during the first two weeks of the month, and have great confidence initiating change during the New Moon on October 9. Even though there are a few odd happenings this month, you can deal with them in a manner that suits your needs. But you may feel unsure of yourself or mistrusting of someone else unless you have all the facts. Even then, if you sense that something's missing or that you're not seeing the whole picture, honor your insights and wait to act until you've satisfied your concerns. Most of the obstacles you've grappled with throughout the year do seem to be moving out of the way, but you may still be trampling through leftover emotional debris. That, in itself, could be the source of your sense of instability.

November

Leaving behind old emotional attachments can leave you feeling exhausted on several levels, but you can be revitalized by seeking and experiencing the beautiful things that are part of your life. You may feel a new sense of peace emerging, although the New Moon on November 8 does present a challenge for you to address unfinished issues and deal with your needs more realistically. If you're feeling controlled by someone or something you can see the picture with greater clarity, and you can make sweeping changes in the way you handle these situations during the Full Moon on November 23. From that point forward you're experiencing a new-found confidence centered on taking positive and assertive action to feel more powerful and alive.

December

Close relationships can become the source of emotional upheavals, because you're not willing to leave unanswered questions alone until you feel some satisfaction. It's easy to become too overbearing, particularly if you've run out of patience or if you feel that you've been betrayed. Your quest for truth spurs you on during the New Moon on December 7, and if you're taking responsibility for your own feelings, actions, and needs during this time, you'll find others to be more forthcoming concerning their own deeper feelings. Pressuring or intimidating others, especially those who seem to have little willpower, is all too tempting. But offering them ways to feel empowered is healthier and will leave you with greater satisfaction. Drawing the line between standing up for yourself and stepping on somebody else's feelings is not easy, though!

Virgo Moon

Your Virgo Moon works like a magnet to draw your attention to every detail, and your critical sensibilities help you develop your sense of precision and ability to fine-tune whatever you're doing. Your mind may have a series of filters that allow you to distinguish the most infinite differences when you're called upon to evaluate anything or anyone. But emotionally, it is that keen ability that adds to your sensitivity—and you are likely to be much more sensitive than others realize. You may seem rather conservative, when actually you're just holding back a bit until you know you're in safe territory.

All those lists hovering in the back of your mind reflect the preferences that guide your habits and subconscious choices. Your analytical nature is highly prized in situations requiring objectivity or serious deliberation, but sometimes it gets you into trouble emotionally—because you can be a first-class worrier. You can also sabotage yourself by trying to make sense out of everything, but sometimes your feelings simply don't make sense: they exist in a realm of what is, not what "ought to be." Your mind rarely rests, and you may find it easier to relax when your hands have something to do. Consequently you may have hobbies that reflect your eye for detail.

When you come to the end of the day you're much happier if you've accomplished something. Your soul is uplifted when you give of yourself. Whether you're concentrating on making improvements, strengthening your foundation of knowledge, or teaching what you know, these processes of personal development aid your sense of self-acceptance and build your self-esteem while making a difference in the world.

In your never-ending quest for self-improvement you can be overly critical of yourself and of others, and may fall into that vicious triangle of persecutor/victim/rescuer more frequently than you like. Accept the diversity of life and seek positive outlets for your critical nature, and remove a few requirements from your unwritten list of expectations for yourself; you'll experience renewed inner peace. Getting in touch with nature fills your soul with hope and widens your breadth of emotion, too. Even though you may think you want perfection, in truth you may simply need pure acceptance. It begins by looking in the mirror.

The Year at a Glance for Virgo Moon

Despite continued changes in the world around you (you probably like some of them), you're feeling much more centered and stable during 1999. After a year of broadening your horizons, you're ready to move into a more profound inner focus. This basis allows you to deal with shifting priorities without feeling threatened.

Jupiter's expansive influence last year may have left you feeling a bit overextended, and this year you're challenged to set more reasonable boundaries. But you have help from Saturn, now moving into a cycle that helps to strengthen your emotional self. You're more likely to question cause and effect and to make choices that aid your long-term growth during the next two years. You may also be thinking more about the future consequences of your promises, and you can find it easier to say "no" when necessary.

The deeply stirring effects of spiritual and emotional transformation are highly influential if your Moon is from 0 to 10 degrees Virgo. You're digging up old emotional hurts, bidding goodbye to all that unnecessary guilt, and opening to an expanded consciousness that allows you to see yourself and your needs from a different perspective. If your Moon is from 11 to 20 degrees Virgo you're facing the challenge of balancing your need to break out of stifling situations with your need for stability and consistency. And if your Moon is from 21 to 29 degrees Virgo it's time to surrender to your creative sensibilities and train your internal focus on becoming more open about your needs and desires.

Your spirituality is strongly emphasized this year. Because this is the most intimate aspect of yourself you may feel less inclined to let just anyone know about these changes. However, your closest relationships gain great benefit from these changes, and your relationship with yourself becomes the key to your happiness. Standing on more solid ground, you can choose the best response to the massive modifications as the world greets a new century.

Affirmation for the Year

I set my priorities according to my highest needs.

January

Staying centered may require daily concentration, because you can misjudge your ability to meet all your obligations. Your concentration can seem unreliable through January 6, but you're getting things into perspective from January 7 to 25. If you feel easily agitated, it could be because your expectations are not realized, but you may also be growing impatient with others whose promises fall short. Take a careful look at your responsibilities during the New Moon on January 17, and determine which things need to be eliminated from your priority list. Time away from everyday pressures after January 26 is important, when something as simple as a free afternoon can bring you back to life. Spending a few hours alone may be just what you need during the Moon's eclipse on January 31.

February

Gaining greater objectivity, you're capable of setting limits that will enable you to concentrate on the things you really want to do. But you have a soft spot for romance this month, and if you really want to be happy you'll find time to indulge your fantasies and enjoy the pleasures of love. Your fascination with high-tech innovations may need to be tweaked near the time of the Sun's eclipse on February 16, when discovering devices that can streamline your efficiency sparks all sorts of possibilities! Creative, musical or artistic activities can be especially provocative this month, and finding outlets for your talents and interests in these areas can be the opening for relationships with others whose similar ideals can fill an important need in your life.

March

If you're surrounded by cynicism you may question your own ideals, but your practical approach to spirituality and psychology may offer a positive perspective to even the most skeptical thinker. During the

Virgo Full Moon on March 2 you're feeling pretty sensitive, and you may not appreciate interruptions in your plans or questions about your intentions. Your actions may speak louder than words, but your deeper desires will profoundly influence the outcome. Honesty with yourself about what you want and how you really feel can empower you this month, but hedging will only cost you time—wasting your energy and frustrating your desires. Matters of the heart need careful consideration from March 17 to 31, when you may want to walk away from anything falling short of your high mark.

April

After an intense couple of days, you may feel more calm, although reaching an understanding with intimate others can be cause for consternation. You may be confused by mixed signals, but as long as you keep your focus on your needs and goals you may be able to withstand the distractions presented by others who may not seem to know what they want. A slowdown after April 18 may be the result of truth coming to the surface, but there's also a tendency for deceit, so take your time before making promises and if you're feeling uncertain, then investigate why. If you run into something (or someone) you just don't like, it does not mean you're wrong—so watch than tendency to wonder if you're being too critical. You may be the only one with good taste!

May

Pieces of the puzzle fall together now, and you're feeling much more self-assured. Even though you may be out of the woods, it's still a good idea to trust your sense of caution if it should arise. After careful planning, you're ready to set forth on a new path after the New Moon on May 15, when foundations for long-term growth are more reliable. Family and friends may seem to offer more support, but you may also feel much more confident about defining your differences and targeting those relationships that seem to be a true bond of soul and spirit. More easily distracted after May 22, you may fall victim to situations that center on the needs of others at the expense of your own. Your choices make the difference!

June

Overdoing anything can be costly during the first few days of June, but this can be a good time to let your creative side emerge. Objectivity is easier after June 7. Because you may still be easily swayed by the demands of others, particularly if you're trying to make a good impression, you'll serve yourself by finding out exactly what's expected. Making these determinations gives you the information you need before you go out on a limb. This is a great time to clear out closets or reorganize your files, making room for growth as you eliminate things that are just gathering dust. You're tired of the pressure resulting from procrastination. Feeling more emotionally balanced during the Full Moon on June 28, you're likely to be the one others turn to for advice and support.

July

With the ups and downs of change it's easy to feel that you're losing control of your life, when you're essentially moving through a period of reorientation and renewal. Innovative changes may run into snags, which can be frustrating if you're trying to convince someone else that a new system or different approach can work; but your practical, no-nonsense tactics can win over the most conservative skeptic. Setting out on an important venture from July 10 to 17 can invite unwelcome delays and unexpected interruptions, and if you have a choice, then this would be a good time to do something close to home or to review situations already in progress. Your creative imagination is working overtime and you can easily fall victim to infatuation. Reality catches up with you after the Sun's Eclipse on July 28.

August

You can be the instigator of change and can be successful if you think through the possibilities before you take action. But jumping into something unprepared near the time of the New Moon on August 11 can leave you feeling highly exposed, and may be emotionally unsettling. Use this time to trouble-shoot and re-evaluate, and consider taking action after August 21. Close relationships, partnerships and romance are on your agenda during the Full Moon on August 26, when you can be positively assertive when necessary and may be willing to take a few risks. If faced with a difficult decision concerning someone you love, you're better off taking a firm stand for the things you know to be best for all concerned—even if that's the uncomfortable choice.

September

Second thoughts about an emotionally charged situation lead to better understanding and deeper commitment to your feelings and needs. By acting with conviction during the Virgo New Moon on September 9 you'll gain momentum in personal and professional arenas. But you may run into power struggles mid-month, when differences in values or ideologies may leave you feeling mistrustful. Unless you're really involved, you may need to step aside in the midst of disputes, because getting into battles that don't belong to you can leave you feeling exhausted or abused. But if you do need to take a stand, digging deep into your soul to determine the best course of action will give you the courage you require.

October

Remember those old movies, where the cavalry rides in just in time to save the day? You may feel that the cavalry has finally arrived! With enhanced self-esteem and a strong confirmation of your choices, this is an excellent time to make serious commitments or to initiate changes that can positively alter your reality. You may be a bit unrealistic from October 4 to 9, but these are good days for breaking out of routine and escaping from pressure by enjoying your favorite pastimes. Romance is favored after October 8, and you may be feeling especially amorous during the Full Moon on October 24, when you're ready to be transported into ecstasy, sharing sensual pleasures with your partner.

November

Love continues to prompt your desires through November 9, and you may be drawn to an affair of the heart during the New Moon on November 7. Because Mercury is retrograde from November 4 to 24, you may not be satisfied with the outcome of a new relationship. However, exploring the deeper elements of an existing relationship can be rather illuminating. You may finally uncover the reasons for your reservations or inhibitions, and you may feel like you can finally let go of old issues from the past that have haunted your soul. It's easy to be distracted by the desire to please everyone else after November 20, but with your new-found sense of emotional boundaries you may find it easier to draw the line when necessary.

December

Passion and the need for deeper understanding drive your creative pursuits and underscore the essence of your personal interactions with others. Although you may feel a little out of step from December 5 to 10, you get back in the groove by listening to your intuitive voice. This change of pace can lead you to take a second look at a situation you previously dismissed, allowing you to confirm your feelings from a different perspective. Sometimes something uninvited keeps recurring until you uncover the source of unrest or dissatisfaction within yourself. A sense of emotional calm pervades your soul during the Full Moon on December 22, when you're ready to leave behind old hurts and step into a brighter day.

Libra Moon

That driving hunger for a perfect partner stems from your subconscious need to connect to someone; it is a reflection of your Libra Moon. Even though your top priority may be finding someone to share your life, you also fill your heart with social contacts, friends and family, and you do your best to create harmony in each of your relationships. Your deepest yearning is for a sense of beauty and peace to permeate your life, and the allure of delightful places, beautiful people, and breathtaking artistry is an integral projection of your truest self. Your own creativity is shown by the way you present yourself to the world, and your artistry is an expression of your soul. You prefer refinement in everything, including people.

Although you may prefer true perfection, your sense of balance allows you to incorporate the flaws of life into the lovely tapestry of experiences woven through time and experience. Even in relationships you realize that your primary goal may be to allow space for the ups and downs, the human imperfections, and the ever-changing balance of needs. Your search for the right partner may lead you to explore many possibilities, and it may take some time before you find the right ingredients for a healthy relationship. Your inner conflicts may stem from your desire to have it all—from the thrill of the chase to the passion of surrender—without losing your personal integrity in the process. If you could, you'd rewrite the fairy tales to show a bit more realism, but then, you'd be likely to miss the fanciful qualities!

Achieving balance in your life infiltrates your decision-making processes, too. Sometimes your hesitation frustrates others, but before you choose you do have your own deliberations to consider! Once you take a stand for your needs, you can be passionate about maintaining your position, although you can change your mind if it seems logical to do so. Sometimes, the price you pay for standing up for your utmost needs shatters the peace, leaving you feeling fragile unless you've forged a solid connection to your inner self. Ultimately, you discover that you must become the true reflection of your own perfect partner. Only then is the "other" likely to manifest!

The Year at a Glance for Libra Moon

You're feeling a great sense of relief this year and are ready to expand your personal horizons. Whether you're involved in travel, education, career development, or adding to your family, you're inviting greater abundance into your life. This may include a desire to move, renovate or make more room at home—or to at least rearrange the furniture!

With Saturn moving out of opposition to your Moon, you're recovering from two years of restraint and self-discipline. If you've eliminated unnecessary burdens, you know you're ready to reward yourself. Following on Saturn's heels, Jupiter now moves into the opposition to your Moon, inviting you to open your personal horizons and experience greater joy. But it's tempting to overdo it, partly as a backlash from all the restraint you've been feeling since 1997. So before you agree to spend all that money on new furniture, decide if you really need it, or if slipcovers will do! Another key to dealing with this cycle with grace is to know your limits before you overextend them. Saying "no" is difficult during this time. Fortunately, you've just learned the price you pay when you've not listened to your limits, so it might be easier than in the past.

The degree placement of your Moon determines specific cycles correlating to major changes in your life. For those born with the Moon from 0 to 10 degrees Libra, a sense of personal power, renewed hope, and creative vision emerge this year. You're ready to blend your spirituality into every aspect of your life. If your Moon is from 11 to 20 degrees Libra, you're ready to break out of boring ruts and experiment with the true nature of personal freedom; it's time for you to release your inhibitions and honor your highest needs, saying goodbye to the things you no longer need or desire. If your Moon is from 21 to 29 degrees Libra, you're taking the leap into new levels of awareness, and you may feel a bit uncertain as you sense some of your old attachments giving way to change. Honoring your limitations is a crucial part of growth. Realize that this does not mean making excuses to avoid necessary maturation!

All Libra Moons are experiencing a greater sense of personal independence and a year of enthusiastic change. Seeing the individuality in yourself and in others can alter your life direction.

Affirmation for the Year

I embrace the opportunity to express my needs and fulfill my desires!

January

You may be fired up about the possibilities of the year ahead and are inspired to listen to your intuitive urging in regard to love, artistry and accomplishment. Your inner voice speaks volumes, but your logical self may try to sabotage what you know. Tell yourself it's a test, which it is: a test of how effectively you're listening to your deeper needs and what you still fear about trusting love. If you're in the wrong situation, you know it, and may finally feel ready to walk away—except for that security thing. Your assignment centers on deciding what's important to you. Allow your visionary spirit to emerge, and do something fabulously romantic during the Full Moon Eclipse on January 31.

February

Excitement accompanies the early part of this month, although you may feel that you're being entirely too idealistic part of the time. Finding a good outlet for your idealistic inspiration may lead to amazing changes, and initiating something new on or following the Solar Eclipse on February 16 can be self-confirming. Testing your close relationships to determine if they still fit into your life can lead to endings, but may also reveal that you need to renew your promises in accordance with your current feelings and desires. This is one of those times when you may have both endings and beginnings, but those things coming to a close may leave you feeling a bit sad. Reaching closure helps to heal the wounds.

March

Confronted with a pressing need for something to inspire you, you may feel ready to test some of your theories about your changing needs and ideas. Although this is a good time to give a relationship a trial run, you may face a tendency to jump to conclusions. It's crucial that you know your own mind, because you can be swayed by someone else whose influence can lead you down the primrose path—and you really hate to go there unless there's something pretty waiting at the end! Playing the teasing, flirtatious game may be the safest option, particularly if you're not sure you want to go any further—but try to avoid sending mixed signals if you want to stay out of the frying pan! You're extra sensitive during the Libra Full Moon on May 31. Keep things simple.

April

Targeting your need to experience something uplifting and inspirational may prompt you to travel, attend a cultural event, or join a party for people you admire. It's easy to overdo it if you're trying to please somebody else, so before you finalize your plans for something extravagant, double-check with reality. Spending time with others whose ideals and interests compliment your own adds a sense of soul level connection after April 13. But you may have difficulty in situations filled with unfair assumptions or prejudicial attitudes. Duplicitous circumstances may be a signal that it's time to walk away, unless you want to be associated with something completely out of balance with your ideals. Set the record straight and take your power when necessary. Did you ever think that maybe you're the one who's right...?

May

You can be livid if you feel that you've been mislead or deceived, and, as a result, may be tempted to take uncharacteristically angry action. Interesting thing is that you know how to fight back while keeping a smile on your face ... very disconcerting! The problem is knowing how far to carry your revenge. If you go too far, you can end up feeling exposed. Gauge your actions by using your innate sense of objectivity. If you've lost your objectivity, seek out a trusted advisor. Entering the arena of any challenge requires that you be fully prepared this month, since you may be easily unnerved. Your judgment seems to clear after May 21, and by the Full Moon on May 30 you're in a great position to take some time away from the action and have fun.

June

There are ample opportunities for pleasure, and whether you're enjoying something or someone, this is a good time to reach into new emotional territory. If good fortune smiles on you now, you'll be happiest if you're sharing it with a special someone. This is a wonderful time to enjoy your friends, and a social gathering near the New Moon on June 13 may even spark romance. Fantasy and reality may seem to meet—but it could be an illusion, so remember your personal boundaries. You can overextend yourself unless you set limits from the beginning, and this is true emotionally, financially, and energetically. Creative or artistic endeavors offer interesting options, and may inspire a shift in your priorities at least once this month.

July

Your flexibility is tested, especially in matters concerning family. But you may also confront power issues resulting from long-disputed differences, and your objective and diplomatic point of view may be the voice of reason that's required to reach a resolution. Even though you may not enjoy conflict, you're pretty good in a crisis, and you can be fair in your assessments. You may yearn for escape during Mercury's retrograde after July 12, and taking some time away from contentious issues can be miraculously healing. After July 24 you're ready for something playful, but you may not like all your options. Retreat with someone you adore during the Full Moon Eclipse on July 28, when you deserve time out. If he or she is not around, indulge yourself in something you've always wanted to do by yourself—and banish that guilty feeling!

August

It may seem that you're just not making progress—at least not at the level you desire. Take a careful look at your life circumstances, get in touch with your unrealized needs, and determine how you can make supportive changes. (Doing so may require that you stand still for a while.) There may also be situations you simply cannot control, or a crisis can occur near the time of the Sun's eclipse on August 11 that alters your perspective. Focus on your priorities in a responsible manner to help keep your personal boundaries intact.

You might find that you're in better shape than you thought. Recognizing unrealistic demands when you see them keeps you ahead of the game. By the time of the Full Moon on August 26 you may want to attend to something personal.

September

Apparently sudden alterations in matters of the heart may come as no surprise to you, since you've been quibbling over what you want for quite some time. You're in a fabulous position to take the lead, setting the pace for change and identifying the best course of action, although you may meet a little opposition if you're pushing too intensely from September 1 to 5. Friendships can be a source of joy and support, and a meeting of the minds can open the way for a special relationship with a friend after September 14. You're expressing your needs and feelings much more clearly after this time, and may find that others are finally acknowledging you. You're extra sensitive during the Full Moon on September 25, but this is still a good time to surrender to the pleasures of love.

October

Whether you're initiating projects at work or forging the way for important changes in your personal life, you're in high spirits and can be exceptionally persuasive from October 1 to 16. The New Moon in Libra on October 9 is prime time for you to stand in the forefront of developments when you can present your abilities and concerns with panache. Shifting your schedule or bidding farewell to bad habits is much easier now, too. Irritating situations can emerge after October 18, when differences in approach, values, or attitudes can leave you feeling at odds with someone. Allow a little time before you make a final determination, since vague circumstances can cloud the issue. You may feel that you need a period of retreat during and after the Full Moon on October 24, just to rejuvenate or balance your energies.

November

Somehow situations can easily be blown out of proportion. You're alert to signals (you probably saw them last month), but you may still be unable to quell all the conflicts or differences. This is one of those times when talking politics or religion can simply be dangerous. Test the water first. If it's hot, turn the conversation to something like the weather. Even the best parties can be spoiled by crass behavior or uncooperative attitudes near the time of the New Moon on November 8. Concentrate extra time on your favorite artistic pursuits or efforts after November 9, when withdrawing into this arena offers positive respite. Social and family tensions ease after November 22, and during the Full Moon on November 23 there's room for healing and acceptance. Finally—common ground!

December

You're inspired to break free of old customs in favor of establishing a new order. Because you can be the master of diplomacy, you may even garner support from traditionally conservative individuals—particularly if your way of doing things promises to be more enjoyable! Innovations at home can also be on your agenda, and whether you're redecorating, moving, or working a little feng shui magic in your environment, changing the energy at home can alter your sense of well-being. You're in high gear, able to work wonders from the time of the New Moon on December 7 until December 23. After that time you may have to pull back just a little, especially if your ideas fly in the face of something someone considers sacred territory!

Scorpio Moon

You may seem calm to the casual observer, but in truth, you can be an emotional extremist. Anyone who knows you well will attest to the fact that you can be intense. Your Scorpio Moon adds a quality of mystery to your aura, and your penetrating gaze can be mesmerizing. You know the depths of emotion, and you are capable of piercing the veil of polite exterior and reaching into experiences that others might find impossible to fathom and even more difficult to express. Driven by a need to probe the once-unspeakable taboos—sex, birth, pain, death, abuse, or anything else easily denied—you're fascinated by the processes of transformation.

The world of secrets and profound emotion and their roles in true healing is part of your subconscious domain, and you may attract others who need the same level of emotional bond you crave. If someone wants to be close to you, he or she must first prove trustworthy. You cannot abide dishonesty, and you may flush it out when necessary; this can be intimidating to those who have something to hide. This can be great when applied to certain life situations, but it can complicate one-to-one relationships. You're not all that keen about anyone knowing your secrets, and you may even keep secrets from yourself. You know well that place within your psyche that's like a vault containing unresolved anger, guilt, self-doubt, and shame. The barriers you've constructed over time to protect your emotional vulnerability can keep you from realizing the very state of ecstasy and closeness you deeply desire to share with someone you love.

Fortunately, you are also capable of purging yourself of old emotional traumas, and as a result you may have experienced phenomenal changes over the course of your life. By welcoming the process of regeneration and peeling away the many layers of life, you discover the core of your true power. This amazing experience equips you to deal with others facing a crisis, and helps you maintain an insightful level of awareness about the true essence of life itself.

The Year at a Glance for Scorpio Moon

You're laying strong foundations for long-term growth during 1999. This can be a year of stabilization, and a time when you may feel ready to take on greater responsibilities. The choices you make now can have far-reaching effects, and whether you're forging new beginnings or saying goodbye to things you've outgrown, you're creating milestones.

Jupiter's influence through this year gauges your ability to set limits. You're testing the differences between overindulging and true prosperity consciousness. You're ready to open to the possibility that life can bring you more, but you must carefully examine the price you'll pay and the appropriateness of your choices. It's easy to push too far, thereby limiting yourself in the process instead of opening avenues for true expansion. Your philosophy of life may need careful examination.

Saturn moves into Taurus, and for the next two years will be transiting in opposition to your Moon. This cycle feels like cosmic brakes grinding to a halt. Periods of separation, testing and emotional losses can be benchmarks of Saturn's influence, and you may feel that you're being unnecessarily victimized by heavy responsibilities. In essence, this period is about learning what you do and do not need. By dealing with unfinished emotional issues you'll go a long way toward becoming free. But this is not the time to shirk the responsibilities you've taken on, because if you do, you'll quickly discover the true meaning of karma. Many times, this cycle presents a return to the past in some way. Whether someone comes back into your life or you experience a visitation from long ago through study, travel, or moving, you can sense that it's time to finally embrace your deepest yearnings.

Your spirituality beckons, but setting emotional limits can be difficult if your Moon is from 0 to 5 degrees Scorpio. If your Moon is from 6 to 11 degrees Scorpio, you're making breakthroughs and saying goodbye to things and people you've outgrown. If your Moon falls between 11 to 20 degrees Scorpio, you're feeling rather rebellious, but are unable to completely give in to the temptation to burn all your bridges; you're continually reminded of your personal responsibility for fulfilling your needs. If your Moon is from 21 to 29 degrees Scorpio, you may feel that you have more control over the changes you're making, and this is a good time to adjust your habits to more healthy choices.

Knowing the difference between positive uses and abuses of power continues to be a strong theme for anyone with Scorpio Moon this year. To be uplifted, you may have to keep your feet on the ground.

Affirmation for the Year

I am safe in the face of change.

January

You can be highly persuasive during the Full Moon on January 1, although you may not be interested in taking unusual risks and you may feel cautious about getting involved in situations you mistrust. There may be changes happening all around you, and some of them could present a chance for you to advance. Before you bank on any of them, clarify those vague issues, since you're not interested in groping your way through a fog of empty promises. Technological or innovative alterations in your daily life can create havoc if you're unprepared, but you may still have to deal with them. Taking a break from stressful situations may be the only way to cope with your mixture of emotions during the Moon's Eclipse on January 31. A day of retreat might be a perfect choice.

February

Because Mars is transiting in Scorpio this month, you may feel more easily angered or irritated, particularly if fulfilling your desires is inhibited by situations you cannot control. Your sensuality is intensified, and if you're involved in an intimate relationship you may be exploring highly charged emotions that can carry you into ecstasy or send you plummeting into despair. Much depends on whether or not you're pursuing healthy choices and if your relationship is ready for more profound honesty. The Sun's eclipse on February 16 stimulates a period of visionary insight which allows you to establish a new set of personal goals. Your creativity and imagination are operating in a supercharged mode throughout this time, but you may not feel like exposing your creations to criticism just yet.

March

Unpredictable or unexpected changes can throw you off balance, although you're quite capable of making the most of them. When others seem perplexed, you can look into a realm of possibility and expose options not readily visible to those of weaker emotional stamina. Pleasurable activities are favored during the Full Moon on March 2, particularly if you want to make a good impression on someone. Yet even in your close relationships you may see things you'd almost prefer not to know; fortunately your sense of compassion is powerful and your need to surrender to unconditional acceptance overrides your need to take charge during the New Moon on March 17. After that time you're experiencing a new understanding.

April

If you feel that you're being misled, it could simply be that unanticipated changes have taken place and your expectations are left out in the cold. Review your emotional vulnerabilities early in the month, and consider the challenges you're now facing. By organizing your time to accommodate unusual changes you'll be less frustrated when they occur. The organizational structure of your life is probably shifting, and whether you're dealing with a schedule change or exposure to different people, you may feel overexposed. By maintaining an awareness of your emotional boundaries and honoring your needs for privacy you can avoid some of the vulnerable circumstances possible during these cycles. Take an emotional inventory during the Scorpio Full Moon on April 30, when you're most in tune with your inner self.

May

The problem for the next couple of months centers on the potential of situations mushrooming out of control. Concentrating on your priorities becomes highly important, and recognizing the needs of others may leave you wondering when you should step in and when you should allow someone to take the consequences. Even if you could make a difference, if you pick up a burden that does not belong to you, you could rob another of the chance to face up to reality. Turn over a new leaf and allow someone to show his or her own strengths during the New Moon on May 15, and feel the freedom that dawns in your own soul. The essence of shared responsibility in partnership may also emerge, particularly if things are out of balance. You may find great comfort in spending time at home. Concentrating on making improvements in your personal environment can be a good outlet for your creative energies.

June

Although it gets easier to talk about your feelings or express your needs, you may discover that your priorities and tastes are in stark contrast to another's. In situations where the variations are too wide, you may lose interest or decide that you're not in for the duration. Since you're used to looking beneath the surface, you may not be fooled by the line you hear from others about "what they really meant to say or do...." The exaggerations can run rampant from June 20 to 26, and you may be the one standing on terra firma while others are buying their tickets to paradise. However, you can lose your objectivity if you're feeling too insecure. Take time for quiet reflection and get away from the press of everyday hassles during the Full Moon on June 28.

July

Philosophical or ethical dilemmas test your ideals, and you may feel that you must take a stand for your beliefs. Before you get into battle gear, question your true values, and determine whether you're simply responding to an emotional threat. It's sometimes difficult to draw the line between one's insecurities and beliefs, but this is a time when truth can win out. Practical matters may ultimately determine your priorities after the New Moon on July 13, when you may find that your connection to your spiritual center is more secure. But you may have trouble determining your limits from July 4 to 20, and you can get into situations that leave you treading water if you're not careful. With Mars in Scorpio for the next two months you can easily overpower others. Your need for a soulful connection is stronger now, and during the Moon's eclipse on July 28 you may reach a new spiritual plateau.

August

You're forging ahead this month, taking positively assertive steps to get what you need and want. But you may face challenges—like rules, responsibilities, and requirements—before you experience the satisfaction of fulfilling your desires. The manner in which you view the obstacles in your path can have a significant effect on your ability to deal with them, so if you're feeling stymied, take a look inside to determine whether or not you're creating more problems by your actions or attitudes! This can be a time of endings, and tension is high during the Sun's eclipse on August 11, when a crisis reaches its apex. But by the Full Moon on August 26 you're past the most painful part of breaking into new territory and you may feel more comfortable with your choices and actions.

September

Although some of the situations you're involved with now may seem like a repetition of what you've experienced before, there's a new twist. You're more capable of standing outside crisis-oriented situations and power struggles that do not involve you. In fact, your presence can be the catalyst for others to face their own dragons— and you don't have to slay them (the dragons, that is). In love relationships, it can be your lover who's changing. Granted, you may also feel the need to get out if it's not working now, and this could be the perfect time to face unhealthy attachments and break free. Think of this as a period of preparation. You're clearing the foundation of your heart to make room for a more secure and trusting circumstance to grow.

October

As illusions fall away, your sense of realistic needs and desires is confirmed. Fresh possibilities emerge on October 5, when you may find it much easier to talk about your feelings and share your innermost thoughts. Feeling that you're now standing on solid ground, you may be more confident about making commitments, or at least getting closer to the experience! After several months of mixed signals, overstated needs and unrealistic expectations, you'll welcome the comfortable options now emerging. Most at ease after September 24, when the Full Moon entices you to let your hair down and indulge your need for passionately sensual moments with your sweetheart, you may have visions of what could be. The momentum is building...and the possibilities are sweet.

November

Although they say you rarely get second chances, it's in the stars this month for you to have another chance to set the record straight. Mercury's retrograde in Scorpio opens the way to explore a different dimension of a situation already in place. Even though this is not the best time to make a final decision, it's the perfect time to take another look at your opinions or conclusions and determine any changes you want to make. The Scorpio New Moon on November 7 marks a significant period of emotional sensitivity, and a time when you may step onto an entirely different platform for fulfilling your needs. You may feel that your soul is drawing you toward your destiny, but remember that you have choices about how you will fulfill it!

December

Love is in the air, and your ability to tap into the pure flow of loving energy that emerges from the core of your being is immensely powerful now. The essence of passion is difficult to describe, but when you feel it, you can certainly recognize it! Experimenting with your fantasies can be delightful from December 1 to 18, but you may feel insecure if those fantasies take you face to face with your inhibitions. This is a time to be open with someone you trust, but new relationships may not be what they seem, and reasonable caution can protect your vulnerability. During the Full Moon on December 22 you're in safer territory, and may feel that you can exercise your imagination without fear of exposing feelings you're not ready to address.

Sagittarius Moon

Your Sagittarius Moon stimulates a deep sense of questioning and a need to experience the grand adventure of life with un-fettered freedom. Whether you're reading, traveling, learning, or pontificating, you're always eager to explore boundless possibilities. Many times, you're physically on the move, and you appreciate the variable features of culture, climate and terrain which encourage you to keep an open mind. Wide-open spaces are very appealing, physically, philosophically and emotionally, and you may prefer living in a place with plenty of room for expansion.

In all relationships you expect to feel independent, and you may have difficulty in emotionally charged situations that require your continual presence or attention. You can be exceptionally loving, although those who are less secure may feel that you're hard to pin down, particularly if you give in to your needs to travel or follow your own path. When you're inspired, your generosity is un-matched, and you have a flair for uplifting others. But you may resent feeling smothered or personally inhibited, and may feel that your spirit withers under the influence of excessive restraints. You can be easily distracted by situations appearing more promising that your current circumstance, and sometimes your wanderlust, leaves you feeling emotionally spent.

Your needs for home may be more esoteric than concrete: you feel at home when you know you're on the right quest, and place may be secondary. Your ability to adapt to new environments is excellent, especially if you're excited by the things you're learning; if your spirit feels connected, you can feel at home almost anywhere. Wherever you nest, you prefer surroundings that inspire you, and may enjoy living close to nature. In your mind, heart, and soul you will forever be journeying, questioning and wondering about the vast reasons and possibilities—ever following your search for the grail of truth.

The Year at a Glance for Sagittarius Moon

A year of excitement and enhanced personal confidence is supported by the planetary cycles that influence your Moon during 1999.

Practical matters take on more significance and may sometimes feel a bit limiting, but you can almost always figure out how to make the most of any delays or challenges you may face. Overall, this can be a year of emotional strength, when you feel better about your choices and see excellent options for continual growth.

The influence of Jupiter to your Moon during 1999 is confidence-building. You may feel that you're ready to accept the abundance life offers. By making the most of your resources you can inspire those who share your life. Others may look to you for answers, but you're probably used to that. The difference this year is in your sense of hope for the future and your need to give others the tools they require to make their own paths. Since you prefer relationships that support mutual independence, you may have more options to assure this type of support. However, Saturn's cycle presents a challenge. You may have to make adjustments, take on new responsibilities or alter your priorities in order to have what you want. It's like learning the language of a different culture—once you've gotten the basics in communication you feel much more at home. If you resist the lessons and demands of Saturn, you may simply feel frustrated about the fact that you're not getting everything you want when you want it. During this year and next year you're dealing with the test of adapting your life to include and honor the demands of those who are part of your world.

If your Moon falls between 0 to 11 degrees of Sagittarius, you're experiencing a renewed sense of power. Satisfying your deepest needs and desires works like magic to make your life more fulfilling on every level—this is your time to let go of the past and move into a brighter future. You're feeling some frustration actualizing your needs for freedom if your Moon is from 10 to 19 degrees Sagittarius, but if you keep your priorities clear and take your responsibilities seriously you'll have more independence! If your Moon is from 21 to 29 degrees Sagittarius, you may feel highly optimistic about your options and choices and may move, make changes in your personal environment or set off on a new life path.

All Sagittarius Moon individuals are releasing unnecessary restraints. It's the manner in which you accomplish this task that determines whether or not your life remains on solid ground!

Affirmation for the Year

I am inspired by the amazing possibilities life offers me;
abundance is mine on every level!

January

Your enthusiasm can get the best of you unless you maintain an awareness of your limitations. By incorporating these limits into your long-range plans, or acknowledging the role stability plays in helping you feel truly free, you can make monumental progress. New ideas about forging emotional satisfaction, personally and professionally, can be like the light on your path, emphasizing the importance of taking measured risks in order to move forward. The manner in which you gauge those risks is the key to success or failure. To prepare for the inner illumination stimulated by the Moon's eclipse on January 31, give yourself a means to step away from the distractions presented by the world and listen to your intuitive voice. It speaks volumes.

February

You may feel emotionally drained by those who clamor for your attention, particularly if you have other plans. Some of the problems that may have been small irritants in the past can seem like boulders in the path to your personal satisfaction. You can run roughshod over another's feelings if you're too impulsive, although you may simply be suffering from differences in values. Fascinated by the allure of something new or different, you can be easily swayed by appearances and may be tempted to leap into something unprepared. If you can afford the diversion, it may be worthwhile, but you may feel differently after the Sun's eclipse on February 16.

March

Your inner gyroscope seems to be functioning more reliably this month, although you can run into problems centered on misunderstandings or poor communication. Pressures escalate during the Full Moon on March 2, although your words and actions can be healing. Fresh ideas and innovative possibilities may fill your mind continuously from March 1 to 17, when you're quite adept at inspiring others to think positively and look forward. If you're exposed to new situations or fascinated by fresh ideas, you may feel that your heart is overflowing with joy, although you'll be more easily distressed if confronted by another's pessimism. You're attracted to those who look with optimistic eyes. Despite outside suspicions, you're more likely to feel hopeful during the Full Moon on March 31.

April

Disruptions or delays last month may have given you a chance to finish something you'd been putting off, and now you're ready to move ahead. Enlisting the help or support of others who share your aims and ideals can be reassuring, and after the New Moon on April 15 you may be considering entirely new options. If the weaker links in your plans seem to leave a few holes during the last half of the month, you may be inclined to abandon problematic situations and seek out simpler paths. Abandoning something or someone you really care about can leave you too vulnerable, though. If you have a change of heart you may not know how to tell someone, but the pressure of projecting a false face can prompt you to confess what's in your soul.

May

Pursuing your dreams keeps you in top form and your enthusiasm is unlikely to falter this month. Practical matters may slow you down a bit near the time of the New Moon on May 15, when re-evaluating your plans can help you avoid previously unseen pitfalls. Proceeding blindly through the fog is not your idea of a good time, and you'll prefer knowledge that requires you to take a detour over ineffective delusion that prevents you from reaching your destination. Fun-filled or adventure-oriented situations capture your imagination during the Sagittarius Full Moon on May 30, so be sure to leave your agenda open for the possibility of spontaneously inspired interests. If you're far from home this month, pay attention to the differences in value systems—there's no need to pay excessively for a good time!

June

Loving relationships may be the primary attention-grabber for you this month, and you may discover someone whose love of adventure rivals your own. The New Moon on June 13 challenges you to look into new directions or to listen to another's questions with genuine interest. Spiritually uplifting situations or a connection that stirs your soul so deeply that you feel transported to another realm may have been the stuff of fairy tales before. But you're in the perfect position to experience what all those artists, mystics, poets and philosophers have been writing about. Come to think of it, you might want to write a few words of your own to aid your reflection of where you've been. You're off balance just enough to allow yourself to suspend some of that skeptical "show me" stuff and let your heart soar. Enjoy the ride!

July

Probing more deeply into emotionally charged territory, you're experiencing a period of release. Letting go of old illusions is sometimes triggered by seeing others fall victim to their own self-deception, and vicarious learning can save you the agony of your own fall. Unsecured commitments fly away like dandelions on a windy day, but those feelings that warm the core of your heart grow brighter, and you may be learning what it's like to lose something that was once sacred. If these emotional bonds are truly forged in love, you're simply removing the crass material that has repressed the brilliant flame. Forgiveness is the key experience of the Moon's eclipse on July 28, and through letting go of unnecessary expectations and allowing the power of love to carry you can journey into the far reaches of awakened living.

August

Free to open your heart to someone you trust, you're feeling the powerful solar eclipse on August 11 stimulating your ego to take a back seat to the calling of your soul. You may be surrounded by changes you simply cannot control, but by listening to the urging of your deepest needs you can make choices that alter your priorities so that you feel more secure. If you're having doubts about a love relationship, you may be failing to address your own fears surrounding commitment, but you may also be seeing things more objectively now. Simply burning your bridges may not accomplish the desire for a true bond of soul and spirit, although letting go of the past is part of your journey during the Full Moon on August 26. Release your old attachments, so your present needs have more room for gratification.

September

You're feeling more assertive, and you may become so enthusiastic about pursuing your desires that you stir up controversy. Others may respond defensively if you go too far. And you may be easily hurt if someone you care about seems less passionate than you had hoped. This can be a highly productive, although unsettled, period, and you may be burning the candle at both ends as you push toward your goals. Getting to the core of your feelings is easiest mid-month, but you may be vulnerable if you've exposed your concerns or desires and don't get the response you'd anticipated. New pursuits fare best after September 19, when your emotional boundaries are more firmly supported. The Full Moon on September 25 marks a time of high passion, and you're quite likely to take full advantage of the opportunity!

October

From October 1 through 18 you're still driving intensely toward personal realization, but after the New Moon on October 9 you may experience hesitation or questioning from those whose previous support had fueled your confidence. Some of the illusions that had led to unrealistic assumptions are finally breaking apart, and even though you may still feel that you can continue onward, you may have to walk a singular path toward your aims. This is a period of testing and clarification, when reality's stark light exposes situations for what they are. In many ways, these experiences allow you to align yourself with truth and integrate your personal desires with your highest needs. You're not likely to retreat from something that's really important, but you may prefer to keep your new visions to yourself until you've had a chance to test them against the backdrop of the current situation.

November

A flash of insight inspires you to traverse new territory emotionally, and you're not likely to be disappointed in your efforts. It is easy to go too far, but you've run into trouble before and seem to have a knack for getting out of situations that cause others to question their sanity. Your faith in yourself grows, and through trusting your creative instincts you can open avenues that were previously closed to you after November 10. This can be a period of strong ingenuity, and you will be tested to define your limits after November 17. A meaningful relationship blossoms during the Full Moon on November 23, and following this time you may finally know how someone really feels about you. If you're comfortable with a relationship, this is an excellent time to think about the future and determine your vision for life together.

December

It's easy to feel excited now! After carefully considering how you want to accomplish the fulfillment of your deepest needs you may be ready to take steps into untried territory during the Sagittarius New Moon on December 7. Carried on the wings of hope, you confidently move toward manifesting long-held dreams and desires, and may feel the stirring of insightful visions about your future. Nurturing joy heals many wounds in your life, and through developing your ability to see joy in every life experience you can alter the nature of your relationships with everyone your life touches. Travel can be more than going somewhere; it may, instead, symbolize a journey that carries you further toward your union with divine wisdom, which is, after all, your ultimate goal.

Capricorn Moon

You are driven to overcome the challenges of life on the physical plane. You are equally fascinated by the promise of success. Accomplishment is the elixir of life to your Capricorn Moon, and even as you climb steadily toward your goals you are recharged by the self-respect that accompanies your powerful desire. You take your responsibilities seriously, and you keenly appreciate others who have the dignity to honor their own. Even as you stand at the summit of achievement, you yearn to strengthen your security. That prompts you to reach toward new peaks, and you may foster the same desire in others who follow your example.

You have a wonderfully dry sense of humor, something that keeps you going when times are tough. Your ability to build solid foundations lends a supportive quality to your relationships with friends and family. Sometimes others may think you're too somber or overly cautious, but when you complete the tasks at hand, you love to play—just not for long! Wasting precious time and effort is just not your style, and because you feel most satisfied when you're producing tangible results, you're not likely to repeat mistakes. (Though these are not necessarily admitted in a public forum!) You need to feel that you are in control of your needs and your life, and you may try to exert excessive control over your emotions. If someone tries to control you, you're very likely to resent their attitudes or actions; but you may not find it easy to give others the autonomy you demand for yourself.

Finding the right partner can take a bit of time, because you need someone who understands your priorities and who can accommodate your practical sensibilities. It's tempting for you to overemphasize work, but you can be exceptionally dedicated to home and family. Giving those who love you time to enjoy your company can provide a level of contentment that may surprise and delight you. Opening your heart, expressing your feelings, and allowing yourself to experience the flow of love and tenderness can be tough if you keep your walls too tightly sealed. Protecting yourself is one thing, but shutting out the joy of life diminishes the returns on your hard work…and that just would not be very sensible!

The Year at a Glance for Capricorn Moon

Because you've been feeling the pressure of increased responsibility and intense challenge during the last two years, you'll have great appreciation for the stability and consistency to come during 1999. There are still unsettling changes in the world around you, and you'll continue to take steps to keep up with the times; occasionally you'll even be ahead of the game! Don't allow anticipation to frustrate your sense of emotional stability; this can be a year of exceptional progress.

Saturn moves into Taurus this year, where it will remain until the early part of 2001. This shifting cycle works to your advantage, because the overall nature of this period may be to honor a conservative approach—right up your alley! This is a good time to accomplish your practical aims. You may side with the traditionalists, but you need to innovate if you are to stay on top of the proverbial heap!

If your Moon is from 0 to 10 degrees Capricorn, you may feel caught between the desire to spend more time developing your spirituality and the need to grow in the outside world. If your Moon is from 11 to 20 degrees Capricorn, you're feeling an urge to develop new directions in career or to incorporate change in your family while creating a stable platform for long-term growth. And if your Moon is from 21 to 29 degrees Capricorn, you'll feel alternating periods of highs and lows as you reach a number of your goals and then begin the uphill climb to your next set of objectives.

For all Capricorn Moons, this is a good time to stabilize your home or to make lasting improvements in your environment. If you're moving or purchasing property, you can attract situations that will retain their value. Strengthening the bonds of commitment in your family or in an intimate relationship seems entirely plausible, too, and may be at the top of your priority list.

Affirmation for the Year

I consciously take actions that show reverence for the past and respect for the power of the present moment.

January

Even though you may feel that you're making progress, you can be anxiety-ridden if others are not giving you the type of feedback you need during the Full Moon on January 2. The disparity could fall somewhere between the cost and the quality you get in return; whether it's money, time, or energy, you expect to see *quid pro quo*— and you may be shorted on the *quid* side! Step away from outside pressures and turn toward your inner needs and desires to gain perspective on the best approach, and during the Capricorn New Moon on January 17, you could be in an excellent position to make your break. Despite the challenges, you have hope, and it is that sense which illuminates your path on the darkest nights and adds sparkle to each day.

February

Some of the sharp edges have been smoothed away by your persistence, and you're feeling more self-assured. Compassionate support from those who understand your intentions emphasizes the importance of your long-standing commitments, and if you've hoped to forge a better-defined promise with someone, you're getting the right signals to go ahead. You may uncover deception or weaknesses, but this can actually be illuminating and allow you to do a little emotional clearing so that you feel more free. But you're not likely to be comfortable with inconsistencies, and if you're faced with flaky attitudes from others you may withdraw until they can make up their minds. Many of the trials you've faced are reaching their final stages. If you're not relieved already, it's around the corner!

March

Differences between what others expect from you emotionally and what you feel prepared to share can create problems unless you illustrate the distinction between clear understanding and unrealistic anticipation! This can be difficult if you don't want to disappoint somebody, but your down-to-earth approach during the Full Moon on March 2 allows you to set reasonable boundaries. Feeling stable, you're in a great position to deal with everyday concerns, but you may feel out of sync with highly idealistic people. Finding the common thread between your spiritual ideals may strengthen intimate ties, but if you feel threatened you might withdraw. Think about what you really want from your relationships, and after the New Moon on March 17 spend time with those who share an important part of your life and explore your hopes for the future. You may be more aligned than you thought.

April

This is a productive month. Even though some of the finer details may escape your priority list, you're moving forward with the things that mean the most to you. Because you may be focused on financial or material matters as a means to maintain your personal security, you're experiencing a positive series of cycles to support these concerns. But your approach to handling these situations is changing, particularly if your old strategies are no longer working. Take a careful look at your needs—emotionally and financially—during the New Moon on April 22, and pay attention to the situations that seem to be losing their luster. By watching for trends and listening to your intuitive sense of what's useful and what's losing power, you'll be on the inside track. Romance is favored during the Full Moon on April 30, so don't forget to allow a little time to savor the sweet things of life!

May

Daily concerns seem to be fairly reliable, but there are pressures building that may leave you feeling stressed by month's end. Riding the ups and downs of sensitive issues can leave you feeling exposed, especially if you're trying to maintain control in a stormy situation. Changes can precipitate turmoil, and if you're overreacting because you don't want to deal with these "minor" matters, you may alienate the very people you're trying to protect. Listen to the concerns of others, and formulate plans you wish to put into action during the New Moon on May 15. Now is the time to establish lasting foundations, because the fluctuations that follow may not undermine the quality of a strong base. But if you're overdoing it or trying too hard to impress someone after May 23, you may feel completely strung out emotionally by the Full Moon on May 30.

June

The friction between Mars and Jupiter builds the potential for adding to your impatience, and can be indicative of changes in your daily routine. As a rule, you don't mind alterations that increase your productivity, but frittering away precious resources connected to issues that should have been settled long ago can leave you in a sour mood. It's time to dust off your sense of humor and look for the silly side of frustrations, because laughing off some of the tension adds momentum. You may be trying too hard to make sense out of everything when this could just be a period of dealing with each issue moment to moment. Staying focused on the present is crucial to your emotional stability and is more empowering than worrying about all those "what ifs." Because you may be extra-sensitive during the Capricorn Full Moon on June 28, honor your limitations, but seek out little indulgences that comfort your soul.

July

This month you're the one who seems to have the solutions to problems that others find too daunting. If you're in a serious relationship your partner may look to you for supportive understanding, and you may find that sharing your concerns forges a deeper bond. Because progressive changes are on hold for a while, you're also concentrating on making the most of what's on hand. Although you may uncover a wide gap between idealistic hopes and practical concerns from July 4 to 10, by choosing the practical side of the matter you may be able to ultimately reach loftier goals. Breakdowns in communication are likely after July 11, when clarifying anything of importance minimizes tension. The Moon's eclipse on July 28 brings problems to the surface, and after that time you may have to make adjustments in your priorities.

August

This cycle tests your competitiveness, and if you know your strengths you can accomplish amazing things. Because you are accomplishment-oriented, you may feel that your focus should be to tackle the tasks at hand and forget the little daily niceties. But this is one of those times when paying attention to the special needs of your family or those who work around you can endear them to you.

If you're moving or making changes on the home front you'll see progress, but may run into problems you had not anticipated. When you're not working, you can experience wonderful enjoyment from being at home in your nest, and after August 23 may feel like staying close to home for a while. During the Full Moon on August 26 you're ready to indulge in some of the pleasures resulting from your hard work.

September

From September 1 to 16 you're feeling confident about expressing your feelings when circumstances call for you to "confess" what's in your heart, and even though you may be having some inner conflict about what you really want you still need to get issues out in the open. You're clearing away some cobwebs from your emotional stockpile by letting go of old habits that drain your energy during the New Moon on September 9. Getting used to the new responses that emerge as a result can be somewhat disorienting, but you'll feel happy about making choices that are ultimately more satisfying. The potential for emotional conflict emerges and intensifies during the Full Moon on September 25 when you may be called on the carpet for your lack of attention to another's needs. Before you feel guilty, ask yourself if the criticism is valid!

October

Look for the pitfalls in unresolved issues to create problems through October 7, but after that time you're in a fabulous position to reach closure and concentrate on building trust. Communication (which involves more than talking!) of your needs may be a bit awkward if the situation leaves you feeling out of place, so to feel more comfortable, change the ambiance to complement your needs. Taking some time off to play adds to your emotional vitality after October 18, when a hike in the woods, gardening, camping or, if you'd prefer not to rough it, a nice hotel with fabulous food can feel great. You're ready for something out of this world during the Full Moon on October 24, and you can actually feel a bit giddy with excitement. Let someone entertain you!

November

With Mars transiting over your Moon this month you'll feel more assertive. That can be in your favor if you use it positively, but you can also run roughshod over another's feelings if you're not careful! During Mercury's retrograde from November 4 to 24, you have a chance to review important matters, and may want to use this time to get back in touch with someone you've missed. Even if everything is not what you want it to be now, you may be more willing to deal with the reality of situations and go on from there. It's the unrealistic expectations from others that can be disconcerting, particularly if you can't get through the fog to show the importance of what you know to be true. Try to be alert to the times when you may push too hard. A gentle touch may be more effective.

December

Financial worries can bother you through the first few days of the month, but after December 6 you're probably doing damage control for problems resulting from the actions of others. Once you've taken care of that, you're free to enjoy some of the pleasures of the season. You're feeling like breaking a few old traditions in favor of doing something memorable, although you're not likely to go too far out of bounds! During the Full Moon on December 22 you're scaling back a little and allowing time to focus on family and those who are a special part of your life. For the remainder of the month you're willing to put some pressing problems on hold and catch your breath. This is your time to let go and feel the glow of love in your life.

Aquarius Moon

You're attracted to the unique qualities of life. Because of the influence of your Aquarius Moon, you're most comfortable when your individuality shines through. The desire to break away from the commonplace leads you to follow a singular path toward self-realization. Along the way, you're likely to forge friendships with those whose understanding and interests uplift the human spirit. You may lead the charge for revolutionary changes for liberation from ignorance and prejudice, and in so doing illuminate that which is extraordinary within yourself and in the world around you.

You can be highly intuitive, but you may argue with yourself when your intuitive sensibilities defy your need for logical understanding. By blending your intuitive and logical intelligence you strengthen your ingenuity and make room for your artistry to emerge. You may love being around others with special talents, and you feel at home in unusual circumstances and around innovative ideas. You can be a trendsetter, and your sense of rebellion can be triggered in the face of abuses of power or when you feel forced to adhere to ideals or values that compromise your principles and sense of integrity.

The ideal of unconditional love lingers somewhere deep in your soul, and to express this fully you may strive to connect to the collective of humanity in a special way. Your friends are the jewels of your life, but sometimes, when you're off on your own journey, you can seem aloof—even to those who are close to your heart. Because you can be difficult to tether, you can have difficulty with intimate relationships. Your need for freedom can feel like a cold shoulder when someone needs to feel special to you, and even though you may not mean to break hearts, you sometimes do. The powerful urging to experience and become that which shatters the boundaries of ordinary reality always wins, and ultimately can lead you to a sense of unity with divine intelligence.

The Year Ahead for Aquarius Moon

You're still feeling the urge to eliminate anything from your life that's standing in the way of your personal growth. But this year, you're challenged to balance freedom with responsibility, and you may feel impatient with the progress you'd like to make. There are more chances to break ground during 1999, and overall you're experiencing a remarkable period of self-realization and personal empowerment.

Throughout this year you're feeling the uplifting influence of Jupiter, and you may be able to see the silver lining in almost any cloud. This can be a good year to travel, study, or write, and your creative drive can be intensified. Because Uranus and Neptune are both transiting in Aquarius for the next several years, you're also experiencing a lengthy period of awakening and a new sense of personal autonomy. Saturn moves into a tense square to your Moon sign until early 2001, slowing your progress a bit and limiting some of your options. But this restraint can be helpful when you learn how to use it. Perhaps you need to complete educational plans, or you may be taking on more significant responsibilities in your personal life—this is a growing time.

If your Moon is between 0 and 9 degrees Aquarius, your spiritual development takes top priority, and you may feel more aligned with your inner self. This can be a phenomenal period of awareness and creative inspiration. If your Moon falls from 10 to 20 degrees Aquarius, you're experiencing a profound need to manifest changes in your life. You may want to move, break out of difficult circumstances or start a new career path, but before you can accomplish these things you're facing a series of tests to determine whether you're really serious about taking on the responsibility that will be associated with these changes. If your Moon is from 21 to 29 degrees Aquarius, you're ready for breakthroughs and your sense of independence is enhanced. The alterations you make this year will set the stage for the future, and by discovering the vision directed by your higher self you can manifest amazing possibilities.

Although you may not feel you have much time for self-reflection, as you open your mind more fully through the influences you're feeling now you'll see fabulous changes in the world that reflect the potential for true enlightenment. The world may need your insights and, just as important, you may relish the world's support of them.

Affirmation for the Year

*I joyfully embrace the challenge to change and free my soul
so that I may fulfill my true destiny!*

January

Love fills your heart as you enter the new year, and you may feel more open to the enriching flow of unconditional acceptance. Whether you're focusing your energies on an existing intimate relationship, your friends, or your family, the compassion that drives your soul can alter even the most difficult circumstances and brings true joy into your life. You may begin a new relationship or find dimensions of love you've never known before. If you're involved in creative or artistic pursuits, you'll appreciate the importance of your intuitive insights and can open to levels of awareness that set you far apart from the ordinary. During the Moon's eclipse on January 31, you're releasing barriers to accomplishing the things you've dreamt and hoped to achieve. Unanticipated events can be unsettling, but can illuminate amazing possibilities!

February

The confusion surrounding you can be the result of changes beyond your control, and as long as you keep a cool head you can remain objective. It's easy to overreact or feel that you've lost control, but when you step back and look at the situation you may find that you had simply lost touch for a moment. The Moon's eclipse in Aquarius on February 16 stimulates a period of emotional release, and may mark a significant ending. This can also be a period of new direction, and a crisis surrounding your personal transformation can simply be the result of stepping into a different conceptual reality. Whether you're thinking of moving, changing the furniture, or rearranging your schedule, this is the time to streamline your life and make room for the things that feel most comfortable. Relationships may also undergo their own rearrangements!

March

For some reason you may feel under attack, and it could be coming from someone who sees you as a threat or feels that the changes you're making undermine his or her effectiveness in some way. If you're responding in an understanding manner or staying alert to the possibility of confrontation, you'll handle things just fine. But trying to escape through irresponsible actions will only cause problems to escalate! Fortunately, your ability to deal with trouble through communication and clarification works beautifully through March 19, but then differences in values and emotionally charged situations can trigger problems. You may be able to step out of the picture and deal with your personal priorities during the Full Moon on March 31, but be alert to others' reactions to avoid being pegged as selfish!

April

You may be amazed by the people who seem to be holding grudges, and you may even be dealing with problems that stem from something hearkening back to the summer of last year! Unrealistic situations are exposed for their weaknesses, and the test to define truth versus fiction can permeate situations that affect your life in a personal way. Although maintaining a stubborn position may not work to your advantage, holding fast to your values and truest ideals can serve you well in the face of adversity. You're feeling more confident about your choices after the New Moon on April 16, and experience a surge of uplifting optimism during the remainder of the month. This is a great time to develop plans that will ultimately simplify your existence.

May

Scientific or intellectual pursuits may go smoothly, but some problems still arise from prejudicial or stubborn attitudes. By extracting excessive emotion from some situations you may be able to arrive at a more objective point of view, but you could also be facing the possibility that you're avoiding emotionally charged circumstances because they're just too uncomfortable for you! To reach the spiritual planes you strive for, you may have to incorporate space for your deep emotional needs and feelings, allowing for the fact that they may never make sense. Connecting with someone through a meeting of the minds after May 22 inspires you to be more holistic in your approach to life, and during the Full Moon on May 30 you're ready to experience a purely magical and uplifting period of awakening.

June

Concentrating on your creative ideas and making space in your life to test them or put them to use, you're feeling more in touch with the rhythm of the times. During the New Moon on June 13 you may feel like reaching out to someone previously out of your scope, and you can inspire revolutionary change in the lives of others. Loving relationships become more passionate, and by engaging another in the experience of freely expressing your feelings you can reach heights that leave you breathless with rapture. But if you're stepping over boundaries that expose either of you to unnecessary vulnerability, you can feel immediate regret. Avoiding contact is not the answer. Instead, you may need to deal with your expectations of the situation before you dive into it!

July

Separation from someone or something you adore can leave you feeling vacant for a while, particularly if you have been unaware of the extent of your attachment! Sometimes love works that way— you don't know how far you've gotten into it until you're somehow removed from its warm glow. Angry situations can be divisive after July 6, particularly if you've been in the midst of excessive romanticizing (by yourself or someone else). It's more likely that you'll feel confronted by someone else, and to avoid escalating the conflict you may have to break contact for a while. During the Moon's eclipse in Aquarius on July 28 you can feel exceptionally open to attack, or you may be in the throes of situations that have finally reached a crisis point. By paying attention to your deepest feelings and allowing your intuitive insights to work their magic, you can rise above anything.

August

Although you may try to step aside from conflict-ridden circumstances, fiery emotions may be unavoidable, even in situations that are usually more businesslike. Hidden feelings seem to be coming to the surface just as readily as claims of denial are bandied about the board room near the time of the Sun's eclipse on August 11. This is an amazing period of adjustment, and some of the tempers flaring can be the result of unexpected changes that challenge the status quo. Now, that's just the stuff that gets your heart pounding, and the delicious part is that your creativity may be at an all-time high. But getting everyone else to understand exactly what you have in mind is another story.... To strengthen your position, align with friends whose influence adds breadth to the situation.

September

Finally! Progress resumes, even though it may be limping along for a while. Your work-oriented relationships may be improving, but you may still be at odds with your partner or significant other until you find common ground. Search your spiritual aims for the point where your paths converge. From this level you create new visions for your future, and if you see positive possibilities you may feel like continuing onward. But if you uncover greater divergence, then this could be the time to bid farewell or to transform the relationship to a different level. You can probably make the transition from lover to friend, but everyone does not possess the key to that door. Talking over your thoughts and feelings is easier after September 17, and accomplishing a meeting of the minds and hearts is entirely possible during the Full Moon on September 25.

October

From October 1 to 17 you're making significant strides in reaching agreements. Misunderstandings can arise if someone's operating with a hidden agenda and this can cause frustrating problems that slow progress. Because you may be dealing with things that keep you apart from the action, you could fail to see the floodwaters rising from October 6 to 18, so try to take a few minutes each day to learn what's happening around you. Even though practical considerations seem to take top priority after October 19 you can still deal with the changes because you're feeling more confident about long-range outcomes. This is a time to remain flexible, because holding stubbornly to your way of thinking without understanding the importance of what someone else needs can thwart your progress.

November

Your confidence may be stronger, and even though you may be making concessions you're feeling more like you're part of the action. Your artistic nature is stimulated by the transit of Venus after November 8, when it's easier to win the favor of others—even those who don't really understand you! Clearing the way for future progress now can involve finishing something that's been on the back burner for a while, but procrastination can be your enemy. By being attentive to the hopes and needs of others you're strengthening friendships and showing your loyalty, but you may have to do a few things you don't like. The payoff can be a more significant balance of power that leads to greater freedom and more satisfaction during the Full Moon on November 23.

December

Your patience wears thin, but you can also get a lot accomplished. Following your vision, you're ready to break away from outworn circumstances or unhealthy relationships in favor of situations that support your deepest yearning during the New Moon on December 7. It's easy to misjudge from December 9 to 18, when you can get into something you're not quite prepared to handle. Unexpected changes can precipitate developments that require you to utilize every ounce of your ingenuity—but that's why you have it! Unrealized promises come to blossom after December 20, when the obstacles to progress seem to loosen up a bit, and when your persuasiveness can overcome the resistance of others.

Pisces Moon

You've learned that your deeper feelings are frequently a powerful barometer for the essence of what's really happening. Through your Pisces Moon you connect to life by absorbing the vibrational energy surrounding you and developing your keen sensibilities to things others may never experience. Poised on the thread between illusion and reality, those sensibilities enable you to sail beyond ordinary reality into the realm of imagination. You can bring magic into any situation.

When others show prejudice, you can bring acceptance. Where there is pain, you bring compassion. Sometimes everyday life is difficult, because your emotional boundaries can be easily penetrated. You prefer to think of the world as it should be—filled with peace, forgiveness and serene beauty, and when confronted with harsh situations you may feel drawn to reach out and help in some way. In your personal relationships you sometimes go too far, and need to create an emotional filter that allows you to distinguish between your own higher needs and the pressing demands of others. To compensate for your sensitivity, it's important that you give yourself time to learn what a situation or person is like before you emotionally immerse yourself. Meditation can be a necessary tool for balancing your inner awareness with your connection to the world around you.

Sometimes the abrasive realities of life are too stressful and may overwhelm you, and it is then that you can be a true escape artist. The extent to which you escape is important, because you can go too far or fall victim to addictive patterns. By creating a safe home space where your dreams can lift your soul you feel whole, and by finding outlets for your artistry and creativity you can attain emotional balance. Ultimately, you can manifest the perfect acceptance and tranquillity you feel deep within your soul—if not to the entire world, at least along the path of your life journey.

The Year Ahead for Pisces Moon

As you shift your focus to stabilizing the expanded opportunities you've experienced during the last year, you discover you're more interested in pursuing practical concerns. This is a year of building lasting commitments, releasing situations you've outgrown and moving toward the realization of many of your deepest needs. Changes in the world during 1999 can be unsettling; however, you're more trusting of your instincts to guide you.

When Jupiter moves out of its cycle in Pisces in February you may feel a little let down, but there's every reason to welcome this change. Your judgments concerning your needs and abilities become more realistic during 1999, and caring for your soul-level concerns involves concentrating more on how to utilize the good fortune you've been experiencing for the last year. Saturn transits in supportive aspect to your Moon this year, and you're looking for stability and practical ways to manifest your vision. Where discipline may have been difficult in the past, now you're ready to put yourself to the tests that will secure your safety and stability.

If your Moon is from 0 to 11 degrees Pisces you may feel a bit unsettled, because you're coping with changes beyond your control that transform the very core of your emotional needs. By seeking solutions that encourage healing and restoration you can become more completely at home with your inner self during this year. You may also feel a strong urge to move or "transplant" yourself in some manner. If your Moon is from 12 to 20 degrees Pisces you're facing a series of adjustments as you make strides toward manifesting your hopes and dreams; by becoming more honest with yourself about your feelings you gain power and momentum. You're taking a leap of faith this year if your Moon falls between 21 to 29 degrees Pisces. If you've never quite learned to trust your connection to your inner self, this is the time; developing a powerful link to your intuitive and psychic ability is part of the expanded awareness you're experiencing this year.

For Pisces Moons, this is a profound period of releasing illusion in exchange for grasping the power of your creativity and the strength of faith. Despite the fact that it's hard to find tangible evidence for faith, you're uncovering it now, and by so doing can inspire others who may have lost touch with this valuable quality of life.

Affirmation for the Year

*I can feel the connection between my consciousness and
divine presence. I am one with my higher self.*

January

The connection to your inner self can be powerfully self-confirming
during the Full Moon on January 1, and by spending time doing the
things that fill your soul you're setting the stage for a profoundly interesting year. Caring for your soul may not have been a top priority, but that's been changing, and blending your spiritual needs into
your everyday life seems quite natural to you. You may not feel ready
to put your plans or ideas into motion until after the New Moon on
January 17, but progress can be a little slow. Conflicts may brew
around you, so keep your emotional boundaries set and try to get involved only if it's necessary. (This grows stronger as the Moon's
eclipse on January 31 grows nearer.) Sometimes watching teaches
you the most. Think of yourself as the nurse during a battle. It's suf-
ficiently dangerous to minister to the wounded!

February

Your imagination and creative sensibilities are working overtime,
prompting you to seek out new avenues for expressing your deeper
feelings. Emotions run high, and you may be faced with endings that
have been on the horizon for a while. Pursuing the process of letting
go can seem more difficult than actually doing it, and surrendering
to the truth in your heart will ultimately lighten your burden. Even
if you're maintaining an existing relationship the manner in which
you're involved can change and you may discover that you need
something different from your partner now. Look for indicators of
new options during the Sun's eclipse on February 16. Then, after
February 20, be attentive to the best ways to define your role in your
close relationships. You're realigning your expectations.

March

While you may feel extra-sensitive during the Full Moon on March 2, you're also more aware and can see through the veil of illusion. That does not guarantee that you'll pay attention to the truth, particularly if it's not what you want to see, but you'll have a harder time ignoring it! You're probably becoming more clear about what lies beneath the facade, and if you give yourself time to deal with the contrasts between your expectations and reality you can find a creative solution. Mercury's retrograde (March 10 to 31) can work to your benefit, when you have a chance to review something you may have thought to be well established. Whether or not this is a fortuitous turn of events depends on everyone concerned, but you can break away from counterproductive situations during the Pisces New Moon on March 17 and step onto a healthier path.

April

An interesting mix of unexpected change and serious responsibility prompts you to redefine your priorities. Dealing constructively with the pressures of a changing world requires imagination—right up your alley! Your ability to remain flexible is also a precious commodity in this climate of uncertainty, but on an inner level you may feel fairly consistent. Your emotional gyroscope works nicely now, and you're quite adept at dodging the crossfire. As the month draws near its close everything becomes more clearly defined, but outcomes are still uncertain. Spend time advancing your spiritual growth during the Full Moon on April 30, when you can easily connect to the divine essence and extract the serenity you require to see things with clarity. From this perspective you can be the one to initiate necessary change.

May

High activity levels from May 1 to 8 can be distracting, and this is a good time to look into something innovative. Incorporating your emerging sense of renewal into your work and your personal relationships changes the way others see you, but, more important, alters the way you see yourself. Your heart needs ample room to nourish the love you're feeling, and whether you're devoting your time to an artistic project or to an intimate relationship, you're capable of expressing and experiencing ecstasy after May 9. There is a difference between hope and expectation, and in matters of the heart it's crucial to keep one toe on the ground as you occasionally leap into the unknown realm of desire and dreams. Watch for pitfalls (or pratfalls!) during the Full Moon on May 30.

June

It's a mixed bag this month. You can make positive and significant changes in your personal environment, but may be disappointed in the outcome if you're in a hurry. It's probably everybody else seeming to be in a rush, and that can be entirely too distracting if you're not focused. Passionate exchanges seem to fly everywhere near the time of the New Moon on June 13, but you may not trust them to be genuine. The contrast between styles of behavior becomes crystal clear: what you feel and your comfort in expressing those feelings can be distinctively different than what you're experiencing from others. As a result, reaching a conclusion about where a relationship is headed can be complex. Communicating your desires and needs is easiest from June 6 to 25. A romantic exchange can lead you to change course during the Full Moon on June 28.

July

You're feeling more assertive, and after testing the waters you can confidently pursue fulfillment of your desires on or after the New Moon on July 12. Because a change in plans or direction is quite possible due to Mercury's retrograde cycle beginning on that day you may be better off using this time to follow up on something you've already started. This is a powerful time to evaluate a love relationship or listen to the concerns or needs of your partner. You may discover that you're coming from very different places emotionally, and this could prompt you to reconsider the nature of your commitment. The period around the lunar eclipse on July 28 is filled with the potential for crisis and conflict, but you may not be a key player. That's probably a relief!

August

This can be a breakthrough period, but you may feel a bit isolated from those who seem stuck in their own issues. It's important that you consider the demands or concerns from others while keeping your own needs a high priority. Caving into pressure will only leave you feeling spent, used or abused. Even if you're in the midst of something uncomfortable during the Sun's eclipse on August 11, you still have a right to stand up for yourself, your ideals and your needs. You're quite capable of making necessary adjustments that accommodate others without compromising yourself too extensively. You may feel extra-sensitive during the Pisces Full Moon on August 26, although this can be the perfect time to pull away from the action and enjoy the company and comfort of someone you adore.

September

Manipulative situations may seem to be around every corner, and you're feeling vulnerable. If you're overwhelmed by something you cannot control, you do have the power of choosing the way you'll handle the situation. Seeking support or counsel from another can be stabilizing, although you need to choose your confidant wisely. Trust is a primary need, and confirming the trust you have in yourself may come more easily through devoting time to your spiritual and creative pursuits than in materially oriented activities. You may feel more stabilized after September 18, when the power games calm down a bit. This is a great time to clear away debris—physically and emotionally—so that you have room to grow.

October

Even though you may have a change of heart due to the awareness that you need something different from a relationship, you can still salvage your connection if it will promote mutual evolution. You're developing a more solid emotional foundation and building a positive support network after October 6, and may meet some fascinating people whose ideas and artistry inspire you to pursue something extraordinary. During the Full Moon on October 24 you're experiencing a period of initiation into a deeper realm of personal awareness. You may feel like spending time in nature to connect with the core of your being. By grounding yourself during this time you can establish a strong foothold that allows you to fully develop your creativity. A significant mentor or teacher can be part of this experience, but you may also discover that you can have a strong influence on someone else!

November

Forging ahead, you're experiencing a test of your ability to remain balanced. You're uncovering a few things you may have left in the wake of changes some time ago and may feel that you're finally ready to reach closure. Really saying goodbye in a conscious way can be extremely empowering, and your need to feel unattached can drive you to walk away. Heading out on a different pathway during the New Moon on November 7 promises the kind of discovery that keeps your enthusiasm alive. But the funny thing is that you may feel you've traveled this way before, and are likely to find tiny elements of the things you failed to address when you thought you were starting anew. It's all a matter of honesty and attitude, and during the Full Moon on November 23 you're finally ready to face the music and step onto the platform of personal empowerment.

December

Despite a few philosophical conflicts, you're likely to enjoy this month. You're feeling generous, and may be more attuned to the desires of those you love. Romance can blossom, although you're held to the realm of reality until after December 15, when your promises will be tested to determine if you're actually committed or just paying lip service in order to stay on the fence a while longer. Time's up... you need to decide how you feel, what you want and whether you can allow time to test the fantasies you've carefully nourished. Love can blossom rather beautifully during the Full Moon on December 22, and whether you're with somebody or simply embracing yourself more fully, your heart is leading the parade of your desires.

About the Authors

Gloria Star has been a professional astrologer for over twenty years. She has written the *Sun Sign Book* forecasts for Llewellyn since 1990, and has been a contributing author of the *Moon Sign Book* since 1995. Her most recently completed work has been as creator, editor, and contributing writer for Llewellyn's new astrological anthology, *Astrology for Women: Roles and Relationships* (1997). Her astrological computer software, *Woman to Woman*, was released by Matrix software in 1997. She is also the author of *Optimum Child: Developing Your Child's Fullest Potential through Astrology*. Gloria has been honored as a nominee for the prestigious Regulus Award. She has served on the faculty of the United Astrology Congress (UAC) since its inception in 1986. She is a member of the Advisory Board for the National Council for Geocosmic Research (NCGR) and has served on the Steering Committee for the Association for Astrological Networking (AFAN).

Bernyce Barlow leads workshops on the sacred sites of the ten Western states, and is the author of *Sacred Sites of the West*, from Llewellyn.

Chandra Moira Beal is a freelance writer. She has also been published in the magazine *Texas Beat*. The name Chandra means Moon.

Estelle Daniels is a professional part-time astrologer and author of *Astrologickal Magick* from Weiser Publications. She has a small select astrological practice and has been contributing to Llewellyn's annuals since 1997.

Alice DeVille has been a consulting astrologer and writer for twenty-five years. She develops and conducts workshops on a variety of astrological, spiritual, and business topics. You can reach her at *DeVilleAA@aol.com*.

Verna Gates teaches folklore classes at the University of Alabama at Birmingham and has been featured on *NBC Nightside* as a folklorist. She was a writer for CNN and has been a freelance writer for fifteen years.

Penny Kelly has earned a degree in naturopathic medicine and is working toward a Ph.D. in nutrition. She is the author of the book *The Elves of Lily Hill Farm*, from Llewellyn.

Barbara Koval publishes a monthly newsletter on astrology and stock market trends called *Intelligent Market Insights*. She is the author of *Time and Money: The Astrology of Wealth* from Llewellyn.

Gretchen Lawlor combines over twenty-five years experience as an astrologer with over ten years experience as a naturopath into her astromedical consultations and teachings. She can be reached for consultations at P.O. Box 753, Langley, WA 98260.

Kirin Lee writes and does graphic design for a science fiction magazine, and is the managing editor for a rock'n roll magazine. She is currently working on a *Star Trek* novel.

Harry MacCormack is an adjunct assistant professor of theater arts, and owner/operator of Sunbow Farm, an organic farm in the Pacific Northwest.

Caroline Moss runs workshops and gives talks on herb growing, cookery, crafts, history, and folklore and designs herb gardens on commission.

Leslie Nielsen has been an astrologer for thirty-one years. She is a lecturer, teacher, writer, researcher, gardener, and animal lover.

Roslyn Reid is a Druid, yoga practitioner, body builder, and student and teacher of the tarot. She also grows a lot of fruit.

Louise Riotte is a lifetime gardener and the author of several books from Storey Publications, including *Planetary Planting* and *Astrological Gardening*.

Kim Rogers-Gallagher is editor of *Kosmos* magazine and writes columns for *Welcome to Planet Earth*, *Dell Horoscope*, and *Aspects* magazines. Her first book is *Astrology for the Light Side of the Brain* from ACS Publications.

Jeraldine Saunders is the author of *Signs of Love* from Llewellyn. Her experience as a cruise director was the basis for the *Love Boat* TV series.

Bruce Scofield is a professional astrologer certified by the American Federation of Astrologers (AFA) and the National Council for Geocosmic Research (NCGR). His specialties are electional and Mesoamerican astrology.

Jim Sluyter and Marilyn Meller are proprietors of a community supported farm (CSA) and publish a newsletter, *The Community Supported Farm: A Voice for the CSA*. They can be reached at *fsfarm@mufn.org*.

Nancy Soller has been writing astrological weather forecasts since 1981, and is studying the effects of the Uranian planets on the weather.

K. D. Spitzer is an accomplished astrologer and tarot reader, teacher, and workshop leader. Her areas of focus are herbal and musical healing.

Lynne Sturtevant is an accomplished craftswoman and avid collector of folk art. She has a B.A. in philosophy and a life-long interest in folklore.

Carly Wall, C.A. is the author of *Naturally Healing Herbs: Using Tonics to Heal*, and *Setting the Mood with Aromatherapy* from Sterling Publications.

Directory of Products and Services

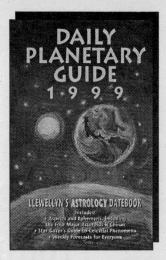

100% OF YOUR DAILY RECOMMENDED DOSE OF MAGIC

It takes more than the right amount of vitamins and minerals to nourish a magaical person—you need a daily dose of magic to satisfy the hunger in your spirit. Instead of fast food, you crave a connection to mystical traditions, the wheel of the year, the divine.

Look no further for soul food. The *Magical Almanac* serves up rich helpings of magic from the global kitchen in portions that will satisfy every taste and appetite. With dozens of savory articles, how-tos, magical crafts and spells, the *Magical Almanac* delivers the info you need to work magic every day. This year's features include: Oujia Board® Magic Out of the Closet; Magical Mishaps; The Magical Job Interview; Aphrodite's Mirror; Elemental Incenses; Teen Witch—Generation Y; Assembling Your Own Athame; and much, much more! The *Magical Almanac* makes magic an essential ingredient in every part of your life. Dig in and enjoy.

LLEWELLYN'S 1999 MAGICAL ALMANAC
384 pp. • 5¼" x 8" • Order # K-940 • $6.95
TO ORDER CALL 1-800-THE MOON

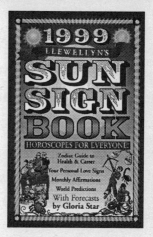

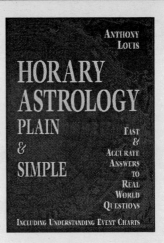

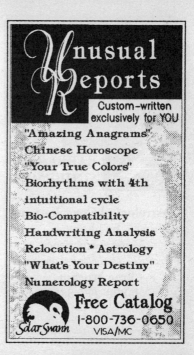

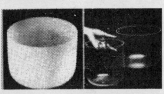

New Poetry Contest
$48,000.00 in Prizes

The National Library of Poetry to award 250 total prizes to amateur poets in coming months

Owings Mills, Maryland – The National Library of Poetry has just announced that $48,000.00 in prizes will be awarded over the next 12 months in the brand new North American Open Amateur Poetry Contest. The contest is open to everyone and entry is free.

"We're especially looking for poems from new or unpublished poets," indicated Howard Ely, spokesperson for The National Library of Poetry. "We have a ten year history of awarding large prizes to talented poets who have never before won any type of writing competition."

How To Enter

Anyone may enter the competition simply by sending in *ONLY ONE* original poem, any subject, any style, to:

The National Library of Poetry
Suite A1261
1 Poetry Plaza
Owings Mills, MD 21117-6282

Or enter online at **www.poetry.com**

The poem should be no more than 20 lines, and the poet's name and address must appear on the top of the page. "All poets who enter will receive a response concerning their artistry, usually within seven weeks," indicated Mr. Ely.

Possible Publication

Many submitted poems will also be considered for inclusion in one of The

Gordon Steele of Virginia, pictured above, is the latest Grand Prize Winner in The National Library of Poetry's North American Open Amateur Poetry Contest. As the big winner, he was awarded $1,000.00 in cash.

National Library of Poetry's forthcoming hardbound anthologies. Previous anthologies published by the organization have included *On the Threshold of a Dream, Days of Future's Past, Of Diamonds and Rust,* and *Moments More to Go,* among others.

"Our anthologies routinely sell out because they are truly enjoyable reading, and they are also a sought-after source-book for poetic talent," added Mr. Ely.

World's Largest Poetry Organization

Having awarded over $150,000.00 in prizes to poets worldwide in recent years, The National Library of Poetry, founded in 1982 to promote the artistic accomplishments of contemporary poets, is the largest organization of its kind in the world. Anthologies published by the organization have featured poems by more than 100,000 poets.

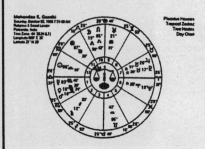
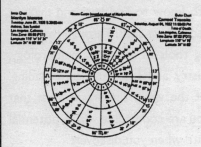

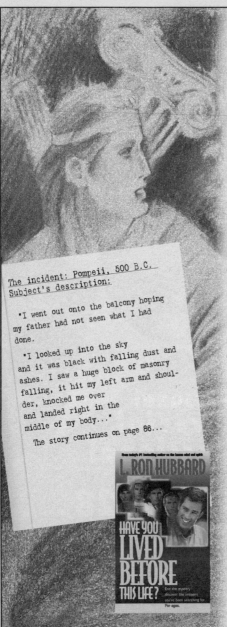

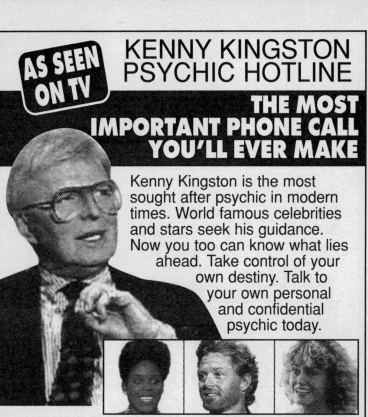